The Harbrace Casebooks in Political Science

Under the General Editorship of
ALAN F. WESTIN, *Columbia University*

Politics in the Soviet Union

7 Cases

CONTRIBUTORS

Robert V. Daniels
THE UNIVERSITY OF VERMONT

Robert Conquest

Bernard S. Morris
INDIANA UNIVERSITY

Grey Hodnett
COLUMBIA UNIVERSITY

Patricia Blake
COLUMBIA UNIVERSITY

John N. Hazard
COLUMBIA UNIVERSITY

Raymond L. Garthoff
THE JOHNS HOPKINS UNIVERSITY

A HARBRACE CASEBOOK IN POLITICAL SCIENCE

Politics in the Soviet Union

7 Cases

EDITED BY

Alexander Dallin COLUMBIA UNIVERSITY

Alan F. Westin COLUMBIA UNIVERSITY

NEW YORK · CHICAGO · SAN FRANCISCO · ATLANTA

Harcourt, Brace & World, Inc.

Library of Congress Catalog Card Number: 66–17594

PRINTED IN THE UNITED STATES OF AMERICA

CONTENTS

INTRODUCTION

The study of Soviet government has long been handicapped by facile generalizations, partisan misconceptions, and a lack of detailed evidence. Only recently has the Soviet political system become the object of searching studies in a comparative context. And only recently has the notion of "case studies" in Soviet politics—or, for that matter, the very existence of Soviet politics—become accepted among scholars.

It seems to us especially important that a basic textbook in Soviet government be supplemented by a volume that presents concrete episodes in detail. The different individuals, interests, and issues that determine the course of Soviet politics are all too often studied as discrete and static entities; yet it is the interaction among them that elucidates the political dynamics of the Soviet system. The seven cases offered here, because they are detailed and specific, reveal that interaction. In addition, they provide the student with the sense of reality that a general textbook often cannot supply, and they permit him to evaluate the evidence presented so that he may judge for himself both what we know and what we do not know about the Soviet system.

Not surprisingly, the Soviet polity shares some but not all the characteristics of other political systems, and it is important that the more common features not be overshadowed by the distinctive ones. Unfortunately, discussions of the nature of totalitarianism, though stimulating, have tended to evoke stereotypes of dictation and obeisance that fail to convey the extent, the significance, or the dynamics of the interaction of different elements in the Soviet government. Yet such an interplay—which may be businesslike and peaceable or may at times involve conflict or even open strife—has been a constant ever since the Bolshevik seizure of power.

Policy differences within the Soviet leadership have occurred across a strikingly broad spectrum of issues. At some times, these issues have been tactical or technical; at other times, they have reflected sharp conflicts among the leaders over values and priorities. They have ranged from the Treaty of Brest-Litovsk to the handling of the Sino-Soviet dispute; from purges to the rehabilitation of their victims; from the allocation of scarce resources to party guidance in the arts; from the prospects of world revolution to quantum physics; from chemical fertilizer to the authority of industrial managers.

The nature and the forms of interaction—and the role of different elements in the policy-making process—have changed considerably in the course of time. "Stalin's Rise to Dictatorship" illustrates a critical aspect of elite politics in the 1920's, and "De-Stalinization and the Heritage of Terror" affords a view of Stalinist terror and its aftermath. "The Twenty-second Party Congress" shows to what extent—and within what limits—the picture had changed by 1961. Whatever interpretation one chooses to adopt regarding change and continuity in the Soviet political process, it is clear that one of the most portentous developments of the post-Stalin era has been the return of politics—and, in some respects, the appearance of politics for the first time—as a vital and visible reality of Soviet life.

But although the Soviet political system has more in common with other systems than is sometimes supposed, many of its patterns are, of course, unique—and these unique patterns may be traced, at least in part, to the nature of the system itself. One may point, for instance, to the impact of the traditional Bolshevik view of a single truth, to the intolerance of dissent, to the Leninist *kto–kovo* (which Stalin applied even within the Communist leadership), and to the illegality of "factionalism" within the elite. In the absence of any accepted mechanism for transmitting legitimacy, the in-stability after each "succession" and the jockeying for power and authority that occurs even before a leader's death or departure place a particularly heavy strain on Soviet politics.

The risks and penalties of noncomformity—the charges of "wrecking," "sabotage," and "treason" so freely attached to political foes, and the almost unbelievable record of the purges—must, it is true, have inhibited many a potential dissenter or special pleader in the Soviet elite. Moreover, the circle of actors on the political stage—and of those waiting or fighting backstage as well—has been far smaller than in open societies, and public opinion has, of course, played but the most indirect role in policy decisions.

Different and at times conflicting views and influences within the leader-ship were apparent even under Lenin and Stalin; others can be shown to have existed, although they remain essentially unknown to us. At the top level, there has generally been a remarkable coincidence of conflicts among personalities, contests for power, and real differences over policy: both "Stalin's Rise to Dictatorship" and "The Twenty-second Party Congress" highlight this phenomenon. In addition, clashes over policy have often arisen from (or have reflected) the different functional responsibilities of segments of the Soviet bureaucracy, as in conflicts between the center and the periphery; industry and agriculture; the advocates of a stronger military establishment and those who favor the production of more consumer goods; the party and the state; the Red Army and the NKVD. Such confrontations are illustrated in "Khrushchev and Party-State Control" and "Khrushchev and the Military."

Even the incomplete evidence now available suffices to put to rest the official Soviet myth (so avidly accepted by many ardent foes of the Commu-nist regime) of a homogeneous ruling party. It now appears almost certain that not only in the years before Stalin consolidated his power but also later, leading Bolsheviks such as Sergei Kirov and Nikolai Bukharin disagreed sharply with some of Stalin's policies. After World War II, the duel between Malenkov and Zhdanov aligned behind each of them different parts of the *apparat,* and Khrushchev's experience demonstrated only too vividly how "his" party and "his" appointees in the end turned against him.

Though at times less visible than the conflicts at the highest levels of power and policy-making, there have also been strains at the lower levels and removed from the capital: between management, trade unions, and party cells in a given enterprise; between representatives of different ministries; between advocates of central direction and those striving to maximize local autonomy—in short, among virtually all the elements of the vast bureaucracy.

Since 1953, Soviet political life has witnessed the adoption of some ground rules, some maturation and routinization. Differences over policy at the apex of the political pyramid no longer need precipitate the ouster of the losers—unless the differences are part of a showdown in which the political survival of the participants is at stake, as it was for Malenkov, Molotov, and Zhukov, and ultimately for Khrushchev himself. As the cases in this volume (especially "Khrushchev and Party-State Control," "Freedom and Control in Literature," and "Khrushchev and the Military") illustrate, such conflicts are resolved in a surprisingly large number of instances by compromise—on issues as well as on personnel policy.

Compromise, however, invites the reopening of arguments and the frequent reexamination of interim policies. On such issues as resource allocation, the relative priority of heavy or light industry, relations with the West, and the organization of the Communist camp, there has in effect been a running debate for over a decade. Fortunes and alignments have changed, and the amount of publicity given the debate has varied; but the basic problems, options, and approaches—and even the jargon in which they are discussed—have been remarkably persistent.

During the post-Stalin era, the circle of participants in Soviet politics has expanded significantly. No longer can the First Secretary or even the Party Presidium make decisions without reference to (or consultation of) elements in the Soviet society and economy who—in fact though not in law —have begun to crystallize into something like "interest groups." One aspect of this development has been the increasing ability of technical, economic, scientific, and military specialists to make themselves heard by the political decision-makers. The process is still at an early stage, and some of the following cases (such as "Freedom and Control in Literature," "Social Control Through Law," and "Khrushchev and the Military") reveal its uncertainties and ambiguities. All the harbingers of change must be balanced against the hard core of inertia, tradition, and continuity so strikingly apparent in "De-Stalinization and the Heritage of Terror" and "The Twenty-second Party Congress."

Unfortunately, the study of Soviet government is distinctive for our relative ignorance of internal political conflicts. Arguments are frequently resolved backstage, without the benefits—or handicaps—of publicity. Transfers, promotions, and dismissals of officials identified with specific policies are often announced without any indication of the actual reasons behind them. And (as, for instance, "Khrushchev and Party-State Control" shows) even the most astute analysts of Soviet affairs can sometimes do little more than record evidence of conflict and on-going debate on a given issue while waiting for further clues because of our inadequate knowledge of (1) the reasons for the debate, (2) the alignment of different personalities and groups on the issue in question, and (3) the mechanisms by which influence is exercised, views are communicated, and decisions are made. This is particularly true of the unofficial, informal contacts and pressures which apparently, as in other systems, loom large indeed. Of necessity, our areas of ignorance have circumscribed both the subjects chosen for the present case studies and the treatment given them.

It is scarcely necessary any longer to do more than dismiss the once-popular notion that disagreements within the Communist world (whether among Communist states or among members of the Soviet leadership) are "orchestrated" by the masters in Moscow for the purpose of misleading the non-Communist world. Later evidence has shown again and again that internal tensions, conflicting pressures, and personal bitterness behind the scenes have been far greater than was apparent or surmised at the time; this was, incidentally, true of Hitler's Germany and Mussolini's Italy as well.

Yet there remains a legitimate area of contention about "Kremlinology." The reading of ambiguous clues, the detection of obscure patterns, the interpretation of esoteric symbols and codes—this is a hazardous business. It is a serious mistake, of course, to fail to detect and analyze the available clues because one assumes that the speeches, editorials, and other public pronouncements reveal no more than an omnipotent and omniscient leadership in Moscow wants them to reveal. But the errors that can result from over-analyzing the scant body of evidence are equally extensive and equally misleading. At its worst, "Kremlinology" is utterly worthless; at its best, it is thoroughly confirmed by later events.[1]

---

[1] For some pertinent discussions, see, for instance, Zbigniew Brzezinski and Alexander Dallin, "Introduction," to Dallin et al., eds., Diversity in International Communism (New York: Columbia University Press, 1963); Robert Conquest, Power and Policy in the U.S.S.R. (New York: St. Martin's Press, 1962), Part I; Barrington Moore, "The New Scholasticism and the Study of Politics," World Politics, Vol. VI, No. 1 (October, 1953), pp. 122–38; Boris I. Nicolaevsky, Power and the Soviet Elite (New York: Praeger, 1965); Sidney Ploss, Conflict and Decision-Making in Soviet Russia (Princeton, N.J.: Princeton University Press,

With the passage of time, the task of following and understanding Soviet political processes becomes somewhat easier, and not only because of the cumulative benefit of research already accomplished and insights already gained. Soviet officials and the Soviet press have become more willing to acknowledge—and sometimes to articulate—conflicting views and interests. The function of the mass media is still not autonomous criticism: they cannot question basic tenets and policies, let alone the competence of the leadership. But lately the Soviet press has begun to ventilate not only past conflicts, but even some current policy disagreements. Soon after Stalin's death different papers began to pursue divergent lines (for instance, some backing Malenkov and others, Khrushchev). More recently, leading organs like *Pravda* and *Izvestia* have openly taken issue with each other in editorials, columns, and letters. But it is well to remember that, however promising and welcome, this process is still quite limited in scope.

Considerable disagreement persists among experts on Soviet affairs concerning facts, judgments, and methodology.[2] Thus, specialists have argued bitterly about the nature of Soviet elite conflicts and of "interest groups." They have differed on the relative importance of the influence of various groups, such as the marshals or the provincial party secretaries or the intelligentsia. They continue to quarrel about which carries the most weight with the leaders: ideology, policies or principles, or the contest for power. They debate whether diversities in the Soviet elite are, to borrow the terminology of another study, "marginal" or "systemic." Some maintain that alignments in Moscow are largely shaped *ad hoc,* depending on the particular issue in question and on the circumstances at the time it arises, while others think that alignments form according to reasonably coherent patterns (left vs. right, soft vs. hard) on whole clusters of disputed issues—domestic, foreign, military, and economic alike.

While not all the major approaches, methods, and points of view can be represented here (not all are, in fact, equally tenable), we have tried in this

1965); John Reshetar, *Problems of Analyzing and Predicting Soviet Behavior* (New York: Doubleday, 1955); and Donald S. Zagoria, "A Note on Methodology," in his *Sino-Soviet Conflict, 1956–1961* (Princeton, N.J.: Princeton University Press, 1962).

[2] See, for instance, Daniel Bell, "Ten Theories in Search of Reality: The Prediction of Soviet Behavior in the Social Sciences," *World Politics,* Vol. X, No. 3 (April, 1958), pp. 327–65; Alexander Dallin *et al., The Soviet Union and Disarmament* (New York: Praeger, 1965); Wolfgang Leonhard, *The Kremlin Since Stalin* (New York: Praeger, 1962); Sidney Ploss, *Conflict and Decision-Making in Soviet Russia,* (Princeton, N.J.: Princeton University Press, 1965); Robert C. Tucker, *The Soviet Political Mind* (New York: Praeger, 1963); and the debates in the pages of the journals *Problems of Communism* (in particular, those by Carl Linden, Thomas Rigby, and Robert Conquest in the issue of September–October, 1963, Vol. XII, No. 5) and *Survey* (in particular, its No. 50 for January, 1964, also available as Walter Z. Laqueur, ed., *The State of Soviet Studies* [Cambridge, Mass.: M.I.T. Press, 1965]).

volume to present a diversity.[3] Indeed, in their orientations and in the implications of their findings, some of the contributing authors disagree. But no
effort was made to impose a single interpretive pattern on the seven case
studies; their diversity will, we trust, be instructive to the student of Soviet
affairs. By the same token, the editors do not necessarily agree with the
interpretations advanced by our contributors.

Political cartoons are customarily used in the Harbrace Casebooks in
Political Science to provide insight into the problems discussed in the cases;
nowhere are such cartoons more significant than in the Soviet Union, where
they reveal the policy of the government rather than the opinions of individual cartoonists. As the reader will gather from the examples reproduced
here, the cartoons on the pages of *Krokodil* and other Soviet publications
amount to a basic course in Soviet politics. They show both what the government will allow and what it will not allow; for example, it is surely
indicative of Soviet sensitivities that there are no cartoons to be found to
accompany the case on Khrushchev and the military.

Thanks are due to many for their cooperation in the preparation of this
casebook, but we would like especially to express our gratitude to Jerome
Gilison and Priscilla Reynolds of Columbia University for their assistance
with research and for their helpful suggestions and comments.

ALEXANDER DALLIN

ALAN F. WESTIN

---

[3] For a sample of other studies that supplement the present cases, see, in particular,
John A. Armstrong, *The Soviet Bureaucratic Elite* (New York: Praeger, 1959);
Isaac Deutscher, *The Prophet Unarmed: Trotsky, 1921–1929* (New York:
Oxford University Press, 1959); Merle Fainsod, *Smolensk Under Soviet Rule*
(Cambridge, Mass.: Harvard University Press, 1958); Roger Pethybridge, *A
Key to Soviet Politics* (New York: Praeger, 1962); Myron Rush, *The Rise of
Khrushchev* (Washington, D.C.: Public Affairs Press, 1958); Howard Swearer,
with Myron Rush, eds., *The Politics of Succession in the U.S.S.R.* (Boston:
Little, Brown, 1964); and Thomas W. Wolfe, *Soviet Strategy at the Crossroads*
(Cambridge, Mass.: Harvard University Press, 1964). In certain fields, such as
resource allocation and foreign policy, good case studies are still lacking.

1

Stalin's Rise to Dictatorship, 1922-29

Robert V. Daniels

"I have come to the conviction that Comrade Stalin cannot fulfill the role of unifier of the Bolshevik general staff. We are against the doctrine of one-man rule. We are against the creation of a 'chief.'" So shouted Leo Kamenev, Chairman of the Moscow Soviet and Deputy Prime Minister of the Soviet Union, above the tumultuous jeers and shouts of the massed Stalinist delegates at the Fourteenth Communist Party Congress in December, 1925.[1] This was the first occasion when Joseph Stalin's growing power in the Russian Communist State was publicly challenged. It was also the last congress with any organized opposition to the leadership. Kamenev and his political alter ego, Gregory Zinoviev, former partners of Stalin, had awakened to the menace of a personal dictatorship by the General Secretary of the Communist Party, but too late. All they did was to seal their own doom; a decade later they were among the first of Stalin's old associates to be rewarded with a bullet in the brain.

Stalin's extraordinary rise to a position of total personal power over Soviet Russia began in April, 1922, when Lenin put him in the new post of General Secretary of the Communist Party (ostensibly an administrative job to assist the top political leaders). Just a month later Lenin suffered the first in his series of strokes, leaving a leadership vacuum in the Soviet dictatorship. From his vantage point in the party Secretariat, Stalin maneuvered with impressive shrewdness, using both organizational and ideological weapons to isolate and discredit all possible rivals for succession to Lenin's mantle.

[1] *Stenographic Report* (Moscow: Gosizdat, 1926), p. 275.

Stalin's struggle with Leon Trotsky, though the most famous of the succession contests, was only one of several. Between 1922 and 1924, while Lenin still lived but did not rule, the Communists who had previously been critical of Lenin rallied around Trotsky in a vain effort to challenge the more dogmatic wing of the party. After Lenin's death and the defeat of the Trotskyists, the scene of the contest shifted to the ranks of Lenin's closest supporters, with the Zinoviev-Kamenev protest against Stalin in 1925 and the split between Stalin and the "Right Opposition" led by Nikolai Bukharin in 1928. In each successive test of strength Stalin's victory was easier, as he consolidated his control over the organizational machinery of the Communist Party and whittled down the ranks of the potential opposition.

One of the secrets of Stalin's success was his step-by-step advance toward power. He always took maximum advantage of his position of the moment but never moved fast enough to provoke more opposition than he could handle. His triumph was a spectacular case of the divide-and-conquer rule of political infighting. No one clash between Stalin and an opposition faction would truly illustrate the manner of his rise. Though, ordinarily, a case study of a decisive political crisis or change can be confined to a brief span of months, Stalin's achievement of personal dictatorship has to be looked at as one continuous process, extending over seven years, from 1922 to 1929.

By 1929, Stalin was the undisputed personal master of the party and of the whole country, though he held no official government position at all. He was finally ready to drive Soviet Russia through a new "revolution from above," to conduct a reign of terror scarcely, if ever, equalled, and to make the Soviet Union a major contender for world power.

The Soviet Power Structure

The Soviet system of government was a product of both ideas and events. It was a dictatorship exercised by a single party, the Bolshevik Party, built up by Lenin for a decade and a half before the revolutions of 1917 and imbued with his attitude of conspiratorial discipline. On the other hand, the formal structure of the government (and of the Bolshevik Party) grew out of the ultrademocratic revolutionary emotions of the year 1917. The actual practices of revolutionary dictatorship, with its suppression of all non-Communist opposition, developed with little prior planning in the course of the violent events of the October Revolution and the Civil War of 1918–20.

Lenin dominated the Bolshevik Party (renamed Communist in 1918) from the time it split away from the Menshevik ("minority") Social Democrats until his death in 1924. He was a powerful, demanding, and inflexible leader who almost always got his way with his party, but he allowed his followers to disagree, debate, and vote, provided they abided by the standards of "democratic centralism." Lenin had defined this as far back as 1906 as "freedom for criticism, complete and everywhere, as long as this does not disrupt the unity of action already decided upon—and the intolerability of any criticism undermining or obstructing the unity of action decided on by the party."[2]

There were several distinct currents of sentiment within the party from 1917 until the 1920's—a utopian and fanatical tendency that took Marxist theory very seriously, as well as an authoritarian tendency that rallied around Lenin's practical policies to win and hold power. The utopian or "left" wing rose in near-revolt against Lenin because of its opposition to the peace with Germany in 1918. Then, divided into the tough-minded faction led by Trotsky and the ultrademocratic groups known as the "Democratic Centralists" and the "Workers' Opposition," the oppositionists of the left resisted Lenin's policies intermittently until he cracked down on them in 1921. They remained ready to resume their opposition when the contest for the succession commenced in 1923.

While Lenin allowed controversy—up to a point—within the Communist Party, he had the utmost contempt for people outside the party, even for Marxist revolutionaries ideologically close to him. After he seized power in November, 1917 (October 25, according to the "old style" Russian calendar), Lenin moved quickly to suppress the political rights of all other parties. After 1918, whoever controlled the Communist Party controlled the government. Complete autocracy was accomplished by creation of a dictatorship *within* the party to correspond to the dictatorship of the party over the country at large. Lenin, in the years remaining to him, moved toward this logical conclusion, but he left the perfection of the dictatorship to the man destined to succeed him.

The organization of the Communist Party at that time—and ever since—was made to appear entirely democratic. Each local "cell" of party members chose its own secretary and elected delegates to a city or district conference, which in turn elected a committee and a secretary for the locality and delegates to the provincial conference. Provincial committees and secretaries were chosen in the same way, along with the delegates to the party's theoretically sovereign body, the Party Congress, which met every year until 1925. The Congress chose the Central Committee, responsible for policy-making during the year, and beginning in 1919, the Central Committee appointed three small executive bodies for day-to-day work—the Politburo (Political Bureau) for policy decisions, the Orgburo (Organiza-

---

[2] Lenin, "Freedom of Criticism and Unity of Action," *Collected Works*, 3rd Russian ed. (Moscow: Marx-Engels-Lenin Institute, 1928), Vol. IX, p. 275.

tional Bureau) for general problems of party organization, and the Secretariat, to keep the records and supervise party personnel.

Political practice quickly ran counter to the democratic forms of the party's structure, as the Communists waged a life-and-death struggle against both democratic and reactionary enemies in the Civil War of 1918–20. Lenin and his top associates found the Communist Party the best organization at their command for mobilizing forces, controlling the country, and generally getting things done. They entrusted the provincial and local party secretaries with major responsibility in local government. To ensure reliable men in these key slots, the central party leadership began to "recommend" candidates for the local committees to choose. In effect, the secretaries were appointed, and often they were transferred from one part of the country to another. If local opposition to such procedures arose, bigwigs from the center went out to shame the dissenters, and the leaders of the opposition could be ordered to another area or even expelled from the party.

By the early 1920's, the real structure of power in the Communist Party was a nearly perfect bureaucratic pyramid, save for the top level of the Politburo and the Central Committee. The Secretariat controlled the appointment of the provincial secretaries, and, through them, the lesser secretaries even of the basic cells. The whole process of electing the party committees that chose the secretaries at each level was under the thumbs of the very secretaries who were supposed to be elected. Soon after Stalin took over the Secretariat the circular flow of power was completed, as he used his machine of secretaries to control the election of delegates to the Party Congress, which, through the Central Committee, was supposed to elect the General Secretary himself.

Adding to the concentration of power at the upper levels of the party organization was a shift of *de facto* power and influence from the official organs of government to the corresponding bodies of the party. In the absence of any non-Communist voice, the Communist Party members who controlled all levels of the government made their decisions in party meetings, leaving only the execution of policy to the governmental offices. The party Politburo became the real nerve-center of governmental decision-making, while the nominal cabinet—the Council of People's Commissars—merely worked out the details. The executives and legislative bodies in both central and local government became mere rubber stamps for the decisions of the party. As a consequence, the internal politics of the Communist Party became the decisive arena for settling all questions of real power.

Early in 1921, the whole Communist regime was shaken by strikes, peasant uprisings, and a rebellion by the sailors at the Kronstadt naval base near Leningrad (then "Petrograd"). Lenin proclaimed a retreat from "War Communism" to the "New Economic Policy" (NEP), giving up attempts

The Circular Flow of Power
in the Communist Party Organization (by 1923)

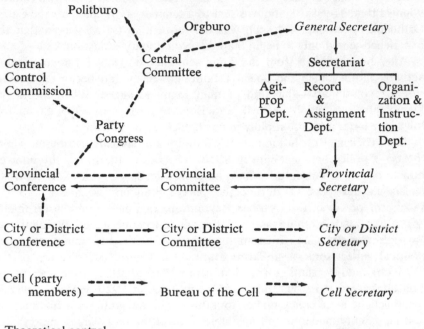

Theoretical control -------
Real control   ―――――――

at moneyless equality and allowing the peasants to produce for their own profit. At the same time, he cracked down on the left-wing idealists inside the Communist Party and banned what he called their "petty-bourgeois deviation" (though their crime was to take Lenin's own line of 1917 seriously). In March, 1921, he had the Tenth Party Congress prohibit organized opposition factions within the party on pain of expulsion.

To implement this rule, Lenin ousted the top men in the party Secretariat (led by Nikolai Krestinsky) because they had supported Trotsky in the recent controversy, and replaced them with a less distinguished but more reliable group headed by Vyacheslav Molotov. Behind these people was the influence of the one man who held seats in both the Politburo and the Orgburo, Joseph Stalin. It was perhaps natural that the following year Lenin should recommend to the Central Committee that it create for Stalin the office of General Secretary, to supervise the Secretariat. Lenin is supposed to have commented, "That cook will concoct nothing but peppery dishes."[3]

---

[3] Leon Trotsky, *Stalin: An Appraisal of the Man and His Influence*, p. 357.

When he became General Secretary, Stalin was only forty-two years old, but he had been in the top ranks of the party for ten years, having been "co-opted" into the Central Committee in 1912. He was, of course, not a Russian but a Georgian, born to a shoemaker and his wife in the village of Gori near Tiflis (Tbilisi) on December 21, 1879. He was just two months younger than Trotsky. Stalin was sent to a seminary to prepare for the Greek Orthodox priesthood, but such was the ferment in tsarist Russia that the experience served only to begin Stalin's revolutionary education.

After his expulsion from the Tiflis seminary in 1899 for revolutionary activity, Stalin joined the Social Democratic Party and became a professional revolutionary—the kind of man Lenin idealized. When the Social Democrats split into Menshevik and Bolshevik wings in 1903, Stalin followed the latter and rose rapidly in its clandestine organization.

The February Revolution of 1917 found Stalin an exile in Siberia, where the tsar's police had sent him in 1913. The fall of the monarchy allowed him to return to Petrograd, where he took a leading part (as an editor of Bolshevik newspapers) during the party's buildup preparatory to the seizure of power in the October Revolution. In Lenin's new government, Stalin was made Commissar of Nationalities to superintend the affairs of Russia's numerous non-Russian minorities. He was the commissar (i.e., political supervisor) of an army during the Civil War, director of the "Workers' and Peasants' Inspection" from 1919 to 1922, a member of the Politburo from 1919 on, and of the Orgburo after 1920. He was never in the limelight as a policy-maker, but his ambition grew with his success, and he quickly made himself available to head the party organization after the party shakeup of 1921. "Few important developments in history," writes Stalin's biographer Isaac Deutscher, "are so inconspicuous and seem so inconsequential to their contemporaries as did the amazing accumulation of power in the hands of Stalin, which took place while Lenin was still alive."[4]

Lenin's Illness and Stalin's Machine

Stalin's political skill and ambition continued to blossom with advancement and opportunity. Within weeks of his appointment as General Secretary, he was promoting or reassigning party personnel in order to consolidate his personal hold on the party organization. He was aided at the top level by two cosecretaries, Molotov and Valerian Kuibyshev, a 34-year-old Siberian Communist with experience as a military commissar and as head of the electric power industry. Under the Secretariat were several administrative offices—the Agitation and Propaganda Department, the Record and Assignment Department that kept records on the party's offi-

---

[4] Isaac Deutscher, *Stalin: A Political Biography,* p. 228.

cials and employees, and the Organization and Instruction Department that supervised the work of the local organizations by means of a roving staff of "responsible instructors." The man Stalin brought in to head the latter unit was Lazar Kaganovich, a former provincial party secretary and trade-union executive, who later on moved up to the Politburo and remained in the topmost rank of the Soviet leadership until Khrushchev ousted him in 1957.

Using the departments of the Secretariat as his levers of power, Stalin moved quickly to appoint provincial secretaries who could rally the provincial party conferences behind his wishes. During 1922 and the first three months of 1923, party secretaries were replaced in thirty-seven of the fifty provinces of the Russian-speaking part of the country (the Russian Socialist Federated Soviet Republic or R.S.F.S.R.). Replacements were sent in by the Secretariat with the "recommendation" that they be voted in by the local party conferences. In several provinces, the secretary was changed twice during this brief period, and in unruly Samara Province three times. A new party rule specified that only people who had joined the party before the October Revolution could be provincial secretaries. Stalin was able to take advantage of this provision to remove the secretaries in no less than eighteen provinces, though he suspended the rule in provinces where the incumbents suited him. Only in Moscow and Leningrad, where the party membership was large, active, and much harder to manage, was there substantial resistance to Stalin's control.

Stalin naturally made all his initial organizational moves in the name of Lenin, but Lenin did not remain the actual leader for long. During the crucial twenty-month period that followed Stalin's appointment to the Secretariat, the political history of Soviet Russia was governed by the medical bulletins. On May 24, 1922, Lenin suffered the first in a series of cerebral attacks that were eventually to kill him. His place was taken temporarily by a "collective leadership" of the Politburo, then consisting (apart from Lenin) of Trotsky, Zinoviev, Kamenev, Stalin, Alexei Rykov (Deputy Prime Minister), and Mikhail Tomsky (chief of the trade unions), with Bukharin, Molotov, and the chief-of-state, Mikhail Kalinin, as candidate members. Stalin held back from the limelight, contenting himself with a place in an unofficial "troika," or triumvirate, with Zinoviev and Kamenev. The immediate concern of this troika was to forestall the transfer of Lenin's power to Trotsky, whom both Zinoviev and Stalin regarded as a personal enemy and as a potential "Bonaparte," i.e., a military dictator on the model of Napoleon Bonaparte. Bukharin later revealed in a frank remark to Trotsky (quoted in Trotsky's autobiography) why the rest of the leadership banked so heavily on the discipline of the Secretariat: "We have no democracy because we are afraid of you."

Meanwhile Stalin made a point of keeping in close touch with Lenin while Lenin was recuperating at his country estate during the summer months of 1922. This contact, however, did not prevent serious friction between Lenin and Stalin when Lenin returned to work in September.

The autonomy of the national minorities was the first point at issue. The rights of the non-Russian peoples in Russia to use their own languages and develop their own cultures had always been a matter of controversy, among the Communists no less than under the tsars. Lenin wanted to appease the minorities by giving them the appearance of political autonomy, and allowed *de jure* independence for the Ukrainians, the Byelorussians, and the peoples of Transcaucasia, as long as they were all "Soviet Republics" under Communist control. Stalin pushed for a formal union of the Soviet republics and made a special effort to control the Communists in his native republic of Georgia. Lenin took alarm: "In my mind the question is super-important," he noted. "Stalin has a little tendency to hurry."[5] Nevertheless, Stalin continued to use the powers of the Secretariat to curb the Georgian Communists. He appointed Sergo Ordzhonikidze to head the Transcaucasian Regional Bureau of the party and directed him to purge the entire Georgian Communist leadership.

Lenin got word of the situation in Georgia just after he had suffered a second stroke in mid-December, 1922. While he had no scruples about excesses of central authority, he found the arbitrary and violent tactics of Stalin and Ordzhonikidze highly objectionable. Lenin was bedridden, but he was able to dictate to his wife, Krupskaya, a note reproving Stalin. In reply, as Krupskaya wrote, "Stalin allowed himself . . . an unusually rude outburst directed at me," with "vile invective and threats."[6]

What Lenin had learned about Stalin's approach to the national minorities and about the state of the Soviet government in general impelled him to dictate a lengthy memorandum for the 1923 Party Congress, a document that could have been disastrous for Stalin.[7] It called for a complete shakeup in the party and governmental bureaucracy and in the planning of the Soviet economy. On the nationality question, Lenin wrote,

> I think that here Stalin's haste and administrator's enthusiasm have played a fatal role, and also his anger. . . . Anger in general usually . . . plays the very worst role in politics. . . . It is known that Russified non-Russians always go too far in taking on a truly Russian attitude.

In conclusion, Lenin noted: "We should, of course, make Stalin and Dzerzhinsky [a Pole] politically responsible for all this truly Great-Russian nationalist campaign."

[5] Lenin to Kamenev, September 27, 1922, Trotsky Archive, Document No. T754.
[6] Quoted in Khrushchev's "secret speech" to the Twentieth Party Congress, February, 1956, in *The Anti-Stalin Campaign and International Communism,* p. 8.
[7] Complete Russian text, including the "Testament," published in V. I. Lenin, *Pismo k s'ezdu* (Moscow: Gospolitizdat, 1956).

Meanwhile, Lenin had written the note known as his "Testament," an assessment of the Communist leaders available to succeed him. Like the rest of the memorandum, it remained unpublished in the Soviet Union until 1956 (though it had been known abroad since the 1920's).

In the "Testament," Lenin expressed serious misgivings about the future leadership:

> I have in mind stability as a guarantee against a split in the near future, and I intend to examine here a series of considerations of a purely personal character.
>
> I think that the fundamental thing in the question of stability—from this point of view—is such members of the Central Committee as Stalin and Trotsky. The relation between them constitutes, in my opinion, the major part of the danger of that split . . . .

Then Lenin turned frankly to individual character:

> Comrade Stalin, since he became General Secretary, has concentrated enormous power in his hands, and I am not sure that he will always know how to use that power with sufficient caution. On the other hand, Comrade Trotsky . . . is distinguished not only by his exceptional ability. Personally, he is, I suppose, the most able man in the present Central Committee, but he is also excessively caught up in self-confidence and excessively fascinated with the purely administrative side of affairs.
>
> These two qualities of the two most eminent leaders of the present Central Committee might, quite innocently, lead to a split, and if our party does not take measures to prevent it, a split might arise unexpectedly.

A week or so later, on January 4, 1923, after receiving new information on the affair in Georgia, Lenin wrote a blunt postscript to the "Testament":

> Stalin is too rude and this fault of his, which is tolerable in our circle and in contacts among us, becomes unbearable from one who holds the post of General Secretary. I therefore suggest that the comrades should discuss the question of dismissing Comrade Stalin from this post and appointing to it another person who in all respects would have but one asset, compared to Stalin, i.e., that of being more tolerant, loyal, civil, and considerate toward the comrades, less moody, etc. This circumstance may seem an insignificant trifle, but I think that from the point of view of preventing a split and of the relations between Stalin and Trotsky discussed above, it is not a trifle, or it is such a trifle as may acquire a decisive significance.

With these explosive comments in his file, Lenin went ahead during January and February, 1923, to dictate plans for sweeping administrative reform. These plans were published as a series of articles in *Pravda,* and they produced no small degree of alarm among his lieutenants. Stalin, again, was the chief target because it was he who had supervised for three years the "Workers' and Peasants' Inspection," the control and supervisory agency that Lenin now singled out for attack as "incapable." Boldly, Stalin held up the publication of Lenin's article, "How We Should Reorganize the Workers' and Peasants' Inspection," and referred it to the Politburo. There he got a majority of six to two against publication. Kuibyshev (as a party Secretary he was allowed to sit with the Politburo) proposed to print a fake number of *Pravda* so that Lenin could see his article in print. Only when Trotsky and Kamenev insisted that the secret could not be kept did the Politburo finally agree to publication.

By March, the personal and political tension between Lenin and Stalin had come to a head. Lenin finally learned the whole story of Stalin's altercation with Krupskaya, and on March 5 sent him the following note:[8]

To Comrade Stalin:
Copies for: Kamenev and Zinoviev
Dear Comrade Stalin:

> You permitted yourself a rude summons of my wife to the telephone and a rude reprimand of her. Despite the fact that she told you that she agreed to forget what was said, nevertheless Zinoviev and Kamenev heard about it from her. I have no intention to forget so easily that which is being done against me, and I need not stress here that I consider as directed against me that which is being done against my wife. I ask you, therefore, that you weigh carefully whether you are agreeable to retracting your words and apologizing or whether you prefer the severance of relations between us.

Sincerely,

Lenin

Simultaneously Lenin sent a note to Trotsky (who was also bedridden at the time) asking him to intervene against Stalin in the Georgian affair; he followed this with a copy of his December, 1922, notes on the national question. Trotsky replied with the suggestion that Kamenev be given the documents, since he was departing for Georgia. Lenin's private secretary brought the answer, "It is entirely out of the question. Vladimir Ilyich [Lenin] says that Kamenev would show the letter to Stalin and Stalin would make a rotten compromise in order then to deceive."[9] The secretary then added, according to Trotsky's account, "Ilyich does not trust Stalin. He

---

8 Quoted in Khrushchev's secret speech, *The Anti-Stalin Campaign,* pp. 8–9.
9 Trotsky to the Bureau of Party History, October 21, 1927, in Trotsky, *The Stalin School of Falsification,* translated by John G. Wright (New York: Pioneer Publishers, 1937), p. 71.

wants to come out openly against him before the whole party. He is preparing a bombshell."[10]

Later that very day, fearing the worst for his own health, Lenin showed his hand on the Georgian matter:[11]

> *To Comrades Mdivani, Makharadze, and others:*
> *Copy to Comrades Trotsky and Kamenev*
> *Esteemed Comrades:*
>
> I am with you in this matter with all my heart. I am outraged at the rudeness of Ordzhonikidze and the connivance of Stalin and Dzerzhinsky. I am preparing for you notes and a speech.
>
> *With esteem,*
>
> *Lenin*

Trotsky thereupon discussed the whole matter with Kamenev and proposed his own compromise. As he later recorded the conversation,

> The last thing I want is to start a fight at the Congress for any changes in organization. I am for preserving the status quo. . . . I am against removing Stalin. . . . But I do agree with Lenin in substance. I want a radical change in the policy on the national question, a discontinuance of persecutions of Georgian opponents of Stalin, a discontinuance of the administrative oppression of the party. . . . In addition, it is necessary that Stalin should write to Krupskaya at once to apologize for his rudeness and that he revise his behavior. Let him not overreach himself. There should be no more intrigues, but honest cooperation.[12]

Three days later, on March 9, Lenin was half-paralyzed and left speechless by his third and most severe stroke. Stalin was saved. His men, led by Ordzhonikidze, went ahead to purge the oppositionists in Georgia. This guaranteed that the delegates sent to the Party Congress from Tiflis as well as from most of the other provincial party organizations would support the Secretariat solidly.

To accomplish this objective Stalin threw in all the resources of the Secretariat. His opponents complained, "The secretarial hierarchy of the party to an ever greater degree selects the membership of conferences and congresses, which to an ever greater degree are becoming executive meetings of this hierarchy."[13]

Stalin saw to it that the provincial conferences nominally empowered

---

[10] Trotsky, *Stalin,* p. 362.
[11] Trotsky, *The Stalin School of Falsification,* p. 69.
[12] Trotsky, *My Life,* pp. 485–86.
[13] Declaration of the Forty-Six (October, 1923), Trotsky Archive, T802a.

to elect Congress delegates were attended by members of the Central Committee (in more than half of the cases) or else by "responsible instructors" from the staff of his Secretariat. Almost invariably the recently appointed provincial secretary was designated a delegate, and in some provinces and national minority regions, the central instructor was returned as a local delegate to the Congress. As a result of these efforts the composition of the Party Congress from 1923 shifted toward the older type of professional party agitator from the prerevolutionary "underground," at the expense of the intellectuals and the newcomers.

The Twelfth Party Congress, in session from April 17 to April 25, 1923, was the first without Lenin and the last with a genuinely uninhibited debate. But for all the behind-the-scenes sparring that had gone on, no clear factional lines developed, and no one ventured to attack Stalin. Trotsky, perhaps because he lacked the talent for political infighting, perhaps because he hesitated to grasp for power while Lenin lived, perhaps because he thought of working with Stalin against Zinoviev, passed up the strategic opportunity to use Lenin's notes and ruin Stalin. Lenin's comments were either unknown or unauthorized for open distribution, and Stalin was able to avoid the limelight and remain unscathed.

Top billing at the Congress was traditionally reserved for the "political report of the Central Committee," a sort of keynote address that had always been given by Lenin. Avoiding an early showdown, Stalin proposed that Trotsky give the speech; Trotsky held back; and finally Zinoviev claimed the honor for himself. This made Zinoviev, in effect, the titular leader of the party until his break with Stalin in 1925.

Stalin followed Zinoviev with the number-two speech, the "organizational report of the Central Committee." In this account of his first year as General Secretary, Stalin established a style of public presentation that he was to follow throughout his career—simple, didactic, organized to the point of pedantry, practical but highly self-righteous. "I speak of the party as the vanguard, and of the working class as the army of our party," he began. He was frank enough to admit that his appointment methods had produced "squabbling and frictions" in the provincial party committees, but he brushed these troubles aside as mere symptoms of what he termed "the healthy striving to create a solid core capable of directing the work"—and ready, one might add, to impose Stalin's will firmly on the party and the people.[14]

Stalin's political strength was shown by the victory of his plan to expand the party's Central Committee from twenty-seven to forty members and by his success in persuading the Congress to approve his slate of new Central Committee members. Stalin did nothing to threaten the carry-over

[14] Joseph Stalin, *Collected Works,* Vol. V, p. 200.

membership: of the twenty-seven, only one was voted out. Of the nineteen alternate or "candidate" Central Committee members, most were either promoted or shifted to the Central Control Commission (the body that enforced party discipline and expelled recalcitrant oppositionists from the party).

The seven candidates promoted to full membership in the Central Committee were (with the exception of one Trotsky supporter) key members of Stalin's secretarial apparatus. They included the first secretaries of the party for the Ukraine and Azerbaijan, the second secretaries of the Moscow and Leningrad provinces, and the party chief of the Ural region. Another was Anastas Mikoyan, then supervisor of the party organizations in the ethnically conglomerate triangle between the Don River, the Caucasus Mountains, and the Caspian Sea, and active until the end of 1965 as President of the Soviet Union. Nine men were promoted directly to Central Committee rank, four representing Zinoviev's influence, but another four clearly aligned with Stalin.

At the level of Central Committee candidate members, Stalin brought in fourteen new names, including Kaganovich and ten more provincial party secretaries (mostly Stalin's appointees). This pattern of selection made clear what Stalin meant when he spoke of strengthening the Central Committee with practical workers in close touch with the masses. When one delegate welcomed a reference Stalin had made to "independent people," the General Secretary hastened to correct the impression of any relaxation of discipline in the party leadership. "I did not say independent of what," he quipped, to the amusement of the audience.

> We need independent people in the Central Committee, but people independent of Leninism—no, comrades, God forbid! We need independent people, people free from personal influences, free from the habits and traditions of the internal struggle in the Central Committee. . . . They should serve as the mortar, so to speak, to cement the Central Committee as a single and indivisible collective body leading our party.[15]

Stalin's Struggle with the Left Wing

The Trotskyists

Stalin wasted no time before beginning to build on the power base he had established at the Twelfth Congress. To consolidate his hold over the party organization, he had the Secretariat push its controls down through the provincial secretaries to the district and local organizations. More complete personnel records were compiled, secretaries were transferred

---

[15] *Ibid.,* p. 320.

about, and local party functionaries were brought to Moscow for organizational instruction.

The Communist leaders in some of the non-Russian minority regions still resisted domination by Moscow, and Stalin continued to give them special attention. In the Ukraine, the government was in the hands of a Trotskyist, Christian Rakovsky. Stalin had him removed in May, 1923, and sent him to Great Britain as head of the Soviet diplomatic mission. This followed the precedent of ex-secretary Krestinsky's assignment to Germany in 1922 and set a pattern for the temporary disposal of Soviet oppositionists in foreign ambassadorial assignments (a device later used by Khrushchev). Against the Tatar Communist leader Mirza Sultan-Galiev, who wanted to set up a large and autonomous Moslem Soviet Republic, Stalin used less diplomatic means. Sultan-Galiev was arrested, accused of treason, and imprisoned.

This was the first such action ever taken against a Communist official. However, Felix Dzerzhinsky, former head of the secret police, soon proposed as a general rule that party members be required to report all signs of opposition among Communists to the GPU—the State Political Administration or secret police. Little is known about Stalin's exact connections with the GPU, but Dzerzhinsky and his successor, V. R. Menzhinsky, collaborated fully with the party Secretariat and the Central Control Commission.

By the summer of 1923, Stalin felt politically strong enough to involve himself in the affairs of the Communist International, which had up to then been handled by his more intellectual associates. The burning issue in the Comintern was the preparation for revolution in Germany. Stalin expressed his characteristic skepticism about the foreign revolutionaries: "If today in Germany the power, so to speak, falls, and the Communists seize hold of it, they will fall with a crash. . . . In my opinion, the Germans must be curbed, and not spurred on."[16] Stalin was vindicated when the German Communist revolt erupted abortively in October, 1923, but by then other issues were dividing the Soviet leadership.

There was only one important force that Stalin did not yet have his hands on: this was the army, where Trotsky still held sway as Chairman of the Revolutionary Military Council and People's Commissar of War. Trotsky had actually strengthened his position in 1922 by having Stalin's man Sergei Gusev removed as head of the political commissars in the army and replaced by his own man, Vladimir Antonov-Ovseyenko (a hero of the October Revolution). In the fall of 1923, Stalin tried to drive a wedge into the door by expanding the Revolutionary Military Council and

---

[16] Stalin to Zinoviev and Bukharin, published in the Leipzig *Arbeiterpolitik*, February 9, 1929; English translation in Ruth Fischer, *Stalin and German Communism* (Cambridge, Mass.: Harvard University Press, 1948), p. 306.

joining it himself, but Trotsky parried this thrust by threatening to resign from the Commissariat.

By this time Stalin's growing influence through the Secretariat was clear to his two partners in the party leadership, Zinoviev and Kamenev. In September, 1923, Zinoviev called a group of party leaders down to Kislovodsk, in the North Caucasus, where he was vacationing. They met in a cave and agreed to "politicalize" the Secretariat by putting Trotsky and one other top leader in it along with Stalin. Stalin was warned of the scheme and hastened to Kislovodsk himself. He secured agreement on an alternative proposal to give his leading rivals seats in the Orgburo. As Stalin may have calculated, this made the reorganization meaningless; Zinoviev met with the Orgburo only a couple of times, and Trotsky and Bukharin never attended at all. The policy-makers were too busy to attend to the organizational sources of power.

The need for organized action to set the country's policies right finally became clear to Stalin's adversaries in October, 1923. Trotsky spoke out first in a letter to the Central Committee attacking his coleaders for mismanagement of the economy and the bureaucratization of the party. Trotsky's complaint was followed a week later by a long collective statement, the Declaration of the Forty-Six, signed by a coalition of Trotskyists and "Democratic Centralists."[17] The "Forty-Six" elaborated on Trotsky's issues of bad economic planning and neglect of the workers. They were particularly indignant about the transformation of the party organization under Stalin:

> The party is to a significant degree ceasing to be that living self-acting collective which really embraces living activity, being linked by thousands of threads with this activity. Instead of this we observe more and more a progressive division of the party, now concealed by hardly anyone, into the secretarial hierarchy and the "laymen," into the professional party functionaries, selected from above, and the simple party masses, who do not participate in its group life. . . .
>
> The regime that has been set up within the party is absolutely intolerable; it kills initiative in the party, subjects the party to an apparatus of appointed officials, which undeniably functions in normal times, but which unavoidably misfires in moments of crisis, and which threatens to reveal itself as completely bankrupt in the face of the grave developments ahead of us.

Such laments counted little with most of the members of the Central Committee and the Central Control Commission, who had been selected by Stalin or gave their favor to him. They were joined by the followers of Zinoviev, who still regarded Trotsky as his main enemy, in passing a resolu-

---

[17] Text in the Trotsky Archive, T802a.

tion to condemn the opposition for "factional-splitting politics." However, the majority did feel it necessary to allow a pro-forma public discussion in the party about the issues that the opposition had raised. Stalin piously called for more democracy in the party, but he cautioned a Moscow party meeting against "unlimited discussion" and urged vigilance to "safeguard the party, to safeguard this fighting unit of the proletariat against degenerating into a debating society." By December, public protests by Trotsky and his supporters prompted Stalin and Zinoviev to launch a wholesale propaganda campaign against the opposition—the so-called New Course Controversy, from the title of Trotsky's pamphlet that provoked the attack. In this effort, Stalin and Zinoviev were effectively aided by Bukharin, who, as editor of *Pravda,* had become in Lenin's absence the chief theoretician of the party leadership.

A month of debate and denunciation in the press and party meetings in December, 1923, and January, 1924, sufficed to cripple the Trotskyites. They had a substantial center of strength in the Moscow party organization, but false vote-counting by the supporters of the leadership and orders from the Secretariat transferring active oppositionists to the remote provinces broke the back of the opposition in the capital. When delegates were chosen to the next party conference (a small-scale congress held between regular Congresses) in mid-January, Stalin's organization succeeded in delivering 125 votes for the party leadership against three for the opposition. This marked the definitive triumph of the apparatus in manipulating the mass party. It rendered future opposition futile unless, somehow, the top organization could be split.

Stalin made the principal report at the party conference and drove his victory home with a blistering denunciation of Trotsky for allegedly trying to split the party and deviating from the policies of Lenin. He condemned the Trotsky group as an illegal faction and set forth his philosophy of the party thus:

> If we were to allow groups in this situation, under these complex conditions, we would ruin the party, convert it from the monolithic, united organization that it is into a union of groups and factions contracting with one another and entering into temporary alliances and agreements. That would not be a party. It would be the collapse of the party. Never, for a single moment, have the Bolsheviks conceived of the party as anything but a monolithic organization, hewed from a single block, possessing a single will and in its work uniting all shades of thought into a single current of practical activities.
>
> But what Trotsky suggests is profoundly erroneous; it runs counter to Bolshevik organizational principles, and would inevitably lead to the disintegration of the party, making it lax and soft, converting it from a united party into a federation of groups. Living as we do in a situation of capitalist

encirclement, we need not only a united party, not only a solid party, but a veritable party of steel, one capable of withstanding the assault of the enemies of the proletariat, capable of leading the workers to the final battle.[18]

Then Stalin cited an unpublished clause in the resolution on discipline passed by the Party Congress of 1921, providing for the removal of Central Committee members and even their expulsion from the party if they committed the crime of factionalism. With this threat in the background, the Conference found the Trotskyists guilty as charged—". . . not only [of] an attempt at the revision of Bolshevism, not only [of] a direct departure form Leninism, but also [of] a clearly expressed petty-bourgeois deviation."[19] Thus, even before Lenin was dead his legacy had hardened from a one-party system into a one-idea system, and it was not long before it narrowed into a one-man system.

Consolidation of Power

Lenin died on January 21, 1924, and Stalin quickly made the most of the political opportunity offered by his funeral. To Trotsky, on the Black Sea coast trying to shake off an infection, Stalin wired a false date for the funeral so that his rival would not hurry back to Moscow. He took for himself the most prominent place in the funeral observances and delivered a funeral oration of singular style and content. "Comrades," he began,

> We Communists are people of a special mold. We are made of a special stuff. We are those who form the army of the great proletarian strategist, the army of Comrade Lenin. . . . Departing from us, Comrade Lenin enjoined us to hold high and guard the purity of the great title of Member of the Party. We vow to you, Comrade Lenin, that we shall fulfill your behest with honor![20]

After each succeeding point in his address, Stalin intoned the same refrain, as though the Orthodox priest were speaking through the mouth of the Marxist revolutionary.

Lenin's official successor as head of the Soviet government was Rykov, a colorless man who deferred in matters of general policy to Bukharin. These two, together with Tomsky, gave the Soviet administration during the remaining years of the NEP—to 1928—its characteristically cautious stamp—caution in dealing with the peasants, caution in directing the intel-

---

[18] Stalin, *Collected Works,* Vol. VI, p. 23.
[19] *KPSS v Rezoliutsiyakh* (*The CPSU in Resolutions*), Vol. I (Moscow: Gospolitizdat, 1954), p. 782.
[20] Stalin, *Collected Works,* Vol. VI, p. 47.

lectuals, caution in planning the economy, caution in foreign policy. Stalin cooperated closely with these men and endorsed their policy guidelines, while he stepped boldly ahead in matters of organization to consolidate the ground won by his apparatus in beating down the Trotsky opposition of 1923. He proclaimed a "Lenin Enrollment" to recruit new party members and opened the party's ranks to the first mass influx since the Civil War. Some 200,000 new members, mostly workers, were added to the half-million already in the party, ostensibly in the name of proletarian democracy. Actually the worker-Communists, old as well as new, were highly susceptible to manipulation by the organization, and Stalin was sure enough of his control to allow the new members to vote for delegates to the Party Congress without waiting for their probationary period to end.

Stalin managed the Party Congress in May, 1924—the Thirteenth—without a hitch. Not a single oppositionist—not even Trotsky—secured election as a voting delegate. There was one sudden embarrassment for Stalin just before the Congress, when Lenin's widow revealed the text of his "Testament" to the top party leaders. They felt compelled to read it privately to each provincial delegation to the Congress, and Stalin faced up to the challenge by offering to resign as General Secretary of the party. But Zinoviev came to Stalin's rescue by assuring the Central Committee that "the fears of Ilyich [Lenin] have not been confirmed." He called for a vote by show of hands, and on this short notice no one ventured to oppose the organizational chief of the party. Stalin was reconfirmed in office unanimously.

The party was even more firmly in Stalin's hands after the Thirteenth Congress made its additions to the Central Committee for the coming year. The committee was expanded from forty members and seventeen candidates to fifty-two members and thirty-four candidates, a step which tended to weaken the body by making meetings and decisions more cumbersome. In composition, the new Central Committee reflected Stalin's growing influence. While all the old members save one (Trotsky's ally, Karl Radek) were reelected without challenge, more than half of the men promoted to the new seats or brought in as candidate members were provincial secretaries representing Stalin's professional apparatus. The secretaries now constituted an automatic majority in the party's official governing body. As for the top policy organ, the Politburo, Stalin did not yet tamper with this group of Lenin's prestigious associates. Even Trotsky kept his membership for the time being.

To aspire to supreme leadership, Stalin still had to make his mark as a theoretician. Despite his prerevolutionary editorial work, he had not yet distinguished himself in doctrinal matters, of which Zinoviev and Bukharin were the leading spokesmen now that Trotsky had fallen from favor. But Stalin was soon to prove an adroit—if not wholly original or sincere—

juggler of Marxist-Leninist phraseology. He made his major theoretical debut in April, 1924, with a series of lectures at the Moscow party training school known as the Sverdlov University. In published form, Stalin called his series "The Foundations of Leninism," and this is exactly what he tried to set forth, in the simple, codified, yet pungent question-and-answer form that was to become his hallmark. "Leninism," Stalin proclaimed, "is the Marxism of the era of imperialism and the proletarian revolution. To be more exact, Leninism is the theory and tactics of the proletarian revolution in general, the theory and tactics of the dictatorship of the proletariat in particular." The bulk of Stalin's exposition, here as elsewhere, was a familiar lesson on the contradictions of capitalism, the vacillations of the opportunists, the sanctity of Lenin's doctrines, the utilization of the peasants and the national minorities, and the military conception of revolution.

Where Stalin was rather more original was in spelling out his theory of what the ruling Communist Party had become in practice. "The proletariat needs the party," he declared, "not only to achieve the dictatorship; it needs it still more to maintain the dictatorship, to consolidate and expand it in order to achieve the complete victory of socialism." This task, Stalin maintained, required a premium on "solidarity and iron discipline," which in turn were "inconceivable without unity of will, without complete and absolute unity of action on the part of all members of the party." Any factional disunity or opposition, he now asserted, could come only from "petty-bourgeois groups" that "penetrate into the party and introduce into it the spirit of hesitancy and opportunism, the spirit of demoralization and uncertainty." From this proposition Stalin drew the rationale for his subsequent fight with the Communist opposition groups. "Ruthless struggle against such elements, their expulsion from the party, is a prerequisite for the successful struggle against imperialism."[21]

The second major step in Stalin's ascent to the ideological high priesthood came in the fall of 1924, after Trotsky had published some unguarded remarks about the party leadership and brought down on his head the wrath of the party's massive propaganda machinery. Stalin, Zinoviev, Kamenev, and Bukharin joined in denouncing Trotsky's "theory of permanent revolution." At first sight this was an odd target, for the theory (vintage 1906) had proved to be a reasonably good prediction of the quick transition from "bourgeois" to "proletarian" government during the continuous or "permanent" state of revolution in 1917. But Trotsky had further predicted a permanent state of revolution as the proletarian movement spread from Russia to the West. In 1917, all the Bolsheviks thought such a development essential to the survival of their own regime amidst the more backward conditions of Russia. The revolution, of course, had failed

[21] Joseph Stalin, *Problems of Leninism,* pp. 2, 80–83.

to spread abroad, and the question now was what would happen to the
"socialist" state left standing alone in Russia. Trotsky and his followers
began to hint that this state, under the cautious direction of men like Stalin,
Bukharin, and Zinoviev, was in danger of becoming unsocialist.

In this ticklish situation Stalin undertook a bold ideological gambit.
"According to Lenin," he asserted in December, 1924,

> the revolution draws its strength primarily from among the workers and
> peasants of Russia itself. According to Trotsky, the necessary strength can
> be found only "in the arena of the world proletarian revolution."
>
> But what if the world revolution is fated to arrive with some delay? Is
> there any ray of hope for our revolution? Trotsky offers no ray of hope,
> for "the contradictions in the position of a workers' government . . .
> could be solved only . . . in the arena of the world proletarian revolu-
> tion." According to this plan, there is but one prospect left for our revolu-
> tion: to vegetate in its own contradictions and rot away while waiting for
> the world revolution. . . .
>
> What difference is there between this "theory of permanent revolution"
> and the well-known theory of Menshevism which repudiates the concept
> of dictatorship of the proletariat?
>
> Essentially, there is no difference.
>
> There can be no doubt at all. "Permanent revolution" is not a mere
> underestimation of the revolutionary potentialities of the peasant move-
> ment. "Permanent revolution" is an underestimation of the peasant move-
> ment which leads to the repudiation of Lenin's theory of the dictatorship
> of the proletariat.
>
> Trotsky's "permanent revolution" is a variety of Menshevism.[22]

To undergird this charge Stalin cast about in Lenin's collected writings
for some substantiation of the notion that Russian socialism did not need
foreign support. He found one passage which, taken out of context, could
be read to that effect. Lenin was writing in 1915 to suggest that one country—he meant the industrially most advanced—might experience the socialist revolution before others. Stalin quoted the passage and made bold
to interpret it: "Lenin . . . opposed to the opportunists his theory of the
proletarian revolution and the victory of socialism in one country, even if
that country is one in which capitalism is less developed." On this basis
Stalin pronounced Trotsky a heretic:

> Trotsky's permanent revolution is the negation of Lenin's theory of the
> proletarian revolution; and conversely, Lenin's theory of the proletarian
> revolution is the negation of the theory of "permanent revolution."
>
> Lack of faith in the strength and capabilities of our revolution, lack of

---

[22] *Ibid.,* p. 93.

faith in the strength and capabilities of the Russian proletariat—that is what lies at the root of the theory of "permanent revolution."[23]

The point in all this is not Stalin's scholarship, which the Trotskyists easily tore to pieces whenever they were given a chance. Nor does Stalin's formulation reveal the social nature of the Soviet system. Although on the surface Stalin's "socialism in one country" suggested a shift away from international revolution and toward emphasis on developing Russia, there was little practical difference between Trotsky and Stalin on the need for caution internationally and the desirability of strengthening the Russian economy while they waited for world revolution. The real significance of Stalin's reasoning is (1) that he regarded textual justification against the opposition as important; and (2) that he dared to venture so novel an interpretation of Communist theory.

Behind the move, of course, was Stalin's assurance that he could back his ideological pronouncements with organizational power, to make his view obligatory for the party. Thus he began what remains Communist practice to this day, the revision of doctrinal interpretations to square them with the practical political needs of the day, and the suppression of any effort to preserve within the movement some unadulterated image of the party's original philosophy. Freedom for the leader to do and to say what he wanted and the tightest control over what all the rest of the Communists thought about it—these were the really important consequences of Stalin's theory of "socialism in one country."

Zinoviev

By the spring of 1925, the collective leadership that had taken over from Lenin was beginning to show strains. Zinoviev and Kamenev, Stalin's partners in the informal troika, saw their colleague amassing a degree of personal power through the Secretariat that threatened to eclipse everyone else among the heirs of Lenin. To combat Trotsky, Zinoviev and Kamenev had endorsed the party discipline and the cautious economic and foreign policy upheld by Stalin and Bukharin, but now to fight Stalin they took the position of the earlier opposition and accused him of neglecting Marxist orthodoxy. At the Fourteenth Party Congress in December, 1925, they attempted to challenge Stalin's power head-on, but only to suffer an ignominious defeat.

Stalin had prepared himself well for the Zinoviev-Kamenev attack. He reorganized the central offices of the Secretariat in May, 1924, and concentrated the key functions of organizational supervision and personnel assignment in one department under Lazar Kaganovich. Kaganovich and Andrei Andreyev, a dutiful trade-union functionary, joined Stalin in the Secretariat.

---

[23] *Ibid.*, pp. 95, 100.

At the same time, Stalin tightened up the Orgburo, temporarily weakened in 1923, and packed it with his own supporters. Then it was comparatively easy for him to move against Isaac Zelensky, the Moscow provincial secretary and a key follower of Zinoviev. By virtue of his office Zelensky had been a member of the Orgburo and the Secretariat. Stalin removed him from all three positions in November, 1924, and sent him out to Tashkent as secretary of the Central Asian Bureau of the party. This sort of transfer was a form of political punishment that Stalin was in a good position to use to get his opponents temporarily out of the way.

Zelensky's replacement in Moscow, Nikolai Uglanov, succeeded to the seat on the Orgburo and Secretariat. He was ready to assure the loyalty of Moscow to the party leadership when the crisis with Zinoviev came the following year.

Zinoviev began to maneuver against Stalin and Bukharin in the spring and summer of 1925. He picked up Trotsky's arguments and tried to turn them against Stalin and Bukharin—that in accepting "socialism in one country" and a long postponement of world revolution, Stalin and Bukharin were betraying the proletariat and condoning a trend toward "state capitalism" in the U.S.S.R. But despite the similarities of their views, Trotsky refused to support Zinoviev. Personal animosity in fact almost led him to come out in favor of Stalin. Such political and doctrinal bickering caused a total disarray among the former lieutenants of Lenin who might, had they had the unity and foresight, have curbed Stalin before he had consolidated his own personal power.

Zinoviev and Kamenev brought their challenge of Stalin to a showdown at the Fourteenth Party Congress in December, 1925. Zinoviev came to the Congress with a solid bloc of delegates from the Leningrad province, where, like Stalin, he had rooted out all opposition to his own leadership. However, he found every other party organization in the country massed on the side of Stalin and Bukharin.

At this point, Stalin ventured to assume the titular leadership of the party implied in delivering to the congress the "political report of the Central Committee." As was customary, he started with a review of the international situation in which he noted the "stabilization of capitalism," the Soviet Union's acceptance in the international community, and the potential for the "national revolutionary movement" in the "colonies and dependent countries." Domestically, Stalin stressed the prospects for independent economic growth:

> We must build our economy in such a way as to prevent our country from becoming an appendage of the world capitalist system, to prevent it from being drawn into the general system of capitalist development as a subsidiary enterprise of this system, so that our economy develops not as a

subsidiary enterprise of world capitalism, but as an independent economic unit.[24]

But when it came to the details of economic planning Stalin was still close to the cautious views of Bukharin. On agriculture, Stalin conceded that the prosperous individual farms of the "kulaks" (well-to-do peasants who produced for the market) were a challenge to socialism, but he put more stress on "another deviation—the deviation of overestimating the kulak danger, in the direction of consternation in the face of the kulak danger, in the direction of panic."[25]

Zinoviev threw down the gauntlet by choosing to make a minority report—an old party custom that had not been exercised at a congress since 1918. He drew up against Stalin and Bukharin an impressive array of embarrassing theoretical issues—coddling the peasants to the detriment of the dictatorship of the proletariat; failing to move ahead from "state capitalism" to a more proletarian socialism; and above all, neglecting international revolutionary progress in favor of "socialism in one country." It was during the spirited debate that followed between the Zinovievist minority and the Stalinist majority that Kamenev made his frank appeal to the congress (quoted earlier) to put a halt to Stalin's personal dictatorship.

According to custom the principal speaker had the last word in the debate, and Stalin used this opportunity for some clever counterthrusts. He revealed that Zinoviev had wished to expel Trotsky from the Politburo, and commented:

> We disagreed with Zinoviev and Kamenev because we knew that the policy of amputation was fraught with great dangers for the party, that the method of amputation, the method of blood-letting—and they demanded blood—was dangerous, infectious; today you amputate one limb, tomorrow another, the day after tomorrow a third—what will we have left in the party? (*Applause*.)

On the kulak question Bukharin was the main target of the opposition, but Stalin came to his defense: "Why . . . does all this unwarranted slander of Bukharin continue? They demand the blood of Comrade Bukharin. . . . You demand Bukharin's blood. We won't give you his blood. (*Applause*.)"[26] (This was the sort of remark that Stalin expurgated from his collected works, published after he purged Bukharin himself.)

Stalin's victory at the Fourteenth Congress was a foregone conclusion. The delegates approved his report by a vote of 559 to 65 (all Leningraders). Four of the nine Zinovievists on the Central Committee were

[24] Stalin, *Collected Works,* Vol. VII, p. 305.
[25] *Ibid.,* p. 343.
[26] *Stenographic Report,* pp. 504–08.

dropped or demoted to candidate. War Commissar Frunze (Trotsky's successor), rumored to be a Zinoviev sympathizer, died while undergoing an operation (ordered, some said, by Stalin to get him out of the way). The Politburo now felt Stalin's first blow, as Kamenev was demoted to candidate status and three of Stalin's cronies—Molotov, Kalinin, and Voroshilov —were made full members. But more importantly, representatives of the central leadership, led by Molotov, moved into Leningrad to destroy Zinoviev's hold there. After touring the factories and making speeches, the Stalinists put the formally democratic procedures of the party into play and ousted the Zinoviev leadership. So ended the last open split within the party command.

The Final Blows

In the spring of 1926, Stalin found arrayed against him a new combination of political forces—forces which might have been unbeatable if they had had the foresight to coalesce before Stalin had systematically broken the organizational power of each. Trotsky and Zinoviev finally came together, composed their differences, and prepared to do battle with Stalin and Bukharin in whatever arena of the press or the party organizations was open to them. They drew up a program—the "Platform of the Thirteen" —packed with bitter criticism of the policies and practices of the leadership.[27] Their protest centered on "bureaucratism":

> The immediate cause of all of the sharpening crises in the party is in bureaucratism, which has grown amazingly in the period following the death of Lenin, and continues to grow.
>
> The Central Committee of the ruling party has at its disposal for action upon the party not only ideological and organizational, i.e., not only party means, but also governmental and economic means. Lenin always took into account the danger that the concentration of administrative power in the hands of the party would lead to bureaucratic pressure on the party. . . .
>
> Those who are dissatisfied, disagree, or doubt are afraid to raise their voices in party meetings. The party mass always hears only the speech of the party command on the one and only text. The mutual tie with and trust in the leadership are weakening.
>
> An official show prevails in the meetings, together with the apathy which is unavoidably connected with it. Frequently only an insignificant minority remains at the time of voting; the participants in the meeting hasten to leave so that they will not be compelled to vote for decisions dictated earlier. No resolutions anywhere are ever adopted otherwise than "unanimously." All this is gravely reflected in the internal life of the party organizations. Members of the party are afraid openly to express aloud their most cherished thoughts, wishes and demands.

---

[27] Text in the Trotsky Archive, T880a.

Stalin—and Bukharin—now had no compunctions about using the instruments that they were criticized for fashioning. After a series of debates and public demonstrations by the opposition, the Central Committee majority cracked down and voted the opposition leaders out of the Politburo. In their places, Stalin installed Ian Rudzutak, the trade-union official, and Valerian Kuibyshev, who had just moved up from the Central Control Commission to become the top administrator of Soviet industry. This shakeup—in October, 1926—finally gave Stalin an absolute majority of his own appointees in the Politburo, not counting his allies Bukharin, Rykov, and Tomsky.

Controversy broke out once again in 1927, when failures in Soviet foreign policy—the collapse of the Communists in China and the severance of diplomatic relations by Great Britain—gave Trotsky and Zinoviev a final chance to discredit Stalin's leadership. The issues were the same, as the opposition attacked Stalin and his allies for favoring the peasants over the workers, letting the tempo of industrialization lag, neglecting the international revolution, and violating democracy within the party. The oppositionists accused Stalin of "the most extreme usurpation of the supreme powers of the party." But the results of the struggle were as dismal as before: debate was met with denunciation, and recantation was followed by excommunication.

Such was the pitch of bitterness by the fall of 1927 that the party leadership could brook no solution short of physically destroying the opposition. When the Central Committee met in October, Trotsky declared, "The dictatorship of the proletariat is in danger." He finally got the matter of Lenin's "Testament" into the record, with the remark,

> The rudeness and disloyalty of which Lenin wrote are no longer mere personal characteristics. They have become the character of the ruling faction, both of its political policy and its organizational regime. . . . The fundamental character of our present leadership is its belief in the omnipotence of methods of violence—even in dealing with its own party.[28]

Stalin proved himself a master at debate as well as organization when he replied:

> Now, on the "Testament" of Lenin. Here the oppositionists have cried out —you have heard this—that the Central Committee of the party "has concealed" the "Testament" of Lenin. Several times this question has been discussed among us at the Plenum of the Central Committee and the Central Control Commission—you know this. (*Voices:* "Dozens of times.")

---

[28] Published in Trotsky, *The Real Situation in Russia,* translated by Max Eastman (New York: Harcourt, Brace & World, 1928), p. 7.

It has been proved over and over again that nobody has concealed or is concealing anything, that Lenin's "Testament" was addressed to the Thirteenth Party Congress (cries of "quite true!"), that the Congress resolved unanimously not to publish it, among other reasons because Lenin himself did not wish or demand its publication. . . .

It is said that in this "Testament" Comrade Lenin suggested to the Congress that it consider, in view of Stalin's "rudeness," the question of replacing Stalin in the post of General Secretary by another comrade. This is quite true. Let us read that passage, although it has already been read repeatedly at the plenary session: "Stalin is too rude and this fault of his, which is tolerable in our circle and in contacts among us, becomes unbearable from one who holds the post of General Secretary. I therefore suggest that the comrades should discuss the question of dismissing Comrade Stalin from this post and appointing to it another person who in all respects would have but one asset, compared to Stalin, i.e., that of being more tolerant, loyal, civil, and considerate toward the comrades, less moody, etc." Yes, I am rude, comrades, in regard to those who are rudely and disloyally ruining and splitting the party. I have never concealed this and will not conceal it. . . . At the very first session of the Plenum after the Thirteenth Congress, I asked the Plenum of the Central Committee to relieve me of the duty of General Secretary. . . . The Congress itself considered this question. . . . All the delegates, including Trotsky, Kamenev, and Zinoviev, unanimously *obliged* Stalin to remain in his post.

The "Testament" means that neither Trotsky . . . nor Kamenev and Zinoviev . . . can be trusted politically. It is a characteristic fact that not a single word, not a single allusion in the "Testament" touches on Stalin's mistakes. Only his rudeness is mentioned. Lack of civility, however, is not a shortcoming in Stalin's political attitude or political position and cannot be so.[29]

Stalin ended the session of the Central Committee by having Trotsky and Zinoviev dropped from its membership. One desperate public demonstration by the opposition followed—on the tenth anniversary of the Bolshevik Revolution, November 7, 1927. It was the last public manifestation of political opposition in the history of Soviet Russia. It was broken up by the police and party vigilante groups, and immediately afterwards the Central Control Commission officially expelled Trotsky and Zinoviev from the Communist Party.

All that remained was to dispose of the opposition followers; this was accomplished at the Fifteenth Party Congress in December. Stalin again gave the political report and sarcastically asked why the opposition had proven so weak:

[29] *International Press Correspondence,* No. 64 (November 17, 1927), pp. 1428–29; published in London by the Executive Committee of The Communist International.

How could it happen that the entire party, as a whole, and following it, the working class too, so thoroughly isolated the opposition? After all, the opposition are headed by well-known people with well-known names, people who know how to advertise themselves (*voices:* "Quite right!"), people who are not afflicted with modesty (*applause*) and are able to blow their own trumpets.

It happened because the leading groups of the opposition proved to be a group of petty-bourgeois intellectuals divorced from life, divorced from the revolution, divorced from the party, from the working class. (*Voices:* "Quite right!" *Applause.*)

. . . The opposition utterly break away from the Leninist principle of organization and take the path of organizing a second party. . . . On all these questions the opposition have slipped into Menshevism. Can these Menshevik views of the opposition be regarded as compatible with the party's ideology, with our party's program, with its tactics, with the tactics of the Comintern, with the organizational principles of Leninism? Under no circumstances; not for a single moment![30]

The opposition had not a single voice at the Congress and in fact was allowed to record no more than two thousand votes out of a million in the "election" of delegates by the membership. The Congress ruled unanimously to expel the entire group of active oppositionists from the party. Some—the Zinovievists—then recanted. Others—the Trotskyists—were turned over to the police to be sent, in old tsarist style, to forced residence in remote parts of the country.

Stalin's Struggle with the Right Wing

At the end of 1927, all that stood between Stalin and total power were the reputations and compunctions of his three old colleagues in the top leadership, Bukharin, Rykov, and Tomsky. He had worked intimately with them all through the years of the NEP, in the decision of policy, the manipulation of theory, and the debates with the opposition. In matters of policy and doctrine their line was his guide; in matters of organization, his power was their support.

How long in advance Stalin calculated the move it is impossible to say, but no sooner had the Trotsky-Zinoviev opposition been broken than he started to work against Bukharin, Rykov, and Tomsky. His tactic was to force them into a position where he could attack them for deviation just as he had the Trotskyists and Zinovievists, though to accomplish this he chose an opposite set of issues. Starting in the winter and spring of 1928, Stalin

---

[30] Joseph Stalin, *Political Report of the Central Committee to the Fifteenth Congress of the CPSU(B)*, pp. 92, 105.

gradually took the Trotskyist position (without, of course, acknowledging it) on curbing the peasants and pushing industrial development, and began to call for a vigorous campaign against all "bourgeois elements" of society. Bukharin and his associates were truly alarmed, as they had been by Trotsky, because they feared such radicalism might provoke the peasants into overthrowing the Communist regime altogether. By June, 1928, Bukharin was privately attacking Stalin for representing a "Trotskyist danger."

The Central Committee met for a decisive session in July. Stalin had laid the groundwork with every means at his disposal, including blackmail of wavering supporters such as Voroshilov. (In one key spot Stalin's preparations went awry. Nikolai Uglanov, secretary of the Moscow province party organization, sided with Bukharin.)

Debate in the Central Committee waxed bitter over the issue of extorting produce from the peasants. As Bukharin saw some of the people he counted on going over to Stalin—Voroshilov, Kalinin, Kuibyshev—he must have realized the need for a political miracle to save himself from the Secretariat. On July 11, even before the Central Committee session had ended, he paid a secret visit to Kamenev at Kamenev's Moscow apartment. Kamenev recorded the conversation:[31]

> KAMENEV: Is the struggle really serious?
>
> BUKHARIN: That's just what I wanted to talk about. We feel that Stalin's line is ruinous for the whole revolution. We could be overthrown on account of it. The disagreements between us and Stalin are many times more serious than the disagreements which we used to have with you. . . . I have spoken with Rykov and Tomsky about this quite frankly. I have not spoken with Stalin for several weeks. He is an unprincipled intriguer, who subordinates everything to the preservation of his own power. He changes his theory according to whom he needs to get rid of. . . .
>
> The Petersburg [Leningrad] people are, in general, with us, but they got scared when the talk got to the possibility of removing Stalin. . . . Our potential forces are vast, but 1) the middleranking Central Committee member still does not understand the depth of the disagreements, 2) there is a terrible fear of a split. Therefore, when Stalin conceded on the extraordinary measures [against the kulaks] he made it difficult for us to attack him. We don't want to come forth as schismatics, for then they would slaughter us. . . .

At the end of his notes Kamenev added the comment, "Stalin knows only one method . . . , to plant a knife in your back."

So far only rumors of the controversy had reached the party rank and file and the general public. While Bukharin and Rykov mistakenly tried to

---

[31] Copy of Kamenev's notes in the Trotsky Archive, T1897.

preserve the appearances of party regularity by keeping their opposition to Stalin secret, Stalin began preparing the public issues he would use against them. To the question of peasant policy he added the Communist International, where he now pushed for a "left turn" in revolutionary endeavor and denounced a vaguely defined "right deviation" and the "tendency" to conciliate this deviation. By fall, Stalin had also begun to develop a new issue in the area of industrial development, where he pressed for such a high rate of construction that the Right Opposition was bound to voice its objections.

Many historians have explained Stalin's decision on rapid industrial development and the collectivization of the peasants as the logical implementation of the Communist program or as the best response to Russia's economic realities. Stalin's approach was, to be sure, one of the economic alternatives, but the question here is whether he adopted it for economic reasons or for other—political—ones. This writer's study of the month-by-month development of Stalin's case against Bukharin suggests that Stalin was only feeling his way toward policies that would embarrass the Right Opposition. In fact, some of the extremeness of Stalin's stand on industrialization and collectivization was due to the efforts of the Bukharinists to save themselves by compromising. Stalin had to keep jumping ahead—notably in the preparation of the Five-Year Plan—by having Kuibyshev's Supreme Economic Council prepare ever more ambitious proposals to discredit the more careful and cautious drafts of the rightist-dominated State Planning Commission (Gosplan).

These programmatic maneuvers were complemented in the fall of 1928 by a swift move to break the organizational center of the Right Opposition in Moscow. In much the same manner as they had during the campaign against Leningrad in January, 1926, officials of the Central Secretariat went to the party's ward organizations in Moscow to agitate against the provincial secretary, Uglanov. When the time was ripe, Stalin himself intervened in the Moscow provincial committee to denounce what he slyly described as the "conciliationist" tendency. "The elections in Moscow," he alleged, "are taking place on the basis of self-criticism, and the active party members in each district have the right to change their secretaries."[32] So again the top leadership went to the rank and file to use them "democratically" against the middle-level officials. Uglanov's opposition collapsed ignominiously, and he resigned from the provincial secretariat.

To consolidate his success in the Moscow party organization, Stalin announced a new party purge—a systematic weeding out of allegedly unfit or undisciplined members from the party such as Lenin had ordered in 1921. Stalin's purge continued well into 1929 and sufficed to dispose of most of

---

[32] Stalin, *Problems of Leninism*, p. 528.

the rank-and-file support for the Right Opposition even before its leaders had been openly condemned. Another center of Right Opposition strength lay among the Communist leaders of the trade unions, still headed by Tomsky. Using the power of party discipline over the trade-union organizations, Stalin moved his men in to win control of the trade-union congress held in December, 1928, and packed the Central Trade Union Council with leading Stalinist party officials.

In response to this new blow Tomsky and Bukharin threatened to resign from their party and government positions and thus to bring the fight out into the open. Stalin countered in February, 1929, by summoning Bukharin before a joint session of the Politburo and the Presidium of the Central Control Commission to answer charges of factionalism.

In April, Stalin presented his indictment of Bukharin to the Central Committee, which automatically endorsed it and at the same time gave the nod to Stalin's most ambitious draft of a Five-Year Plan of industrialization. Official sanctions against the Right began in May, with the removal of Uglanov as a candidate member of the Politburo. In June, Tomsky was ousted as trade-union chairman and replaced by Nikolai Shvernik. In July, the Executive Committee of the Communist International accepted the unpublished "recommendation" of the Soviet Central Committee and deposed Bukharin as Comintern Chairman. In November, Bukharin, Rykov, and Tomsky recanted their views completely, with the statement (printed in *Pravda,* November 26, 1929), "We consider it our duty to declare that in this dispute the party and its Central Committee have proven right." But this did not long avert the final step in Stalin's installation of his own men in all the key offices of government, society, and the international Communist movement: in December, 1930, Rykov was removed as Prime Minister and replaced by the ever available Vyacheslav Molotov.

By the end of 1929, Stalin's establishment of a complete personal dictatorship was accomplished, though he did not liquidate his defeated rivals until the late 1930's and did not assume formal leadership of the government until he took over as Prime Minister from Molotov in May, 1941. The new tone in Soviet public life was struck on the eve of Stalin's birthday in December, 1929. Three days before the event *Pravda* carried a full page of greetings to Stalin, under the headline, "For the Fiftieth Anniversary of the birth of Comrade Stalin, faithful Comrade-in-Arms of Lenin, Unwavering Bolshevik." On the day itself, December 21, the entire issue was devoted to Stalin:

> To the true continuator of the cause of Marx and Lenin, the unwavering fighter for the purity of Marxism and Leninism, for the steeled unity of the ranks of the All-Union Communist Party (of Bolsheviks) and the Communist International, for the international proletarian revolution; to the

organizer and director of the socialist industrialization and collectivization
of the Soviet country; to the chief of the party of the proletariat, which
is building socialism in one-sixth of the world; to the oldest *Pravda* man;
to Comrade Joseph Vissarionovich Stalin, from *Pravda*—fighting Bolshevik
greetings.

The inevitable editorial recounted Stalin's virtues, damned his enemies, and
concluded, "Long live the iron, united Leninist Party! Long live its chief,
Comrade Stalin!"

So Russia had a "chief" once again. His response was printed the next
day, in the tone of selfless modesty that was to become his stock in trade:

> Your congratulations and greetings I accept on behalf of the great party of
> the working class, which has borne and raised me in its image and like-
> ness. And just because I accept them on behalf of our glorious Leninist
> Party, I take upon myself the boldness to answer you with Bolshevik
> thankfulness.
>
> You need not doubt, comrades, that I am ready again to render to the
> cause of the working class, to the cause of the proletarian revolution and
> world Communism all my efforts, all my capacities, and if necessary all my
> blood, drop by drop.

Stalinism Triumphant

Stalin's emergence as sole ruler in Russia was the signal for a period of
violence and turmoil that rivaled the Revolution itself. This time, however,
it was a "revolution from above," as Stalin described it, commanded by
the dictator and carried out through the machinery of the party organization that he had been perfecting during his rise to power.

This "Stalin Revolution" stemmed directly from the last phase of Stalin's
political contest with his opponents—his fight with the Right Opposition.
The program of the Stalin Revolution was adopted, it appears, for the
short-run purpose of outmaneuvering the Bukharinists. It was, in essence,
an exaggerated and inhuman version of the Trotskyist program of exploiting the peasants and rapidly building heavy industry. Collectivization brought violent revolution to the countryside, while the Five-Year
Plan meant toil and privation for the city dwellers. By extension of the
party's authoritarian pattern to society at large, the enduring foundations
of the totalitarian state were laid down.

Between 1930 and 1934, Stalin took no further direct action against his
former adversaries, but signs of a new harshness accumulated in 1932 and
1933 as he struggled with disaster in agriculture. In December, 1934,
Stalin's second-in-command, Sergei Kirov, was assassinated, and Stalin

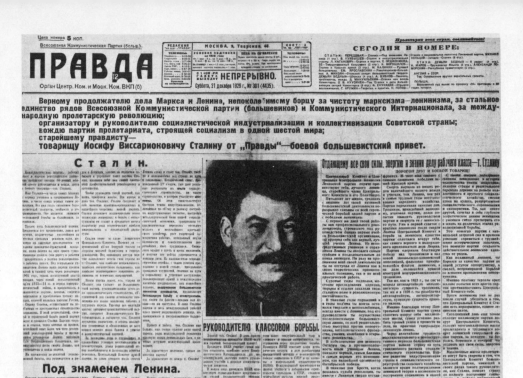

On Stalin's fiftieth birthday, December 21, 1929, *Pravda*'s front page was devoted in its entirety to extravagant eulogies of the "chief." The headlines read:

> TO THE TRUE CONTINUATOR OF THE CAUSE OF MARX AND LENIN, THE UNWAVERING FIGHTER FOR THE PURITY OF MARXISM AND LENINISM, FOR THE STEELED UNITY OF THE RANKS OF THE ALL-UNION COMMUNIST PARTY (OF BOLSHEVIKS) AND THE COMMUNIST INTERNATIONAL, FOR THE INTERNATIONAL PROLETARIAN REVOLUTION;
>
> TO THE ORGANIZER AND DIRECTOR OF THE SOCIALIST INDUSTRIALIZATION AND COLLECTIVIZATION OF THE SOVIET COUNTRY;
>
> TO THE CHIEF OF THE PARTY OF THE PROLETARIAT, WHICH IS BUILDING SOCIALISM IN ONE-SIXTH OF THE WORLD;
>
> TO THE OLDEST *Pravda* MAN;
>
> TO COMRADE JOSEPH VISSARIONOVICH STALIN, FROM *Pravda*—FIGHTING BOLSHEVIK GREETINGS.

The same page included messages of salutation to the "chief" from the Central Committee and the Central Control Commission of the party, from the Executive Committee of the Communist International, from the Moscow party organization, and from the Central Council of the Profintern (Red Trade Union International). They were featured under such headlines as "To the one who is giving all his strength, energy, and knowledge to the cause of the working class" and "To the beloved leader, indefatigable fighter, and dear Comrade Stalin."

Lenin and Stalin in the city of Gorki, 1922. During the Stalin era, this photograph —unique in showing Lenin and Stalin together on an informal occasion—was often used to show a close relationship between the two men.

Sovfoto

Deni in *Pravda*, 1923

Тов. Зиновьев произносит речь...

The cartoon hints at the embarrassment caused to Soviet diplomacy by the inflammatory efforts of the Comintern. People's Commissar for Foreign Affairs Georgi Chicherin is visibly discomfited while (the caption reads) "Comrade Zinoviev Makes a Speech . . . ."

took the murder as a pretext for one of history's bloodiest and yet most mysterious episodes, the Great Purge. From 1936 to 1938, he caused most of the old oppositionists, Left and Right, to be arrested and to "confess"; then, systematically, they were liquidated. At the same time, Stalin turned the secret police against his own Stalinist party apparatus, wiping out almost the entire Central Committee, most of the regional party secretaries, most of the commissars both in the central government and in the union republics, and most of the marshals of the Red Army, in a purge that extended from the Soviet officialdom and professional class up to the Politburo itself.

From the time of the purges on, Stalin ruled as an oriental despot, terrorizing his lieutenants and subjects alike. Only his death permitted his successors to begin to discuss and question the manner of his rule, and still their real revelations have been few. The complete story of Stalin's rise and rule remains untold.

The Keys to Dictatorship

Like every significant historical event, Stalin's rise to dictatorship was the product of so many different factors that a definitive explanation is very difficult. There were personal factors of ambition, ability, and good fortune, as well as political reasons, in the story of Stalin's struggles with his rivals. There were impersonal factors in the nature of the Communist Party and the circumstances of postrevolutionary Russia that made dictatorship possible by someone, if not Stalin. And there was the specific historical development brought about by Stalin himself, as he built his personal dictatorship in the course of perfecting the instruments of dictatorial rule.

In the first place, Stalin was lucky. His appointment to the office of General Secretary in 1922 gave him access to what was unobtrusively becoming the key to power in the Communist Party, that is, the professional apparatus of secretaries. To be sure, he had shown some ability before then as a political handyman, and this no doubt was the function he would have fulfilled even in the new job had Lenin gone on as the Soviet leader. Lenin's untimely illness and death was Stalin's second stroke of luck, opening the field of contest for the succession and enabling Stalin to make his own position something it was never intended to be, boss of the party.

The evolution of Stalin's personal aims can only be guessed at. Retrospectively it is clear how he was fired by ambition and vindictiveness. When the succession struggle was brewing in 1923 he reportedly confided to a couple of associates, "To choose one's victim, to prepare one's plans minutely, to slake an implacable vengeance, and then to go to bed—there is nothing sweeter in the world."[33] Many critics have seen in Stalin the blood-feud mentality of the Caucasus mountaineer. But it is doubtful whether he lifted his sights from vengeful party infighting to the goal of supreme power until he was well on his way to success in the mid-1920's. Not until the succession struggle was under way did Stalin's distinctive political talent show itself. Stalin personified the tactics that make for success in any power struggle in a dictatorial government or bureaucratic organization. He was a master of machine politics with a keen appreciation of the power of organization, a shrewd capacity to get the right man into the right job, and a readiness to employ any tactics—favors and doctrinal arguments, threats and blackmail—to keep his followers in line. He had an instinctive sense of political strategy—of when to move and when to hold back; of whom to attack, whom to befriend, whom to betray; of how to divide the opposition and how to identify himself with symbols of loyalty and unity. He knew how to stay out of the limelight of great issues until his rivals had assumed vulnerable positions and he himself had prepared for battle in the party organization. Without caring for theoretical rigor per se, Stalin knew how to manipulate theory to shame and discredit his opponents in debate.

The place of Communist doctrine in Stalin's thinking is hard to assess. He identified himself in every public statement with the virtue of undeviating doctrinal orthodoxy and made the dead Lenin a living prophet. Throughout his career Stalin acted in the name of the dictatorship of the proletariat and the future classless society of Communism. There is no reason to doubt the sincerity of his convictions or to wonder at his belief, common in most ambitious politicians, that his own power was essential for the good of the movement. There is more room to question the extent to which Stalin's theoretical convictions actually guided his actions, and to ask how his actions may subtly have influenced his convictions. Stalin's use of Marxist doctrine challenges the common-sense assumption that one either acts on one's convictions or is a cynic. Stalin believed, but he believed in what was most convenient to his own pursuit of power, and he crushed with wrathful vengeance those who questioned the Marxian correctness of his successive stands. In the end, the worst devils in Stalin's mind were not capitalists or fascists, with whom he could do business at arm's length, but his opponents in the Communist movement itself.

As an individual, Stalin could doubtless have been stopped at several points in the succession struggle, but his own political skill and luck were matched by the weakness and blunders of the opposition. First and most obviously, the potential opposition to Stalin was divided—divided so badly that it never even agreed on Stalin as the enemy until too late. As it hap-

---

[33] Quoted in Boris Souvarine, *Stalin: A Critical Survey of Bolshevism*, p. 485.

pened, the opposition came only in waves, beginning with the more anti-authoritarian Communists. Stalin was able to beat off each wave singly and to enhance his own power each time. His victories were facilitated, moreover, by the inhibitions imposed on each opposition group by the accepted principles of the Leninist party—that there should be no factional challenge to party discipline and that any separate organization would be "unproletarian" and hence treason to the supposed government of the working class. The principles of Leninism and the circumstances of party dictatorship allowing no political life outside the Communist ranks boxed the opposition in so much that they never dared to oppose effectively. In the end, of course, the result could have been no worse, for Stalin sooner or later expelled all the opposition groups from the party on grounds of "petty-bourgeois" deviation and then had them liquidated as "enemies of the people."

The unique institution through which Stalin accomplished his political triumph was, of course, the apparatus of the Communist Party—the hierarchy of secretaries that Stalin built into a personal instrument of power. The apparatus was itself considerably refined and vastly upgraded in its power, as Stalin built his own power by expanding that of the apparatus. Through the circular flow of power—*de facto* down through the secretaries and over to the membership, *de jure* up through the party's conference and committee structure, Stalin brought the whole party under the bureaucratic control of the Secretariat. Through the party, he had ultimate control of the government at every level. Outside of the metropolitan party organizations (Moscow in 1923 and 1928, Leningrad in 1925), there was no institutional foothold from which any challenger could seriously threaten him.

Much has been made of the deviation in the history of the Russian Revolution from the model of the French Revolution because of the failure of a military dictator like Napoleon Bonaparte to emerge and overthrow the Communists. But there is an underlying likeness. Any country after a violent revolutionary upheaval needs order but lacks the institutional stability for a legal order to work. The field is open for the man with the most powerful extralegal organization to put himself in power. Bonaparte did this with his army. In Russia, not the army but the apparatus of the Communist Party was the most powerful organization in the country, and so it fell to the man with the good fortune to be in command of this organization at the decisive moment to assume the role of dictator.

Study Questions

1. Explain the circular flow of organizational influence that Stalin used to obtain control of the party.

2. How and why did the various party leaders, especially Trotsky, Zinoviev, and Bukharin, react to Stalin's growing power? How did Stalin "divide and conquer"?

3. Compare Stalin with the American political "boss" or with the "Organization Man." Do such comparisons help explain his success?

4. How did Stalin use Communist theory? Did he use it the same way his rivals did? Why did he bother with it?

5. Why did all the opposition to Stalin fail? Was there anything the later oppositionists might have learned from the earlier ones that could have stopped Stalin?

Selected Bibliography

The detailed research on Russia in the 1920's by the present author is set forth in *The Conscience of the Revolution: Communist Opposition in Soviet Russia* (Cambridge, Mass.: Harvard University Press, 1960). Among the sources principally used in that work are the stenographic reports of the Congresses of the Russian Communist Party, the party press, and Trotsky's personal archive (now in the Houghton Library at Harvard University).

The serious historical study of Stalin's rise began with a polemical but detailed book by a French ex-Communist—Boris Souvarine, *Stalin: A Critical Survey of Bolshevism* (London: Secker & Warburg, 1939). A Russian Menshevik émigré, A. S. Michelson, had previously published a valuable though little-known study on Stalin and the Communist Party organization— Aleksandrov (pseud.), *Kto upravliaet Rossiei* (Who Rules Russia?), Berlin: Parabola, 1933. The best official history, biased but factual, was N. N. Popov, *Outline History of the CPSU,* 2 volumes (New York: International Publishers, 1934). All Soviet histories since Stalin's purges have been much more distorted.

Most of the important recent books are by British scholars: E. H. Carr's monumental work, *A History of Soviet Russia,* 7 volumes in 8 parts to date, extending from 1917 to 1926 (London and New York: Macmillan, 1950 to date); Isaac Deutscher's two biographies, *Stalin: A Political Biography* (London and New York: Oxford University Press, 1949) and *The Prophet Unarmed—Trotsky, 1921–1929* (London and New York: Oxford University Press, 1959); and Leonard Schapiro's history, *The Communist Party of the Soviet Union* (New York: Random House, 1960). Trotsky's posthumously published study, *Stalin: An Appraisal of the Man and His Influence,* edited and translated by Charles Malamuth (New York: Harper, 1946), is good for the years up to 1923.

Stalin's own writings have been published in English translation by the Foreign Languages Publishing House in Moscow. The *Collected Works* (13 volumes, 1952–55) is ostensibly complete up to 1935 but actually slightly expurgated. Numerous editions of selected speeches and articles by Stalin were published under the title *Leninism* or *Problems of Leninism*.

The texts of Lenin's revealing notes of 1922–23 were published in translation in a U.S. Department of State press release of June 30, 1956; the original Russian texts were soon afterward released by Moscow in the journal *Kommunist* and in pamphlet form. Khrushchev's "secret speech" attacking Stalin at the Twentieth Congress of the CPSU is available in *The Anti-Stalin Campaign and International Communism,* edited by the Russian Institute of Columbia University (New York: Columbia University Press, 1956).

2

De-Stalinization and the Heritage of Terror

Robert Conquest

On October 30, 1961, following the first full public denunciation of a selection of Stalin's crimes at the Twenty-second Party Congress of the Soviet Communist Party, delegates proposed "that the sarcophagus with Joseph Stalin's coffin be removed from the [Lenin-Stalin] Mausoleum. To leave it there would be blasphemy." An aged woman delegate, D. A. Lazurkina, rose to say: "Yesterday I asked Ilyich [Lenin] for advice, and it was as if he stood before me alive and said: 'I do not like being next to Stalin, who inflicted so much harm on the party.' (*Stormy prolonged applause.*)"

The Congress adopted a resolution for removing Stalin. That evening a gang of workmen, escorted by police detachments, descended on Red Square, lifted the embalmed body from the showplace where it had lain for eight and a half years, and reburied it in a less distinguished spot under the Kremlin wall.

It had been laid beside Lenin in a bitter time. In 1952–53, Stalin had been tightening his already harsh and horrible system in preparation for another great blood purge. Calls for vigilance against hidden enemies, the secret slaughter in August, 1952, of the leading Yiddish writers, and a wave of arrests for economic crimes culminated in January, 1953, with the announcement of the "Doctors' Plot." A dozen of Russia's leading medical specialists, mainly Jews, were charged with murdering Soviet leaders and preparing further assassinations in the interests of the Western powers and of Jewish circles generally.

The terrible winter dragged on. The population was hungry as well as frightened. (It was later revealed that, owing to Stalin's statistical falsification, the tolerable figure of eight billion poods for the harvest had been false: it was only five and a half billion, near starvation level.) A violent campaign in all the mass media made it clear that hidden enemies—"live people," as the press repeatedly insisted—were to be implicated in a vast anti-Soviet plot. On March 5, 1953, at the height of the tension, when all Russia was gripped with gloom, Stalin died.

Over the ensuing years, the process we call "de-Stalinization" began, picked up momentum, and produced political events of the highest drama.

Yet it is at once necessary to examine our definitions. What is meant by "de-Stalinization"? As we shall see, "Stalinism" might be described as those elements in Communist practice in the U.S.S.R. over the period before 1953 of which one disapproves. Evidently, different people disapprove of different things. Thus it is most important, when we hear of the Soviet government practicing "de-Stalinization," not to assume automatically that they are ridding the country of *all* those elements which Western observers might find deplorable. Even at the height of the attacks on the dead dictator, important elements of his system remained intact.

Stalin secured his grip on Russia by the Great Terror of 1936–38. During these two years it is estimated that there were about a million executions, while at least seven million other victims went to the vast labor camps of Siberia and the Arctic, where many of them perished. These figures mean that every other family in Russia suffered a casualty, usually among its adult males. (And there had already been the minimum of more than five million deaths admitted by Stalin to Winston Churchill as having been lost among the peasantry as a result of his collectivization campaign.) During the rest of Stalin's rule there was no comparable burst of mass destruction, but a large and steady flow of victims still went to the firing squads and labor camps.

The effect of the Terror is reflected even in the census figures of 1959. These show a great deficit of males among the younger groups that provided the fighting troops for World War II. But they show an even larger deficit of males in the older age groups that bore the brunt of the Terror. It is easy to deduce that the often-mentioned resentment of the Russians against Germany is likely to be paralleled to some degree by a similar resentment against another enemy that took about the same toll of Russian life—the Stalin regime. And this is evidently the case. In *Doctor Zhivago* Boris Pasternak says that, compared with the thirties, "the war came as a breath of deliverance. . . . Its real horrors, its real dangers, its menace of a real death were a blessing compared with the inhuman reign of the lie." Even an official publication was able to remark, during the brief relaxation of censorship that took place in 1956–57, that "many are aware of this theme much more strongly than of any other that had been dealt with in Soviet literature"—more strongly, that is, even than the war.

But it is necessary to recall that Stalin was not *simply* a bloodthirsty tyrant—a Nero or Domitian. He was a bloodthirsty tyrant with an ideological cover story. He had, by successive purges in the name of Marxism, reduced a party with a genuine intellectual and even moral basis to a disciplined organization for enforcing his whims—while retaining in a debased form the phraseology, and the emotional self-justification, of the original humanist vision. He and his adherents were not just terrorists, they were self-righteous terrorists.

To induce a body of men trained in this tradition to abandon terrorist practices is anyhow a formidable task. And it is made much more so by the fact that the basic justification for terror was the idea, central to Communist doctrine, of the party apparatus' divine right to rule the country.

Moreover, the repudiation of the Stalinist past means, in effect, repudiation of the processes that brought the present leaders to the fore within the party by the elimination of so many of their opponents and established the party's power in the face of general hostility. Past history has seen many attempts to liberalize autocracies. But these have almost always found themselves in self-contradiction—for the reason Tolstoy gives in connection with the "liberal" landlords, who would do anything for the peasant except get off his back.

Stalin's method of rule sought its economic justification in the idea that Russia needed a crash program of industrialization. Marx's own view was that only societies that were already highly industrialized could be taken over by a socialist party. The Russian Marxists, having, on the contrary, taken over a comparatively backward country, spoke—in terms that would have been meaningless to Marx—of "constructing" socialism, by which they meant the creation *ex post facto* of the economic and social base that they should theoretically have had in the first place. This is not the context for entering into the argument as to whether the industrial advances achieved under Stalin could not have been at least equaled or more probably bettered by less violent and destructive methods, even under Communist Party rule. What is certain is that in 1953 the economy had reached an impasse.

Stalin left the Soviet Union a disproportionately industrialized country of great military strength, with a grotesquely inefficient agriculture; a country in which the self-perpetuating party bureaucracy was the repository of power and was equipped with dogma justifying its sole right to rule.

Even in 1953, it was plain that Stalin's legacy had many disadvantages to the new rulers. The extreme unpopularity of the Terror, even in party circles, made it advisable for them to seek other methods of maintaining their power. At the same time, the concentration of the dictatorship in one unquestioned leader of immensely forceful character was no longer practicable. In relations with the foreign Communist parties, too, the removal of Stalin damaged the status of the Soviet Union as the sole source of right doctrine, and rendered some attempt at devolution unavoidable.

Changes in policy were thus, to some degree, inevitable. These could have been made without attaching any open blame to the different policies of the Stalin era, and at first this was the method pursued. But plainly the motives for not merely changing the old arrangements but also denouncing them and their patron were powerful ones.

1953—55: Beria's and Malenkov's De-Stalinizations

The first reversal of Stalinist measures is associated with the Secret Police chief, Beria. He alone of the Soviet leaders, Khrushchev tells us, "did not deem it necessary to conceal his joy at Stalin's coffin."

Beria had himself been threatened by Stalin's actions during the last eighteen months of his life. These had included a purge of Beria's supporters in Georgia and, in connection with the "Doctors' Plot," censure of the organs of State Security at a time when they had been under Beria's control (for, meanwhile, Stalin had replaced Beria's nominees in the Ministry of State Security with a group of hostile officials—Semyon Ignatiev as Minister; Mikhail Ryumin, Stalin's personal security man, as one Vice-Minister; and Alexander Yepishev, of Khrushchev's old Ukrainian party machine, as the other. These men had ruled the police during the Doctors' Plot episode.)

When Stalin died Malenkov and Beria grasped the main instruments of power and, as was later said, "presented the Central Committee with a *fait accompli.*" Malenkov, remaining the leading Secretary of the party, took over the Premiership as well, while Beria regained control of the police ministries, now united in a single MVD. But other veteran leaders like Molotov and Khrushchev, though weakened, were not eliminated. And within two weeks Malenkov was forced, evidently with the approval of Beria, to give up his party post—leaving Khrushchev as the senior Secretary, though still ranking only fifth or sixth in the leadership as a whole.

Beria continued to maneuver. On April 4, 1953, his MVD issued a statement repudiating the "Doctors' Plot." Ignatiev was censured and Ryumin arrested. Shortly, the rulers installed by Stalin in Georgia were publicly condemned and dismissed, and a number of Beria's supporters who had been arrested early in 1952 were rehabilitated and restored to power.

These measures, though bluntly directed against Stalin's final arrangements, were in themselves no more than a reconsolidation of Beria's personal power. But other moves more genuinely established a political theme and program in some degree opposed to Stalin's. On May 6, 1953, *Pravda* published a decree dated April 28 awarding the Order of the Red Banner of Labor to G. I. Petrovsky on the occasion of his seventy-fifth birthday. Petrovsky was the only survivor of those leading Bolsheviks who had been removed from the Politburo during the 1930's. He had meanwhile held a minor post in a Moscow museum, and no public reference had been made to him for fifteen years. That this was a conscious demonstration against Stalin is even clearer when we note that Petrovsky's seventy-fifth birthday had actually occurred on February 4, when Stalin was still alive!

Meanwhile, another announcement (in contrast to violent propaganda about the dangerous increase in economic and other crimes that had marked Stalin's last period) appeared in a Decree of the U.S.S.R. Supreme Soviet, "On the Amnesty," which provided for the release of a large number of short-term, nonpolitical prisoners, on the grounds that "observation of the law and socialist order has grown stronger" (*Pravda,* March 28, 1953).

During the whole period of Beria's ascendancy—from March until June, 1953—there was a greater abstention from praise of Stalin and a greater implied criticism of him than at any time up to a few weeks before Khrushchev's "secret speech" of February, 1956. Emphasis was given to "collective leadership," as in a key *Pravda* article of April 16: "Collectivity is the highest principle of party leadership." It is extraordinary and notable, considering the enormous emphasis given to the feats of the Generalissimo during the war, that no reference to Stalin occurred in Nikolai Bulganin's speech as War Minister on May 1, 1953, or in his Order of the Day for the VE Day Anniversary of May 9. *Kommunist* in May, 1953, described the "cult of personality" as "exceedingly harmful." The published theses on the fiftieth anniversary of the party referred to Stalin only four times and very much in passing, while Lenin was given many mentions.

The two expressions "collective leadership" and "cult of personality" were to become the key phrases of de-Stalinization over the following years. "Collective leadership" was much spoken of even in Stalin's time. The old dictator frequently stated the convention that the party was ruled by a group of elected leaders, in the Central Committee and the Politburo, through mutual consultation. The successive constitutions of the Soviet Communist Party provided for such a process. But there had been no reality in it during the period when Stalin would, if he felt like it, simply order the arrest and shooting of a Politburo member who took a line he disapproved of. And in fact, the party and the Soviet state were organized to put into practice the will of Stalin alone. Through the forthcoming period, a severe political struggle for the leading position took place. It has always been doubtful whether a centralized one-party state of the Soviet type can in fact be ruled effectively except by a single leader. But for four years after Stalin's death none of the contenders was able to achieve unchallenged leadership. The old slogan of collective leadership was thus given a certain meaning—even though it was later explained that the majority of the Presidium were antiparty schemers who, far from cooperating as a friendly group, each contributing his wisdom to the common cause, were viciously intriguing for power. And, ironically enough, the leader who finally came to power, Khrushchev, did so by accusing the others of addiction to Stalin's undemocratic practices. In any case, through all the political crises right up to the present, collective leadership became the orthodox description of whatever form of leadership happened to be current. And at least this may have had some effect in preventing any easy transition to untrammeled one-man dictatorship.

The "cult of personality" is a far more direct challenge to the Stalin tradition. Increasingly, for twenty years, the genius of Stalin in every field, his unique competence to rule in war and peace, and the lavish gratitude due him by the entire world were a constant theme of Soviet press and propaganda. While the new talk of "collective leadership" was, as it were, a defensive slogan carrying only oblique criticism of Stalin, the "cult of personality" was an offensive one directly challenging the past.

It became, and has remained, the target of all attacks upon Stalin and his system. Two points should be noted at once. First, during the period of the strongest attacks upon this "cult," other leaders built themselves a similar if much lesser body of personal adulation. In particular, it is now alleged— quite truly—that Khrushchev during his period of ascendancy had thrust himself into the history books and grabbed totally unwarranted credit for his role in war and peace, and had built himself up as the single infallible figure. Second, and more important, the "cult of personality"—which is, in effect, an allegation of vanity and flattery—is not quite the essential that made Stalin's rule deplorable. It mattered much less to his victims that towns were being named after him and that this abject applause was being granted to him than that he was ruling them by terror and falsehood. The centering of attention on the "cult" is a curiously oblique maneuver: as will be seen, it seems to have reflected a certain ambiguity in the whole treatment of Stalin and his system by the new rulers.

Beria was arrested in June, 1953, and probably killed at once by his colleagues, though it was later announced that he was tried, in secret, in December. His defeat did not lead to a restoration of Stalin's policies. The references to Stalin became, it is true, cool rather than cold, and some of Beria's more "liberal" notions, such as concessions to the national minorities, were withdrawn. But on the whole, for the next eighteen months, a fairly consistent trend of reform was pursued. Beria's fall involved the ruin of the police apparatus as an independent repository of power. Henceforth, it came under the full control of the party leadership. And, just as Beria had started to rehabilitate some of Stalin's victims, now the cases of those liquidated by Beria himself were to come up for review.

The leading figure in the country was now Georgi Malenkov, whose domestic policy may be summed up as an attempt to conciliate the population by economic means. The grip of the bureaucracy remained unaffected, though the terrorist extremes of the Stalin years were repudiated amid execrations against Beria. But it was now proposed to give some thought to the consumer. In August, 1953, Malenkov announced that the consumer-goods industries were to be given as much emphasis as heavy industry itself. This was the first sign of a modernization of Stalin's ideas on the development of industry. Stalin had operated on the principle of hard discipline and minimum incentive for the workers. His view was that the building of heavy industry was so urgent that it left no spare resources for the production of more than the minimum of goods required by the Soviet consumer. It seems clear that a regime feeling obliged to relax its tight political control on the population would also find it sensible to provide the Russian worker with better incentives: if the whip was to be used less fiercely, the carrot would have to be juicier.

There is no doubt that this course was popular, as far as it went. But Malenkov's position was not secure. Nikita Khrushchev, who had been elected First Secretary of the Central Committee in September, 1953, gradually raised allies against Malenkov. Late in 1954, a campaign in favor of the old line on heavy industry was launched, supported by Khrushchev and Molotov. Other policies of Malenkov's, including proposals he had made for the relaxation of international tension, also came under attack. At the same time, the police chiefs responsible for the execution of the victims of the "Leningrad Affair" of 1949–50, by which Malenkov had destroyed his then rivals for Stalin's favor, were tried and shot. This attack led to Malenkov's resignation from the Premiership (though not from the Party Presidium), in February, 1955.

During 1955, Khrushchev, though still not in full control, continued to advance. He effected a degree of reconciliation with Tito, whom Stalin had denounced as an imperialist agent in 1948–49; but Khrushchev as yet blamed only the already denounced Beria, not Stalin, for the breach— to Tito's obvious chagrin. Having rehabilitated Malenkov's victims of 1949–50, and on the pretext of investigating cases criminally framed by Beria, Khrushchev sponsored a delving into the massacres of party officials in Stalin's lifetime.

Still there was no direct attack on Stalin. On the contrary, his birthday on December 21 was celebrated more warmly in 1955 than it had been in 1954.

Meanwhile, the Twentieth Party Congress, the first since Stalin's death, had been set for February, 1956. As it approached, there were a few signs of increasing coldness to Stalin, but nothing to foreshadow the dramatic events now impending.

Thus, all in all, the period from 1953 to 1956 had seen some important changes as compared with Stalin's time. There had been a reversal of some of his policies and a certain coldness toward his prestige. As a result of Beria's fall, the power of the police had been curbed, and rehabilitation of victims of the past had commenced, though Stalin still had not been blamed openly. In fact, everything had been implicit, gradual, undramatic.

This was now to change. At the Twentieth Party Congress, held in February, 1956, Khrushchev delivered his Confidential Report, or "secret speech," and for the first time, many of the crimes and errors of the past were denounced and blamed squarely on the old dictator.

1956: The "Secret Speech"

It was late in February, 1956, just after the Twentieth Party Congress had closed, that extraordinary rumors began to sweep Moscow. Khrushchev, it was said, had made, *in camera,* a speech attacking Stalin that had caused a violent sensation among the assembled delegates. No confirmation was forthcoming. The *Stenographic Report* of the Congress (Vol. II, p. 402) simply stated that, on February 25, "in closed session the Congress heard a Report by the First Secretary of the Central Committee of the Communist Party of the Soviet Union, N. S. Khrushchev, 'On the Cult of Personality and its Consequences,' and adopted a decision on the question."

But the reports were persistent and detailed. Finally in June, 1956, the U.S. State Department published a version that it had obtained from an east European source (probably in Poland, where the speech was circulated outside the party ranks for which it was intended). The authenticity of this version has never been openly confirmed by the Russians, but outside the U.S.S.R. it has long been accepted as genuine by Communist and non-Communist alike.

Khrushchev's open references to Stalin in his Report to the Congress on February 14 had been fairly friendly. In his speech on February 16, Mikoyan had made several remarks that constituted the first direct criticism naming Stalin and a hint that more was required. He had called for a revision of Stalin's last work, *Economic Problems of Socialism in the U.S.S.R.,* and described a well-known dictum of Stalin's as "hardly helpful, hardly correct." He had referred not very indirectly to "Lenin's Testament" —the document hostile to Stalin that had long circulated in the West but had been suppressed in Russia. He had dropped other anti-Stalinist hints, such as one to the effect that histories of the Transcaucasian party organization had falsified the facts. And he had spoken of "Comrade Kossior" and "Comrade Antonov-Ovseyenko," victims of the Great Purge of the thirties never named meanwhile, as "wrongly declared enemies of the people."

On February 24, 1956, a substantive resolution was adopted on Khrushchev's Report. It instructed the Central Committee "not to weaken the struggle against vestiges of the cult of the individual." This was very different from the line taken the next day.

It was plain, even at the time, that there were elements who wished to go no further. In his speech on February 18, 1956, Lazar Kaganovich, veteran member of the Presidium and one of Stalin's closest aides in the Terror, almost directly condemned any "unprincipled" personal attack on Stalin:

> After the Nineteenth Congress of the Party [in 1952] the Central Committee boldly (I have in mind the boldness that has to do with ideas—that is principled, theoretical) raised the question of the struggle against the cult of the individual. This is not an easy question. But the Central Committee gave a correct, Marxist-Leninist party answer to it.

We learn from Khrushchev's speech to another Party Congress, five years later, that a severe struggle was in fact going on among the top leadership on the issue:

> Comrade delegates, 1 want to tell the Congress how the Antiparty Group[1] reacted to the proposal to raise the question of abuses of power in the period of the cult of the individual at the Twentieth Congress. The proposal was violently resisted by Molotov, Kaganovich, Malenkov, Voroshilov, and others. We told them in reply to their objections that if they resisted consideration of this question, we would put the matter to the Congress delegates. We had no doubt that the Congress would express itself in favor of the consideration of this question. Only then did they agree, and the question of the cult of the individual was reported on at the Twentieth Congress.

We need not take this account as wholly objective. But at least it shows —and this is a major key to the whole "Stalinism" issue over the years that followed—that the struggle between the political factions in the Presidium was an important element in the whole process.

And so the "secret speech" was delivered. It was a sustained invective against Stalin's role in the party after the Seventeenth Party Congress in 1934 and, more particularly, since the commencement of the Great Terror

---

[1] A misnomer for what should be called the Anti-Khrushchev Group. The term is used here and elsewhere in this volume because it has become common usage and appears in the cited Soviet materials.

in 1936. It painted an atrocious picture of Stalin's actions. Starting with a denunciation of the cult of personality and the suppression of "party democracy," with many quotations showing the ostensible opposition of Marx and Lenin to such phenomena, it then revealed the documents long known to the outside world, dating from 1922–23, in which Lenin had denounced Stalin as unsuitable for such a powerful position as that of General Secretary of the Party, and in other ways showed his disapproval of him. At first (Khrushchev said) Stalin had heeded Lenin's strictures, but in the latter part of his rule his negative characteristics had predominated, and he had "used extreme methods and mass repressions." These iniquities had only come to light recently, "especially after the unmasking of the Beria gang," when, for instance, it had come out that "of the 139 members and candidates of the party's Central Committee who were elected at the Seventeenth Congress [in 1934] 98 persons, i.e., 70 percent, were arrested and shot (mostly in 1937–38). (*Indignation in the hall.*)"

After the murder of Sergei Kirov, Secretary of the Central Committee and Party Secretary in Leningrad, on December 1, 1934, the Terror had begun, directed against "honest workers of the party and of the Soviet State." At the Central Committee meeting of February-March, 1937, members had "questioned the rightness of this course," and as a result many high officials perished. Khrushchev quoted declarations made by executed leaders saying that their cases were frame-ups and that torture had been employed. He cited, for the first time, a telegram of January 20, 1939, issued by Stalin on behalf of the party's Central Committee: "The application of methods of physical pressure in NKVD practice is permissible from 1937 on, in accordance with permission of the Central Committee."

Dealing next with World War II, Khrushchev accused Stalin of failure to prepare the country militarily, refusal to listen to warnings of impending German attack, and pessimism and incompetence in the handling of the campaigns. Soviet defeats were also attributed to "Stalin's annihilation of many military commanders" in the years 1937–41.

In 1943–44, Stalin had ordered the wholesale deportation of a number of minority nationalities from the Caucasus and elsewhere in collective punishment for alleged disloyalty during the war. Khrushchev denounced this as "monstrous" and "un-Leninist" in the case of five of the seven nationalities involved, while remaining silent on the other two (the Volga-Germans and the Crimean Tatars).

Going on to the period after the war, Khrushchev referred to the later cases of intraparty terror—the "Leningrad Affair" of 1949–50, in which Politburo member Nikolai Voznesensky and a number of others perished, and the so-called Mingrelian Affair of 1951–52, which decimated the Georgian party leadership. Referring to the "Doctors' Plot," Khrushchev revealed that Stalin issued orders to arrest a group of eminent Soviet medical specialists. He personally issued advice on the conduct of the investigation and the method of interrogation of the arrested persons. He said that Academician Vinogradov should be put in chains, another should be beaten. Present at this Congress as a delegate is the former Minister of State Security, Comrade Ignatiev. Stalin told him curtly, "If you do not obtain confessions from the doctors we will shorten you by a head." (*Tumult in the hall.*)

Stalin personally called the investigative judge, gave him instructions, advised him on which investigative methods should be used; these methods were simple: beat, beat, and, once again, beat.

Khrushchev then attacked Stalinist historiography, and in particular charged that the "Short Course" history of the party—the most widely circulated of all the publications of the Stalin period—had been written solely with a view to adulating Stalin. Stalin had inserted in his own hand such sentences as: "Although he performed his task as leader of the party and the people with consummate skill and enjoyed the unreserved support of the entire Soviet people, Stalin never allowed his work to be marred by the slightest hint of vanity, conceit, or self-adulation."

Stalin's passion for statues of himself, films glorifying his role in the war, and so on, was then attacked. This was followed by the assertion that Stalin had totally mishandled the country's agriculture in the postwar period— for example, by attempting to increase taxes on the peasantry by a sum larger than their entire income.

He knew the country and agriculture only from films. And these films had dressed up and beautified the existing situation in agriculture. Many films so pictured *kolkhoz* [collective farm] life that the tables were bending from the weight of turkeys and geese. Evidently, Stalin thought that it was actually so.

Khrushchev went on to maintain that members of the Politburo had not been in a position to resist Stalin, who arrested or suspended them at will and, during the last months of his life, was planning to get rid of them—in particular, Molotov and Mikoyan.

The speech ended with a general appeal for "Leninist principles of party leadership, characterized above all by the main principle of collective leadership," at the same time calling for the correction of "widely spread erroneous views connected with the cult of the individual in the sphere of history, philosophy, economics and other sciences, as well as literature and the fine arts," and for the restoration of "socialist legality."

The speech was a dramatic and, at first sight, devastating and complete demolition of Stalin. But there are certain important reservations to be made. The routine appeal to Marx and Lenin against the "personality cult" has a certain basis; it is perfectly true that Marx and Lenin were not themselves men of great personal vanity, as Stalin was. Nevertheless, almost anything can be justified by appeal to these texts (a practice that has been attacked in Communist literature as "Talmudism"). In this case, for instance, a supporter of Stalin might well have quoted the view of Lenin (no liberal) that "Soviet socialist democracy does not in any way contradict one-man management and dictatorship; the will of the class is sometimes given effect by a dictator . . . ." It might also be said that in substituting one authority for another (Lenin for Stalin) Khrushchev was very near a "personality cult" of Lenin. Certainly he gave many of Lenin's pronouncements in a way that implied, "Lenin said it, so it must be right," rather than as argument.

Justification from Lenin is nothing new in Soviet life. Stalin employed it continually—though incorrectly, in Khrushchev's view. For example, Khrushchev's speech condemns Stalin for holding that Leninism implies the sharpening of class war as socialism becomes more firmly established. What Stalin argued and Lenin had explicitly denied was that as the Communist Party's grip became firmer and firmer, the internal enemies of the regime would become more and more desperate and dangerous; this was the theoretical justification for the Great Terror.

But though correct on this important general point, Khrushchev proceeded to support his theme of Lenin's comparative humanitarianism by saying that the death penalty had been abolished in February, 1920, on Lenin's orders. This was an absurd piece of special pleading. In the first place, shootings did not cease in practice, and the penalty was officially restored almost at once (as Khrushchev does not mention) in May, 1920. Moreover, Khrushchev was in no position to resort to this type of argument, for, Stalin's successors having made no effort to abolish it, the death penalty is still in force! In fact, political executions—of Beria's associate Mir Dzhafar Bagirov and his followers—took place only two months *after* Khrushchev's speech.

Moreover, since Stalin's death a decree of May 6, 1954, had already extended the death penalty to cover murder as well as treason. In 1958 it was again extended to cover acts of terrorism or banditry. On May 5, 1961, certain cases of embezzlement, forgery, and violence on the part of prison inmates were added to the list of capital crimes. In July, 1961, "serious" currency offenses were added (and two offenders were executed by retrospective application of this law). And on February 15, 1962, the death penalty was yet again extended, to cover attacks on the life, health, or dignity of policemen, and certain cases of rape and bribery. Over the years increasing numbers of executions have been announced.

This is a minor example of Khrushchev's inconsistency. Much the same could be said on the major issues. Lenin held, as Khrushchev said, that repression should become less and less necessary as Soviet power became more firmly consolidated. In fact, repression in present-day Russia, though less than in Stalin's time, is far stricter than in Lenin's. Again, on "party democracy," Khrushchev made much of the early Party Congresses and of how Lenin insisted that "the party discuss at length" the problems facing it. But the Twentieth Congress, itself, to which Khrushchev put this point, simply heard a series of agreed speeches from the leadership, accepted them unanimously, and dispersed, precisely as in Stalin's time. Nor has there been much improvement since.

It is also significant to note Khrushchev's general attitude to terror as such. His main denunciation of Stalin was for directing terror against his own accomplices and disciples. Apart from this, he was concerned only with terror against loyal Army officers and with the mass deportations of some national minorities. It will be seen that there were considerable omissions in his register of victims of Stalinism. It was nowhere implied that it was not perfectly legitimate to "liquidate" non-Communists. On the contrary, Khrushchev invoked Lenin as having "without hesitation used the most extreme methods against enemies." He condemned Stalin for using "physical annihilation not only against actual enemies" but also against loyal Communists. Again, Khrushchev virtually confined his attack on the Great Terror to its effect on the top ranks of the party, the odd thousands of whose execution Stalin personally approved. Actually, of course, the Terror affected the population on a mass scale.

A touchstone of the party's attitude to terror may be found in Khrushchev's references to a class intermediate between "enemies" and good comrades—that is, the Communists who in the twenties had formed oppositions within the party objecting not to Leninist essentials, but to particular policies of Stalin's. Here Khrushchev's attitude was ambiguous. He implied that Stalin had ordered the Kirov murder of 1934; but he did not exonerate Zinoviev, who was shot for it. He asked whether it was "necessary to annihilate" people who "broke with Trotskyism and returned to Leninist positions"; but this is rather different from pleading for Trotskyists proper. He defined the political line of the "oppositionists" as leading "actually toward the restoration of capitalism and capitulation to the world bourgeoisie," which would seem to make them "enemies." On the other hand, he noted with approval that in Lenin's time "during the furious ideological fight . . . extreme repressive measures were not used against them." Perhaps this uncertain attitude is best summed up in Khrushchev's carefully qualified comment: "In regard to those persons who in their time had opposed the party line, there were often no sufficiently serious reasons for their physical annihilation." If this is what was felt, even twenty years later, about "companions of Lenin," it is natural enough that Khrushchev did not conceal his approval of "extreme measures" against the rest.

Even more striking was the extraordinarily varying nature of Khrushchev's remarks about Stalin. On the one hand we read, "You see to what Stalin's mania for greatness led. He had completely lost consciousness of reality." And we read denunciations of Stalin on the grounds that his agricultural plan was based on no facts or figures, since "a genius does not need to count"; that he approved of "loathsome adulation"; and that he personally ordered the beatings of prisoners. On the other hand we are told that he was not a "giddy despot" but looked at matters "from the position of the interest of the working class, the interest of the laboring people, the interest of the victory of socialism and Communism"; and that he was "one of the strongest Marxists," possessed of "logic, strength, and will."

At the same time Khrushchev was careful to say that he himself, and Stalin's surviving associates, had no responsibility whatever for anything that had happened. As we have seen, Khrushchev stated that the Central Committee of 1934 was largely massacred. But Khrushchev and his colleagues are precisely the men who survived those and later massacres. Khrushchev denounced Stalin for planning to eliminate the members of the Party Presidium in 1953 in order to replace them with younger and more pliable men. But (commentators asked) were not Khrushchev himself and his colleagues the beneficiaries of an identical operation fifteen years previously?

In general, the other reasons Khrushchev gave for his and his colleagues' inaction—or rather collaboration—were these: first, the members of the Politburo "viewed these matters in a different way at different times," which seems to mean that they believed Stalin to be right as often as not. Secondly, Khrushchev pleaded fear of arrest. And lastly, the members were in a "very difficult situation"; since the Politburo met only occasionally, "we will understand how difficult it was for any member of the Political Bureau to take a stand against one or another unjust or improper procedure." This seems to mean that no one could open an attack on Stalin without the virtual certainty that the others would throw him to the wolves.

More basically yet, the attempt to reconcile denunciation of Stalin with acceptance of the society he constructed was bound to lead to odd results. Khrushchev's central themes were that Russia had been ruled by a ruthless dictator, but that the state was at the same time essentially sound and "socialist"; that Stalin had seized and maintained power through the illegal shooting of the elected Central Committee, but that his nominees, still ruling after his death, were in the legitimate line of party succession. It is these considerations, more than anything else, that affected the reliability of the speech. Although it was of extraordinary value in confirming various long-suspected crimes of the old dictator and in giving some real idea of Soviet political life, it was in certain respects almost as much a falsification of history as the Stalin versions it denounced. And the political reasons for this falsification were obviously compelling.

Moreover, there was complete evasion of any serious Marxist or other analysis. The formula was to attribute all errors to the "cult of personality." But, as the Italian Communist leader, Palmiro Togliatti, said:

> First, all that was good was attributed to the superhuman, positive qualities of one man: now all that is evil is attributed to his equally exceptional and even astonishing faults. In the one case, as well as in the other, we are outside the criterion of judgment intrinsic in Marxism. The true problems are evaded, which are why and how Soviet society could reach and did reach certain forms alien to the democratic way and to the legality that it had set for itself, even to the point of degeneration. ["Nine Questions on Stalinism," *Nuovi Argomenti,* June 16, 1956.]

Revolt and Repression

In the Soviet Union, the "secret speech" remained unpublished. But it was certainly read and discussed throughout the party, and there can have been few who did not learn of it. A Central Committee Resolution on the personality cult, on June 30 (published in *Pravda,* July 2, 1956), was of a much more formal nature than the "secret speech," condemning the "cult" in general terms as leading to violations of Leninist principles, but not adducing particular crimes. It argued that "the people" would allegedly have been against any attempt to take action against Stalin:

> Any action against him would have been assessed under those conditions as . . . an action against the building of socialism, as a blow against the unity of the party and the entire state, which would have been extremely dangerous under conditions of capitalist encirclement. In addition, the successes that the working people of the Soviet Union were achieving under the leadership of the Communist Party . . . created an atmosphere in which individual errors and shortcomings seemed less significant against the background of tremendous successes.

And again, it asserted,

> No personality cult could change the nature of the socialist state, which is based on public ownership of the means of production, the alliance of the working class and the peasantry, and the friendship of peoples.

It is curious that it can be baldly asserted that one-man rule could not change such things as the "friendship of peoples," when Stalin—as Khrushchev had admitted—actually ordered the deportation of entire nationalities.

The denunciation of the cult of Stalin's personality presented a number of technical problems. Russia was littered with statues of Stalin, with towns (ten of them), streets, institutes, and factories named for him—as was eastern Europe. Some of the east European towns were now renamed (together with streets like Stalin Street in Prague—formerly Adolf Hitler Street, and, before that, Marshal Foch Street), as were the highest peaks in the Pamirs, the Carpathians, and the Balkan Mountains. But for the time being, Stalingrad retained its name, as if to show that the attack was on the "cult" of Stalin rather than on the man himself. In the same way, his body remained, for another five years, in its honorable mausoleum on Red Square. Statues presented a problem: the monstrosity in Prague lasted until 1963. A particularly trying task was the removal of the busts of Stalin that had been placed on Russia's forty-odd highest peaks by a generation of Soviet alpinists.

But while such symbolic actions were slowly put into effect, movements of opinion at a deeper level were changing the mood of Russia. There are many points to be raised about the Khrushchev speech. But its *impact* derived from the forthright and detailed exposure of Stalin's cruelty and vanity. There were many nuances and saving clauses and a number of limitations on the scope of the political criticism of Stalin. But, for the moment, these were scarcely noted. Everywhere in the Communist and the non-Communist worlds, the speech appeared as completely destructive of the claims put forward over twenty years by the Soviet regime, and as a complete recognition of the truth of criticisms made by its enemies. The Communist parties in the West were severely shaken; and the Communist regimes in eastern Europe, still mainly headed by Stalin's personal nominees and imitators, were struck by a profound trauma that led eventually to the overthrow of the Polish Stalinists in favor of Gomulka and to the Hungarian Revolution of 1956. These events in their turn had a profound effect in Russia, recalling the leadership and Khrushchev personally to the old duties of securing the party's monopoly of rule, by repression where necessary.

Within the Soviet Union itself, the people and the party membership at large were severely shocked. There were attempts to press things to their logical conclusion, beyond the inconsistent position now adopted by the leadership. An article in *Pravda* of April 5, 1956, mentioned that a number of Communists, mainly in "intellectual" branches of the party, had "permitted themselves to make inaccurate and essentially demagogic statements." Student meetings, too, demanded more liberty, under the slogan "Democracy—from below!"

A crucial barometer of all Soviet relaxations, both under Stalin and since his death, has been on the literary "front." The first hint of any degree of relaxation has always been taken up promptly by writers wishing to tell the truth, as they saw it, or to express their personal moods. As early as the mid-thirties "socialist realism" was made the official line in Soviet literature, and it was made clear that the party was the final arbiter of what was permissible under that phrase. The first burgeonings of independent thinking, manifesting themselves in fiction and verse, have invariably attracted the close vigilance of the ideological bureaucracy. A minor "thaw" in 1954 had petered out under severe attacks. Now, the attacks on the Stalinist past again encouraged the writers to speak up. Poems, novels, plays, and essays took up the dual theme of the sufferings of the past and the aspirations of the present—themes that came to be known in 1957 as "last year's errors."

Writers and historians welcomed the revelations concerning the Stalin era as an invitation to reveal the whole truth. For the moment, the cultural authorities permitted the publication of such works as Vladimir Dudintsev's significantly named novel, *Not by Bread Alone,* or poems about the purges like those of Olga Bergholtz and Margarita Aliger. Such slackening of vigilance was eventually "corrected," but even then it seems to have been difficult to get agreement in ruling circles about what constituted the truth about the past—or how much could now be told. The new history of the party designed to replace Stalin's did not appear until 1959, and (as we shall see) it had to be radically altered in its second edition in 1962.

Meanwhile, the historians also pressed on. Even before the Twentieth Congress, at a Conference of Readers of *Problems of History,* the major historical journal, on January 25–28, 1956, its Assistant Editor Burdzhalov had attacked Stalin's "Short Course" (the pro-Stalin party history). He was counterattacked by historians from the party apparatus. But after Mikoyan had supported his view in his speech to the Twentieth Congress, Burdzhalov, backed by most of his editorial board, made a powerful attempt to use the new atmosphere to secure objective treatment of party history. In particular, in his article on Bolshevik policy in March-April, 1917, and in a number of articles on Caucasian history by various other "liberal" historians, several long-suppressed truths began to emerge. Attacks were made on him, but for most of 1956 he was able to reply. In October and November, however, he and the magazine were officially attacked (in *Kommunist,* No. 10, 1956, and *Pravda,* November 20, 1956) for ideological error due to "rotten" or at best "hasty" elements. After intervention by Mikhail Suslov and the party authorities, on March 9, 1957, the party's Central Committee adopted a resolution condemning the historical journal. Burdzhalov and seven other members of the board were removed and the controversy was silenced.

Similarly, in March, 1957, Khrushchev personally harangued and threatened a meeting of the leading literary figures for their lack of discipline, and the comparative freedom of the year past petered out amid silence and apologies.

It had been no part of the attack on Stalin to fall into "rotten liberalism." By now, even the view of Stalin himself put forward earlier in the year began to be modified. On December 23, 1956, *Pravda* published an article by the ideologist Azizyan, which pointed out that

> Such a teaching—Stalinism—is unknown to us. It must be clear to those who are versed in Marxism-Leninism that Stalin has not left any separate teaching of his own. He was a major Marxist and was guided by the teaching of Marxism and Leninism in his activity.

Khrushchev's own—temporary—"rehabilitation" of Stalin took place at a Chinese reception in Moscow in January, 1957: he publicly declared his belief that "the term Stalinist, like Stalin himself, is inseparable from the high title of Communist."

The Rehabilitation Issue

And yet it was no longer possible to put the genie back in its bottle. The past had been made a political issue: even though the concern of the rulers was now to prevent a breakdown of their authority in any field, a fierce struggle for supremacy was going on, and the theme of vengeance or injustice awaiting correction was a valuable weapon. One particular process, once started, was difficult to halt. This was the appeals for rehabilitation of those whose imprisonment had already been admitted to be unjust, and of relatives and friends of the unjustly executed, followed by similar appeals for men whose cases had not yet been covered.

The first rehabilitations in 1953 had been the product of Beria's need to repudiate and abort the purges of Stalin's last period, which were directed at himself and at others in the leadership. For instance, the public rehabilitation of the doctors of the "Doctors' Plot" and of the Georgians of the "Mingrelian Affair" was complete by mid-April, 1953.

The fall of Beria, the same year, involved accusations against him of having illegally persecuted and executed certain Communists. Although only a few were named at first, the possibility of rehabilitation was thus extended to the victims of the late thirties.

That such cases led only gradually to the key crimes of the Stalin era with which Beria had *not* been associated seems to be shown by Khrushchev's statement (in the "secret speech") that the cases of two prominent Communists shot in the thirties—Rudzutak and Komarov—were examined in 1955. Meanwhile, as we have seen, the "Leningrad Case" victims had been rehabilitated in December, 1954.

Khrushchev, in the "secret speech," mentioned that the Central Committee of the party had "looked into" Beria's crimes. Any investigation of the Secret Police records in the Soviet Union was bound to turn up a good deal of interesting material, especially if the Central Committee was not responsible to a single man who could tell it what to find and who could suppress anything he did not like.

In any case, by the time of the "secret speech," the issue had been thrown wide open. Khrushchev said,

> Having at its disposal numerous data showing brutal wilfulness towards party cadres, the Central Committee has created a party commission under the control of the Central Committee Presidium: it was charged with investigating what made possible the mass repressions against the majority of the Central Committee members and candidates elected at the Seventeenth [1934] Congress of the All-Union Communist Party (of Bolsheviks).
>
> . . . The commission has presented to the Central Committee Presidium lengthy and documented materials pertaining to mass repressions against the delegates to the Seventeenth Party Congress and against members of the Central Committee elected at that Congress. These materials have been studied by the Presidium.

In the course of the struggle for power these "materials" were to prove irresistible. And even if they were not intended only, or even primarily, as weapons against Stalin, henceforth they inevitably involved him.

The way in which this aspect of anti-Stalinism was linked with the vagaries of the power struggle and of day-to-day policy considerations was revealed by the treatment of the generals of the Red Army, executed by Stalin in June, 1937. In the "secret speech," Khrushchev referred in a general way to "Stalin's annihilation of many military commanders and political workers during 1937–41," but the only names he mentioned were those of three generals then surviving (Rokossovsky, Gorbatov, and Meretskov) plus one who had been killed in the war (Podlas). These had all been released and rehabilitated even in Stalin's time, and thus no direct attack on the Great Trial of the generals was made—a notable contrast to the open rehabilitation of various political Stalinists who had been shot in the purge. Over the next two years, the rehabilitation of the generals began. That is, their names were again mentioned, though still without overt reference to their final fates. They simply reappeared, one by one, in historical and military journals as former good comrades, now dead. In 1958, a supplement to the *Large Soviet Encyclopedia* was published, in which biographies were given of several former "unpersons" who had been omitted in the main body of the encyclopedia. These included Marshal Mikhail Tukhachevsky and other purged soldiers. But in the ensuing months a curious process of what has been called "de-rehabilitation" set in, and in the 1959 *History of the Communist Party of the Soviet Union,* Tukhachevsky was no longer mentioned in the lists of outstanding Soviet commanders. It was not until the Twenty-second Party Congress, in October, 1961, that, quite unexpectedly, Khrushchev himself and others delivered powerful defenses of the generals and attacks on their persecutors. This coincided with the first open attack on Marshal Voroshilov, who during the purges had been Stalin's Commissar for Defense. There is no doubt that these vagaries and inconsistencies reflect a contest between representatives of the army (whose press often took the initiative in making neutral or friendly references to the generals who had gone into oblivion) and political elements wishing to hold the line against too much, or too hasty, exposure of the past.

1957: The Antiparty Group

In June, 1957, came the showdown between Khrushchev and his enemies within the Party Presidium—henceforth labeled the Antiparty Group—Molotov, Malenkov, Kaganovich, and Dmitri Shepilov, who now tried, and failed, to overthrow him. That other prominent figures had also formed part of the Group was revealed at later dates—Bulganin (1958), Mikhail Pervukhin and Maxim Saburov (1959), and Voroshilov (1961). It was natural that they should be accused, among other things, of having been Stalin's accomplices, or of having egged him on to his worst excesses. But the theme of the "Stalinism" of the Antiparty Group could be developed in two different ways: its members could be charged with complicity in criminal terrorism or accused merely of adhering to outdated, "dogmatic," and erroneous political views. The original public accusation against them —the Resolution of the Central Committee of June 29, 1957—referred in passing to "the errors and shortcomings born of the personality cult," and to attempts to "drag the party into the erroneous methods of leadership condemned by the Twentieth Party Congress," but in general emphasized rather their "sectarian and dogmatic" attitudes on various matters of policy. Stalin's name does not appear in the Resolution, and no definite criminal accusations are made against members of the Group. (It was later revealed that during the "debate" in the Central Committee, various near-criminal charges had indeed been made, but they were not then published.)

However, during the weeks that followed, various attacks were made on the "criminal" activities of members of the Group. For example, Khrushchev soon accused Malenkov openly of having taken an active part in organizing the fabricated "Leningrad Affair." He repeated his allegations against Malenkov the following month, this time bringing in Stalin, though to some extent as a dupe of Malenkov's:

> Great blame in this matter attaches to Comrade Malenkov, who fell completely under the influence of Beria, was his shadow, and was a tool in his hands. Occupying a high position in the party and state, Comrade Malen-

kov not only failed to restrain J. V. Stalin, but very adroitly exploited Stalin's weaknesses and habits in the last years of his life. In many cases he egged him on to actions that merit severe condemnation. [*Pravda,* August 28, 1957.]

Again, the *motives* of the opposition were analyzed as stemming from fear of the truth:

The Antiparty Group put up a constant resistance to the measures that were introduced by the party [i.e., by Khrushchev and his allies] for the liquidation of the consequences of the personality cult, for the removal of the infringements of socialist legality that had occurred in the past, and for the creation of conditions that make it impossible for them to be repeated. No small part was played in this by the fact that Malenkov, Kaganovich, and Molotov were particularly deeply implicated in the grossest errors and shortcomings that had happened in the past. [*Party Life,* July, 1957.]

This is not the place for detailed consideration of the struggle for power among the Soviet leadership. But we may note in the circumstances of this June, 1957, clash clear indications that strictly ideological, or even policy, divisions are not in themselves crucial and that a very important, if not decisive, role is played by simple rivalry for power. The struggle was, indeed, debated in terms of policies and of political failures and successes. But as the attack on the Antiparty Group in the Central Committee's June Resolution shows, they were not themselves united on most policy issues. The single important policy matter that brought them together was opposition to a scheme Khrushchev had just launched for decentralizing industry and dissolving many of the ministries in Moscow concerned with it. Most—but again not all—of the Group held posts in the state machine, and the breakup of much of that machine would have affected them. But again, the struggle can only to a limited degree be represented as one between representatives of the state machine on the one hand and the party machine (which Khrushchev headed) on the other. Naturally, all the contenders used, and tried to strengthen, the institutions that they themselves controlled. But that this was a matter of convenience rather than principle was seen in 1964–65 when the post-Khrushchev rulers—all of whom had backed him against the Antiparty Group in 1957—largely reversed his attenuation of the state's control over the economy.

In the theoretical arguments whose terms have been employed in all Soviet controversy for the last decade, the twin and opposite errors have been labeled "dogmatism" and "revisionism." The former is used to indicate policies linked with the Stalin attitude—policies regarded as out-of-date, rigid, and inclined to rely too heavily on simple force. "Revisionism" is the error of relaxing controls so far as to endanger the party's monopoly grip on Soviet life, and of introducing policies that depart from basic party theory. The words are fairly vague. When the regime is pursuing "hard" policies, it is normal to attack revisionism; when it is on the tack of relaxation, dogmatism becomes the main target.

While the Antiparty Group was accused of "dogmatism," some of its members were also made responsible for the excessive "liberalism" of 1956 in arts and letters. Shepilov, who had been party Secretary in charge of culture at the time, "displayed rotten liberalism towards the antisocialist ideological propositions of a certain section of our literary and artistic intelligentsia" (*Problems of Philosophy*, No. 4, 1957); and it was even said that the Group as a whole had inspired these hostile *littérateurs*.

In actual fact, the Group was a coalition of reactionaries and reformers, united only by its opposition to Khrushchev and to certain of his policies (such as his vast scheme for the agricultural development of virgin lands in Central Asia) that cannot be categorized as either Stalinist or non-Stalinist. Initially, Malenkov was always named first among the Group's members. *His* policies, far from being dogmatist, had over the period of 1953–55 been more "liberal" than Khrushchev's own. Khrushchev's own coalition, moreover, was also a power grouping by no means united on any general anti-Stalinist principle.

When, later on, the struggle against dogmatism became stronger and that against revisionism weaker, Molotov was promoted to the leading role in the fallen Group. (In the first [1959] edition of the new *History of the CPSU,* Malenkov is still named first, but in the 1962 edition, Molotov takes first place, as he does in the great majority of references to the Antiparty Group at the Twenty-second Party Congress in October, 1961.)

Molotov himself can legitimately be accused of "dogmatism." To a lesser degree, the same appears true of Kaganovich and Voroshilov. Against the remainder, the accusation is not very impressive. The propaganda solution has been, as is natural, the smear by association. The Antiparty Group as a whole, and—by implication—all opposition to Khrushchev, was now treated as Molotovist, and this in turn was equated with "Stalinism."

1957–61: Rallentando

During the period 1957–61, de-Stalinization was not much emphasized. Direct attacks on Stalin were comparatively few and undramatic. Even in the renewed assault on the Antiparty Group in November, 1958–January, 1959, it was the Group's own responsibilities for the past, rather than Stalin's, that were stressed.

This is not to say that one clear policy was pursued on the issue. A continuing struggle in a minor key was waged, for example, between the conservative and liberal elements in the cultural field.

There was progress in other spheres. In December, 1958, as part of the penal reform, a new Decree on State Crimes replaced the relevant articles of the Criminal Code dating from Stalin's time. Certain notorious excesses, such as Article 58 i.c, which openly inflicted penalties on the families of "traitors" fleeing abroad, even if they were totally unimplicated, were dropped. On the other hand, the Decree remained draconic and provided severe punishment for all forms of action, organization, or discussion hostile to the government.

Legal practice, too, received some degree of reform. Andrei Vyshinsky, the notorious Prosecutor in the Great Trials, was denounced, together with his theory that confessions are the main element in a good case (but confessions are still used and treated as valid, as in the Powers and the Penkovsky Cases, in 1960 and 1963 respectively).

As to the actual rather than theoretical improvement in the penal camp system, we are on dubious ground. Estimates of the number of prisoners in Stalin's time vary widely, though there were certainly several millions by the lowest count. In 1953, after Stalin's death, there were riots and uprisings in a number of camps. These were followed by some attempt at least to ensure that the minimum rations the prisoners were supposed to get actually reached them. Various amnesties released mainly nonpolitical prisoners, but many of these were professional criminals arrested again in fairly short order. The only semiofficial hint of the number released was given by the Assistant Prosecutor General of the U.S.S.R., P. I. Kudriavtsev, to Professor Harold Berman of Harvard Law School in May, 1957. He "apparently wanted to convey the impression" that there were three million camp inmates at the time of Stalin's death but that only 800,000—900,000 remained in them in 1957. ("Soviet Law Reform," by Harold J. Berman, *The Yale Law Journal,* Vol. 66, No. 8.) There is some reason to believe that these figures are too small for both dates. As for the claim by Khrushchev that "there are no political prisoners in the prisons of our country at present" (speech to the Twenty-first Party Congress, January, 1959), this followed the announcement, only the previous month in the new Decree on State Crimes referred to above, of penalties from ten years' imprisonment to death for a whole series of specifically political offenses. And as the Chairman of the KGB (Secret Police), Alexander Shelepin, said in his speech to the same Congress, "We shall continue to punish mercilessly all the enemies of our people." (Shelepin spoke in even stronger terms to the Twenty-second Congress in October, 1961.) Khrushchev, in practice, seemed to be claiming all the kudos attached to a liberal attitude. But the system has been reformed and rationalized rather than abolished. An example of this oblique method became widely known when Olga

Ivinskaya and her daughter were arrested in August–September, 1960, and sentenced in December to terms of imprisonment, ostensibly not for defying the authorities in assisting Pasternak to have *Doctor Zhivago* published abroad, but for "currency offenses." Several other writers who had published abroad were charged on similar grounds, or else confined in mental institutions.

Another ideological event of key interest in this period was the appearance of the *Sta* volume of the *Large Soviet Encyclopedia* (Vol. 40) in 1958. The encyclopedia volumes normally appear at intervals, in alphabetical order. But in this case there had been a delay of over eighteen months, during which all the subsequent alphabetical volumes had appeared. The trouble was plainly the Stalin biography. Its final form may be taken as representing the then considered position of the regime on the subject.

The article is only six pages long, as against forty-four in the previous edition. Stalin's role in the Revolution is toned down, though not to the extent of giving credit to the "oppositionists." He is praised for exposing deviationists and carrying out collectivization of agriculture and industrialization. The biography, unlike the "secret speech," has little to say on the purges in the thirties, and what it says is far more moderate in tone. Stalin is said to have applied unnecessary mass repression against ideological opponents. This he did, it is stated, on the basis of the mistaken thesis he advanced in 1937 that the class struggle would become increasingly intense during the construction of socialism. The encyclopedia places most of the responsibility for the liquidation of the innocent on other shoulders: "In this situation the accursed enemies of the people, [Genrikh] Yagoda, [Nikolai] Ezhov and [Lavrenty] Beria, who had wormed their way into J. V. Stalin's confidence, slandered and destroyed many honorable and devoted party people."

As far as his policies during World War II are concerned, Stalin is credited with making "a serious contribution to the defense of the country and the struggle against fascism" and with taking all possible measures for strengthening the antifascist coalition. On the other hand, he is said to have attached excessive significance to the Nazi-Soviet Pact and thus to have been partly responsible for the early defeat of the Soviet Army.

Considerable space is given to the "personality cult" theme. Arguing that the cult is not endemic in the Soviet system, the biography attributes its emergence both to negative features in Stalin's character and to specific conditions that prevailed during "the period of the construction of socialism," i.e., the thirties. As a result, although the lower party organizations continued to function normally, Central Committee Plenums and Party Congresses were not held for a number of years, and Stalin became impervious to all criticism.

In conclusion it is emphasized that while the cult inflicted considerable damage on Soviet life, it had no great influence on the development of the Soviet state. In the peroration we read:

> His name is inseparable from Marxism-Leninism, and it would be a most flagrant distortion of historical truth to spread the mistakes made by Stalin in the last years of his life to all his party and state activity extending over many years. The campaign undertaken by reactionary imperialist circles against the "Stalinism" they themselves have invented in fact constitutes a campaign against the revolutionary workers' movement. The attacks by revisionists against so-called Stalinism are also essentially a form of struggle against the fundamental positions of Marxism-Leninism.

This is a striking indication of the strength and nature of the pro-Stalin side of the party's attitude, even at a time when considerable reservations were being made about the old methods.

1961: The Twenty-second Party Congress

The Twenty-second Party Congress, of October, 1961, is dealt with in detail elsewhere in this volume.[2] Here it is appropriate to note that its most striking theme was the sudden renewal of the attack on Stalin and the "Stalinists" of the Antiparty Group, which had for some time been conducted only in a comparatively formal and sporadic fashion. Although widely known throughout the Soviet Union, the "secret speech" had, technically speaking, remained confidential, and the Twenty-second Congress was, out of the blue as it were, made the occasion for the first major public assault on the dead dictator.

Khrushchev's opening Report of the Central Committee at the Congress was fairly moderate. He mentioned Lenin's demand that Stalin be removed from the General Secretaryship, and criticized "mistakes" and "distortions" associated with the personality cult, but he made no specific charges and even said, "Of course, Stalin had great merits in the party and the Communist movement and we give him his due."

But as the Congress went on, junior Khrushchevites gave cases proving Stalin's brutality. In his concluding speech, Khrushchev attacked Stalin more strongly than any of them. In particular, he made it clear that Stalin had been personally responsible for Ezhov's actions in the killings of the Great Purge.

None of this was on the set-piece scale of the "secret speech." The acts and atmosphere of terror of Stalin's rule were clearly developed. But much

---

[2] See Chapter 3, "The Twenty-second Party Congress, 1961."

more detail was given on misdeeds by Molotov, Malenkov, and Kaganovich under his aegis than on Stalin's own actions. Only a few of these latter were cited. It was implied, though not asserted flatly, that Stalin had been responsible for the Kirov murder in 1934, and Zinovi Serdyuk, a speaker, stated that Stalin and his accomplices had taken advantage of that crime "by deceiving the party, to launch antiparty methods of struggle to maintain a leading position in the state." Otherwise a few unjust executions were blamed on him, or jointly on him and the others.

Molotov, Kaganovich, Voroshilov, Malenkov, and Beria nevertheless attracted fiercer and more extensive denunciation, until, on the last day of the Congress a set of short speeches demanding the removal of Stalin from his tomb gave a most powerful impact to the attack on the old leader in person.

Stalinist Survivors?

Even at the 1961 Congress, Stalin had been granted some positive qualities. But the Antiparty Group received no quarter (except for a partial pardon issued to Voroshilov). "Stalinism" was attacked more strongly in their persons, and in the policies attributed to them, than in Stalin himself.

Molotov, it was now revealed, had sent the Central Committee a letter or manifesto attacking the new party program as revisionist. He was certainly urging a return to stricter measures of control, and to old-style economic and social policies. Yet even Molotov (as was admitted in an attack on him by Pavel Satyukov at the Congress) had amended Stalin's views in certain respects. Secondly, Molotov was an isolated figure even among the conservative elements of the Antiparty Group. At the debate in the Central Committee on the Yugoslav issue in July, 1955, for example, he alone had opposed a *détente* with Tito. Even Kaganovich seems to have favored it. As for the "Stalinists" still in high position (see Evtushenko's poem, below), it seems clear that there were elements opposing certain of Khrushchev's economic plans, too much relaxation of control over the writers, and aspects of his foreign policy. But allowing for the fact that all leading elements in the party remain devoted to the principle of political and ideological monopoly operated from above by members of the party elite, we may ask if there remained in reality any specifically "Stalinist" grouping, and if so, in what sense.

As Khrushchev pointed out, some of those who openly opposed him had grave responsibilities for the Stalinist past. So did many of his own faction, including himself. Again, reference is sometimes made to the younger members of the leadership as a "young anti-Stalinist trend." Yet all those referred to, such as Dmitri Polyansky, Alexander Shelepin, and Vladimir

Semichastny, already had records of indoctrination and service; they rose to moderate prominence precisely in the bad time of Stalin's last years. This is only to say that elements were present in the party leadership who, while willing to make relaxations as a matter of tactical maneuver, were also, on their records, prepared to undertake swings back to more repressive policies. Allowing for the changed circumstances of the times, it seems legitimate to call tendencies in such a direction "Stalinist" without thereby implying a total reversion to the worst period of Stalin's rule.

It is interesting that the new Party Program adopted at the Congress itself, while generally moderate in wording, openly reserves the right to revert to tougher methods of rule if the circumstances seem to require it:

> The general trend of class struggle within the socialist countries in conditions of successful socialist construction leads to consolidation of the position of the socialist forces and weakens the resistance of the remnants of the hostile classes. But this development does not follow a straight line. Changes in the domestic or external situation may cause the class struggle to intensify in specific periods. This calls for constant vigilance in order to frustrate in good time the designs of hostile forces within and without.

Meanwhile, we should note that, by the time of the Congress, the quarrel within international Communism had become acute. The Chinese (not yet quite openly) and the Albanians (quite openly) had become the repositories of opposition to Khrushchev on issues of doctrine and power. Although the Chinese Communists had in practice resented and resisted Stalin, they could as of 1961 be properly regarded as more dogmatist than the Russians (and indeed than Stalin himself). The Congress, therefore, was a set operation against all the "dogmatist" opponents of the Khrushchev regime—Molotov, the Albanians, and, by implication, Mao Tse-tung, who were lumped together and blamed as adherents of Stalin-type rule.

But Khrushchev again confused several issues. There is a general sense in which, within the fairly narrow limits of current party practice in Russia, Khrushchev stood for a less repressive and more modern political and economic style, but the distinction between his and his *Soviet* opponents' views was one of degree rather than principle. This was again shown in a Soviet-sponsored organ, almost at once: "Unrelenting struggle against . . . manifestations of the personality cult does not of course imply making concessions to petty-bourgeois liberalism or countenancing any attacks by the revisionists." (*World Marxist Review,* December, 1961.)

Even what might appear to be a matter of deepest principle—the dispute between Molotov and Khrushchev about whether war was inevitable—remains abstractly doctrinal to a high degree. The Stalin-Molotov policy involved postponing the "inevitable" war for as long as possible—which in practice obviously means indefinitely. Both parties, in any case, were committed to a forward policy, and Khrushchev's approach to the Berlin problem strongly resembled that of 1948–49. This is not, of course, to assert that the tactical *nuances* do not differ: the Molotov *style* of diplomacy is one that was rather too lacking in day-to-day dynamism for the Khrushchev, though not perhaps for the post-Khrushchev regime.

It is true that such doctrinal differences *might* involve important differences of policy. When the Chinese speak of the inevitability of war, they pretty clearly mean also to indicate its desirability. But we must distinguish, in this as in other matters, between Molotov and Mao. Even from the Stalin point of view, the Chinese are "left," deviationist adventurers. Though the struggle for power to some extent obscures the fact, even Molotov was, as far as practical policy is concerned, far closer to Khrushchev than he was to Peking. And, on the other side, Chinese support of Molotov and adulation of Stalin were tactical attachments to what they conceive to be the least bad of a bad lot. When Stalin was actually there, the Chinese resented him bitterly: there is, after all, a record of friction between Stalin and Mao, as there never was between Stalin and Khrushchev.

In fact, as ever in Communist life, politics come first. Intelligent opinion in the West, saturated in Marx, Tawney, and the others, has forgotten Machiavelli. It is a Soviet poet and philosopher, Yesenin-Volpin, who can now note that "a purely political tendency toward power or authority is prevalent in the Soviet Union."

1962: Interrupted Progress

Following the attacks on Stalin at the Twenty-second Party Congress, there came a certain swing back. There were many calls at the Congress for the expulsion from the party of Molotov and the rest of the Antiparty Group —though it is noteworthy than many speakers abstained from supporting this demand. During the following months there was somewhat of a reaction. After a period of doubt, Molotov's expulsion was not proceeded with. At the same time, there were various changes in the newly elected leadership that reflected the renewed struggle. There was a certain tendency, too, to say no more of Stalin's crimes. As before, Khrushchev himself supplied the back-pedaling. Even while criticizing "abuses of power" on Stalin's part, he asked, "Does anyone doubt that Stalin was a Communist, that he was dedicated to Communism? If there is such a person, he must be quite without understanding. Stalin was dedicated to Communism with his whole being; everything he did was for Communism." (*Pravda,* April 27, 1962.)

Yet progress had again been made and steps had been taken that were difficult to revoke. And later in 1962, the theme of the horrors of the Stalin period again gathered momentum. After a return to several important positions of literary "reactionaries," summer saw a certain advance for "liberals." A recrudescence of attacks on Stalin started in editorials on party history in *Pravda* of June 22–24, 1962. In *Pravda* on October 21 came Evgeny Evtushenko's poem, "The Heirs of Stalin." It attacked Stalin and Enver Hoxha of Albania and strikingly asserted the persistence of the "Stalinist" mind:

> We bore him out of the mausoleum.
> But how, out of Stalin, shall we bear
> > > > > Stalin's heirs!
> Some of his heirs trim roses in retirement
> secretly thinking
> > > > their discharge is temporary.
> Others,
> > > from rostrums, even heap abuse on Stalin
> but,
> > at night,
> > > > > hanker after the good old days.[3]

This definite allegation that "Stalinists," concealing their true feelings, remained in positions of power, is obviously of the highest significance, as is the fact that the poem was published (again, reportedly on Khrushchev's personal instructions) in the official organ of the Communist Party itself.

Likewise, in the autumn of 1962 came the publication, again apparently on Khrushchev's direct orders, of Alexander Solzhenitsyn's *One Day in the Life of Ivan Denisovich,* a staggeringly frank and well-written account of life in a labor camp in Stalin's time. A Soviet comment on the book was that for the first time it "establishes the truth about the camps in which honest Soviet people—from the armed services, workers, peasants, artists —did penal servitude and perished."

Party "History"

The development of anti-Stalinism between 1959 and 1962 is most revealingly (and of course authoritatively) demonstrated by a comparison of the two editions of the *History of the CPSU* (designed to replace the condemned "Short Course") appearing in those two years. It also demonstrates the Soviet method of treating history as "politics projected back into the past," with amendments made to suit the political attitudes of the time of publication. It need hardly be said that, though the latter version is an im-

---

[3] Translated by George Reavey and reprinted with the permission of Encounter Ltd.

provement, it still does not approach what would normally be regarded as objective historical truth.

Many other instances could be given of the change of attitude to Stalin in Soviet publications over the period. But direct comparison of equivalent passages in the two editions of the *History of the CPSU* are particularly striking, and a few examples from the dozens that occur should be sufficient to show the general change.

1959 EDITION	1962 EDITION
Stalin adopted the mistaken position of advocating pressure on the Provisional Government but soon renounced it and adhered to Lenin.	Stalin adopted the same position of advocating pressure on the Provisional Government [as Kamenev]. He failed to grasp the meaning and role of the soviets as a new form of state power. . . . He also spoke out in favor of uniting with the Mensheviks, a suggestion that ran contrary to the party's policy and Lenin's instructions. In the middle of April, 1917, Stalin renounced his mistaken position and adhered to Lenin's platform.
[In February, 1918, the "left-wing" Communists opposed the signing of a peace treaty but proved to be in a minority.]	[The "left-wing" Communists opposed the signing of a peace treaty.] Stalin wavered: he spoke in favor of negotiations but was against signing a peace treaty on new terms. After being criticized by Lenin, he stated that peace on these terms ought to be signed. [The left-wingers proved to be in a minority.]
Stalin's works, *Trotskyism and Leninism* and *The October Revolution and the Tactics of the Russian Communists,* played a great role in the unmasking of Trotskyism. In them Stalin defended Leninism. . . . Stalin exposed Trotsky as a willful saboteur con-	Prominent party figures, primarily those who had fought together with Lenin for the triumph of the October Revolution, spoke against Trotsky. . . . Trotsky's new outburst against Leninism was discussed [at the January, 1925, Plenum, which described] Trot-

stantly attacking the party. . . .
Stalin unmasked all of Trotsky's
fabrications and his scheme to
foist Trotskyism on the party in
place of Leninism.

sky's unceasing speeches against
Bolshevism [as an attempt to]
substitute Trotskyism for Leninism.

[Stalin's *Foundations of Leninism*]
sets out concisely and clearly the
basic questions of Leninism, of
the theory and tactics of the proletarian revolution, of the theory
and tactics of the dictatorship of
the proletariat, and elucidates the
new elements that Lenin contributed to Marxism.

[Stalin's *Foundations of Leninism*] sets out concisely the basic
questions of Leninism.

[Kirov's murder in December,
1934] showed that a party membership card could be used as a
cover for vile anti-Soviet actions
[and that] the party had to be
shielded against alien elements so
as to render impossible all actions
hostile to socialism and the interests of the Soviet state, whatever
cover they masqueraded under.

[The murder] was committed in
the atmosphere of the personality
cult. Stalin utilized the murder as
a pretext to organize reprisals
against those who were in his dis-
favor. Numerous arrests followed. A start was made with the
mass repressions and gross infringements of socialist legality.

[By 1937 Stalin had] started to in-
fringe the norms of party life
worked out by Lenin and the
principle of collectivity.

[Stalin] infringed the norms of
party life worked out by Lenin
and the principle of collective
leadership. After the Seventeenth
Congress [1934] Stalin completely
ceased to heed the collective opinion of the party and its Central
Committee. The cult of personality created fertile soil for such
negative phenomena as arbitrariness, abuse of power, careerism,
toadying, suspicion, and mistrust,
and, in the field of ideology, for
dogmatism, quotation-mongering,
and the divorce of theory from
practice.

A shameful role was played during that period by Ezhov, who held the post of People's Commissar of Internal Affairs.

Ezhov was appointed to the post of People's Commissar of Internal Affairs on Stalin's direct instructions.

In 1938, the *Short Course of the History of the CPSU(B)* appeared, and an intensive study of party history was set in motion.

Work on the study of party history was set in motion. In general this played a positive role, though the *Short Course of the History of the CPSU(B)*, which came out at that time, suffered from serious shortcomings. It was impregnated with the cult of Stalin's personality and failed to give a truthful and objective account of many of the questions of party history.

[No comparable passage.]

At the beginning of the Great Fatherland War [1941] the activity of the Communist Party was directed toward mobilizing all forces, bringing the enemy to a halt, and keeping him from utilizing the suddenness of his attack and the mistakes committed as a result of Stalin's underestimating the danger of military attack by Hitlerite Germany.

[No comparable passage.]

Stalin considered that he alone was entitled to a decisive say on all questions of theory. . . . Stalin perpetrated major errors in his works. [In his *Economic Problems of Socialism in the U.S.S.R.* he] ignored the importance of commodity-money relationships in the economy, denied the possibility of selling technical equipment to collective farms, . . . mistakenly asserted that collective farm ownership had outlived its usefulness [and gave an incorrect analysis of] the paths of gradual transition from socialism to Communism. . . .

[Stalin's mistaken and anti-Marxist-Leninist thesis that] under socialism, production must always outstrip consumer demand [served to justify] shortages of basic consumer goods [and misled party, state, and economic functionaries].

Although the mistakes committed as a result of the cult of Stalin's personality did act as a brake on the development of Soviet society, they did not put a stop to this development, nor *a fortiori* could they change the socialist character of the Soviet regime. The entire activity of Stalin himself was bound up with the implementation of vast socialist transformations in the Soviet land.

Although Stalin's cult of personality did act as a brake on the development of Soviet society, it could not arrest its forward development, alter the character of the socialist system or weaken the Leninist foundations of the party. Despite the cult of personality, the party and its local organizations pursued an active, spontaneous life.

The essence of the party criticism of the cult of personality consisted in the elimination of the harmful consequences of this cult and in the strengthening by this token of the positions of socialism, *not* in the wholesale denial of Stalin's positive role in the life of the party and the country. Under the leadership of the Communist Party and its Central Committee, in which Stalin played a leading role, the Soviet Union achieved enormous successes of world-historic significance. J. V. Stalin did much that was useful for the Soviet land, for the CPSU, for the entire international workers' movement.

The essence of party criticism of the cult of personality consisted in the elimination of the harmful consequences of the cult and in the strengthening by this token of the positions of socialism.

[Remainder omitted.]

Stalin up . . .

. . . and down

The "personality cult" was exemplified by the profusion of Stalin portraits throughout the Soviet Union and eastern Europe—here shown in a May Day parade. Removed from the mausoleum on Red Square by decision of the Twenty-second Party Congress, Stalin's remains were relegated to an obscure spot near the Kremlin Wall, alongside the graves of other Bolsheviks.

Zolnierz Polski (Warsaw), February, 1957

Grzesznicy bez winy

A Polish cartoon, entitled "Innocent Culprits," illustrates the tendency to "pass the buck" for all wrongdoings, ultimately blaming it all on Stalin.

Krokodil, July 20, 1956

— Что это вы мне двойку поставили! Я же признал свои ошибки!

Another allusion to those officials who behave as if a perfunctory admission of past errors (in the Stalin era) gave them the right to proceed as before:

"Why did you give me a failing mark? I've admitted my mistakes, haven't I?"

1963–64: Further Maneuvers

By now, the area in which the party was trying to stabilize both its image of Stalin and its attitude to the principles of the Stalin regime had become clear; since then, there has been little in the way of major development. At the same time, it was clear that the exact line and tone taken within the prescribed limits varied considerably with the effects of the political forces involved—personal or factional advantage in the struggle for power, the pressures upon the leaders of a society and economy not well adapted to their style of rule, the aspirations of writers and others wishing to take advantage of and to extend any relaxations, and so on. Over the ensuing years, the same processes have been at work, and the oscillations have repeated themselves; but the central ambiguity remains.

During the first three months of 1963, a tougher and more "dogmatic" line, manifesting itself most obviously on the literary question, led to a major, though temporary, political setback for anti-Stalinism. Attacks on the Antiparty Group continued, but it is noticeable that Khrushchev, in his speech to the writers on March 8, 1963, again spoke favorably of Stalin and attacked Malenkov and Beria rather than Molotov, for insufficient hostility to the West rather than for dogmatism. Continued and extremely violent assaults on the "liberal" writers produced moods of utmost gloom among the intellectuals. But this "black" period lasted only through the first quarter of 1963. Khrushchev, who had evidently been on the defensive on several issues, was able to regain the initiative in April-June, and a general, though still unexciting, anti-Stalinism returned.

It is of interest that the period of Stalin's errors and crimes now began to be put back in time. The original (1956) attack on Stalin dates his "bad" period from 1934. And although individual errors dating earlier than this were often attributed to Stalin thereafter, for some time no criticisms of the policies and actions of the first period of Stalin's rule were made. But now attacks appeared on the process of collectivization of agriculture, going back as far as 1929–30. A novel, *People Are Not Angels,* by Ivan Stadnyuk, which began to appear (in serial form) in 1962, was openly critical of the forced collectivization of 1929–31. A more formal statement by M. L. Bogdenko in the May, 1963, issue of *Problems of History* said that for excesses committed at that time "a tremendous share of the guilt" lies with Stalin. (The article was almost equally concerned to blame Molotov, which may account in part for its harsh tone.) Had the facts changed? No, but some rethinking on agriculture had begun.

Rehabilitations took place in 1963–64, but in a partial and erratic way. Some of the loyal followers whom Stalin executed in the thirties were rehabilitated with considerable honor; others were more briefly dealt with; and others again have still to be mentioned. Of those who were shot during the Great Trials, half a dozen have been rehabilitated. It has even been conceded in an obscure lecture session that some of the main figures were not guilty of espionage and terror; but, in general, justice has not been done them; and a number of oppositionists who simply disappeared and have not since been spoken of are now mentioned coldly as having been expelled from the party and sentenced for anti-Soviet activity. The murder of Sergei Kirov in 1934 has still not been openly attributed to Stalin—though an extremely direct hint of his guilt was made early in 1964—and the oppositionists accused of it have not been cleared.

After the fall of Khrushchev in October, 1964, an end was put to speculative and risky initiatives in every field. This applies also to the matter of Stalinism. The rehabilitation process again slowed down, as did written discussions of the more sensitive areas of the Stalinist past. Stalin himself began to be treated with a rather cold respect. The system of government he created, as amended and improved under Khrushchev, was consolidated.

Conclusions

We may summarize two main strands in the long and erratic campaign against Stalin.

First, immense advantages accrue to the rulers of the U.S.S.R. if they can dissociate themselves as far as possible from the burden of the past, from the memory—enormously unpopular even in party circles—of both the *Ezhovshchina*—the Great Terror—and Stalin's last few years, when no one at any level was safe.

Yet the present regime owes its legitimacy to its descent from Stalin, and is committed to the correctness of Stalin's "general line" as against both the Left and the Right Oppositions of the twenties and thirties, and hence to his doctrinal correctness on basic policy matters. De-Stalinization, therefore, has to be kept within bounds and confined to a special and partial denunciation. Stalin's body has been removed from Lenin's tomb, but it still lies in a fairly honorable position under the Kremlin wall, among the bodies of important "positive" figures of the second rank—and, perhaps significantly, next to that of Felix Dzerzhinsky, founder of the secret police.

The second main element in the de-Stalinization campaign has been its use as a weapon in the day-to-day political struggle. The more the Stalinist position is repudiated, the less is it possible for any opposition to rally under a "conservative" banner.

The particular errors and excesses associated with Stalin that have now been denounced include:

1. "Mass repression," in particular when exerted against loyal Communists, army officers, and certain cultural figures.

2. One-man rule and excessive adulation of the leader, and in general the "cult" of Stalin.

3. Certain theoretical "errors" of Stalin's, some of them harmful to the economy, some—in particular the thesis of the increasing sharpness of the class struggle in the U.S.S.R.—justifying the Terror.

4. Certain foreign policy errors, in particular the mishandling of the quarrel with Tito.

5. Peripheral abuses harmful to the Soviet image abroad, such as the mass deportation of minority nationalities.

The rejection of Stalinist falsehoods about the past does not automatically mean a return to objective truth. A falsehood may be replaced either by the truth or by a different or even an opposite falsehood. In Stalin's time, discussions or histories of the Revolution and the Civil War assigned all the major roles to those who remained in favor with Stalin. History has now been amended to give prominent roles to a number of Stalinists purged by Stalin, while removing such discredited leaders as Molotov from the list. But it has not yet been granted that the man who played a role second only to Lenin's—Trotsky—was of any significance.

The Stalin era was a past so atrocious that its repudiation brought obvious dividends to any succeeding regime, but its successors also inherited a set of institutions and a ruling caste indoctrinated in certain habits and beliefs. A point sometimes neglected is the extraordinary rigidity of the leading political stratum in the Soviet Union concerning political thought. And "political," in the Soviet context, covers a very wide field indeed, since a basic principle of the Communist Party is that final decisions on literature and history, for example, as well as on agriculture and foreign policy, must remain in the hands of the party's Central Committee. It is difficult enough to induce the bureaucrats of the party machine to accept changes that do not affect their right to rule. No sort of approach to eroding that right has been made, and probably none could be made with any chance of success unless a high degree of disintegration were to enter the Soviet political scene. Yet, in an important sense, the essence of Stalinism is less the particular periods of terrorism or special views on industrial organization than the establishment of the political setup. And that remains substantially unchanged.

"Stalinism" in its normal usage is an undefined or inadequately defined term. It is common to equate "de-Stalinization" with "liberalization." But the "de-Stalinization" that has taken place in the Soviet Union consists of the abandonment (or at least the denunciation) of a specific set of excesses associated with the late dictator. It does not amount to any change of sub-

stance in the *system* of political rule in the U.S.S.R., or of the basic principles behind that system. Russia is still ridden by the party machine, and
the principle of *partinost*—that is, the doctrine of the party's right to ride
and to decide on all questions of speed and direction—remains untouched.
What has taken place, in effect, is simply the denunciation and renunciation
of excessive use of whip and spur.

As Leonard Schapiro has written:

> I think one must distinguish two categories of change since Stalin's death:
> the change in "political climate," and institutional change. The former has
> been enormous; the latter, virtually nil—so far as essentials are concerned.
> To put it another way: the *method* of government has changed enor-
> mously; its basic *mechanism* is the same, because no new institutions have
> taken the place of the old. [*Survey,* April, 1963.]

This point was well illustrated by the circumstances of the coup against
Khrushchev in October, 1964.

The climate has changed. But there is no institutional guarantee against
a re-Stalinization. It is the experience of all political systems that even
those politicians who are brought up in the most demanding circumstances
need the continual check of free institutions and a free press if they are
not to accumulate, and abuse, power, and the cadres who rule Russia today
—even the youngest of them—were brought up in a far more dangerous
tradition. It is a political generation that regards the use of terror to maintain its position as an acceptable, even if not actively desirable, method of
rule.

Current de-Stalinization is not comparable to the de-Nazification program in Germany, and perhaps the reason is to be sought precisely in
the fact that it has not involved the removal from public life of more than
a handful of old Stalinists. It is appropriate to recall that a Stalin-style
regime builds up its own cadres, institutions, and habits of mind. The terror
at the heart of Stalinism penetrated everywhere. Ilya Ehrenburg speaks of
it as "not a blow aimed at a political idea. It was a blow aimed at the people of my generation." Evtushenko characterizes Stalin's period as one of
"careerism, servility, spying, cruelty, bigotry, hypocrisy."

The Italian Left-wing Socialist leader Pietro Nenni, who had always
been a good friend of the Communists, wrote confidentially to Suslov after
the "secret speech" that the destruction of the Stalinist myth must also call
in question

> the juridical and political structure of the state, the very idea and practice
> of one-party government, and the conduct of economic and social affairs—
> in short, the entire system. . . . What is more, despotism and abuse have
> become systems of government, and one cannot but fear that despotism

and abuse will rear their heads again tomorrow as they did yesterday, if the denunciation of the "shameful facts" of the Stalin era is not followed by a full and complete restoration of democracy and liberty.

When Khrushchev fell, eight years later, Nenni published this letter, adding the comment that the new coup proved the point that "the good will and good faith of human beings, even those endowed with exceptional personalities, are powerless against the vices of a system."

A start, a partial step, has been ventured. It is not to denigrate what has been done to insist that much more is necessary before we say that de-Stalinization has removed the Old Man from Russia's back. Truth must no longer be condemned as "bourgeois objectivity." The oligarchy must forfeit, permanently, the *power* to repeat the excesses of the old autocrat.

Meanwhile, with all the general denunciations of Stalin's terror and despite the particular crimes alleged against him, the regime has not yet fully and frankly repudiated the Terror. Executed military men, writers, Stalinists who fell out with their leader, and many other individual victims have been cleared. But there has as yet been no serious attempt to deal with the Terror as a whole. That is, the great plot ostensibly headed by Trotsky, backed by the Nazis, involving politicians, generals, engineers, doctors, and ordinary citizens by the thousand, has not been explicitly denounced as a fabrication. Statements have been made that demolish the authenticity of some of the main accusations in the Great Trials of the thirties. The doubt cast on the circumstances of the Kirov murder affects the Trials of 1936 and 1938. The revelation (at the Twenty-second Congress) that an alleged assassination attempt on Molotov was a fraud disposes of one of the main charges in the 1937 Trial. The rehabilitation of several of those tried or named as fellow conspirators in the 1938 Trial undermines it to a considerable degree. But there has been no frank and formal exculpation of Trotsky and the opposition leaders such as could alone signify a true repudiation of the heritage of Stalin's terror.

Russia is in a transitional stage, and such stages are associated with illogical compromises. But it is hard to see how they can endure.

Study Questions

1. How has "Stalinism" been defined in the case, both explicitly and implicitly? Do you find the definition accurate?
2. In what ways was de-Stalinization used as a weapon against the Antiparty Group? How effective a weapon was it?
3. What advantages and disadvantages for the government has the official Soviet treatment of political history, as represented by the 1959 and 1962 editions of the *History of the CPSU?*

4. What differences do you note between earlier—i.e., pre-1956—and later attempts at de-Stalinization?
5. What is the present official attitude toward Stalin?

Selected Bibliography

The two volumes that contain most of the major revelations about the Stalin period to have been officially put on record in the Soviet Union are: Leo Gruliow, ed., *Current Soviet Policies II, The Documentary Record of the Twentieth CPSU Congress and Its Aftermath* (New York: Praeger, 1957); and Charlotte Saikowski and Leo Gruliow, eds., *Current Soviet Policies IV, The Documentary Record of the Twenty-second Congress of the Communist Party of the Soviet Union* (New York and London: Columbia University Press, 1962). Volume II also carries Khrushchev's "secret speech" of February, 1956.

In addition, the student may want to consult: Boris Souvarine, *Stalin* (London: Secker & Warburg, 1939), the best biography of Stalin, though it goes only as far as the end of the first great purge; Leonard Schapiro, *The Communist Party of the Soviet Union* (New York: Random House, 1960), useful for political background; Robert Conquest, *Power and Policy in the U.S.S.R.* (New York: Harper Torchbooks, 1966), covering the postwar political struggle; Simon Wolin and Robert M. Slusser, eds., *The Soviet Secret Police* (New York: Praeger, 1957); Zbigniew K. Brzezinski, *The Permanent Purge* (Cambridge, Mass.: Harvard University Press, 1956); Alexander Weissberg, *The Accused* (New York: Simon & Schuster, 1951), one of the best of several good accounts of life under the Terror; Alexander Solzhenitsyn, *One Day in the Life of Ivan Denisovich* (New York: Praeger, 1963), the Soviet classic of concentration-camp life; and Robert C. Tucker and Stephen F. Cohen, eds., *The Great Purge Trial* (New York: Grosset & Dunlap, 1965), a transcript, with notes, of the most important of the faked trials of Stalin's time.

Other instructive sources include: David J. Dallin and Boris I. Nicolaevsky, *Forced Labor in Soviet Russia* (New Haven: Yale University Press, 1947), a detailed account of the huge labor-camp system at a time when its existence was denied; S. Swianiewicz, *Forced Labor and Economic Development* (New York: Oxford University Press, 1965), a careful examination of the extent and economic significance of the labor-camp system; Priscilla Johnson, *Khrushchev and the Arts* (Cambridge, Mass.: M.I.T. Press, 1965), an admirable documentation of the struggle for greater literary freedom in the early sixties; Robert C. Tucker, *The Soviet Political Mind* (New York: Praeger, 1963), a most useful conspectus of various aspects of Stalinism and of de-Stalinization; Abraham Brumberg, ed., *Russia Under Khrushchev* (New York: Praeger, 1962), a large collection of essays on the Russia of the late fifties and early sixties; Herbert Ritvo, ed., *The New Soviet Society* (New York: New Leader, 1962), a fully annotated version of the current Program of the Communist Party of the Soviet Union; and Robert Conquest, *Russia After Khrushchev* (New York: Praeger, 1965), dealing with the political background and perspectives.

3

The Twenty-second Party Congress, 1961

Bernard S. Morris

There have been many public figures in history who proved themselves at certain periods in their lives and played a notable role but then came to a standstill, as it were, and even began gradually to fade out.

Such phenomena happen for various reasons: One person's powers deteriorate; another loses touch with life, becomes conceited, does not work; a third proves an unprincipled, spineless turncoat without stanchness in the struggle for the cause of the party. Meantime, in the course of the struggle, new political figures arise who oppose everything that hampers the development of the new and who overcome the resistance of the old. What happens is something like the phenomenon that astronomers call light from extinct stars. Some very distant stars continue to shine even though they have actually been extinct for a long time. The trouble with some people who have found themselves in the position of stars on the public horizon is that they think they are continuing to radiate light although they have long since turned into dying embers.[1]

This statement of Khrushchev's at the Twenty-second Congress of the Communist Party of the Soviet Union (CPSU) in October, 1961, characterized the so-called Antiparty Group who in 1957 had unsuccessfully banded together to deprive him of power. It acquired a special poignancy in the light of his ouster, almost three years to the day later, by a younger combination of politicians. Khrushchev, the innovator, had broken his op-

---

[1] This and other excerpts from speeches quoted in this chapter are reprinted, with minor changes, from *The Current Digest of the Soviet Press,* published weekly at Columbia University by the Joint Committee on Slavic Studies appointed by the American Council of Learned Societies and the Social Science Research Council. Copyright 1962, the Joint Committee on Slavic Studies. Reprinted by permission.

ponents by linking them with the Stalinist past of terror and oppression. Having embarked on a new course, Khrushchev rode the crest of popularity until he was called to account for failures in internal and external policies, many of his own making. His star had shone brightly at the Congress, although, in retrospect, it may already have been turning into a dying ember.

Introduction

The Twenty-second Congress held on October 17–31, 1961, afforded a brilliant spectacle of Soviet politics in the making. An internal power struggle was linked to the struggle for mastery of the international Communist movement. The necrophiliac excavation of the past was set off against the promise of future Soviet society. The carefully orchestrated reports of the delegates were upset by the violent Soviet attack on Albania and the Chinese delegate's unscheduled departure. Peaceful coexistence was affirmed against the background of Soviet nuclear explosions and reports of 100-megaton bombs.

What did it all mean? How much credibility can be attached to the renewed denunciation of Stalin's crimes by those who took part in them?[2] Why was it necessary to return to the attack against the so-called Antiparty Group if it no longer represented a threat to the party leadership? Was there perhaps an organized (or an unorganized) opposition to Khrushchev's policies? Why was it deemed necessary virtually to read the Albanian Communists out of the Communist fold? What was the end of the "dictatorship of the proletariat" to mean for the average Soviet citizen?

A "case study," as this is designed to be, implies the availability of a record from which motives, events, continuity, and meaning can be abstracted and on which generalizations can be based. A "record" of the Congress, running into hundreds of pages, is in fact available. Unavailable are the intraparty debates, the Molotov correspondence, the various positions of the individuals in the Antiparty Group—in short, the inside information that would validate or invalidate conjectures from the published record. Yet many other studies of contemporary politics, whether of open or closed societies, face similar problems of lacunae in crucial data. A reconstruction of the Twenty-second Congress is probably easier and may well be more accurate than, for instance, an attempt to reconstruct the motives and political interplay in the Bay of Pigs fiasco. However, a description and analysis of the Twenty-second Congress necessarily takes the form of a reading of the record against the development of Soviet society and its international relations.

---

[2] For the attack on Stalin at the Twentieth CPSU Congress in February, 1956, see Chapter 2, "De-Stalinization and the Heritage of Terror."

The Setting

More than 4,800 delegates[3] of the Communist Party of the Soviet Union and representatives from eighty-seven foreign Communist parties gathered in the Kremlin's new Palace of Congresses to participate in the proceedings of the Twenty-second Congress. This was more than triple the number of delegates who had attended the Twenty-first Congress in 1959, as a result of a change in the ratio of delegates to party members from 1 to 6,000 in 1959 to 1 to 2,000 in 1961. (The party claimed 9,716,005 full and probationary, or "candidate," members in September, 1961.) Increased representation was part of Khrushchev's on-going campaign to revitalize the party and to promote what in Communist parlance is called "intraparty democracy."

This huge audience—for the role of the party delegate was more that of a witness than of a participant—was comfortably seated in the modern Palace of Congresses, built to hold 6,000. Contrasting sharply with the onion domes, ramparts, and spires of the old buildings, the Palace, constructed of white marble pylons and glass, had been sunk deep underground so that its silhouette would not overshadow the ancient buildings of the Kremlin. The delegates, dressed mostly in black and gray and many of them wearing flowers in their buttonholes, could be impressed by this building of the Khrushchev era, equipped with the latest conveniences: escalators, air conditioning, indirect lighting, and acoustic tiles. Aesthetically, and no doubt functionally, the Palace was a vast improvement over such Stalinist wedding-cake architecture as the Ukraina Hotel and Moscow University.

Although the setting may have been more pleasant and the delegates more representative, the function of this Party Congress was the same as that of earlier ones: to legitimize decisions already made by the party leaders, this time by Khrushchev and the party's Central Committee. These decisions concerned Soviet domestic and foreign policy and the policy of the international Communist movement as well. Soviet Party Congresses have traditionally served as occasions for caucuses or informal international meetings of Communist party representatives. It was customary that the pronouncements of the Congresses themselves were generalized for the guidance of the foreign Communist parties.

The delegates, from all accounts, had expected the proceedings to focus on the new Party Program that, commissioned by the Twentieth Party Congress in 1956, had been presented in draft form to the Central Committee on June 19, 1961, by its First Secretary, Nikita Khrushchev, and

---

[3] According to the Credentials Commission Report by Vitaly Titov, 4,408 voting delegates and 405 delegates with consultative votes—4,813 in all—were elected to the Congress. Fourteen voting delegates were absent for "valid reasons."

published for discussion on July 30. Promulgation of a new Program was in itself a major occasion: there had been only two previous Programs—in 1903 and 1919—and plans in 1939 and 1952 to devise a new one had not materialized. The new Program, outlining the Soviet Union's "transition to Communism,"[4] was bound to be of interest to the Soviet citizen at the very least because it codified Khrushchev's ideas for the development of Soviet society.

The months preceding the Congress had been devoted to discussion of the Party Program and Statutes. Innumerable meetings had taken place at all levels; articles and letters to the editor flooded the press; in short, all the devices of communication at the disposal of the party had been used to engage the population's interest in Khrushchev's policies that would be formalized at the Congress. Moreover, the agenda of the Congress, published as follows, did nothing to prepare the delegates for the actual turn of events:

1. Report of the Party Central Committee
2. Report of the Central Inspection Commission
3. Draft Program of the Communist Party of the Soviet Union
4. On changes in the Party Statutes
5. Elections of central party bodies

The formal conduct of the Twenty-second Congress, moreover, was cut to the pattern of previous Congresses: a major address by the First Secretary—which this time took the better part of two days; comments by key Soviet figures on one or another aspect of the address from their own special area of competence; expressions of support from the foreign Communist delegates, who also recounted the activities of their respective parties; election of officials, adoption of resolutions, and a closing address by the First Secretary. The Twenty-second Congress conformed to this pattern, putting to test the fortitude of the delegates condemned to listen for days on end to figures on output of poods of grain and square meters of housing construction. Yet the speeches of the foreign delegates, especially those concerning Khrushchev's attack on Albania—and implicitly on China—were transformed from their routine character of greetings into a virtual roll call for or against Khrushchev.

Khrushchev's Rationale: An Overview

Whereas the Soviet society of the future had been presumed to be the main feature at the Congress, Khrushchev startled the audience by return-

---

[4] "Transition to Communism" is a doctrinal phrase used to designate the process of change from the present Soviet "socialist" system to a more advanced stage in which there would be material abundance and a gradual disappearance of the state machinery.

ing to an excoriation of Stalin and of the so-called Antiparty Group. This is how Khrushchev developed the attack in his Central Committee Report:

> The Leninist course expressed by the Twentieth Congress was at first carried out against the fierce resistance of antiparty elements, zealous partisans of the methods and practices prevailing under the cult of the individual [i.e., under Stalin's dictatorship], revisionists and dogmatists. The factionalist Antiparty Group consisting of Molotov, Kaganovich, Malenkov, Voroshilov, Bulganin, Pervukhin, and Saburov, and Shepilov, who joined them, came out against the Party's Leninist course.[5]
>
> At first the party's line on condemning the cult of the individual, fostering intraparty democracy, condemning and rectifying all abuses of power, and exposing the individuals guilty of repression was strongly resisted by Molotov, Kaganovich, Malenkov, and Voroshilov. Their stand in this matter was no accident. They bear personal responsibility for many mass repressions against party, soviet, economic, military, and Komsomol [Young Communist League] cadres, and for other similar manifestations that took place during the period of the cult of the individual.
>
> At first this group was only an insignificant minority in the Presidium of the Central Committee. But when the party launched the struggle to restore Leninist norms of party and state life, when it set about such urgent tasks as developing the virgin lands, reorganizing the management of industry and construction, enlarging the rights of the union republics, improving the well-being of Soviet people, and restoring revolutionary legality, the factional group activized its antiparty subversive work and began to recruit supporters in the Central Committee Presidium. It added Bulganin, Pervukhin and Saburov, and Shepilov joined them. Sensing that they had managed to gather an arithmetical majority in the Presidium, the members of the Antiparty Group went over to open attack, seeking to change the policy in the party and the country—the policy set forth by the Twentieth Party Congress.
>
> Having reached agreement at their secret gatherings, the factionalists demanded an extraordinary meeting of the Presidium. They counted on carrying out their antiparty designs, on seizing the leadership of the party and country. The Antiparty Group wanted to confront the members of the Central Committee and the whole party with a *fait accompli.*
>
> But the factionalists miscalculated.

Noting the defeat of the Antiparty Group at home and the "approval" of the Twentieth Congress' policies at the meetings of the international movement in 1957 and 1960, Khrushchev went on to attack the Albanian Communist leaders, virtually offering them the choice of recantation or excommunication:

---

[5] "Revisionists" and "dogmatists" represent critics from the "right" and "left" respectively. "Factionalism" implies the existence of organized opposition within the party.

> The course drawn up by the Twentieth Party Congress is a Leninist course, and we cannot concede on this fundamental question to either the Albanian leaders or anyone else.
>
> .   .   .   .
>
> If the Albanian leaders hold dear the interests of their people and the cause of building socialism in Albania, if they really want friendship with the CPSU, with all the fraternal parties, they should renounce their mistaken views and return to the path of unity and close cooperation in the fraternal family of the socialist commonwealth, the path of unity with the whole international Communist movement.

The attack on Albania might just as well have been directed at Communist China, whose disagreements with the Soviet leadership—not yet openly acknowledged—had brought Sino-Soviet relations to a virtual impasse. Unable to still the Chinese criticism of his strategy of peaceful coexistence and its various ramifications, Khrushchev, in his charges against the Antiparty Group and against Albania, now appeared to have given up his attempts to bring the Chinese into line.

On the face of it, the objects of Khrushchev's displeasure were separate and unrelated items. Molotov, advocate of traditional Stalinist approaches, does not seem to have much in common with the "revisionist" Malenkov, who after Stalin's death made himself something of a champion of consumer goods. As obstacles to Khrushchev's rise to power, they were nevertheless both labeled "antiparty," i.e., anti-Khrushchev, in a manner reminiscent of the Left and Right Opposition of the 1920's and 1930's that Stalin successively eliminated during his consolidation of power. Khrushchev's rationale, then, was to link the Antiparty Group opposing him to Stalin's malpractices and to the intransigent policies of the Chinese Communists who in passing had backed Albania's revolt against the Kremlin. By tarring the group with the rejected past, he hoped to rally support for his liberalization of Soviet society.

The use of the word "liberalization" requires explanation. Various Western commentators have applied the terms "normalization," "liberalization," and "controlled relaxation" with more or less similar value meanings to Khrushchev's policy. But the terms are troublesome. What are the "norms" for Soviet society? "Liberalization" is the most justifiable term if only because it denotes the difference between the use of terror, purge, and the police under Stalin and under Khrushchev. But the word "liberal" with its Western connotation is bothersome. "Controlled relaxation," though cumbersome, strikes a more neutral note and conveys Khrushchev's attempt to satisfy the demands for domestic reform and a more temperate foreign policy without letting matters get out of hand. At any rate, Khrushchev led the attack on the late dictator and the Antiparty Group to the accompaniment of the other Soviet speakers, who provided the chapter and verse of indictment.

Stalin Revisited

"Of course," Khrushchev declared in his opening Central Committee Report, "J. V. Stalin [no longer "comrade"] did make great contributions to the party and the Communist movement, and we give him his due." So much for the man who built Soviet state and society and for the Chinese complaint about the unbalanced nature of Khrushchev's evaluation of Stalin. Khrushchev's discussion at the opening of the Congress amounted to a general defense of his decision to attack Stalin at the Twentieth CPSU Congress and justification for another installment of the same at the Twenty-second Congress in the light of some domestic and international Communist deprecation of the effort. However, his concluding remarks indicted Stalin openly for crimes suspected but heretofore concealed by euphemism and innuendo. He virtually accused Stalin, for example, of having used the assassination of Sergei Kirov in 1934 as a pretext for the great purges of the following years. He revealed that torture was used during the same period to elicit confessions in the case of Soviet military commanders alleged to have conspired with the German military staff. He was most effective in playing on the emotions of the audience by revealing Stalin's behavior in private toward his victims. Thus, he related how Stalin simply cursed on being informed that the army commander, Ion Yakir, had exclaimed before he was shot: "Long live the Party, long live Stalin!" And Khrushchev told the story of Alyosha Svanidze, the brother of Stalin's first wife:

> He had been an old Bolshevik, but Beria made it appear, through all kinds of machinations, that Svanidze had been planted near Stalin by the German intelligence service, although he was a very close friend of Stalin's. And Svanidze was shot. Before the execution, Svanidze was told that Stalin had said that if he asked for forgiveness he would be pardoned. When Stalin's words were repeated to Svanidze, he asked: "What am I supposed to ask forgiveness for? I have committed no crime." He was shot. After Svanidze's death, Stalin said: "See how proud he is: he died without asking forgiveness." It never occurred to him that Svanidze had been above all an honest man.

Not much could be done for Stalin's victims: Khrushchev proposed that the newly elected Central Committee consider erecting a monument in Moscow to the memory of outstanding figures who had perished. Stalin himself was not so fortunate. By formal resolution of the Congress, his body was removed from the mausoleum—now renamed the Lenin Mausoleum—in Red Square and interred in the more modest surroundings under the Kremlin wall that hold the remains of other honored Communists.

The Antiparty Group

Not being dead, the Antiparty Group posed problems of a different order. It seems established that the principals—Molotov, Kaganovich, Malenkov, Voroshilov, Bulganin, Pervukhin, Saburov, and Shepilov—had conspired in June, 1957, to oust Khrushchev. Shepilov, who was called a "political prostitute," achieved special distinction in this catalog of names because of his political opportunism. He was said to have carried around a little notebook to jot down bits of gossip about leading officials, trying to set the members of the Presidium quarreling among themselves. Bulganin, it was also revealed at the Congress, had, during the June affair, posted his bodyguard in the Kremlin and stationed additional guards around the building in which the Presidium was meeting to seal it off. The oppositionists, having secured a majority against Khrushchev in the Presidium, no doubt intended to present the Central Committee with a *fait accompli*. Khrushchev nevertheless managed to defeat the maneuver and had the conspirators expelled from the Presidium. Since then, they had been assigned lesser posts or were living in political obscurity.

To what extent, if any, the members of the group were able to keep their hands in political affairs is a mystery. However, it was revealed at the Twenty-second Congress that in April, 1960, Molotov had submitted "his first ideological statement since his 1957 defeat." It had arrived in the form of a letter to *Kommunist,* the party's theoretical journal, on the occasion of the ninetieth anniversary of Lenin's birth. It was—ominously—also the occasion on which the Chinese Communists started their public attacks on Khrushchev, with an article called "Long Live Leninism!" published in their theoretical journal, *Red Flag.* Among other things, the Chinese attacked Khrushchev's strategy of peaceful coexistence by reaffirming the validity of Lenin's theory of inevitable war between capitalism and Communism, and stressing the need for Communists to maintain a revolutionary tempo.

Did Molotov's letter, as yet unpublished, parallel the Chinese attack? As Soviet Ambassador to Mongolia, Molotov presumably could have been in contact with the Chinese. Within a few weeks after the receipt of the letter, he was recalled from Ulan Bator. Evidence is lacking to establish a link between Molotov and the Chinese, but the Congress made the attempt by innuendo:

He [Molotov] apparently has decided to stir up the waters in order to try later on to fish in these muddy waters. Perhaps the bait will be swallowed by some bony sprat (*laughter*) if not here in domestic reservoirs, then at least somewhere in foreign waters. (*Stir in the hall; laughter.*)

The Sins of the Father . . .

Precisely what significance can be attached to Molotov's move is open to speculation. It was ridiculed at the Congress by Otto Kuusinen, the veteran Finnish-born Secretary of the Party Central Committee, in a sort of afterthought stating that an opposition group at least ought to have a written political platform. On the other hand, even if the members of the Antiparty Group had no direct influence in channeling the opposition to Khrushchev on various issues, it may be hypothesized that the Antiparty Group still represented a point of attraction, a source of legitimacy, so to speak, for the opponents of Khrushchev. Whatever the significance of Molotov's venture, it was used by Khrushchev forcibly to dissociate his policies once again from those of the past.

Khrushchev struck back by identifying the Antiparty Group with Stalin's malpractices. The "revisionism" of the Antiparty Group when Malenkov was the number one man was all but forgotten in an all-out campaign to tar the Group with Molotov's "dogmatism" and intransigence. A document was produced to show Molotov's prior approval, along with Stalin's, of the execution of persons including "wives of the enemies of the people" who were being brought to trial. To illustrate Molotov's inhumanity, Nikolai Shvernik, chairman of the Party Control Committee, related the story of a professor who in 1937 asked for Molotov's intercession on behalf of his father, who had been arrested through a misunderstanding. "Instead of looking into this very human request," Shvernik said, "Molotov wrote a memorandum: 'To Ezhov: Can it be that this professor is still in the People's Commissariat of Foreign Affairs and not in the [hands of the] NKVD?' Whereupon the writer of the letter was unlawfully arrested." Finally, the authority of Lenin was invoked in the form of a letter from him to Molotov in 1922, which was used to suggest that even then Molotov was a hopeless bureaucrat.

The other leading members of the Antiparty Group were also implicated in Stalin's crimes. When Yakir wrote Stalin pleading his innocence, Stalin wrote on his letter, "Scoundrel and prostitute." Voroshilov added, "A perfectly accurate description"; Molotov signed the letter and Kaganovich appended: "For the traitor, scum and [next comes a scurrilous, obscene word] one punishment—the death sentence." Malenkov was associated with Beria's murder of innocent Armenian party members and the slaughter of honest Communists in Byelorussia. Kaganovich was called a "degenerate," and accused of arresting workers in the Ministry of Transportation without grounds and torturing them. The chorus against the Antiparty Group reached the point of the absurd when Vladimir Kucherenko, President of the U.S.S.R. Academy of Construction and Architecture, accused Kaganovich of practicing Stalinism by "crudely implanting false architectural solutions, as in the case of the Theater of the Soviet Army and certain tall buildings and apartment houses on the main thoroughfares of Moscow." It is true, however, that those who have seen these buildings may sympathize with Kucherenko's indignation.

Serpents Without Fangs

However guilty of the heinous crimes attributed to them—and the presumptive evidence is on the side of the accusers—the crime with which the Antiparty Group was charged at the Twenty-second Congress was political rather than legal. There was a certain defensive note at the Congress on the question of why the matter of the Group—"political corpses"—had been brought up at all. At one point they were characterized by Nikolai Ignatov, Vice-Chairman of the U.S.S.R. Council of Ministers, as:

> harmless . . . serpents [who] have had their fangs pulled. Some of them are now crawling and others hissing, but none of them can bite any longer. If we talk about them, it is not because they constitute any danger to the party but in order that the party and the Soviet people will know the nature of these renegades who had lost touch with life and will know what they were out to do.

What specific forms the "crawling" and "hissing" took we do not know, but the bill of particulars drawn up against the Group amounted to a defense of Khrushchev's policies. Thus the Group, it was alleged, was opposed to de-Stalinization, to the reorganization of state and economic administration, to the reorganization of planning, especially in agriculture, to the development and utilization of virgin lands and, in short, to the "general line" of the party. Molotov—now promoted to "ideologist" of the Group—was charged with undercutting the premises of Khrushchev's plans for building communism by denying, for instance, that socialism had been built thus far in the U.S.S.R. The logic of Molotov's position—if one is familiar with Communist categories of development—was that if the U.S.S.R. had not yet constructed a socialist system, the other Communist states were in various earlier stages of presocialist development. Thus, in those states the class struggle against bourgeois elements had to be pursued—the Khrushchev leadership maintained that there were no longer any antagonistic classes in the U.S.S.R. and that the class struggle was therefore obsolete—and heavy industry demanded absolute priority over the production of consumer goods.

On international policy, Molotov was said to reject the major tenets of the Khrushchev line: peaceful coexistence, avoidability of war, relaxation of international tensions, and personal contacts with Western leaders. Paul Satyukov, editor-in-chief of *Pravda,* revealed that Molotov had on the eve of the Congress criticized the new draft program for its alleged pacifism and revisionism and for failing to coordinate "Communist construction" in the U.S.S.R. with the worldwide revolutionary struggle. "His contentions lead to the conclusion," Satyukov declared, "that it is impossible to continue the advance to Communism without the most serious political conflicts with the imperialist countries, and hence without war."

The parallel between the views attributed to Molotov and to the Chinese is suggestive. In his concluding remarks defending his policy of peaceful coexistence, Khrushchev stated:

> The world socialist system has today grown mightier than ever. It already takes in more than a third of mankind, and its forces are growing swiftly; it is the great bulwark of world peace. (*Applause.*) Under present circumstances the principle of the peaceful coexistence of states with different social systems assumes vital importance.
>
> The only people who fail to see this are the hopeless dogmatists who, having learned by rote general formulas on imperialism, stubbornly turn away from life. This continues to be the position of the diehard Molotov. He and his like fail to appreciate the changes in the world situation, the new developments in life. They have not kept up with the times and have since become a drag, a needless burden.

Saved from Expulsion

The crescendo of attacks on members of the Antiparty Group was accompanied by proposals for their expulsion from the party. One of the last speakers, Peter Pospelov, Director of the party Central Committee's Institute of Marxism-Leninism, declared:

> There is no doubt that the Twenty-second Congress will unanimously approve the proposal of a number of delegates to exclude these schismatics and factionalists from the party's ranks. (*Applause.*) They should be held responsible both for their criminal actions during the period of the Stalin cult and for the attempt to counterpose their own antiparty, anti-Leninist line, dangerous and harmful to the cause of Communism, to the party's Leninist course!

This was presumably a suggestion that they be brought to trial. Yet nothing happened to them at the time. Was Khrushchev too insecure to carry it off, or had he never intended to do so?

They had expected the worst, according to Khrushchev: "When the

Antiparty Group was smashed, its participants expected that they would be treated in the same way they had dealt with people at the time of the cult of the individual—the way they hoped to deal with those who favored the restoration of Leninist norms of party life."

Khrushchev then recounted a "typical" conversation with Kaganovich after the expulsion of the Antiparty Group from the Central Committee in June, 1957:

> "Comrade Khrushchev, I have known you for many years. I ask you not to let them treat me in the vindictive way people were treated under Stalin."
>
> And Kaganovich knew how people had been treated because he himself had been a participant in these reprisals.
>
> I answered him: "Comrade Kaganovich! Your words once more confirm the methods you intended to use to achieve your disgusting ends. You wanted to return the country to the state of affairs that existed under the cult of the individual, you wanted to indulge in reprisals against people. And you measure other people by your own yardstick. But you are mistaken. We firmly observe and we shall adhere to Leninist principles. You will be given a job," I said to Kaganovich, "you will be able to work and live in tranquility if you labor honestly, as all Soviet people labor."

The opposition, out of power for years, was now spared by Khrushchev's "magnanimity," more particularly by his purpose of graphically demonstrating the break with Stalinist methods of treating opponents. Sanctimonious as his statement sounds, it is plausible. One can, of course, speculate that the Antiparty Group had sufficiently powerful friends in court to block punitive action.

It can be argued that Khrushchev was so implicated in the crimes of the Stalin era that he could not bring himself to expel them from the party or, alternatively, that he feared the consequences of their expulsion. Speculation on Khrushchev's motives for spelling out the misdeeds of the Antiparty Group prompts the question of his moral right to indict others without implicating himself. The answer, at least in part, is that moral issues all too often yield to the exigencies of power. In this case, moreover, Khrushchev had popular backing for his efforts to do away with the Terror and other oppressive conditions. No matter how guilty of malpractice in the past, he after all was the leader who had the courage to denounce the evils of Stalinism and start a new course. In psychopolitical terms, as Professor Philip Mosely has pointed out, "By naming scapegoats for the Stalinist crimes, Khrushchev actually makes it easier for himself and the party members to localize the diffused sense of shared guilt in a few powerless individuals."[6]

---

[6] "Khrushchev's Party Congress," *Foreign Affairs*, pp. 183–95.

Of the Antiparty Group, only Marshal Voroshilov was pardoned. Aged and compromised, he had been relieved in 1960 of his post of Chairman of the Presidium of the Supreme Soviet (formally, the chief of state). Special dispensation was bestowed upon him apparently for switching sides during the crucial 1957 Central Committee meeting and, according to Khrushchev, in some measure influencing the outcome. Unable to speak at the Twenty-second Congress "for reasons of health" (perhaps a valid excuse), the seemingly senile Voroshilov published his recantation in *Pravda* and *Izvestia* during the course of the Congress.

Not until a showdown with the Chinese Communists seemed in the making in 1963 were Malenkov, Molotov, and Kaganovich expelled from the party. Even then, no information was forthcoming which might have clarified the action and its timing.

Opposition to Khrushchev Abroad

The Albanian Disaffection

Stalin had been undisputed master in his own house and by tradition undisputed head of the international Communist movement. The various national Communist Parties were linked to the CPSU through the principle of "proletarian internationalism," that is, unquestioning loyalty to Moscow. So it was until 1948, when Tito successfully defied Stalin's attempt to establish his hegemony over the Yugoslav Communist Party. Tito's stubborn refusal to capitulate when Stalin "shook his finger" marked the beginning of the end of the monolithic international Communist movement. Nevertheless, for the remainder of Stalin's life, the movement, with the exception of Yugoslavia, maintained its cohesiveness.

The death of Stalin in 1953 removed the Primal Father, and discipline and authority in international Communism slowly deteriorated. Riots broke out in Poznan and Berlin; a full-scale revolution in Hungary had to be crushed by Soviet armed forces; the Chinese were invited in by the Russians to help restore order in eastern Europe; subsequently they too challenged Soviet authority; and even the pro-Soviet Italian Communist leadership sniped away at Khrushchev. The ultimate insult to the Russians was the defection of the Albanian (Communist) Party of Labor, rulers over this most backward country in Europe.

In the east European complex, Albania had occupied the unenviable role of a subsatellite, initially subordinated to the Soviet Union through Yugoslavia. The Albanian Party of Labor had been built up—and Enver Hoxha, First Secretary of the Albanian Party, had achieved his position—with Yugoslav help. Albania's second-class citizenship in the Communist camp was illustrated, for example, by its exclusion from membership in the

Cominform (Information Bureau of the Communist and Workers' Parties) founded in 1947. Moreover, Yugoslavia, with Stalin's seeming acquiescence, had planned to annex Albania. According to Milovan Djilas,[7] once Tito's trusted collaborator, Stalin said in January, 1948:

> "We have no special interest in Albania. We agree to Yugoslavia swallowing Albania! . . ." At this he gathered together the fingers of his right hand, and, bringing them to his mouth, he made a motion as if to swallow them.
>
> I was astonished, almost struck dumb by Stalin's manner of expressing himself. . . . Again I explained: "It is not a matter of swallowing, but unification!"
>
> At this Molotov interjected: "But that is swallowing!"
>
> And Stalin added, again with that gesture of his: "Yes, yes. Swallowing! But we agree with you: you ought to swallow Albania—the sooner the better."

When the Cominform broke with Yugoslavia, the Albanian Party understandably pledged its allegiance to the Cominform, denounced the Yugoslavs, and purged Kochi Xoxe, Tito's man in the Albanian movement and Hoxha's most dangerous rival. While the expulsion of Yugoslavia from the Communist camp had the effect of tying Albania more directly to Moscow, at the same time it removed Albania from direct land access to the other Communist states. This situation provided Hoxha with one of the basic preconditions later to assert his independence of Moscow.

Albania's disaffection with Moscow may be traced back to Khrushchev's and Bulganin's visit to Belgrade in May, 1955, which was intended to end the seven-year rift. The ensuing improvement of Soviet-Yugoslav relations could hardly have led to rejoicing in Albania, and Khrushchev's attack the next year on the "cult of personality," a euphemism for the Stalinist type of rule, must have caused some misgivings to Hoxha, himself a minor Stalin. In time, it became clear that the Soviet-Yugoslav rapprochement was the obverse of the Soviet coin of peaceful coexistence. Watching Khrushchev's wooing of Tito and his conversations with the Greek politician Sophocles Venizelos about the maltreatment of the Greek minority in Albania and the desire of the Greeks for cultural autonomy, the Albanian leaders evidently suspected, rightly or wrongly, that something was afoot at their expense.

At the international Communist caucus in Bucharest in June, 1960, Albania, not yet without some praise of the Soviet Union, sided decisively with the Chinese. In the pre-Congress maneuvering, the Soviet leadership had engaged in extensive politicking among the parties, including the

---

[7] In his *Conversations with Stalin* (New York: Harcourt, Brace & World, 1962).

Albanian, in preparation for its effort to bring the Chinese into line. The Albanians indicated their displeasure with the direction of events by sending their number three man, Hysni Kapo. As matters turned out, the gathering witnessed the first violent debate between top-level Soviet and Chinese party leaders before an international Communist audience.

Soviet-Albanian relations rapidly deteriorated after the meeting: the Russians cut their economic aid and apparently tried to have Hoxha overthrown. When, in September, 1960, the First Secretaries of the east European Communist parties accompanied Khrushchev on the *Baltika* to the United Nations General Assembly, Prime Minister Mehmet Shehu—not First Secretary Hoxha—representing Albania, traveled separately. An attempt to patch up the Soviet-Albanian rift at a private confrontation held during the November, 1960, meeting of the eighty-one Communist parties in Moscow came to nothing. Whatever the dissatisfaction of the Albanians with Khrushchev's policies, it had to be weighed, however, against their almost total economic dependence on the Soviet Union and eastern Europe. Their assertion of independence then became a part of the more far-reaching Sino-Soviet conflict.

The Soviet-Chinese Imbroglio

The Sino-Soviet conflict is sufficiently celebrated already to have attracted its historians, some of whom trace the dispute to the centuries-old clash of Russian and Chinese interests and to Chinese megalomania; some date it back to Chinese Communist distrust of Soviet advice, which virtually decapitated the Chinese movement in the 1920's; others attribute the conflict to Chinese policy and ideological differences with Khrushchev. Since 1962, the Russians and particularly the Chinese have stated their cases in agonizing detail. For our purposes a brief summary at the risk of oversimplification will have to suffice.

The origins of the Sino-Soviet dispute, as distinguished from underlying historical and psychological factors that were brought to bear on the dispute as it unfolded, may be traced to the theses expounded by Khrushchev at the Twentieth Congress. His denigration of Stalin appeared to the Chinese as a rash and unwarranted action. His revision of the Leninist doctrine on the inevitability of war, the doctrinal pivot of his policy to negotiate some agreements with the United States, appeared to be a betrayal of the worldwide revolutionary struggle. His stress on multiple and peaceful roads to socialism was seen as a weakening of the revolutionary *élan* of the Communist parties.

Insofar as the more traditional state-to-state relations were concerned, the Chinese leaders were angry with Khrushchev for subordinating Chinese national interests in Asia to Soviet negotiations with the United States, for abrogating the agreement to develop China's atomic power—ostensibly to "appease" President Eisenhower in the Camp David talks—and for failing to supply the Chinese more generously with economic aid. In short, they challenged the premises of Soviet foreign—and in some key aspects domestic—policy, as well as Soviet fitness to establish policy for the international Communist movement. To the Chinese, the Russians had become "revisionists" on the order of the followers of Marshal Tito and of Eduard Bernstein, who had revised Marxian theory at the turn of the century to bring it into line with the growing constitutional and democratic practice of the socialist parties. There is something to this analogy. While the Chinese have been experimenting with such radical domestic policies as the "great leap forward" and the communes, the Soviet Communists have shifted toward more moderate policies suitable to their maturing industrial economy. Contemporary Chinese Communist fundamentalism is more akin to early Bolshevik revolutionary fundamentalism than the latter-day Russian "Bolsheviks" who view societal development more nearly in terms of Bernsteinian "determinism," that is, gradual evolution.

From 1956 to 1960 the Sino-Soviet debate had been conducted by innuendo and by proxy, as it were. Neither side called the other by name. "Revisionists" and the "Tito clique" were the epithets the Chinese hurled at the Russians; "dogmatists" and "Albanians" were the Russian labels for the Chinese. Attempts to resolve the quarrel at the November, 1960, meeting in Moscow of eighty-one Communist parties failed. After the meeting, at which the Chinese fought off a Soviet attempt to impose discipline on them, a patched-up, contradictory document was issued. The Chinese had made it clear that they would not be bound by the "arithmetical majority," that is, the majority of Communist parties responsive to Soviet command, and that they would not accept either majority decisions of which they disapproved or Soviet party policy positions as binding on them. In effect, they demanded that the Russians change their policies to accord with the Chinese in order to restore Communist unity. The Chinese had developed their own veto power.

The Sino-Soviet conflict was fortuitous for the Albanians. Though far removed from China in space, the Albanians fell in easily with the Chinese ideological outlook. Distance had its advantage; Albania's erstwhile Yugoslav allies had been too close for comfort. China had the prestige of being the second-ranking Communist power. Poor as it was, China could help fill the economic void left by Soviet withdrawals. Indeed, one thing China and Albania had in common was that they were both poor and proud. To China, the link with Albania was advertisement for the justice of its cause. Although the Tirana-Peking axis did not yet outflank the Soviet Communists, it marked the beginning of China's successful search for allies in the international Communist movement.

Russia's Loss Is China's Gain?

By the time of the Fourth Albanian Party Congress, in February, 1961, Khrushchev had apparently written off Albania. In June, 1961, the Soviet submarine fleet was withdrawn from its base at the Albanian port of Valona. Shortly afterwards, the Soviet Union cancelled military training for Albanians; Soviet specialists were withdrawn; and on August 19, Soviet Ambassador Shikin left Tirana and was not replaced.

Soviet-Albanian relations had reached the breaking point. The Albanian Communists had not even been invited to attend the Twenty-second Party Congress. A Tirana-Peking axis was in the making. What did Khrushchev hope to accomplish by his ostracism and denunciation of Albania and implicit censure of China? Surely he could not have anticipated that the Albanians, now backed by the Chinese, would heed him more carefully than they had in the past. Nor could he have expected the Chinese, committed to their tiny European ally, to back off simply because he again accused the Albanians of views that after all they shared in large part with the Chinese. The temptation is strong therefore to argue that by October 17, 1961, Khrushchev had written off both the Chinese and the Albanians. Be that as it may, Khrushchev's attack on the Albanians precipitated one of the sensational episodes of the Congress.

Khrushchev's opening statement censuring the Albanian Communists was one of patronizing reasonableness. All the same, the bill of particulars was clear enough. The Albanian leaders had disagreed with the Twentieth Congress' repudiation of the "cult of personality," and were, moreover, using Stalinist methods in their own country. "The course drawn up at the Twentieth Congress of our party," Khrushchev declared, "is a Leninist course, and we cannot concede on this fundamental question to either the Albanian leaders or anyone else [the Chinese?]." Khrushchev called upon the Albanian leaders to "renounce their mistaken views" and return to the path of unity. Khrushchev in effect unilaterally suspended the Albanian Party from membership in the international Communist movement.

From the first, the senior Chinese delegates to the Congress, Chou En-lai, Party Vice-Chairman and Premier of the State Council, and P'eng Chen, member of the party Secretariat, indicated their disapproval of the proceedings by failing to join in the applause for Khrushchev's attack on the "cult of personality" and on the Antiparty Group. According to a Yugoslav observer, when the Congress rose to applaud Khrushchev, Chou En-lai was the only one to remain seated. The Chinese delegates, moreover, sat on their hands on the second day when Khrushchev expanded on the new CPSU program and on the building of Communism in the U.S.S.R.

On the third day of the Congress, Chou En-lai spoke, rejecting the notion that the CPSU had the right willy-nilly to excommunicate a Communist state or party. "Our socialist camp of twelve fraternal countries," he said, "from the Korean People's Democratic Republic to the German Democratic Republic and from the Democratic Republic of Vietnam to the People's Republic of Albania, constitutes a single whole." Disputes between Communist parties should be settled patiently, privately as between equals, and not by "open unilateral condemnation." Lest words be inadequate, the Chinese also said it with flowers by laying two wreaths at the mausoleum where Stalin was still buried alongside Lenin. To make certain that this gesture would not be interpreted as a mere formality, the Chinese wreath dedicated to Stalin bore the legend "the great Marxist-Leninist." That was on October 21. On October 23, Chou abruptly left Moscow to attend the All-China Assembly of People's Representatives, which suddenly required his presence. Protocol, nevertheless, was observed: Khrushchev and a delegation of notables saw him off; P'eng Chen was left behind to head the Chinese delegation; and as Chou flew over the Soviet border, he dispatched a message to Khrushchev thanking him for the "cordial welcome and warm concern."

Chou had remained long enough, however, to hear the Soviet Communists unleash a particularly nasty diatribe against the Albanians. On the day after he had addressed the Congress, Chou heard Anastas Mikoyan, First Vice-Chairman of the U.S.S.R. Council of Ministers, allegedly quote Prime Minister Shehu's statement at the recent Albanian Party Congress "that anyone who disagreed with the leadership on a question would be . . . 'spat in the face, punched in the mouth, and, if need be, have a bullet put into his brain.' " Albanian crimes against humanity were linked to such political crimes as failing to publish the complete text of the CPSU's Party Program. Khrushchev recounted how the CPSU Central Committee had interceded a few years ago on behalf of Albanian Politburo member Liri Gega, who together with her husband had been sentenced to death:

> In approaching the Albanian leaders at the time, we were guided by considerations of humanity, by anxiety to prevent the shooting of a woman, and a pregnant woman at that [and one who had probably been involved in a pro-Khrushchev plot against Hoxha and Shehu]. We felt and still feel that as a fraternal party we had a right to state our opinion in the matter. After all, even in the blackest days of rampant reaction, the tsarist satraps, who tortured revolutionaries, scrupled to execute pregnant women. And here, in a socialist country, they had sentenced to death, and they executed, a woman who was about to become a mother, thus applying altogether unwarranted cruelty. (*Stir in the hall. Shouts: "Shame! Shame!"*)

The Albanians had even resisted Soviet pressure to "rehabilitate" pro-Titoist Kochi Xoxe, who had been executed in 1949 after the break between Moscow and Belgrade. Khrushchev's interest in the rehabilitation of Xoxe stemmed from his rapprochement with Tito and the general policy of posthumously clearing the reputations of those who had been victimized by Stalin and his collaborators.

These events had occurred in 1956. Now, five years later, Khrushchev continued, the Albanian leaders were calling Comrades Liri Belishova and Koço Tashko enemies of the party:

> And all this merely because Liri Belishova and Koço Tashko had the courage honestly and openly to voice their disagreement with the policy of the Albanian leaders and took a stand for Albanian solidarity with the Soviet Union and the other socialist countries.
>
> People who today advocate friendship with the Soviet Union, with the CPSU, are regarded by the Albanian leaders as enemies.

In other words, there was something to the Albanian charge that the Russians had attempted to unseat Hoxha.

Finally, Khrushchev vented his sarcasm on the Chinese for their alleged concern over the Soviet attack on Albania:

> Comrade Chou En-lai, head of the delegation of the Communist Party of China, voiced concern in his speech over our having openly raised the issue of Albanian-Soviet relations at the Congress. As far as we can see, his statement primarily reflects alarm lest the present state of our relations with the Albanian Party of Labor affect the solidarity of the socialist camp.
>
> We share the anxiety of our Chinese friends and appreciate their concern for the strengthening of unity. If the Chinese comrades wish to apply their efforts to normalizing the Albanian Party of Labor's relations with the fraternal parties, it is doubtful whether there is anyone better able to facilitate accomplishment of this purpose than the Communist Party of China. This would really redound to the benefit of the Albanian Party of Labor and accord with the interests of the entire commonwealth of socialist countries.

On the opening day of the Congress, October 17, Khrushchev had merely called upon the Albanian leaders to "renounce their mistaken views and return to the path of unity"; by October 27, he affirmed that "to put an end to the cult of the individual would in effect mean that Shehu, Hoxha, and others would have to give up their key positions in the party and government." Khrushchev may have felt no more sanguine about the Albanian situation at the beginning of the Congress than he did at the end. Nevertheless, he was sufficiently exasperated to call for the ouster of the key Albanian leaders from their positions, and implied that he had the backing of the international Communist movement.

The fact of the matter is, however, that many of the other Communist parties were reluctant to go down the line for Khrushchev. More than thirty parties, some of which could not possibly be identified with Albanian or Chinese policies, refrained for different reasons from jumping on the Kremlin's bandwagon. Some were evidently surprised at Khrushchev's attack; some preferred noninvolvement. Given all the tributes paid for the preceding five years to equality among Communist parties, many parties were reluctant to place their stamp of approval on the CPSU's unilateral action against Albania. Criticism of Khrushchev on *organizational* grounds —on the way in which he handled the Albanian affair—as distinguished from the substance of the charges against Albania thus added another dimension to the disagreement within the Communist family. The Soviet diplomatic break with Albania was to come a month later, on November 25, 1961, when the Soviet Union announced the withdrawal of its Ambassador to Tirana and demanded the recall of the Albanian Ambassador in Moscow.

"The Communist Manifesto of the Modern Era"

The attack on the Antiparty Group and on the Albanian Communists provided the drama of the Congress; in perspective, the attack against the "old guard" served as counterpoint to Khrushchev's international strategy and his domestic proposals. The ideas and tendencies of Khrushchev's reign emerged from his Central Committee report, his report on the new Party Program, and the Program itself. Behind the verbiage and obfuscation, in spite of rationalizations and contradictions, the main lines of his policy are clear. As architect of the Party Program, Khrushchev submitted his candidacy to the Communist hall of fame after Marx, Engels, Lenin, and (whether Khrushchev liked it or not) Stalin; the achievement of Communism is still the goal of Soviet society. Khrushchev's Communism is something less—or rather, something quite different—from what Marx had in mind, and the Program as a plan, particularly in its economic objectives, is probably unrealizable and should not be taken literally. It represents a hope that in a twenty-year period (1960–80), Soviet society will move from the oriental despotism of Stalin to a more rational technical-industrial order that will be able to satisfy the basic needs of its inhabitants. As such, Khrushchevism represents a transitional phase from Stalinism to a society whose norms and values are still blurred.

Peaceful Coexistence and Revolution

"The issue of war and peace is the principal issue of today," states the Party Program.[8] "The main thing is to ward off a thermonuclear war, to

[8] *Programme of the Communist Party of the Soviet Union* (Moscow: Foreign Languages Publishing House, 1961). Quotations from the Program are taken from this document.

prevent it from breaking out." Although the basic social and national causes of all wars will not be eliminated until "socialism" is victorious throughout the world, the Program continues, there is a good possibility of avoiding war because the balance of world forces has changed in favor of the Communist camp. True, the capitalist countries are gripped by deep and acute crisis, and they tend to try to extricate themselves from their dilemmas by adventurist policies and war. But they no longer will risk war lightly in the face of Communist power supported by other non-Communist "peace-loving forces." Khrushchev was sufficiently optimistic to venture that "matters are reaching a point where even before the total victory of socialism on earth, while capitalism holds on in part of the world, there will be a real chance of eliminating war from the life of society." In simpler terms, the Soviet leadership seems to be saying that, given the development of nuclear weapons systems and the balance of mutual deterrence between the United States and the Soviet Union, it has opted for peaceful coexistence between states of different social systems. Peaceful coexistence or "disastrous war" are the only alternatives.

What precisely does peaceful coexistence mean according to the Party Program?

> Peaceful coexistence implies renunciation of war as a means of settling international disputes, and their solution by negotiation; equality, mutual understanding, and trust between countries; consideration for each other's interests; noninterference in internal affairs of other states; recognition of the right of every people to solve all the problems of their country by themselves; strict respect for the sovereignty and territorial integrity of all countries; promotion of economic and cultural cooperation on the basis of complete equality and mutual benefit.

Some Western commentators have considered Khrushchev's slogan of peaceful coexistence a snare and a delusion designed to lower the guard of the West. They have pointed to Communist commitments to oppose wars of conquest and to support those of national liberation, such as the Algerian war against the French. At the very best, they have argued, peaceful coexistence implies a continuation of the cold war.

Khrushchev, apparently sensitive to this criticism, in effect replied that peace and peaceful coexistence are not the same thing. Peaceful coexistence is not simply the absence of war or an unstable truce between wars. It is the coexistence of two opposing social systems, founded on mutual renunciation of war as a means of settling disputes between states. Moreover, he has invested the peaceful coexistence formula with a special twist: "Peaceful economic competition is the chief arena of the contest between the socialist and capitalist systems." For all his talk about the disintegration of capitalism, Khrushchev recognizes that it is here to stay for some time:

This does not mean, of course, that imperialism is at a total standstill, that its productive forces are immobilized. In particular periods, under the influence of transitory factors, there may be a more rapid economic growth in certain capitalist countries than in others.

Expansion of trade with the West is, moreover, part of the peaceful coexistence strategy. Socialist economic policy, Mikoyan said, is not autarchic; the Soviet Union must take cognizance of the fact that, despite the existence of two world systems, a world market and international division of labor remain. Khrushchev went so far as to state that peaceful coexistence is the most effective form of class struggle in the contemporary epoch. No wonder the Chinese have accused him of diluting revolutionary doctrine!

The Soviet strategy of peaceful coexistence between states was complemented by peaceful prescriptions for the international Communist movement. Due mention was made of the fact that the proletariat may have to resort to violence if the bourgeoisie uses force against it, but the weighting in the Program is on the peaceful attainment of power. The argument runs something like this: the international balance of forces has turned in favor of the "world socialist system"; Communism is capturing the imagination of the people; the capitalistic countries are torn by conflict and dissension; they can no longer resist the pressure of "democracy" and "socialism."

The Program invests the struggle for "democracy" in capitalist countries with special meaning: the bourgeoisie can be compelled to carry out measures that "transcend ordinary reforms": to cease preparations for a new world war, to renounce the policy of starting local wars, and to use the economy for peaceful purposes. The struggle for peace and democracy and against capitalist monopolies does not, the Program hastens to add, postpone the day of revolution but brings it nearer. Against a considerable body of evidence to the contrary, the Program argues that "the more profound the democratic movement, the higher becomes the level of the political consciousness of the masses and the more clearly they see that only socialism clears for them the way to genuine freedom and well-being."

But if revolutions occur, they need not be accompanied by war. Given the favorable conditions prevailing today as compared to the past, Communist parties "seek to accomplish the socialist revolution *by peaceful means.*" It is possible for a Communist-led political coalition to win a solid majority in parliament and then use the instruments of power to achieve a socialist revolution. (This is precisely what the Communists claim happened in the Czech coup of 1948.) And there was even more optimism for the future:

It may well be that, as the forces of socialism grow, as the working-class movement gains strength and the positions of capitalism are weakened, there will arise in certain countries a situation in which it will be preferable for the bourgeoisie, as Marx and Lenin foresaw, to agree to the basic means of production being purchased from it and for the proletariat to "pay off" the bourgeoisie.

The peaceful coexistence strategy also provides the key to Soviet policy in the underdeveloped areas. Far from calling upon the Communist parties in these areas to engage in direct revolutionary action—and most of the parties are powerless to do so anyway—the Program exhorts the Communist movements to form a national "front," or alliance, with various other, non-Communist groups, classes, and interests so as to establish a state of "national democracy." The Communist view of the new states is that their independence is tenuous. The United States and the Western powers, through aid and other devices, are trying to maintain or reestablish indirect control over these former colonies—what the Communists call "neo-colonialism." Given the possibility of help from the Communist countries, the new states have the option of taking the noncapitalist road of development and, by radical economic and social transformation of their societies, ensuring their independence. In doing so, Khrushchev declared in his report on the Party Program, these states can draw on the experience of the Communist movement in by-passing the capitalist stage of development and transforming the countryside even "without nationalization of the land, taking into account the lingering tradition of deep peasant attachment to private ownership of land." As if to demonstrate the plausibility of the Soviet prescription for the underdeveloped areas, delegations from the ruling parties of Guinea, Ghana, and Mali attended the Twenty-second Congress as guests. Not since the Kuomintang was associated with the Comintern in autonomous ("sympathizing") membership in the 1920's had a non-Communist party been accorded such an honor.

Prospectus for a Communist Society

The prospectus for Soviet society is set out in the new Party Program, which was labeled "the Communist Manifesto of the modern era," purportedly realizing the ideas of Marx, Engels, and Lenin on the "transition to communism."

Communism [the Program states] is a classless social system with one form of public ownership of the means of production and full social equality of all members of society: under it, the all-round development of people will be accompanied by the growth of the productive forces through continuous progress in science and technology; all the springs of cooperative wealth will flow more abundantly, and the great principle, "From each according to his ability, to each according to his needs" will be implemented. Communism is a highly organized society of free, socially conscious working people in which public self-government will be established, a society in which labor for the good of society will become the prime vital requirement of everyone, a necessity recognized by one and all, and the ability of each person will be employed to the greatest benefit of the people.

On basic principles, however, the connection between the Program and Marx is purely verbal. This is apparent, for example, in juxtaposing Marx's and the Program's views on labor. For Marx, the entire thrust of historical development was to free man from toil, to secure for man a nonrepressive society in which he would recover his spontaneity and be able to identify himself with nature, work, and his fellowman. (Whether Marx's vision is realizable is irrelevant to this discussion.) In contrast, the Program paralleled the aims of a welfare state, holding out the prospect of a shorter work week—certainly a precondition for the liberation of man from toil—but maintaining withal the repressive aspects of the state in one form or another. Similarly, the Program pays lip service to the Marxian idea of eliminating the gap between town and country. A countryside organized on industrial lines and wage labor complete with the amenities available to the city is projected for the "future," but the chief problem at the Twenty-second Congress, as it was in the following years, remained agricultural productivity and the concomitant problems of decentralization, individual material incentive, and investment priorities. Though not without interest, it is unrewarding, therefore, for our purpose to conduct an exegesis of the Program in the context of Marxian thought.

The Program also sought to come to grips with the old Marxist forecast of the inevitable (and desirable) "withering away of the state" by introducing the concept of the "all-people's state." It is difficult to imagine that Soviet leaders take the concept of "withering away" seriously, yet Communists have something of an obsession with this doctrine, conceived by the idealistic social theorists of the nineteenth century. Its operational significance in the Soviet Union today has less to do with the disappearance of the state apparatus than it does with efforts to secure the loyalty and active involvement of the people in affairs of state.

As set forth in the Program, the "all-people's state" has replaced the "dictatorship of the proletariat" which "has fulfilled its historic mission and has ceased to be indispensable in the U.S.S.R. from the point of view of the tasks of internal development." That is to say—and the ambiguity of the Soviet pronouncements restricts precision of analysis—the Soviet state which had heretofore obtained in the guise of the dictatorship of the proletariat, expressing by definition the interests of the working class, no longer reflected the needs of Soviet society. It was to be replaced by the "all-people's state," reflecting the interests and the will of the people as a whole. This state would survive until the "complete victory of Communism," presumably worldwide. Meanwhile, "the dictatorship of the working class will cease to be necessary before the state withers away," meaning presumably that the class interests of the workers would come to coalesce with the interests of the rest of the population.

While these formulations on the state are far from clear, the thrust of the doctrinal innovation is comprehensible. It was to provide a greater measure of political involvement and a greater measure of political democracy—if such a possibility is meaningful in a one-party state. The principle of rotation in office, provided for by the new Party Statutes, called for a turnover of at least one-quarter of the members of the Presidium and Central Committee at all regular elections and the renewal of at least one-third of the membership of the Central Committees at the union-republic, territorial, and regional levels. With certain exceptions for highly qualified individuals, members were limited to three consecutive terms of office.

Soviet "democracy" was also to be expanded by the involvement of the citizen in "public self-government." As the Communist society is being built, state functions were progressively to be transferred to such "public organizations" as the trade unions, the Komsomol, the cooperatives, and cultural and educational groups. Since the process would encompass "an entire historical epoch," the "withering away of the state" remained an academic problem for the Soviet rulers. Meanwhile, "public self-government" performed a two-fold function: it provided an unpaid civil service to perform certain administrative and quasi-judicial functions, such as the comrades' courts, and it promoted conformity through education, persuasion, and social pressure.

If the dictatorship of the proletariat was acknowledged to be dead, and if the state was destined for transformation (and—in theory—for eventual extinction), the party's role in Soviet society was by contrast on the increase. The new Party Statutes adopted at the Congress were designed to enhance the role of rank-and-file members by increasing turnover at local, county, and regional levels in order to broaden recruitment of new leaders and break the monopoly of local party leaders. The revised Statutes were also designed to afford a real choice in the election of party officials and to provide greater freedom of discussion. It is of interest to note that the proposal to replace secret by open voting was turned down.

The Khrushchev Program, as the preceding pages show, was revisionist by comparison with orthodox Marxism-Leninism. Within Communist circles, it was sure to be attacked by all those who represented the more rigid, more "leftist," more militant wing of the movement. For it is this hostility to the "revisionism" of the Khrushchev line that all the (real and imaginary, live and dead) enemies assailed at the Twenty-second Congress had in common: Stalin himself; the Antiparty Group (as reinterpreted); the Albanians; the Chinese; and unnamed die-hards at home, who formed what

1924

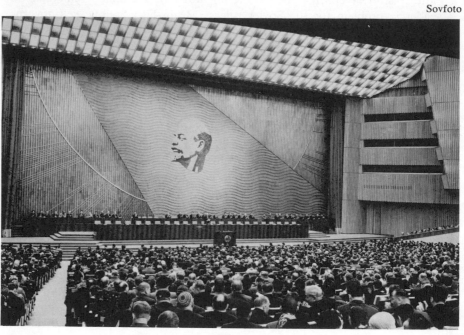

1961

From Lenin's death to the Twenty-second Party Congress, the hall in which the leading Communists assembled was not the only thing that had changed.

Sturshel (Sofia), October 11, 1963

The caption of this Bulgarian cartoon reads: "New Chinese saying: 'So what if half the world perishes? The other half can still have a good time.'"

Politika (Belgrade), January 21, 1962

A Yugoslav cartoon suggesting the "evolution" of an Albanian into a Chinese.

became known as the "domestic Chinese" contingent. While we have a rather good idea about the actual stand of most of these opponents of the new line, we do not know who within the Soviet elite and bureaucracy disagreed with what part of the Khrushchev "package."

The Twenty-second Congress in Perspective

In retrospect, the Twenty-second Congress confirmed and continued the general policy pursued by Khrushchev since the Twentieth Party Congress in 1956. His main line in foreign policy was to reduce the risk of war by arriving at a *détente,* above all with the United States, and in domestic affairs to transform the rule of terror into a rule of Communist rationality.

It is sometimes argued that the liberalization of Soviet society after Stalin's death was an inevitable response to the demands of a highly complex industrial order. That may be so; perhaps there is some correlation between the political superstructure and the economic base, which by the 1950's rendered a centralized rule of terror obsolete. In the particular case, the absence of legitimized rules of succession and the consequent competition for power among equals, from 1953 on permitted a freer expression of various interests, which Khrushchev used to consolidate his power and which, in turn, limited his exercise of power.

In any case, once controls were relaxed, ideological precepts questioned or discarded, and new objectives set, the way was open to controversy and political pressure within both the U.S.S.R. and the international Communist movement. Since, moreover, Khrushchev's policies, especially in the second half of his rule, can hardly be said to have met with unqualified success, he was all the more vulnerable to challenge by those who felt he was undermining the system.

Khrushchev undoubtedly had the support of the Soviet rank and file in exploring a new course free of many of the terroristic, repressive aspects of Stalinism; he also had the backing of important elements in the society disposed to favor a more rational order. His struggle to consolidate power was inextricably meshed with his policies, which were opposed (on principle or on tactical grounds) by others from among Stalin's epigoni—and by such important Communist figures outside the U.S.S.R. as Mao Tsetung. International strategy was directly linked to Khrushchev's attempt to reallocate resources in the Soviet Union or, more simply, to provide for an enlargement of the consumer economy. This linkage of domestic and international strategies provided targets of opportunity for critics who did not necessarily see eye to eye on all points. The struggle over power and policy gave additional opportunity to various interest groups—e.g., military and economic—not to form a cohesive opposition but to exert sufficient pressure to account for the backing and filling of Khrushchev's policies over the years.

Khrushchev's attack on Molotov reflected in part his attempt to break down the resistance of those "conservative" forces in the Soviet Union that, among other things, preferred to concentrate on the development of heavy industry, Stalin style, to the exclusion of any significant reinvestment in consumer goods. The traditionalists had their counterparts in the military establishment, who have tended to emphasize heavy-industry defense policies in opposition to those who, with Khrushchev, have favored a weapons system based on modern technology—such as missiles and rockets—which would permit substantial savings through reduction of the traditional theater forces.[9] This controversy among the military was not yet settled; Minister of Defense Malinovsky's speech at the Twenty-second Congress was eclectic: "Although nuclear weapons will hold the decisive place in a future war, we are nevertheless coming to the conclusion that final victory over an aggressor can be achieved only through combined operations by all branches of the armed forces."

Similarly, the controversy of heavy *vs.* light industry went on. Although consumer goods fared better in the Party Program than they had in the Seven-Year Plan for 1959-65, for example, there was considerable ambiguity with regard to the relative stress on heavy or light industry.[10] Unresolved policy differences, ambiguity of data and characteristic inflation of goals suggest that the economic goals were hortatory. Whether the Program's goals are considered fantastic or merely exaggerated, the Program did indicate the direction in which Khrushchev was attempting to point Soviet society, its economic perspectives, and social and political arrangements.

Khrushchev's denigration of Stalin perforce called into question the legitimacy—and purpose—of the Soviet system. Palmiro Togliatti, the late chief of the Italian Communist Party, for example, made the point that for Marxists the distortions in the social system could not be explained away satisfactorily by ascribing them to the guilt of one individual. There must have been more fundamental causes, rooted in social institutions and structure. While Togliatti was ideologically distant from the positions attributed to the Antiparty Group, he nevertheless put his finger on a crucial point. For if the methods and practices for which millions of persons had suffered and died for a generation were wrong, the authority of the Soviet leaders associated with Stalin and the *raison d'être* of socialism were undermined. Moreover, Molotov and others may indeed have been convinced that the

---

[9] See Chapter 7, "Khrushchev and the Military."

[10] See Naum Jasny, "Plan and Superplan," in Walter Laqueur and Leopold Labedz, eds., *The Future of Communist Society*, pp. 29-43.

U.S.S.R. had a long way to go in building up its industrial power and therefore had to continue the general patterns of the past.

While the Soviet internal order was able to withstand the shocks of de-Stalinization, the external order began to disintegrate: Khrushchev's attempt to place relations with other Communist countries and parties on a new basis got out of hand. The international Communist movement was fragmented. Albania, under Chinese cover, declared its independence of Moscow; the Chinese made their bid for leadership in the movement; Communist countries like Rumania proceeded to assert their independence of Moscow on economic policies; and anti-Moscow parties and factions appeared throughout the world. Khrushchev's policies at this point appeared to be leading to disaster.

The Twenty-second Party Congress testified to the strength of Khrushchev's position which permitted him to pursue his domestic and foreign policies in the face of predictable damage to the international movement already badly splintered. While his opposition within the U.S.S.R. was neutralized, or perhaps beaten, the situation internationally was quite different.

The Chinese had established themselves as the leaders of a well-defined ideological and political tendency. Not only were they arrayed against Khrushchev on foreign policy, but they had challenged him on Soviet internal policies including his prescription for the achievement of Communism. The Chinese, for example, ridiculed the pronouncement of the "all-people's state," maintaining, contrary to Soviet doctrine, that exploiting classes still existed in the U.S.S.R. and that, consequently, the dictatorship of the proletariat must inevitably continue until the higher stage of Communism was reached. The Chinese position thus held out the prospect of alliance—whether in fact or in the logic of the argument—with the militant opposition in the U.S.S.R. to oust Khrushchev and restore the unity of the Communist movement. Yet nowhere does the evidence confirm that such an alliance, except tacitly perhaps, existed. Nothing, moreover, but inference suggests that Russia's "domestic Chinese" were organized or even willing to speak out.

The conflict over policy in the CPSU invites a comparison with the revisionist trend that transformed the international socialist movement in the late nineteenth and early twentieth centuries from one of revolutionary Marxism to social democracy. At that time, the revisionist trend, which more nearly reflected the actual condition of the European socialist movement, won out. Was Khrushchev's revisionism an analogous development? The Chinese in accusing Khrushchev of a Bernsteinian sell-out avoided discussion of this point. Rather, they preferred to compare the situation to that in 1903 when Lenin constituted the "Bolshevik" faction as a temporary minority. Like Lenin, the Chinese have hoped to convert their temporary minority into a permanent majority.

But even if they succeed, will the international balance of power and the needs of the Communist states and parties permit them to execute those policies with which they are now identified—policies no doubt partly conceived in principle, but just as much shaped by the exigencies of immediate interests and the irresponsibility permitted the opposition? At any rate, the CPSU Program's description of the growing cohesion of the Communist state system and of the international Communist movement is belied by the facts and was so even before the Twenty-second Congress met.

Khrushchev's renewed attack on all the real and ostensible varieties of Stalinism provided the drama of the Twenty-second Congress, obscuring its stated purpose of defining the future Communist society. Whatever the results of the split in the international Communist movement, which in turn will undoubtedly have repercussions on Soviet politics, the Congress represented a landmark in the domestic development of the U.S.S.R. The Party Program, though not to be taken literally as a blueprint or plan, reflects the goals and aspirations of Khrushchevism, which may be characterized most simply as the achievement of a collectivist welfare state. If this has little to do with Marxist humanism, it is nevertheless a significant improvement for the Soviet citizen over Stalin's terrorist, bureaucratic order.

Study Questions

1. What significance do you attach to the Twenty-second Party Congress? What impact do you think it had on Soviet society and the international Communist movement?
2. What is the function of a Soviet Party Congress? Who attends, how are the delegates chosen, how often do they meet, and what power do they have?
3. What are the chief points of the Program adopted by the Twenty-second Congress? What operational significance do you think the Program had?
4. What significance do you attach to Khrushchev's attack on Albania? What were his motives and what did he hope to achieve?
5. To what extent do you think Khrushchev's policies represented a liberalization of Soviet society?

Selected Bibliography

The handiest source containing a condensed record of the major speeches of the Twenty-second Congress together with the Party Program and Party Statutes, is Charlotte Saikowski and Leo Gruliow, eds., *Current Soviet Policies IV, The Documentary Record of the Twenty-second Congress of the Communist Party of the Soviet Union* (New York and London: Columbia University Press, 1962). The texts of the speeches in Russian are collected in *XXII s'ezd Kom-*

munisticheskoi partii Sovetskogo Soyuza (Moscow: Gospolitizdat, 1963), 3 volumes.

The Congress has prompted the publication of a number of books containing pertinent documents and commentary on the proceedings and Program. Among these are Thomas P. Whitney, *The Communist Blueprint For The Future* (New York: Dutton, 1962), which includes the program of the Russian Social-Democratic Labor Party, the 1919 Party Program and the 1961 Program in draft together with an introduction by the author; Jan F. Triska, ed., *Soviet Communism: Programs and Rules* (San Francisco: Chandler, 1962); Herbert Ritvo, *The New Soviet Society* (New York: The New Leader, 1962) reproduces the final text of the Program with extensive annotations. Harrison E. Salisbury, *Khrushchev's "Mein Kampf"* (New York: Belmont Books, 1961) includes the draft Program and Statutes with background by the author. Harry Schwartz, *Russia Enters the 1960's* (Philadelphia and New York: Lippincott, 1962) contains major speeches delivered at the Congress and the author's commentary on anti-Stalinism and Soviet economic growth to 1980.

Among the useful articles relating to the Congress are Walter Laqueur and Leopold Labedz, eds., *The Future of Communist Society* (New York: Praeger, 1962), a collection of articles on the Program; Merle Fainsod, "The Twenty-second Party Congress," *Problems of Communism*, Vol. 10, No. 6 (November–December, 1961), Special Supplement; Philip E. Mosely, "Khrushchev's Party Congress," *Foreign Affairs*, Vol. 40, No. 2 (January, 1962), pp. 183–95; Oscar Gass, "Soviet Economic Developments," *Commentary*, Vol. 37, No. 2 (February, 1964), pp. 54–68; and "The Congress and Its Aftermath," *Problems of Communism*, Vol. 11, No. 1 (January–February, 1962), pp. 1–42.

On the "interest group" approach to Soviet politics and the problem of the Antiparty Group, see Roger Pethybridge, *A Key to Soviet Politics* (New York: Praeger, 1962), and the discussion in *Problems of Communism*, Vol. 12, No. 5 (September–October, 1963), pp. 27–46.

Finally, on the Soviet–Albanian-Chinese controversy, two leading books are Donald S. Zagoria, *The Sino-Soviet Conflict* (Princeton, N.J.: Princeton University Press, 1962); and William E. Griffith, *Albania and the Sino-Soviet Rift* (Cambridge, Mass.: M. I. T. Press, 1963).

4

Khrushchev and Party-State Control

Grey Hodnett

In November, 1962, not long after the humiliating withdrawal of Soviet intermediate-range ballistic missiles from Cuban soil, Nikita Khrushchev confronted a plenary meeting of the Central Committee of the Communist Party of the Soviet Union. The members of this congregation of top leaders, drawn from all the various elites of Soviet society, listened to Khrushchev's speech with intense interest and applauded as if on cue. Yet many of them must have questioned his deftness in the handling of Soviet foreign relations and have been even more concerned with the radical party and state reorganization plan he was at this very moment unveiling—a plan that not only jeopardized the jobs of some of them but threatened to create dangerous instability in the Soviet political system. From their point of view, as became clear after his premature departure from political life, Khrushchev was engaging in "harebrained scheming."

One of the features of the ill-fated reorganization that managed to survive Khrushchev's fall—for but a year—was the new Committee of Party-State Control of the Central Committee of the CPSU and of the Council of Ministers of the U.S.S.R. (CPSC). This organization was to be formed, Khrushchev implied at the Plenum, through a merger of two previously independent bodies: the *State* Control Commission (SCC), whose duty it had been to detect various forms of cheating commonly practiced by officials in Soviet state agencies, and the *Party* Control Commission (PCC), whose main task had been to supervise the imposition of party disciplinary measures against party members who violated the party Rules. Khrushchev selected as Chairman of the CPSC Alexander Shelepin, who was known to the Soviet public as the former head of the Committee of State Security (KGB)—the Soviet secret police.

To a Russian-speaking person raised in the Soviet Union, the word "control" (*kontrol*) means something different from what it means to an Englishman or an American: ordinarily it connotes the power to investigate and oversee rather than the power to give commands. For a Soviet citizen, "control" means primarily checking to make sure that officials adhere to codified rules and regulations, and it ordinarily involves the verification of documents. "Control" in this sense is an important task that must be performed if the Soviet system is to function with even moderate efficiency, given the central direction of most aspects of economic and political life and the absence of a critical political opposition.

The Soviet leadership has two major channels available through which it may exercise "control," each with its own particular advantages and liabilities. It may choose to stress the role of "public" (i.e., voluntary, nonpaid, party-led) organizations in performing "control" duties, thus maximizing the advantages of grassroots participation by people likely to be aware of what needs checking. This technique, however, sometimes leads to amateurish results, disrupts administrative routine, fails to overcome the resistance of local officials, and makes central direction difficult. Or the leadership may choose to exercise "control" through various bureaucratic instruments legally authorized to conduct investigations. This approach helps overcome the defects of "public" methods, but it sacrifices coverage and ease of access to incriminating information. In practice, the leadership blends these techniques, varying the combination in response to specific circumstances.

Deciding whether to merge the State Control Commission with the Party Control Committee was a political choice of considerable importance for the Soviet leaders. In making the decision, they had to determine whether the new agency should have extraordinary administrative and/or party disciplinary powers, and whether the scope of its activity should extend beyond routine checking of legal violations to matters that would entail serious intervention in the political process. More specifically, they had to decide whether the agency should be a party (or party-police) establishment, and whether it should also exercise a certain degree of control over the party apparatus itself.

In a multitude of ways, the resolution of these issues affected the vital interests of various individuals and groups—Presidium members, lower party *apparatchiki,* Soviet state officials, Goskontrol functionaries (*Goskontrol* refers to the state control agency, whatever its official title), enterprise managers, KGB officers, prosecutors and judges, academicians, rank-and-file party members, and even the "nonparty masses."

An examination of how these issues came to be resolved casts light on the ways in which "ideology," group interests, and situational pressures impinge upon Soviet decision-making. But it also illustrates the hazards of attempting to determine the ultimate meaning of a major Soviet political event. Although an understanding of one event requires an interpretation of the broader political scene, in recent years even the most knowledgeable Western observers have held opposite views on the most important single feature of Soviet politics—the leader's power. Those who believe that Khrushchev obtained absolute power in 1957 (whatever may have happened to it later on) would be inclined, in interpreting the emergence of the CPSC, to look for certain kinds of information—especially signs that the creation of this great "watchdog" agency was a response by Khrushchev to increasingly serious economic difficulties in the U.S.S.R. On the other hand, those who stress the instability of Khrushchev's position after 1957 would tend to look especially for suggestions, however subtle, that in order to consolidate his power Khrushchev was considering the drastic expedient of a full-fledged purging instrument that would facilitate the removal of leaders disloyal to his own person and policies.

As will become clear, both types of information can be found. But, here as elsewhere, the reader should ask himself whether the evidence goes beyond providing factual foundations for the alternative hypotheses about Khrushchev's power to actually prove one or the other of these hypotheses and the related interpretation of the CPSC.

Background

Khrushchev's "Historical Precedent"
Whether simply to provide the public with some explanation for the CPSC and to maximize the leverage provided by an official unchallengeable party "line," or also to buttress his own personal position, Khrushchev felt the need at the November Plenum to produce an ideological rationale for his innovation. He and his spokesmen justified the establishment of the CPSC as a "restoration" of the "Leninist principle of combining party and state control." Lenin's policy of drawing "the masses" into the conduct of public affairs, they asserted, had been implemented by the merger in 1923 at the Twelfth Party Congress of the People's Commissariat of Workers' and Peasants' Inspection (WPI, or Rabkrin—the state control organ headed by Stalin) and the Central Control Commission (CCC) of the Party. Stalin, it was argued, had never really accepted Lenin's policy. His distrust of the masses became manifest in 1934 when he abolished the CCC-WPI and established two separate bodies: the Party Control Commission and the Soviet Control Commission.

This use of "precedents" to legitimize current policy is a good example of how ideology can be put to work in Soviet politics. By the same token, it reveals how little—or how ambiguous—a relation to historical reality such references to party history may have.

Lenin and the CCC-WPI

In 1920, Lenin had played a major role in creating both the CCC and WPI, which he viewed in part as weapons to suppress political opposition; soon after, he strongly supported Stalin and Rabkrin against those who wished to eliminate the CCC and the WPI. These included Stalin's opponents among the party elite, economic administrators, advocates of industrial democracy who feared bureaucratic tutelage, professional Rabkrin "controllers" who were eager to do their job unhampered by "politics" or mass "democratic" participation, and some lower-level party officials who feared excessive interference from above—roughly the same office-holders who, we may assume, have more recently looked askance at the creation of the CPSC.

As the ailing Lenin became increasingly concerned in late 1922 over Stalin's grasp for power and even further convinced that it was vital to pursue a conciliatory policy toward the peasantry, his views on the control agencies began to change. In a series of notes and five articles written between December, 1922, and March, 1923, for the forthcoming Twelfth Party Congress, Lenin articulated a "rightist" resource-allocation policy (i.e., one not implicitly geared to a large-scale application of compulsion), proposed the removal of Stalin from the General Secretaryship of the party, and advocated a sweeping reorganization of Rabkrin.[1] Lenin premised the continued existence of the Soviet regime on adherence to a policy of moving the peasantry toward "socialism" only gradually and by means of tangible incentives—a policy that was anathema to some Communists because of the slow tempo of development in heavy industry and the discrimination in favor of the peasantry that it implied. Lenin feared that the consistent pursuit of his policy would be prevented by a schism in the party leadership. The reorganization would help avert a split by bringing some 50 to 100 "workers" and "peasants" into the top party ranks, thus ensuring well-informed and ideologically correct debate in the Central Committee

---

[1] Lenin's reorganization schemes were presented in the articles "How We Should Reorganize Rabkrin" (January 23, 1923) and "Better Less, but Better" (March 2, 1923). Three earlier drafts of "How We Should Reorganize Rabkrin," which presented a significantly different proposal from that of the final article, were not published until 1959. The distinction between the two proposals was that, according to the first, fresh "workers" and "peasants" would participate in Rabkrin as full-fledged representatives of the Central Committee. According to the second, they would participate in both Rabkrin and the Central Committee as members of a third body (the CCC) which, Lenin knew, was legally elected by the Party Congress but was at the time dominated by Stalin and his Secretariat. Under both plans the size of the Central Committee would be increased. In neither plan did Lenin discuss the local agencies of Rabkrin or of the CCC.

and Politburo, and increasing the power of the Central Committee vis-à-vis the Politburo and central party bureaucracy.

Stalin and the CCC-WPI

Shortly before the Twelfth Party Congress in April, 1923, when action was to be taken on his suggestions, a paralyzing stroke reduced Lenin to silence. The Congress' resolution on reorganizing Rabkrin, drafted beforehand by a special committee composed of Zinoviev and four Stalinists (including Dzerzhinsky, head of the secret police), decreed a reorganization of the control network that failed to reflect Lenin's intention of curbing the party apparatus.

Discussion at the Congress revealed a pronounced bias of the party bureaucracy against economic administrators; a clear intention of the party bureaucracy to intervene even more vigorously in appointments at all levels in the economic bureaucracy; and a continuing interest by the party leadership in utilizing the control commissions as watchdogs to supervise local *party* functionaries.

Following the Congress, Valerian Kuibyshev, the head of the new CCC-WPI and a staunch Stalinist, turned this joint party-state control apparatus into one of the major instruments with which Stalin purged the party of his opponents in the 1920's and early 1930's.[2]

The Great Purges

By 1934, strengthened secret-police controls, the rise of a new Soviet managerial stratum, and the instituting of centralized industrial chains-of-command had diminished the political and economic utility of the CCC-WPI. In addition, Stalin might have feared that the joint control organ —an "elective," nonbureaucratic body—could still become a focal point of opposition. Whatever his motives, he split the CCC-WPI in 1934 to establish the Soviet Control Commission and the Party Control Commission. Soon after, he began to put together a completely new purge mechanism by installing figures from his private secretariat in the key positions of head of the secret police, Secretary of the Central Committee in charge of personnel, head of the Central Committee Party Organs (formerly Personnel Assignment) Department, head of the Party Control Commission, and head of the Soviet Control Commission.[3] Thus was the organizational groundwork laid for the Great Purges.

---

[2] The CCC-WPI worked closely with the Personnel Assignment Department of the Central Committee apparatus and the secret police. It enjoyed both state and party disciplinary powers. Local CCC organs were independent of the local party apparatus, and this centralization of command within the party control agency continued to exist after 1934.

[3] In 1934, Yagoda replaced V. R. Menzhinsky as head of the secret police. In February, 1935, Ezhov replaced Lazar Kaganovich as secretary of the Central

For a decade and a half after 1934, little was said about joint party-state control. Only in the ominous postwar years, as Stalin prepared for new purges, was Rabkrin—the predecessor of the Ministry of State Control —resurrected in "historical" literature as the embodiment of "intraparty democracy," "mass control from below" and "criticism and self-criticism"; that is, as a positive symbol of ideologically legitimized denunciation of superiors by inferiors.[4] Once again the key positions in the purge network began to change hands.[5] Stalin's death in March, 1953, however, prevented this dark drama from progressing to its destined end. The newly constituted purge mechanism was rapidly dismantled, and approving "historical" articles on the CCC-WPI ceased to appear in Soviet journals.

The Post-Stalin Period

The silence surrounding Rabkrin was broken in February, 1954, by an "historical lecture" in the back pages of the official party theoretical journal, *Kommunist*. It mentioned the CCC-WPI, referred to party "unity" in the context of the Twelfth Congress, and recalled the opposition of "Trotskyists and Bukharinists" to party policy. It was soon followed by a major unsigned article in *Kommunist* (March, 1954) that cited Lenin's last works and mildly criticized the Ministry of State Control; a review article in the official party organizational journal, *Party Life* (August, 1955), of a collection of Lenin's writings on public administration, which tangentially criticized Goskontrol; and then a scathing attack on Goskontrol that took the form of a critique in *Kommunist* (September, 1955)

Committee in charge of personnel and as head of the Party Control Commission. Ezhov's two associates, Georgi Malenkov and Matvei Shkiriatov, were promoted to head of the Party Organs Department of the Central Committee and deputy chairman of the Party Control Commission, respectively. And Kuibyshev conveniently died in January, 1935.

[4] In addition to the appearance of "historical" articles on Rabkrin, on April 9, 1949, *Pravda* celebrated the "Thirtieth Anniversary" of Goskontrol with an editorial, an announcement of the awarding of medals to 36 top Goskontrol officials, and a long article on Goskontrol's glorious traditions by Leo Mekhlis, then Minister of State Control. The timing of this publicity could not have coincided more closely with the purge of Andrei Zhdanov's followers then being set in motion in Leningrad, suggesting a reward to Goskontrol for services rendered.

[5] Mekhlis, who himself had long-standing ties with the secret police, was replaced as Minister of State Control in October, 1950, under obscure circumstances by Vsevolod Merkulov, a former head of the secret police. In late 1951, Stalin moved Beria's dependent Viktor Abakumov out as head of the secret police and put Semyon Ignatiev in his place. Shkiriatov was moved up to replace Andrei Andreyev as Chairman of the Party Control Commission. (At the Nineteenth Party Congress in 1952, Khrushchev announced the decision to upgrade the PCC into a Party Control Committee with representatives officially independent of the local party apparatus in republics and oblasts [an administrative division corresponding to a province].) In the fall of 1952, Stalin transferred jurisdiction over personnel assignment in the Central Committee Secretariat and apparatus from the hands of Malenkov to those of Averki Aristov.

of Goskontrol's news sheet for its employees. This article charged Goskontrol with failing to investigate the implementation of major party and state policies, to take any interest in instituting major reforms of the Soviet administrative structure, and to correct shortcomings on the spot, and it asserted that Goskontrol shrouded the results of its checkups in the deepest secrecy. These accusations were undoubtedly true; indeed, there were good reasons that Goskontrol should have behaved in this manner.[6]

It is impossible to say who caused these articles to be written, or for what reason. If later attacks are any clue, the hypothesis might be entertained that Khrushchev may have passed the word. But why? One possible explanation is that Khrushchev may have seen in Goskontrol a potential lever of power that he wished to capture.[7] Alternatively, Goskontrol may have been a Stalinist stronghold that Khrushchev wanted to neutralize. Or, Goskontrol may simply have been doing a poor job.

The Twentieth Party Congress, 1956

Khrushchev precipitated public attack upon Goskontrol by major party leaders at the historic Twentieth Party Congress in February, 1956. Goskontrol, Khrushchev declared, was "poorly carrying out Lenin's injunc-

---

[6] Goskontrol was a centralized union-republic ministry with a large proportion of its personnel concentrated in Moscow. The Ministry operated through its own "chief state controllers" attached to other union and republic ministries, to important industrial enterprises and transportation sectors, and to military regions. It had no apparatus below the oblast level, and its local staffs were small, scattered, and frequently unqualified to judge technical production problems. According to law, Goskontrol had the right *not* to authorize expenditures of money and raw materials, which gave it "extraordinary powers to interfere in the administrative and economic activity of many state organs"—or so a Soviet author has recently claimed. It is uncertain, however, how widely this right was invoked after 1953. The Ministry did not have the right to summon guilty officials before its Collegium to explain their actions—much less the right to punish them. Local Goskontrol investigators could not impose reprimands without gaining the permission of the republic Council of Ministers, nor could they impose fines. They had no power to order violations stopped. And they were specifically forbidden to inform local party and administrative officials of their findings. In general, the field inspectors had little contact with local party officials. Goskontrol also seems to have been weakened after 1953 by an apparent attenuation of its ties with the secret police. Before 1953, Goskontrol could be considered a "front" operation of the secret police. This relationship was apparently modified after Stalin's death and Beria's downfall when V. G. Zhavoronkov, formerly a party official and then Minister of Trade, became Minister of State Control in the summer of 1953, replacing Merkulov, who was executed as an accomplice of Beria.

[7] He had already succeeded in having his former collaborator, Ivan Serov, appointed head of the secret police in March, 1954. With the demotion of Malenkov in February, 1955, he was able to oust Malenkov's protégé, N. N. Shatalin, from the Secretariat, thereby acquiring undisputed control over the key Party Organs (personnel assignment) Department. By the Twentieth Party Congress in 1956 he also succeeded in gaining increased influence in the Party Control Committee.

tions concerning state control." It failed to raise important questions related
to perfecting the state administrative machinery. (He implied that top
Goskontrol officials were not supporting his reorganization proposals.)
Consequently, the Ministry should be "radically reconstructed." Khrushchev later assured his audience that "life had shown" there was no
need for the provision in the Party Rules permitting independent local
agents of the Party Control Committee; this statement implied that a mass
purge was not in the offing. (In his "secret speech" ten days later, however, he may have been taking a different position by quoting Lenin's
words that the Control Commission "should be transformed into a real
organ of party and proletarian conscience.")

Khrushchev's motives for criticizing Goskontrol remain a matter of con-
jecture. Was Goskontrol a genuine obstacle in the path of his reorganization proposals? Could he have been engaged in the unlikely undertaking of
destroying Zhavoronkov, the Minister of State Control and a very minor
Soviet leader? Might he already have been maneuvering for "party-state
control"? Was Goskontrol a bastion of "conservatism"? Or was Khrushchev
just letting off steam? The evidence provides no answer.

Neither Zhavoronkov nor Andrei Andreyev, Chairman of the Party Control Committee and a former opponent of Khrushchev, spoke at the Twentieth Congress. Andreyev himself was replaced as Chairman of the PCC
at (or perhaps even before) the congress by Nikolai Shvernik, an old
apparatchik who had worked in the CCC-WPI and was later to side with
Khrushchev against the Antiparty Group. At the Congress, Khrushchev's
indictment of Goskontrol was vigorously echoed by Mikhail Pervukhin, a
Presidium member and high planning official who is known to have repeatedly opposed certain of Khrushchev's policies and who was later disgraced
for having been a member of the Antiparty Group. Perhaps Goskontrol
was in some way obstructing Pervukhin's own empire-building plans; perhaps he was settling old accounts with Goskontrol; or perhaps—less likely
—he was simply criticizing its current functioning. Again, the evidence
permits different interpretations.

In delivering the Central Committee report to the Twentieth Congress,
Khrushchev was in theory presenting the agreed position of the entire party
leadership. As we know, this leadership in fact was bitterly divided on
many issues. The final resolution adopted by the Congress contained no
reference to reorganizing state control. Clearly, Khrushchev's proposals
lacked unanimous support.

A New Minister of State Control: Molotov

In the months immediately following the Twentieth Congress, several
articles by close Khrushchev followers referred to Rabkrin and stated in
effect that Goskontrol was sabotaging the reconstruction of the state ap-

paratus. There followed a period of silence lasting from April until November 22, when Molotov, Khrushchev's antagonist, was suddenly appointed Minister of State Control. Zhavoronkov stepped down a rung to become Deputy Minister.

What Molotov's appointment signified is not clear. Molotov had been removed from his position as Foreign Minister on June 1, 1956. Following the events in Hungary and Poland, for which Khrushchev could well be blamed, Molotov unquestionably regained some influence. Did he, or others, hope to use Goskontrol to enhance his own power and restrain Khrushchev? Aside from the offices of Chairman of the Council of Ministers and chief of the secret police, that of head of Goskontrol was perhaps the one *state* position whose jurisdiction and formal powers might be used by a leader with independent political stature to build an autonomous power base. Yet past history and current realities indicated that Goskontrol could not possibly have been a match for Khrushchev's party apparatus. Molotov's appointment may have been a defensive move to block any plans Khrushchev might have had to use Goskontrol to enhance *his* power. Whatever the explanation of this puzzling move, attacks on Goskontrol could now be construed only as direct attacks on Molotov.

Molotov's appointment was greeted on December 12 by a *Kommunist* editorial. The Ministry of State Control, *Kommunist* pointed out, had not been following Rabkrin's example. It had failed to elaborate "proposals concerning the restructuring of the entire system of administration in various areas of state construction." Nor, *Kommunist* implied, had Goskontrol in the "recent past" maintained contacts with "the masses" (i.e., the party). "Now," it added, "these shortcomings are being corrected." This could have been a pat on the back for Molotov; it could also have been a demand that he go along with Khrushchev's reorganization schemes. Although the fate of Goskontrol per se was hardly comparable in importance as an issue in its own right to foreign policy or administrative reorganization, it had become an index of anti-Khrushchev power. Two weeks later, at the December, 1956, Plenum of the Central Committee, at which Khrushchev's opponents mounted their vigorous and partly successful counterattack, Molotov mustered sufficient support to suppress any mention in the final resolution of Goskontrol's "shortcomings."

Soon, however, Khrushchev regained the offensive—in this as in other areas of political activity. Shortly before the February, 1957, Plenum of the Central Committee, a "historical" article in *Kommunist* on "Lenin's Principles of Party-Building" noted that Lenin in his last writings had planned ways for improving the Soviet state and strengthening the party. The author also pointed out that Lenin had advocated expanding the Central Committee in order to increase its authority. (No significant increase in the size of the Central Committee, which presumably would have favored Khrushchev's interests at this time, occurred until the Twenty-second Congress in 1961.) Following Khrushchev's wishes, the February, 1957, Plenum resolved, in line with the first of the *Kommunist* theses:

> Reorganization of the administration of industry and the national economy demands a radical reconstruction of the content and methods of work of conducting state control. It is necessary for basic control work to be concentrated in the economic regions [the local territorial units within which Khrushchev proposed to establish *sovnarkhozy* (councils of national economy)] in order that shortcomings in the activity of the state and economic apparatus may be revealed and eliminated on the spot. The organs of Goskontrol both in the center and at the local level in all their work must lean upon the broad masses of toilers.

After the Plenum, several direct and "historical" attacks on Goskontrol for its failure to "draw the masses into state control" or to "lean upon party organizations" appeared in the press, prior to the publication of Khrushchev's "Theses" on administrative reorganization at the end of March. (Molotov was later charged with having obstructed implementation of the decisions of the February Plenum.) The "Theses" put forward a drastic plan, bitterly opposed on various grounds by the anti-Khrushchev faction, to break up the old ministerial bureaucracies and establish regional economic councils. Goskontrol, Khrushchev repeated, would have to be "rebuilt" to fit in with the administrative decentralization: "A new statute on Goskontrol organs both in the center and at the local level should be worked out, bearing in mind the realization of Lenin's instructions on the arrangement of control and improving the work of the state apparatus." Khrushchev apparently attempted to isolate Molotov from the possible support of economic administrators and perhaps the military by accusing Goskontrol of

> trying to cover literally all questions, including even control over the technical level of development of one or another branch of production, the level of development of science and technology, which is useless. Controllers try to give orders on production problems, which means supplanting the economic organs.

The same day that Khrushchev's "Theses" were published (March 30), a *Party Life* feature article made two important points: Lenin had proposed the obligatory attendance of a member of the CCC at Politburo meetings; and Lenin had stated that the Party *Congress* elected the CCC, and that the CCC ought therefore to act independently of the other leading bodies elected by the Congress. The article may have reflected a preliminary step (or threat) by Khrushchev to employ the Party Control Committee to counter the "arithmetical majority" in the Party Presidium that the "Anti-party Group" was welding together.

A definite decision to reorganize Goskontrol appears to have been made before the second week in April. A correspondent describing a Ukrainian Goskontrol meeting pointedly remarked in *Izvestia* on April 24:

> The main line on reconstructing Goskontrol has been indicated in a number of party documents. *It is clear and nobody objects to it.* Basic control work must be concentrated in the economic regions and must be conducted with the participation of the broad masses of toilers. As for the concrete details of the reconstruction, there is still not complete clarity on this score. It is true that there are variations of different drafts, but much is still subject to clarification and elaboration.[8]

The month of April was devoted to a characteristic ritual of Khrushchevian "democracy"—the comparatively free public discussion of important details of a new policy, within the limits set by a prior decision establishing the policy's broad outlines. Participants in the "debate" included republic Goskontrol ministers, republic Goskontrol inspectors, and local Goskontrol group chiefs, all of whose remarks revealed no particular loyalty to Molotov, their titular chief. There were no spokesmen for the U.S.S.R. and R.S.F.S.R. ministries of State Control. A number of participants referred approvingly to Khrushchev's "Theses." Most of them—especially the republic ministers, whose jobs hung in the balance—ritualistically admitted the truth of Khrushchev's earlier accusations; but they also utilized the occasion to articulate their own professional claims. All strongly urged that Goskontrol be given more disciplinary powers and less paperwork. Those who touched upon relations with the party implied that the party was ignoring *them*—not they the party. Most, but not all, of the participants favored the absorption by Goskontrol of competing watchdog agencies, including the inspection units of the ministries of Finance and Trade. Most seemed genuinely to favor the establishment of volunteer "assistance groups" in enterprises (workplaces) to ferret out information for Goskontrol. Various suggestions were also made concerning the best way to organize mass participation at higher levels, with some proposals betraying a fear of sacrificing professionalism on the altar of "mass democracy." Several republic ministers took issue with the proposal to change Goskontrol from a *ministry* (with one man at the head) to a *committee*. And some of the same ministers implicitly questioned Khrushchev's wisdom by advocating the retention of a centralized structure, thereby contradicting the latter's position.

The suggestions of these lower-level officials who had a large personal

---

[8] Except where noted, italics are mine in all quoted material. G.H.

stake in the outcome had no immediate influence upon policy. At the Supreme Soviet session early in May, called to discuss the great administrative reform, Khrushchev repeated his earlier accusations, asserting that he wished "considerably to strengthen the control work at the local level," but he indicated a desire to postpone any final decision on Goskontrol. He was challenged, however, by a high party *apparatchik,* Tursunbai Uldzhabaev, First Secretary of the Tadzhik Central Committee:

> In our opinion, it would be expedient to preserve the Ministry of State Control of the U.S.S.R. as a union ministry, having abolished these ministries in all the union republics. *This measure will heighten the significance of control conducted from above,* in combination with control by the masses of peoples from below, and will raise the responsibility of local organs of administration and of the sovnarkhozy.

Did Uldzhabaev really wish to strengthen or weaken Goskontrol? Was he simply expressing a personal view? Was he publicly venting the wishes of local party and economic officials? Was he (it is unlikely) siding with Molotov? Or was he manifesting a form of "bourgeois nationalism" by covertly criticizing a tool of Russian domination? His motives were unclear, but the effect of his proposal would have been to strengthen Molotov's position. Khrushchev was compelled to reply:

> In his speech Comrade Uldzhabaev . . . talked about the organization of state control. He proposed abolishing the republic Goskontrol ministries and concentrating the whole job of state control just in the center of the country. It seems to us that Comrade Uldzhabaev is wrong on this question. . . . Obviously the reconstruction of the Goskontrol organs must be done in such a way as to concentrate control at the local level, in the economic administrative regions. It is necessary to strengthen control work in the sovnarkhozy; to heighten the role of local soviets in this affair. It seems to us that at the present session of the Supreme Soviet the question ought not to be decided how, under present-day conditions, it would be best to organize control, and which control organs it is necessary to have. This question must be studied more deeply, and proposals worked out; after this the appropriate decisions will be made.

At this moment in the struggle between Khrushchev and his opponents, attacking or threatening Molotov as Minister of State Control may have served Khrushchev's purposes better than attempting to demolish Goskontrol, which he could not have done in any event. Khrushchev was preoccupied with his vast scheme of administrative reorganization, and Goskontrol was a side issue except as it provided leverage against Molotov and his other opponents. An attempted reorganization of Goskontrol could have precipitated a final showdown between Khrushchev and Molotov under conditions not favorable to Khrushchev. It is hardly surprising, therefore, that the reorganization of Goskontrol did not come about until after Khrushchev's victory over the Antiparty Group at the end of June.

Molotov was then expelled from the Party Central Committee. He was replaced as Goskontrol head by Georgi Eniutin, a long-time party *apparatchik* and protégé of Khrushchev. Some of the fifteen republic Goskontrol ministers were also soon ousted, their replacements being drawn from posts both within and outside the party apparatus. Surprisingly, Zhavoronkov—whose management of Goskontrol had appeared to be under such heavy attack in 1955 and 1956—continued on for several years as Eniutin's deputy.

The Reorganization of Goskontrol, 1957

How Goskontrol would be reorganized and what would be done about the PCC (nothing was) became clear only in August. The July 1 issue of *Party Life* had stressed the "programmatic significance" of Lenin's last five works (which encompassed, among other ideas, his plan to merge the CCC with the WPI). The August 15 issue alluded to the fact that the CCC had been created in 1921 to strengthen party "unity." It might have been surmised, on the basis of these and previous hints, and of Khrushchev's remark about "Lenin's instructions," that a merger of state and party control organs was being contemplated—perhaps aimed partly at purging minor followers of the Antiparty Group.

On August 23, 1957, however, the Ministry of State Control was replaced by an even less powerful Soviet Control Commission (SCC). The SCC was assigned the tasks of checking the implementation of government decisions on the most important economic problems and of conducting financial audits. To accomplish these tasks, the SCC was assigned legal powers that, on paper, went part way toward meeting earlier Goskontrol claims to greater authority.[9]

The reorganization may have brought Goskontrol "closer to production," but its main effect was to dissipate whatever influence Goskontrol did possess, and especially any potentiality it might still have retained of utiliz-

---

[9] Theoretically, organs of the Soviet Control Commission could give binding orders to responsible officials to eliminate shortcomings; impose disciplinary reprimands and fines; and, with the consent of the U.S.S.R. or republic Council of Ministers, remove guilty officials from their positions. The Commission was composed of a chairman and five members. (One of these represented the trade unions, another the Komsomol [Young Communist League], and a third, it seems reasonable to suppose, the secret police.) At the local level, Goskontrol representatives attached previously to production units were removed and combined into small territorial groups covering one or more oblasts. Republic commissions were made entirely independent of the all-union commission in Moscow.

ing its network of local agents as a means of wielding bureaucratic power. This reduction in power reflected on a small scale what was happening to other *state* bodies at this time as Khrushchev strengthened the position of the *party* apparatus. The decentralized structure that Khrushchev had imposed contributed greatly to this result. Without backing from Moscow, the thinly spread 1000-odd republic and oblast Goskontrol inspectors found it difficult to make headway against powerful local economic officials. The punitive rights of Goskontrol turned out in practice to be negligible. Nor did Goskontrol enjoy consistent support from local party authorities, who themselves were frequently involved in various shady undertakings. The low prestige and lack of influence of the organization contributed to a tendency of higher Goskontrol officials to act cautiously and to "live in peace" with influential economic administrators and their party "protectors." This outlook dampened reform enthusiasm at the lower levels.

Newspaper correspondents, republic Goskontrol chiefs, Goskontrol regional group leaders, academicians, and all other persons who spoke in favor of Goskontrol's bureaucratic interests publicly between 1958 and 1962 urged with one voice that the agency be given greater powers to do its job. Almost all persons affiliated with Goskontrol pressed the institution's claim to be *the* state control body; that is, to coordinate or completely absorb such checking agencies as the Ministry of Finance's Control-Revision Administration or the Ministry of Trade's State Trade Inspectorate. Enterprise managers could sympathize with Goskontrol's argument that the uncoordinated actions of some twenty-seven all-union and thirty republic checking organizations produced chaos at the enterprise (workplace) level.

Differences of opinion among Goskontrol spokesmen did manifest themselves, however, over three important questions: the proper way to organize public participation in Goskontrol activities (other than through establishing "assistance groups" at enterprises, which everyone favored); whether Goskontrol should become the central body that investigated complaints from the public at large; and whether Goskontrol staff members should be selected on the basis of their investigative skills or their abilities as mass mobilizers. In essence, all three questions could be reduced to the issue of the degree to which Goskontrol ought to become involved in the risky game of politics; or in operational terms, precisely what its relations with party bodies ought to be.

The May Plenum, 1958

Instead of organizationally merging state and party control systems—the policy later praised as truly "Leninist"—the party leadership chose to introduce gradual changes that brought the former into closer contact with party organs and the latter into closer contact with matters outside the narrow confines of party discipline per se. The metamorphosis of PCC functions began in earnest with the adoption by the May, 1958, Central Committee Plenum of a resolution (which has remained secret) initiating a broader range of activity on the part of the PCC.

The Central Committee's Party Control Committee (PCC) and its republic and oblast branches continued to perform their traditional task of receiving and screening appeals against disciplinary measures imposed by lower party organs which individual party members submitted to obkoms (oblast Party committees), republic party central committees, and the Soviet party Central Committee. And they were involved in the sensitive process of rehabilitating victims of Stalin's purges. Shvernik's speeches at the Twenty-first and Twenty-second Congresses (February, 1959, and October, 1961) revealed the strategic role of the PCC in gathering information on crimes committed during the Stalin era. But the local branches of the PCC were also encouraged to extend their writ into areas hitherto solely within the jurisdiction of ordinary party or administrative bodies: receiving "signals" from rank-and-file Communists and nonparty members concerning cases of professional malfeasance and dishonesty on the part of managers and party officials; acting autonomously to discipline administrative bodies and the secretaries of lower-ranking party organs for failing to enforce production directives; and, to a certain extent at least, criticizing lower-ranking party organs for "mistaken" personnel selection.

By expanding the functions of the party control bodies, the party's leadership evidently hoped to increase its own capacity to force the local party secretaries to exercise *their* power in combating "localistic tendencies"—the particular manifestation of self-interested behavior by regions and production units that arose from the 1957 administrative decentralization, and that was powerfully stimulated by certain effects of a poorly integrated system of economic incentives.

Economic considerations, though important, were not the only ones underlying the assignment of greater authority to the PCC. Concern over a tarnished popular image of party officialdom went hand in hand with an effort to restrict the autonomy of economic managers. Khrushchev may also have considered the possibility of using the PCC to purge high-ranking incompetents (left over in profusion after Stalin's death), or even to deal with opponents of his own policies and power. The enlargement of control functions, which was unquestionably unpopular with—and probably resisted by—the local party *apparatchiki,* took place only gradually and does not seem to have been uniformly implemented.

The expansion of the jurisdiction of the PCC after 1957 was complemented by two further innovations "democratizing" party disciplinary proceedings: the introduction of volunteer (nonstaff) party commissions for the preliminary review of disciplinary cases in city and district party committees; and the expression of a greater commitment to overcoming the *de facto* existence in the party of two systems of justice: one for those party members (especially economic managers) with political influence; and one for the rank and file.[10] While these changes in party control were being set in motion, "historical" articles in the Soviet press (in June and July, 1958, and July, 1959) continued to stress the contemporary relevance of Lenin's last articles and the role of the CCC-WPI in combating schism.

The Twenty-second Party Congress, 1961

The emergence of critical policy problems in the 1958–61 period, as well as the occurrence of important personnel changes in the Soviet leadership, set the stage for the Twenty-second Party Congress held in October, 1961.

After 1958, the rate of Soviet economic growth began to drop sharply. Khrushchev's response to this vexing problem involved a combination of moves that challenged traditional canons of Stalinist orthodoxy and those who benefited from them. These measures included promoting younger, technically trained persons into positions of leadership throughout the administrative and party structures; fostering monetary rather than moral incentives in order to raise labor productivity; increasing the output of consumer goods; allocating greater resources to agriculture; accelerating the development of modern "growth" industries, especially the chemical industry; attempting to reduce the enormous arms burden; encouraging mass-participatory public initiative and "criticism from below" while instituting more repressive measures of social control; and pursuing a relatively cautious "peaceful coexistence" line in foreign policy. How much Khrushchev "conceded" to the potential victims of his largely "rightist" initiatives is much debated. But it is a fact that neither policy affecting the Soviet military establishment nor policy with respect to resource allocation followed an unswerving course from the fall of 1959 to the Twenty-second Party Congress.[11]

---

[10] This campaign was stressed in 1961 and 1962, when it converged with an emphasis on two directly related themes: overcoming the tendency to restrict the obligations of party membership (and hence the scope of party discipline) to extraoccupational misbehavior; and encouraging the state judicial machinery to prosecute economic officials without prior clearance by local party organs.

[11] It strongly appears that some of the top Soviet leaders, particularly Mikhail A. Suslov and Frol R. Kozlov, did not always see eye to eye with Khrushchev in his attempt to pursue a policy line that threatened the stability of the Soviet political system. Kozlov's rise to second-in-command of the Secretariat, as well as other changes in the membership of the Secretariat and Presidium in the spring of 1960, are interpreted by some Western analysts as a sign of successful opposition by a "Stalinist" faction to Khrushchev's policies and personal power. Other observers interpret the same personnel shifts as the last step by Khrushchev in cementing his own dictatorial power.

The Twenty-first Party Congress and the June Plenum, 1959

At the Twenty-first Party Congress in February, 1959, Khrushchev referred in passing to "organizing a campaign, truly embracing all the people, against mismanagement, extravagance, and disregard of public property." On May 8, a book entitled *The Worker-Peasant Inspection, 1920–1923*, written by G. A. Dorokhova, was released for publication after having been held back since September, 1958, indicating the sensitive nature of the author's topic. The volume's sole reference to any current Soviet leader was to Shelepin, the future head of the CPSC, suggesting that he was already involved behind the scenes in the discussion of control.

At the June, 1959, Plenum of the Central Committee, Khrushchev spoke of the control problem in the context of combating economic inefficiency:

> In the work of the Soviet Control Commission there are serious shortcomings. It must strengthen control over the fulfillment of party decisions and of the laws of the Soviet state. . . . Now, when our country has entered the period of developed construction of a Communist society, public control over fulfillment of the directives of the party and government acquires enormous significance. It is necessary to strengthen control in all links of state, *party,* economic, and other organizations. Recently, the Presidium of the Central Committee took a decision on this matter. I think the members of the Central Committee will approve this decision.

Khrushchev was evidently referring to a decision to set up party control commissions within party cells as a means of drawing the rank-and-file membership more actively into criticizing the work of managerial personnel. The Central Committee approved this innovation and resolved that it was necessary to "perfect continually the forms and methods of *party and state control* over the activity of economic organs."

Following the Plenum, *Party Life* announced editorially that the SCC should expand its ties with the "public" by building up a group of volunteer helpers. A month later it signified its approval of joint checkups with trade union and Komsomol organizations, the formation of "groups of assistance to Sovkontrol" (i.e., the Soviet Control Commission) in enterprises, the deputizing of nonstaff controllers, contacts with party cells and their control commissions, and greater publicity for Goskontrol activities in the press.

During the rest of 1959 and 1960 major commentary on the future of control seems to have been presented in the garb of "historical" articles although the meaning of such esoteric commentary, by its nature, cannot conclusively be proved. An article by S. I. Ikonnikov in the February, 1960, issue of *Problems of History* noted that the reorganization of the WPI in 1923–25 was of topical significance; that Trotsky had spoken against Lenin's views on the WPI; and that at the Twelfth Congress the draft resolution on the CCC-WPI had been drawn up by Dzerzhinsky, known as the founder of the secret police. (Shelepin, then the head of the secret police and later head of the CPSC, had revealed an interest in Goskontrol at the Thirteenth Komsomol Congress in April, 1958. Could this have been a reference by analogy to *him*? But if Ikonnikov was speaking analogically, which members of the Party Presidium fitted the Trotsky mold?) In touching upon all the historical analogues of the major issues that were later to be raised overtly, Ikonnikov was clearly suggesting that the details of a proposed merger of party and state control were already under serious debate.

By 1961, there were other indications, too, that the party leadership was reaching a decision about the reorganization of control. After five years of evoking the memory of the CCC-WPI, the time seemed ripe to heed "Lenin's instructions" by unveiling a joint party-state control organ at the Twenty-second Congress. Instead, surprisingly, a decision simply to upgrade the Soviet Control Commission into a more centralized (union-republic) *State* Control Commission was announced on July 25, 1961. Several days later the long-awaited draft Program and then the draft Party Rules were printed for public comment, to be adopted (without substantial change) by the Congress. With reference to control the draft Program read:

> Constant *state and public control* is an important means of accomplishing this task [improving the state apparatus]. In accordance with Lenin's instructions, organs of control must function constantly at the center and at the local level, *combining state control with public inspectorates.* The party regards *inspectorates of people's control* as an effective weapon for drawing the broad masses of the people into the management of state affairs and into control over the strict observance of legality, as a means of perfecting the *governmental* apparatus, eradicating bureaucratism, and promptly putting into effect proposals made by the people.[12]

The draft Rules indicated that no change was contemplated in the status of the Party Control Committee. Thus, it would appear that opponents of a joint control organ had, in July, successfully preempted the "decision" of the forthcoming Congress. The shift from Soviet Control Commission to State Control Commission undermined hopes for a more radical reorganization. And, by failing to mention *party* control, the Program reinforced this conservatism. It limited the planned pre-Congress public "debate" by

---

[12] This excerpt from the draft Program, as well as later quotations from the records of the proceedings of the Twenty-second Congress and from Khrushchev's Report to the November Plenum, 1962, is reprinted, with minor changes, from *The Current Digest of the Soviet Press,* published weekly at Columbia University; copyright 1962. By permission.

seemingly placing changes in the structure of the party beyond the pale of legitimate discussion.

Pre-Congress Discussion

From August until October, when the Twenty-second Congress assembled, the pages of Soviet newspapers and journals were filled with articles that praised the draft Program and Rules but also pressed the special claims of their authors—rationalized, to be sure, to harmonize with the broad principles underlying the Program or the Rules. Three articles were of peculiar relevance to the control issue. They unquestionably reflected the views of various elements of the Soviet elite, including Party Presidium members.

The first of these, signed by an obscure Communist, S. Vorontsov, was "planted" in the September 5 issue of *Kommunist*. Vorontsov stressed the absence of party control bodies below the oblast level and the dependence of oblast and republic control bodies upon the oblast and republic party apparatuses. In his view, what was required was an independent hierarchy of party control organs paralleling the regular party apparatus. He justified his proposal by arguing that, while party policy emphasized the "restoration" of "Leninist norms of party life" and "intraparty democracy," the dependence of party control organs upon the local apparatus led to miscarriages of justice in cases involving rank-and-file members. Vorontsov's proposed reform might have promoted "intraparty democracy" by stimulating "criticism from below." Yet it would also have brought into being an instrument independent of the regular party apparatus and able to watch over, if not purge, local party officialdom.

The second article, written by A. Adoian, a member of the Armenian party's Central Committee and editor of the Armenian party journal, *Leninyan Ugiov,* appeared in the October 12 issue of a major Armenian newspaper also called *Kommunist*. Adoian touched upon the distribution of power at the party summit, while proposing in detail a merger of the PCC and the SCC similar in many respects to that enacted over a year later. A Collegium of Party-State Control would be elected at party *congresses* and *conferences* (thus becoming formally independent of the committees and secretariats) at all levels within the party, including the raion (district) level, and would be headed by one of the secretaries of the given party committee. At the republic and all-union levels, members of the collegiums would enjoy the rights of central committee members and would be given a high salary—a measure presumably felt necessary to guarantee their independence and honesty. The new organ would continue to perform the routine functions assigned to the current party and state control organs. It would also take on the additional tasks of assuring the observance of "intraparty democracy," policing conformity to the "Communist's moral code," and, most important, intervening in personnel assignment:

> It would assume a large role too in [assuring] the strict observance of Leninist principles of selecting and distributing cadres. Who could better know the organizing abilities of a man, his political preparation, than the Collegium of Party-State Control, *which would study people not by looking at their dossiers, but in the process of their practical activity?*

This passage seemed to be a slap at the Party Organs Department, which since May, 1960, had been supervised in the Secretariat by Frol Kozlov. Adoian could not have written the article purely on his own authority.

The same day the Moscow journal *Kommunist* printed another proposal, offered by I. Boliasnyi, an unknown history teacher at the Zaporozhye Machine-building Institute, the implementation of which could equally well have radically altered the distribution of political power at the republic and lower levels. Boliasnyi urged the creation of a "Central Control Commission–People's Control Inspection" resembling the old CCC-WPI. CCC members would be "elected" at republic party congresses and at oblast, city, and raion party conferences, while PCI members would be named at "elections" to local soviets. Local organs would be in "dual subordination" both to the party and state elective bodies that ostensibly appointed them and (apparently to a greater exent) to the top control body in Moscow. The central control commissions were—"in the sphere of control"—to have "equal rights" vis-à-vis the central committees of republics and oblast, city, and raion party committees, and hence plenary meetings of these committees were to be held "jointly with the CCC organs." According to Boliasnyi,

> Such a structure, it seems to me, would provide for the independence of local control organs from the local organs of authority and *the local party leadership,* would strengthen control on the part of the Central Committee of the CPSU and the Council of Ministers of the U.S.S.R. over the work of raion, oblast, and republic institutions and departments, and would aid the effective struggle against localism and its consequences. Such a structure of the control organs would also assist in strengthening mass control from below.

Boliasnyi's tactics in justifying his proposal illuminate the arguments—and in part the motives—of some opponents of party-state control. In contrast to Adoian, Boliasnyi admitted that the dissolution of the CCC-WPI in 1934 had had a certain "positive significance for its time." He therefore chose not to select loyalty to anti-Stalinism as the terrain for political warfare. Instead, he candidly argued the practical proposition that sometimes violations committed by workers in the state apparatus and economic organs are grounded in the actions of local party leaders. . . . In order to provide for operative and all-round control at the local level, it is necessary simultaneously to check both the work of *khoziaistvenniki* and the work of the state and party apparatus. If only the soviet institution is checked or only the economic organization, the local party leaders (who are also responsible for the poor work of these institutions and organizations, but have not been checked because of the functional splintering of our existing system of control) frequently try even to protect the people being investigated and thereby smooth over the implied evaluation of their own shortcomings.

His proposal, he intimated, would *not* undermine the leading role of "the party," since "party organs must head the entire checkup system." Opponents of the plan, he seemed to be saying, might argue that the CCC-WPI was established at a time in which overcoming internal dissension in the party was the main task; that this was now not the case; and that therefore joint party-state control was unnecessary. Boliasnyi adroitly parried the implied charge of wishing to restore practices associated with the "cult of personality" while denying his opponents' conclusions:

If, during the 1920's, the main motivation for creating the CCC-WPI was the threat of schism in the party, at the present the main object is the necessity, first, to overcome localism, the influence of "purely personal and accidental factors" (Lenin) in the activity of republic, oblast, and raion instances, and, secondly, to expand the role of the public in all state administration, including the control system; otherwise, it will be impossible to assure the universal participation of the toilers in nationwide control from below, of which Lenin dreamed.

He reassured those who feared the introduction of a mass purge of "conservatives" by stating, in contrast to Adoian:

In the 1920's, when there was a threat of schism in the Central Committee, it was necessary that the CCC-WPI have rights equal to those of the CC and that it be elected at congresses of the party. At the present time, when there is no danger of schism, there is no need for the [new control organ] to possess rights equal to those of the CC.

He indicated that those (undoubtedly local party and state officials) who charged that such a control organ would contradict the "party policy of broadening the rights of local party and state organs" misconstrued the nature of this policy. Concluding, he stated:

The draft Program of the CPSU says: "In accordance with Lenin's instructions, organs of control must function constantly at the center and at the local level, combining state control with public inspectorates." It seems expedient to us to supplement this formulation and to present it as follows: "combining party, state control with public inspectorates. . . ." (Add the word "party.") The corresponding changes, it seems to us, should also be introduced in the Party Rules.

Several other public statements in the pre-Congress discussion touched upon the control issue. Georgi Eniutin, head of the State Control Commission, who could have sided with the advocates of joint party-state control, chose to say nothing about the CCC-WPI while referring to the draft Program and its "inspectorates of people's control." Eniutin gave the impression that he was satisfied with the July reorganization. In emphasizing that Goskontrol organs were broadening their contacts with the public, however, he did state that councils of "representatives of soviet, *party,* and Komsomol organizations and of advanced production workers" were being formed under oblast Goskontrol groups.

The Chairman of the Supreme Court of the U.S.S.R., Alexander Gorkin, soon thereafter referred to the formation of councils of "representatives of soviet, *trade-union,* and Komsomol organizations and of advanced production workers" under oblast Goskontrol groups. Gorkin's lengthy experience as a party *apparatchik* made it highly unlikely that the difference in phrasing was accidental. The immediate issue posed in this jockeying over a seemingly minor point of "formulation" was the degree to which the control system would be infused with party power; the ultimate issues may well have been—however contradictory it may seem—both the defense of the legal order against the inroads of party-led "popular democracy," *and* the protection of those officials who had compromised themselves under Stalin's reign.

Another important expression of opinion was an article called "Lenin and Party Congresses" that appeared in the October 12 issue of *Kommunist.* Written jointly by an editor of the journal, G. Shitarev, and a well-connected writer on party affairs, A. Sidorov, the article cited Lenin's "How We Should Improve Rabkrin" and "Better Less, but Better," noted that the expansion of the Central Committee at the Twelfth Congress in 1923 had promoted "collegiality" and party "unity," and linked Lenin's sanction of disciplinary measures against Shliapnikov and the Workers' Opposition faction with the steps taken more recently against the Antiparty Group. At the Twenty-second Congress a week later, the Central Committee *was* increased by almost one hundred full and candidate members, leaving little doubt as to the contemporary relevance of this "historical" article. The significance of the change in size of the Central Committee, the first since the Nineteenth Congress in 1952, was obscure, but it might possibly be argued by historical analogy that expanding the Central Committee was linked in some way with overcoming opposition to Khrushchev's policies, and that this in turn was linked to "party-state control."

The Twenty-second Congress

On the morning of October 17 the delegates to the Twenty-second Congress gathered to hear Khrushchev deliver the Central Committee Report. In the section of the Report that dealt with control (though not in the similar section of the Report on the Program, which he also delivered), Khrushchev came out in favor of joint party-state control, linking it with the need to pull in the reins on lower party officials:

> Comrades! At the present time the question of *party, state, and public control* [italics in original] from top to bottom and bottom to top is acquiring importance of the first order. In control lies an effective means for perfecting leadership of Communist construction. The work of this or that organization, of *any leading party organ* must be evaluated first of all on the basis of how they are in fact carrying out the demands of the Program and the Rules of the CPSU, of party directives.
>
> . . . Strengthening control and verification of execution must begin first of all with *party* organizations. It is necessary to establish a strict order of accountability of *local party organs* before higher party committees and before the masses of Communists with respect to the fulfillment of party decisions. We must recall and unswervingly fulfill the Leninist demand: "Check people, check the actual performance of the job."
>
> Much remains to be done in improving state control. Large shortcomings existed until recently in the work of the Soviet Control Commission.
>
> The system of *party, state, and public control* is a mighty means of perfecting leadership in Communist construction on the basis of genuinely democratic principles; it is a wonderful school of Communist education for the broadest masses of people. This is why we must, with due attention to present circumstances, take fuller advantage of the advice given by Vladimir Ilyich Lenin in the article, "How We Should Reorganize Rabkrin."

The debate at the Congress—a debate embodied in subtle shades of emphasis—was intended not to influence the adoption of the new Party Program and Rules, but to shape in advance the frame of reference within which these documents (themselves a series of compromise "formulations") would later be interpreted. Soviet leaders tended to show agreement with Khrushchev's policy proposals by commenting favorably on them and disagreement by remaining silent. Only one Presidium member, Mikoyan, said anything at the Congress which could be interpreted as approval of party-state control. In justifying the suppression of the Antiparty Group, Mikoyan declared:

> These disagreements with the conservative-dogmatic group were not disagreements over partial organizational or separate political questions. No!

They involved the determination of the entire policy of the party for the new stage of historical development, its general line. In his own time V. I. Lenin showed that the reorganization of Rabkrin proposed in 1923 was no simple organizational measure, but involved all our work, our policy, our tactics, our strategy. What was involved was preserving leadership by the working class over the peasantry and facilitating the victory of socialism in the U.S.S.R.

Under present-day conditions, what is involved to an even greater degree is not simply organizational measures, but the elaboration of a policy which may provide for the successful building of Communism in our country and provide the opportunity to avert world war.

Mikoyan's ambiguous statement could be interpreted as linking party-state control with the handling of political deviation and with the maintenance of a "rightist" policy line. (Mikoyan was widely considered a firm supporter of Khrushchev's resource-allocation priorities and "peaceful coexistence" formula.) Yet would Mikoyan, an Armenian, have associated himself with a scheme so clearly aimed at further limiting the autonomy of the local non-Russian elites?

Nikolai Shvernik, a veteran Presidium member and Chairman of the PCC, delivered fulsome tributes to Khrushchev, noted the "crimes" of members of the Antiparty Group uncovered—so he said—by the PCC, and approvingly discussed (as he had at the Twenty-first Congress) the extension of PCC functions. He failed, however, to endorse joint control. His silence contrasted sharply with the speech of his new deputy, Zinovi Serdyuk. Echoing Khrushchev, Serdyuk stated:

The question of *party, state, and public control,* from top to bottom and bottom to top, is now acquiring importance of the first order. The feeling of responsibility of each leader, each Communist, for the job assigned to him must be heightened as never before.

. . . From the rostrum of the Twenty-first CPSU Congress, Comrade N. S. Khrushchev called for organizing a nationwide campaign against every manifestation of waste, extravagance, negligent attitudes toward national wealth. . . . Speaking of the tasks of party control, Vladimir Ilyich Lenin emphasized that he saw the goal of this control as lying "not only or even so much in 'catching,' 'convicting' (this is the court's task)—as in being able to correct. Wise and timely correction—this is the main task." It is just such an effective, creative control that we need. A bureaucratic, paper-shuffling control will not serve in struggling with shortcomings; it will aggravate them and harm the training of cadres. The effectiveness of control—*party and state*—lies in its mass quality, in drawing rank-and-file Communists and the entire public into realizing control functions.

Serdyuk, a long-time beneficiary of Khrushchev's protection in the Ukrainian Party apparatus, had been promoted from his latest job as First Secretary of the Moldavian Central Committee to the newly created post of First Deputy Chairman of the PCC on May 29, 1961. It appears likely that Khrushchev wished to strengthen the PCC, or to place a man of absolute loyalty to himself near its head—or both.[13]

Alexander Shelepin, speaking as head of the secret police, provided further lurid details of the "criminal" deeds of members of the Antiparty Group, and emphatically demanded that they be expelled from the party by the Party Control Committee—implying, perhaps, that the PCC may have possessed the power in some circumstances to block expulsions from the party.

Frol Kozlov delivered the Central Committee Report on changes in the Party Rules. One of his duties was to comment upon the various suggestions made to amend the Rules, including the proposal to institute joint party-state control. Yet he said nothing whatever about it. Kozlov's noncommittal remarks about control seemed to shift all responsibility to Khrushchev:

> It is necessary to draw the toilers more actively into the administration of *state and public* affairs, to improve the selection, distribution, and training of cadres, to organize effective control and verification of fulfillment— which was discussed exhaustively in the Report of the Central Committee to the Congress.

In this case, as in the case of several changes in the Party Rules, Kozlov appeared to speak for the more conservative party *apparatchiki* in his reluctance to endorse innovations that might shake the existing distribution of political power. One other proposed innovation that Kozlov objected to was the revival of periodic party purges. "Socialism," he declared, "has triumphed fully and conclusively in the country. . . . Is there any need, under the circumstances, to revive the party purges? . . . There is no need for a measure of this kind."[14]

Differences in phraseology between the Program and the Resolution of the Congress on Khrushchev's Central Committee Report seemed to mirror an argument over a variety of issues, one of which was party and state control. As on other subjects, slight but symptomatic changes seem to indicate the extent to which Khrushchev had succeeded in altering the frame-

---

[13] The timing of the move, Serdyuk's close ties with Khrushchev, the pre-Congress spotlight on the PCC, the fact that he even spoke at the Congress, his support of party-state control, and his vigorous promise at the Congress to expose those guilty of crimes during the Stalin era argue strongly that Serdyuk's elevation and his support of Khrushchev's position were not coincidental.

[14] This could have been a qualifying reference, at least in part, to the plan, supported by Khrushchev and embodied in the new Program and Rules, of institutionalizing a more rapid turnover among the holders of elective party and state positions.

work of future debate. The draft Program, which in several respects stopped short of Khrushchev's own preferences, spoke of "state and public control." But, the Resolution on the Central Committee Report, as adopted by the Twenty-second Congress, stated:

> *Party, state, and public control* over the proper organization of affairs, over the precise fulfillment of the requirements of the Party Program and the Rules and of directives and instructions of the party and the Soviet government by every official in whatever post is acquiring significance of the first order under present circumstances. . . . In order to intensify control over and verification of actual fulfillment of tasks it is necessary to institute a strict procedure for *accounting by local party organs to higher party organs* and to the masses of Communists about the fulfillment of party decisions. The Twenty-second Congress instructs the Central Committee to devise effective measures for improving and perfecting *party, state, and public control.*

Advocates of joint control now had an authoritative platform, sanctioned by the "highest organ" of the party, from which to argue their case.[15]

The November Plenum, 1962

Foreign and Domestic Difficulties

A peculiar conjunction of developments during the months preceding the November, 1962, Plenum of the Central Committee imposed strains on the party unparalleled, perhaps, by any since the defeat of the Antiparty Group in June, 1957. The embarrassing withdrawal of Soviet missiles from Cuba; the decision not to support China in her border war with India; agricultural stagnation and the continuing decline in the rate of economic growth; aggravated contention between military and other groups over resource allocation; and unrest among urban workers (with rioting in some instances) over food price increases—all contributed to Khrushchev's discomfiture. During 1962 the Soviet leadership had proceeded with a quiet demotion of thousands of economic officials and a press campaign of praise for the secret police. The latter also received wide publicity for rounding up economic "criminals," scores of whom were shot under recently enacted

---

[15] At the end of the Congress, Shelepin was appointed to the Secretariat and replaced by Vladimir Semichastny as head of the secret police. Vitaly Titov became head of the Party Organs Department of the Central Committee apparatus. Ivan Spiridonov, the Leningrad party boss, was also promoted to the Secretariat. Because Spiridonov was ousted from the Secretariat and his Leningrad position with Khrushchev's demonstrative backing a scant half year later, some observers interpret his appointment to the Secretariat as another manifestation of a continuing struggle for power in the Kremlin.

laws extending the death penalty. The tensions created by diplomatic and economic difficulties blended with a simmering controversy over cultural freedom, restlessness among the youth, and even signs of a desire for greater independence in the lower reaches of the party. Thus, a variety of factors—potential instability in the party, popular dissatisfaction with the standard of living, and intractable economic problems—would seem to have provided a strong incentive for Khrushchev to push the debate over control toward resolution.

Debate over Control

Public discussion of control during 1962 brought into sharper relief the contours of two opposing schools of thought: one that associated "Lenin's instructions" with the Program's formulas of "state and public control" and "inspectorates of people's control," and one that identified Khrushchev's slogan of *"party,* state, and public control" with "Leninism." Each formulation indicated a particular set of arrangements.

The first implied that the new control organ was to be strictly an arm of the *state.* Major *de facto* initiative in the appointment and removal of control commission chairmen and members would lie with the government, while the party would perform a more passive ratifying role. Staff employees would be selected on the basis of their "businesslike" (rather than their political) qualifications. The transfigured Goskontrol would become the central structure in the entire network of governmental control agencies. It would either totally absorb or closely supervise (opinions differed) all "departmental" control agencies, including those of the sovnarkhozy, the oblast executive committees, the Ministry of Finance, and the Ministry of Trade. It would also become the nucleus around which a system of volunteer inspection bodies would be organized. Groups of nonstaff (i.e., unpaid) controllers would be directly attached to the control organs, or alternatively, additional permanent commissions of deputies to local soviets could be created to assist Goskontrol. (Opinions also differed here: some Goskontrol officials apparently wished to leave the headaches of organizing mass participation to the soviets. This solution held "the masses" at arms' length and minimized the disruption of tried-and-true control techniques.) While the new control agency would maintain contact with local party officials, it would rely for major assistance in mobilizing public participation upon the less potent trade unions, Komsomol organizations, and local soviets, with their subordinate mass-participatory bodies. At the enterprise level, the less prestigious trade-union committee would have the main responsibility for organizing assistance, though the party cell and its "control commissions" would lend a hand.

The second formulation—"party, state, and public control"—implied much the reverse. In this scheme, the control body would be basically a *party,* or party-police agency. Party officials would entirely dominate the appointment of its leaders. Its personnel would be selected primarily from among political "activists"—a type, needless to say, most likely to be found on the staffs of party or Komsomol committees. It would work through party as well as governmental channels and would make full use of the mass-mobilizing potential of party bodies at all levels.

The first set of views was expressed publicly by a member of the U.S.S.R. Goskontrol, several republic Goskontrol heads, and several academic experts in public law. The second was never fully articulated in public, but the chairman of the Ukrainian Goskontrol indicated his general support for it early in April. Its contents could be inferred from what opponents said and what later happened. The first viewpoint seems to have reflected a majority (but not unanimous) opinion within Goskontrol. It probably coincided with the opinion of those jurists whose genuine attachment to the "liberalization" of the Soviet system has been accompanied by a concern for legality and a distrust of the motives of those in favor of greater "Leninist democracy." Although they did not express themselves publicly, many party bureaucrats probably also preferred the first formula to the second, but for negative reasons. "State and public control" would not seriously threaten their interests and power and would involve less "mobilizing" responsibility. In all likelihood, other government agencies, faced with the prospect of losing their own departmental investigative units to a revivified Goskontrol, were tacitly hostile to *both* plans. These units were, in their estimation, an essential tool for effective administration that could at the same time be trusted not to "wash dirty linen in public." The antimanagerial element implicit in "party-state control" was even less palatable. Factory managers could have found nothing pleasant in either scheme.

Who, then, did support party-state control? Some frustrated Goskontrol personnel may have favored the idea, reasoning that this solution provided the only way to combat the local political power of influential economic administrators. The KGB probably favored party-state control as a front for multiplying secret police channels of activity. Some officials within the Central Committee apparatus undoubtedly voiced their support. But those who did approve party-state control were probably united as much by a common, activist (and typically Khrushchevian) urge to "do something" about the staggering waste, inefficiency, and corruption of Soviet economic life as by a convergence of occupationally derived interests.

Steps taken in 1962 pointed toward a victory for the advocates of "state and public control." In fact, the first stage of the reorganization of Goskontrol that had been formally announced on July 25, 1961, was evidently postponed until after the Twenty-second Congress and undertaken only "at the beginning of 1962."[16] New Goskontrol groups were created in oblasts that did not have them. "Public councils" composed of representatives of soviet, *trade-union,* and Komsomol bodies and "outstanding production workers" continued to be established under oblast Goskontrol groups. The highest trade-union body adopted a resolution obliging local trade-union organs and plant trade-union committees to assist Goskontrol. "Inspectorates of public control" (which dealt primarily with living-condition problems) were formed in three oblasts. On the party side, the Central Committee Resolution of January 11, 1962, seemed to stabilize matters by approving the formation of nonstaff party commissions under oblast, city, and raion party committees, although this could also be interpreted as a move to prepare for the establishment of the CPSC.

Only slowly was the decision to move in the direction of party-state control apparently reached by the party leadership. An article by N. Aleksandrov (*Party Life,* February 16, 1962) reflected indecision:

> Following the instructions expressed by Lenin in the article, "How We Should Reorganize Rabkrin," the party is setting a course toward combining *state and public control.* The system of *party, state, and public control* which exists in our country is a mighty means for perfecting leadership of Communist construction.

In the March issue of the legal journal *Soviet State and Law,* an article linking Lenin's interest in "state and public control" with the "observance of legality" bluntly declared:

> The new Rules of the CPSU provide *all* the necessary organizational conditions for strengthening the leading position of the party in the system of the all-people's state, and also for promoting the development of public control over the activity of state and other organizations in strengthening socialist legality.

A timely "historical" article on the 1922 Eleventh Party Congress (*Kommunist,* March 31), however, stressed a different theme. That Congress, the author noted, condemned "all believers of little faith, who tried to exaggerate the difficulties of economic construction and to sow panic in the ranks of the party." The Eleventh Congress had resolved

> that the CCC was to strengthen work in unifying and leading local control commissions. The control commissions were entrusted . . . with the serious and important task of warding off and struggling with squabbles and illegitimate groupings. . . . Unity of the party was and *remains* the decisive condition of its force and might. Our party has dealt and *deals*

---

[16] A. E. Lunev, *Obespechenie zakonnosti v SSSR* (Moscow, 1963), p. 88.

intolerantly with fractionalists, those who corrupt its ranks, undermining its monolithic structure from within.

On April 19, at the Fourteenth Komsomol Congress, Khrushchev posed the question of control in the seemingly nonpolitical context of the "struggle against parasites." He briefly announced that "the Central Committee and the government are thinking about strengthening control in order to eliminate shortcomings more quickly. The public is the main force in the struggle with shortcomings." Khrushchev's speech was quickly followed by a *Party Life* editorial on April 28 stating that the principles upon which "party, state, and public control" should be based had been enunciated "in the reports of Comrade N. S. Khrushchev, in the decisions of the Congress, and in the new Party Program." (Note the order.) Control, *Party Life* added pointedly, did not mean "sowing a circle of suspicion, of mutual distrust. Only hopeless Philistines could understand and interpret the essence of control in such a fashion." In conclusion, the editorial asserted that "only by uniting *party, state, and public control into one* will we be able to create a genuinely all-people's control over the activity of all organizations, institutions, and officials and thus multiply our opportunities to accelerate the movement forward to Communism."

This editorial, however, was by no means the expression of a final Presidium decision. In *Izvestia* on May 26, Georgi Eniutin, Chairman of Goskontrol, quoted the "state control with public inspectorates" section of the Program and added: "This passage serves us as a compass, as a guide to action." Perhaps the turning point came at the end of May, 1962, when an article by Frol Kozlov appeared in *Kommunist*. Kozlov conceded that:

> perfecting the system of *party and state control,* giving to it a broadly public character, has enormous significance in principle and practice for further improving methods of leadership. What is involved is a rebirth and development of the remarkable ideas on Rabkrin proposed by Lenin in the last years of his life.

But he went on to remark: "V. I. Lenin considered it important to arrange for broad mass control from above and below . . . in perfecting the *Soviet structure.* . . . Now the party is thinking about how to implement concretely Lenin's instructions concerning control."

The available evidence does not reveal when or how the key decisions on the shape of the Committee of Party-State Control were taken. Shelepin was moved to the Secretariat in October, 1961, probably in part so that he could supervise planning for the CPSC. However, the "final" plan seems not to have been authorized until shortly before the November, 1962, Plenum.

The Plenum

On November 19, 1962, the Central Committee convened to hear Khrushchev deliver a report on "The Development of the U.S.S.R. Economy and Party Guidance of the National Economy." In it he announced a major reorganization of the party, intended to enhance its role in economic management. The party reorganization, as Khrushchev must have been aware, could not endear him to the Soviet "Establishment."[17]

Khrushchev went on to declare that a joint party-state control agency, the Committee of Party-State Control, would be formed. The party's republic central committees and obkoms, he declared, were not checking the execution of decisions at the local level because "in effect we do not have special party control agencies." The PCC and oblast party control commissions confined themselves "primarily" to reviewing disciplinary cases. The State Control Commission, Khrushchev charged, relied exclusively on its staff workers, who ignored the most glaring abuses.

Some people, Khrushchev implied, did not think the control agency should "watch over fulfillment of the national economic plan." But he had ready several answers to objections to his proposed party-state control. In "How We Should Reorganize Rabkrin" and "Better Less, but Better," Lenin had provided for a "well-arranged system of party and state control," but "Stalin grossly violated the Leninist principle of the organization of party-state control." (That is, those who objected to party-state control were taking a "Stalinist" position.) The Resolution on the Report of the Central Committee to the Twenty-second Congress—Khrushchev did not mention the Program—assigned prime importance to "party, state, and public control." (The Resolution was approved by the Congress; the Congress was the highest organ of the party; and hence those who opposed

---

[17] The elimination of the existing district (raion) party and soviet structures meant that thousands of party and state jobs would be jeopardized. The decision to split the party apparatus into agricultural and industrial branches from the oblast level down not only institutionalized urban-rural conflict within the party, but meant that there would no longer be a single party "boss" in each locality —a disquieting prospect for the traditionally minded. The emphasis on economics meant that younger, better-educated men would be advanced into posts now held by the older party *apparatchiki*. Organizational, and especially ideological, specialists in the party apparatus were being asked to take a back seat. Factory managers were threatened from three directions: being fired for not taking measures that would decrease their own and their workers' incomes; being subjected to greater party interference; and being further afflicted with time-consuming and potentially disruptive plant "democracy." (Khrushchev advocated experimentation with a form of worker participation in management that vaguely smacked of the "revisionist" Yugoslav workers' councils. As he remarked, apparently alluding to certain Presidium members: "Some comrades may wonder where this will lead.") At the same time, workers were told that output norms would be raised. State planners were notified that their performance would fall under closer party scrutiny. And all party members, regardless of rank, were warned that they would be punished more harshly than nonmembers for violations of the law.

party-state control opposed the will of the party.) The proposals submitted at the Plenum were those of "the Presidium," which had made up its mind after having "lately discussed repeatedly and thoroughly with Central Committee members and heads of local organizations the question of how to improve the organizational structure of party guidance of the national economy at this time." (Thus, the proposals were not simply Khrushchev's own.)

The major function of the CPSC would be to detect and eradicate production shortcomings *on the spot*—whether or not laws, regulations, or plans were technically being violated. Khrushchev now placed less emphasis than he had in 1956–57 on improving the administrative apparatus. When the CPSC discovered major troubles, it was to submit its recommendations directly to the top party and state authorities.

The Khrushchev Report had a certain antimanagerial, populist flavor to it. There was little in it, however, to encourage proponents of an agency that would watch over the party apparatus, except, perhaps, for these surprising remarks:

> In 1948, the then Minister of State Control Mekhlis issued an order that to all intents isolated the apparatus of State Control from other Soviet organizations and institutions. . . . In the period of the cult of personality, when mass repressions began, many important functions of control were turned over to the state security agencies, the heads of which, as is well known, tried to put themselves above the party. The idea of control in its Leninist conception proved incompatible with the ideology of the cult of personality. . . . We have still not taken all measures for fully eliminating major defects in the organization of control. The organizational structure of the control agencies has not yet been restored in accordance with Leninist conceptions.

Khrushchev was evidently criticizing the secret police affiliations of Goskontrol before, and perhaps even after, 1953; yet he seemed to imply that some functions performed by the secret police were to be transferred to the CPSC. The remark could be interpreted as a threat that the new agency would perform tasks long associated with the secret police. On the other hand, it could as easily be interpreted as a promise that the "important functions" would be performed in a "Leninist" manner, because they would be performed under the immediate supervision of the party and not directly by the KGB. Unfortunately, the key to the riddle is missing since it is unclear which "important functions" Khrushchev had in mind.

Once the decision had been reached to create a party-state control organ, its structure and powers became the focus of political infighting. On these crucial matters Khrushchev was almost as vague as he had been earlier on establishing the CPSC. He seemed to imply that party-state control committees would not be established below the oblast level. Although he did not clarify the division of power between the CPSC and the local party apparatus, he appeared to assure the party *apparatchiki* that, at the top, the CPSC would be subordinate to the central party apparatus. He implied, accurately, that Goskontrol had failed in its bid to absorb the "departmental" control units. Broad publicity, he indicated, was to be one of the major weapons of the new agency. There was, of course, to be mass participation; but he said nothing about the form it would take.

Was it Khrushchev's intention to leave organizational details open for further debate and experimentation after the Plenum? Or had he said all that the other leaders would let him say, with the details subject to further negotiation?

Khrushchev's Report was discussed by Plenum participants in painstakingly formulated speeches. Of those who were invited to express their views, forty-seven could reasonably, it seems, have been expected to comment upon party-state control, which was, after all, one of the major innovations announced in Khrushchev's Report. The table on the next page indicates their responses.

Since no explicit negative comments could be made, it would appear that over three-quarters of the speakers were cool toward the idea of party-state control. Enterprise directors, sovnarkhoz chairmen, high government officials (probably including Georgi Eniutin), kraikom and obkom secretaries, and a majority of the republic party secretaries who were not members of the Central Committee Presidium or Secretariat (seven out of nine) fell into this category. Extraneous reasons could have explained—not that they necessarily did—the position of most of those who commented favorably. (It may be argued, of course, that the same could be said about those who did not comment favorably.) The seeming lack of support for party-state control contrasted sharply with the approval generally expressed for the other major features of Khrushchev's proposed reorganization. The chances are that this approval was feigned; but if it was, those who did so at least felt it necessary to mask their true feelings—because final decisions had already been taken, because Khrushchev had solid Presidium support for these elements of his "reform," or because in any event he would have brooked no opposition.[18]

---

[18] An important reason for sentiment against party-state control may have been reflected in Georgi Eniutin's speech, which he was allowed to append to the minutes of the Plenum but not asked to read. Eniutin criticized Stalin's Goskontrol for "isolating itself from the people" and for its "blanket distrust of leading economic cadres." He then remarked, for no apparent reason:

Matters went to such an extreme that in the name of the cult of Stalin's personality, contrary to historical facts, a celebration of the thirtieth anniversary of Goskontrol was organized in 1949, although it is well known that a Collegium of the People's Commissariat of State Control was formed December 5, 1917, by a decree signed by Lenin; whereas Stalin was appointed People's Commissar of State Control in 1919. It was this

Responses of the Plenum Participants

	Total number	No refer-ence	Pro forma refer-ence	Favor-able com-ment	Strong support
Members and candidate members of CC Presidium	6	—	3	2	1
Members of R.S.F.S.R. Bureau	2	—	—	1	1
Secretaries of CC	1	—	—	—	1
First Secretaries of republics and Leningrad Oblast	14	5	4	2	3
Secretaries of krais and oblasts	15	11	2	1	1
High government officials	4	1	3	—	—
Goskontrol Chairman	1	—	1	—	—
Sovnarkhoz Chairmen	4	3	1	—	—
Enterprise Directors	5	5	—	—	—
All-Union Komsomol Chairman	1	—	—	—	1
All-Union Trade-Union Chairman	1	—	1	—	—
Totals (less double-counting[a])	47	25	12	4[b]	6[c]

[a] Four Presidium members and candidate members were also First Secretaries of republics; one Presidium member was First Deputy Chairman of the R.S.F.S.R. Bureau of the CC; one Presidium candidate member was Chairman of the Trade Unions; one member of the R.S.F.S.R. Bureau was First Secretary of Leningrad Oblast.
[b] Those who commented favorably were Voronov, Mazurov, Kunaev, and Komiakov.
[c] Those who expressed strong support were Demichev, Tolstikov, Mzhavanadze, L. N. Efremov, Pavlov, and Snechkus.

The strength of sentiment against party-state control may well have been reflected in a most important disclosure contained in the resolution adopted

---

date that served as the pretext for a jubilee, for every sort of eulogizing and exalting of the role of Stalin in the organization of Goskontrol. In such a way was history falsified.

It is not improbable that Eniutin was obliquely recalling the link between Goskontrol and the "Leningrad Affair" (see footnote 4, p. 118), and more generally, perhaps, Goskontrol's ties with the secret police and its role in the purge preparations of Stalin's last years. He may have intended to convey the message that the CPSC would behave in a "Leninist" fashion. Given his apparently lukewarm support of party-state control, however, this remark could also be interpreted as a subtle warning against the dangers of establishing a powerful purge weapon.

by the Plenum. While a Committee of Party-State Control was to be created and the State Control Commission abolished, the *Party* Control Committee was to continue in existence as the Party Commission—with the task of reviewing appeals by party members against expulsion and other disciplinary measures. The implications of this decision were important. Reference to the CCC-WPI had seemed to suggest that the new joint-control organ would possess the right to recommend the expulsion of members from the party, an assumption that had been reinforced by the expansion of PCC functions after 1958 and that had surrounded the notion of party-state control with much of its aura of power. Suddenly, this underlying assumption was exploded.

It is impossible to say with finality why the choice was made not to assign expulsion power to the CPSC. Did Khrushchev simply lack the necessary support within the Presidium and especially the support of those Presidium members (such as Kozlov) whose approval was particularly necessary? If so, then how had he managed to push through the most radical party reorganization in years? As soon became evident, some "concessions" had been made to various groups whose interests were at stake; perhaps this particular choice, highly desirable from their point of view, was dictated by the importance of their morale if not their political power.

Khrushchev's public speeches do not show how he felt about the matter, but there were certain reasons he might not have wanted to grant the CPSC the power of recommending expulsion. Most obviously, assigning disciplinary powers over party members to a partly nonparty (state) organ would have set a precedent with unforeseeable consequences. Preserving a Party Commission tended to prevent what Khrushchev might have considered an excessive concentration of power in Shelepin's (and the KGB's?) hands. Shelepin was already, after all, a member of the Secretariat. In terms of personal background, Shelepin, a former youth coordinator and policeman, was balanced by Serdyuk, a party *apparatchik* par excellence. "Rehabilitating power" was kept out of Shelepin's hands—*if* Khrushchev did want this, rather than the reverse. A party disciplinary appeals court somewhat removed from the current fray was allowed to stand. Granting the CPSC the right to initiate expulsion could have generated an unhealthy atmosphere at lower levels, deepening the rigid hierarchic pattern of relationships imposed by Stalinism on Soviet life—a pattern that killed production innovation and spawned "reinsurance" against all conceivable risks. Finally, retaining the *threat* of a future merger of the Party Commission with the CPSC gave Khrushchev a type of political leverage that he seems consistently to have wanted to employ.[19]

---

[19] At the end of the Plenum, the Ukrainian Vitaly Titov, head of the Party Organs Department, was made chairman of a new Commission for Organizational-Party

The Establishment of the CPSC

The two months' delay between the November Plenum and the first public announcement of the detailed rights and duties of the CPSC suggested a continued clash of interests behind the scenes, a hypothesis that seemed confirmed by conflicting propaganda treatments of party-state control during the first half of 1963.[20]

For example, one article in *Kommunist,* "The Development of Lenin's Ideas on Party-State Control" (December 26, 1962), cited the "decisions of the Twenty-second Congress" first and the "new Party Program" second; referred to improving the work of the *party* apparatus; quoted Lenin's formula, "Check people, check the actual performance of the job"; declared that the "struggle of the party for unity in its ranks" was a law "in effect even now"; and mentioned the CCC-WPI's function of "assisting the party and state in the selection of leading cadres." But another *Kommunist* article (January 31, 1963), by one of Stalin's top ideologues of the early 1950's, cited at the outset the Program's formula of "state control with public inspectorates"; referred to perfecting the "state and economic apparatus"; did not quote the "check people" formula; and said nothing about party "unity" or cadre selection.

Roughly similar contrasts were evident in two articles celebrating the seventy-fifth anniversary of Kuibyshev's birth, which appeared in *Pravda* on June 6 and *Izvestia* on June 7, 1963. (*Izvestia,* edited by Alexei Adzhubei, Khrushchev's son-in-law, stressed the "unity" theme.) That the question of some degree of CPSC control over the party apparatus was indeed a bone of contention seemed indicated by G. A. Dorokhova's "historical" article in the February 18, 1963, issue of *Problems of the History of the CPSU.* She declared her intention not to discuss "measures for strengthening party unity" taken by the CCC-WPI. "This particular function of the organs of party-state control," she pointedly remarked, "demands special research."

Questions in the Central Committee apparatus and simultaneously appointed to the Secretariat. The implication was that he now exercised an even greater influence over personnel assignment, perhaps at the expense of some of Kozlov's power. In the spring of 1965, after Khrushchev's fall, Titov was demoted to the post of Second Secretary of the Kazakh Communist Party and soon dropped from the Secretariat of the Central Committee.

[20] Some observers argue that Kozlov's "heart attack" and disappearance from public life, which dated from April 11, 1963, signified the failure of an attempt by the "hard-liners" to undermine Khrushchev's power. They believe that a series of later events testifies to his resurgent strength: the appointment of Leonid Brezhnev and Nikolai Podgorny to the Secretariat in June, 1963; the diminished momentum of the 1962–63 literary persecutions; Khrushchev's consumer-oriented remarks about resource allocation in the spring of 1963; the public rift with the Chinese; and the signing of the test-ban treaty with the United States.

The CPSC Statute

On January 18, 1963, *Pravda* published what purported to be a summary of the "Statute on the Committee of Party-State Control" issued by the Central Committee and the Council of Ministers on December 20. According to the summary, economics and administration were emphasized by the Statute, not political deviation. The CPSC and its local organs were to:

> check on the actual execution of party and government directives . . . ; supervise the fulfillment of economic plans and disclose internal reserves . . . ; give assistance to the party in improving the work of the state and administrative-managerial apparatus . . . ; put a decisive end to violations of party and state discipline, to manifestations of localism, narrow departmentalism, and hoodwinking; report padding, mismanagement, and extravagance . . . ; wage a ruthless fight against bureaucratism and red tape, bribe-taking, speculation, and abuse of office . . . ; and exercise control over . . . observance of the socialist principle, "He who does not work, neither shall he eat."

The CPSC was to be a union-republic body; that is, the center in Moscow would exercise a large but ill-defined degree of authority over the republic branches. The U.S.S.R. CPSC would be subordinate to the Central Committee, *not* to the Party Congress. Republic and oblast committees would be "dually subordinate," it was vaguely implied, both to the organ that formally "approved" them—the republic central committee or the oblast committee (a concession to the interests of middle-level party officials?)—and to the CPSC of the all-union or republic central committee. Organs of the CPSC below the oblast level (which Khrushchev had not even mentioned), however, were to be accountable only to oblast or republic party-state control committees, though they required the formal "approval" of plenums of local party committees. This decision probably reflected, on the one hand, the weight of those in favor of a more vigorous control system, and, on the other, the lesser political influence of the lower-level *apparatchiki*. At the same time, subordinating the bottom control organs even formally to the city and district party apparatus would have tended, from the party leadership's point of view, to defeat the purpose of the reorganization of control.

The CPSC of the Central Committee was to be composed of "leading workers of the Committee [i.e., CPSC functionaries], representatives of the trade unions, Komsomol and the press, and workers, collective farmers, and members of the intelligentsia." Republic and oblast committees would contain representatives of these organizations and social classes and, in addition, delegates from subordinate party-state control committees, thus interlocking lower and higher control bodies. Public participation would be arranged by creating nonstaff departments in the CPSC organs and "groups of assistance to party-state control" at enterprises, construction sites, kolkhozes (collective farms), and sovkhozes (state-owned farms).

The summary of the Statute gave the CPSC (at least on paper) impressive powers; for instance, it could "instruct" high *state* officials to eliminate violations; countermand orders by state officials; and fine, reprimand, and even remove from office guilty individuals.

Organizing Party-State Control

In early 1963, a two-pronged propaganda campaign was set in motion to build public support for the policy of party-state control and to deter possible resistance within the party and administrative hierarchies. Obstructionists were warned of the "Trotskyist" character of such behavior.

Meanwhile, the process of reorganizing the control network began. Although the staffing of the new party apparatus—now divided into agricultural and industrial branches—was completed in January, 1963, the establishment of the CPSC and its local branches extended well into March. At no level but perhaps the top could the CPSC therefore have played any role in the massive reassignment of party cadres necessitated by the reconstruction of the party apparatus. The chairmen of republic and oblast CPSC committees were on the *nomenklatura* of the Central Committee—that is, they had been placed in their positions by the Central Committee Party Organs Department, with the probable assistance of Shelepin and his associates. They were referred to as "plenipotentiaries" of the higher CPSC organs and were paid out of the central budget. Below the oblast level in cities, raions, and industrial zones, scattered evidence indicates, the choice of CPSC chairmen and members lay largely in the hands of party secretaries at the same level, with the republic CPSC exercising a veto over nominees. At the very bottom, most chairmen of "groups of assistance" were selected by the secretaries of party cells. Thus the influence of regular party officials in appointing the party-state control chairmen with whom they would have to work became progressively greater at the lower levels. This power was evidently used in certain instances to ensure the nomination of friends, or, at any rate, people who could be counted on not to be troublemakers.

The composition of the group chosen to lead the CPSC provides some insight into the motives behind the reorganization of control. Shelepin's participation in purging the Moscow Institute of History, Philosophy, and Literature in the 1930's; his appointment as First Secretary of the All-Union Komsomol before the anticipated purge in 1952; his tenure as head of the Central Committee's Party Organs Department in 1958; and his appointment as head of the secret police on December 29, 1958 (when, in Robert Conquest's words, "there were at least some signs of the preparation of a purge atmosphere") lend support to the hypothesis that Khrushchev appointed Shelepin head of the CPSC because he anticipated a need for Shelepin's demonstrated bureaucratic-inquisitorial talents.

Shelepin's First Deputy Chairman was Iosif Shikin, a long-time Stalinist who had mastered the art of loyalty investigation as head of the Soviet Army's Main Political Administration, served from 1954 to 1959 as deputy head of the Central Committee's Party Organs Department, and then as Soviet ambassador to Albania. The second deputy, V. I. Zaluzhny, might be called "Shelepin's man" by the usual tests: he had worked under Shelepin as a secretary of the Komsomol from 1952 to 1958, and then under Shelepin's successor, Semichastny, and had also served a tour of duty as a secretary with personnel appointment responsibilities of the oblast party committee in the industrially important Kemerovo region.

At the republic level, though the composition of the CPSC leadership varied somewhat from one republic to another, certain uniformities could be noted. Those selected tended to be men with experience either in Goskontrol, Party Organs departments, other branches of the party apparatus, or the secret police.[21] Judging by its background, the CPSC leadership

---

[21] In the Russian Republic (R.S.F.S.R.), Georgi Eniutin, head of the former State Control Commission, was appointed Chairman of the CPSC and a member of the R.S.F.S.R. Bureau. Before taking over Goskontrol in 1957, Eniutin had risen in the party apparatus under Khrushchev and from 1951 to 1953 had served as a deputy head of the Central Committee's Party Organs Department. His First Deputy, Viktor Churaev, had also been a deputy head of the Party Organs Department in 1952 and he had later headed (at different times) both this department and the equivalent department for the R.S.F.S.R. Having held such politically crucial posts for a decade and having been a member of the R.S.F.S.R. Bureau, Churaev's stature in the party leadership equaled—if it did not surpass—that of Eniutin. The name of the other deputy chairman of the R.S.F.S.R. CPSC, suspiciously enough, was not disclosed.

In the other republics, persons with various backgrounds were chosen as CPSC chairmen: among others there were two former sovnarkhoz chairmen; three former republic central committee secretaries; two former republic Party Organs Department chiefs; and three (probable) former KGB officials. In addition, at least one of the former council of ministers deputy chairmen (A. G. Kerimov of Azerbaidzhan) was known to have had professional dealings with the secret police in the past. Ten of the chairmen could be typed as party *apparatchiki*. Some of them had advanced in the party apparatus during Khrushchev's reign, but the career of only one (the Ukrainian Chairman, Ivan Grushetsky) seems to have depended directly on Khrushchev. One chairman (the Latvian, E. K. Beman) had served under Shelepin in the Komsomol. Three others, if they were recruited from the KGB (A. Vader of Estonia; N. G. Minich of Kirgizia; and M. S. Asimov of Tadzhikistan), might also have qualified as "Shelepin men." The majority, however, had had no known previous contact with him.

Information on the fourteen pairs of republic CPSC deputy chairmen is incomplete, but in over half the cases in which the necessary facts are known, the former Goskontrol heads became deputy chairmen of the CPSC. Of much greater importance is the strong likelihood—based on the absence of any information whatever about the former positions of the men involved—that in most

core seems to have been put together to serve three interrelated functions: to handle important personnel operations; to supervise routine investigations; and to act as an outpost of, or channel of communications with, the KGB.

The elaborate structure of the CPSC apparatus to some extent paralleled that of the regular party apparatus (including an Administrative Organs Department—a section, at least in the party apparatus, that supervises the courts, prosecutor's office, soviets, and secret police). This parallelism did reflect a recognition that the party apparatus as staffed in the past did not have the time, ability, or inclination to keep a close watch over production—above all, over industrial production. The CPSC structure, however, clearly invited jurisdictional conflict between the two.

The CPSC in Action

The CPSC of the Central Committee, with its local organs and assistance groups, soon became involved in a broad variety of activities, including sponsoring various nationwide campaigns against waste, reducing redundant administrative personnel in agriculture, resolving high-level disputes among industrial administrative agencies, and formulating detailed proposals on technical matters. The main targets of the CPSC were industrial managers, engineers, bookkeepers, planners, and high state administrators. Judging from published material, party *apparatchiki* did not seem, directly at least, to have been much affected.

The crucial question, of course, is whether the CPSC engaged in disciplinary action with respect to persons occupying politically sensitive positions. The Soviet press during 1963–64 did not suggest that it had, although one should still be cautious in judging this question, especially in the unstable post-Khrushchev period.[22]

As renewed complaints about failures to "disseminate advanced experi-

---

committees one of the deputies was drawn from the KGB or had done work involving daily contact with the KGB.

[22] The published account of the CPSC Statute, it might be noted, did not reveal the important fact that CPSC assistance groups were established throughout the army to "assist" commanders and political workers in eradicating "theft, embezzlement, mismanagement, extravagance and abuse of authority." (*Krasnaya Zvezda*, April 30, 1964. Cited by Y. Marin in *Bulletin* [Munich: Institute for the Study of the U.S.S.R.], Vol. XI, No. 9, p. 41. Marin also notes a case in which the CPSC assistance group of the Taman Guards Division stationed in Moscow submitted a report directly to the Chairman of the CPSC, Shelepin.)

Since the above was written, evidence has come to light that the CPSC was indeed beginning to remove some high officials from office. An expansion of CPSC activities may have occurred with Shelepin's promotion to full membership in the Party Presidium promptly after Khrushchev's ouster, in November, 1964.

ence," to strive for thorough rather than numerous checkups, and to evoke broad public participation indicated, the CPSC—and especially its local organs—did not function perfectly. It appears that vertical and horizontal ties among different CPSC organs were not strong enough to give local control committees the capacity to respond effectively to transregional problems. Local committees were also limited in their "positive" activities by the fact that nonstaff participation did not always materialize.

Because the CPSC, even without mass participation, was itself a political instrument that Soviet leaders intended to be linked in the public mind with the KGB, conflict between it and those agencies with a stake in legality might have been anticipated. There were signs that although the courts and the Prosecutor's Office on the one hand and the CPSC on the other cooperated with each other in some respects, relations between them were not without friction.

The greatest power possessed by the CPSC, but one hard to weigh with any precision, was in all probability its special mandate to engage in *exposure*—its capacity to uncover embarrassing facts and to communicate them fairly freely. Closely connected with this power was the CPSC's power to arbitrate, more or less compulsorily, the conflicting claims of different planning, administrative, and production units. At the national and republic levels, the CPSC made "proposals" and "suggestions"; it even assigned agencies to take remedial action, although it did not "oblige" them to do so— probably because it lacked the necessary power. Below the republic level, commands by the U.S.S.R. CPSC and republic committees were regularly and publicly addressed to sovnarkhoz chairmen "obliging" them to take action and reprimanding them for their shortcomings. The heavy artillery of removals and fines was seemingly reserved almost exclusively for even lesser state officials. Where such officials were removed from office, it was usually not clear whether the removals resulted from direct CPSC action or from a decision of administrative superiors. Except in clearly criminal cases, the policy seemed to have been to decide upon removals through informal consultations by the CPSC with the official's administrative superiors and the corresponding party authorities. This procedure safeguarded both the power of the party apparatus and the advantages obtained from formally maintaining the state administrative chain-of-command. The CPSC did not, at least in public, order the party apparatus at any level to take specific steps, or invoke sanctions against party officials. It placed local party officials and party cell secretaries in the position of having to *discuss* shortcomings and disciplinary matters that they might have preferred to overlook.

The attempts by statute and leadership appointment to ensure local control committees some independence of the local party establishment seem to have been outweighed by a variety of opposing pressures. CPSC chairmen, while maintaining some leeway by virtue of their status as chairmen, were simultaneously secretaries of their respective party committees. They ranked last among the other secretaries, and most of them were also relative newcomers to this inner seat of party power. The background of a majority of these men presumably induced them to sympathize with the interests and aspirations of their fellow secretaries.

A significant indication of the extent of their power as CPSC chairmen vis-à-vis the party apparatus was the handling of disciplinary proceedings against economic administrators. In a number of cases involving factory managers and their chief engineers, CPSC organs at various levels disciplined the chief engineers "along *state* lines," but had to hand the manager over to the party apparatus (at the same or lower levels) for *party* punishment. Thus, the CPSC did, of course, at least have the power to trigger party proceedings, which could force the hand of the apparatus. But it was the apparatus that decided whether the manager would be disciplined "along party lines"; and in practice (though not in theory) the failure to impose party punishment was still likely to mean that administrative superiors would not take action and the Prosecutor's Office would not press charges. In this way, party officials could suppress attacks against those managers whom they found it in their own interests to protect, leaving the managers' less influential subordinates to "take the rap." They could not, however, prevent word of these incidents from reaching higher levels in both the apparatus and the CPSC. This power relationship reflected the fundamental compromise contained in the decision not to assign party disciplinary powers to the CPSC. Other signs confirmed the dependence of CPSC organs on the party apparatus.[23]

Assistance Groups

The activities of assistance groups received by far the greatest publicity in the Soviet press. The assistance groups were intended as a bridge between party and mass control—the "organizing centers around which all public control is united." According to the CPSC Statute, the members of assistance groups were to be "elected" at general assemblies in enterprises, construction projects, kolkhozes, sovkhozes, apartment dwellings, and "institutions," after having been nominated beforehand at separate meetings of party, trade-union, Komsomol, and other "public" organizations. Counterbalancing this gesture in the direction of democracy was a manifest intent to assure party domination of the groups.

---

[23] The apparatus at any level could review and approve the plan of operations of "its" CPSC; assign tasks to the CPSC; and neglect or deliberately fail to support the CPSC, thereby undermining its effectiveness. The absence of strong vertical and horizontal ties among CPSC organs also weakened the independence of local CPSC officials.

By February, 1964, it was claimed that 711,000 assistance "groups" and "posts," with some 4,000,000 members, had been set up during the first year of the CPSC. It is difficult to determine just how effective they were. According to the Statute, assistance groups were not assigned administrative powers. They did have the power, if they wished to avail themselves of it, to communicate—the power to inform on the inefficient and corrupt. But the strong position of Soviet managers, the self-protective interests of party cell secretaries, and the distasteful nature of the job to be performed made it likely that assistance groups were not overly effective. Many signs pointed in this direction. Descriptions of group activities made it clear that the brunt of their attack was felt by low-ranking officials and ordinary workers, rather than by leading managerial personnel.

Interpreting the Evidence

The evidence presented above does not, by itself, prove any particular hypothesis concerning the history of party-state control; the meaning of the evidence must be sought in the light of a broader perception of Soviet politics. Most observers, however, could probably agree on certain conclusions emerging from the present account of this history.

Areas of Agreement
1. The nature of decision-making. The fact that the decision to establish the CPSC matured for at least seven years before coming to fruition rebuts the common assumption that rapid decision-making is a corollary of Communist dictatorship. The multiplicity of effects that had to be anticipated before the decision was reached helps to explain this delay. These effects included the impact the CPSC would have upon managerial authority and accountability; the way in which it would influence relationships among different parts of the economic-administrative bureaucracy; the effect it would have upon the power and morale of local party officials; and the response it would evoke from the public. During these years, consultation, experimentation, and the expression of divergent ideas and interests—within certain limits—were the rule rather than the exception.
2. The role of ideology. Ideology, in the form of public references to party "history," provided no blueprint for action. Soviet leaders emphasized and distorted certain aspects of Leninist theory and Stalinist practice and ignored others. Nor were the leaders confined in their actions by any outer limits imposed by "Leninism." However, ideology did set boundaries for mass discussion, did help communicate the current party line, and did legitimize the introduction of new policies to the public at large.
3. The pattern of interests. A play of interests occurred at all levels in

the Soviet system—bottom, middle, and top. The division between those for and against party-state control coincided only partially with broad organizational, functional, and social groupings, and with political backgrounds or ideological attitudes. "Stalinists," "Khrushchevists," party *apparatchiki,* and state officials could be found on both sides of the issue. In particular, the split between party and state was hardly as wide as is frequently assumed. Most party *apparatchiki* were probably opposed to the instituting of party-state control, even though it was a step ostensibly intended to strengthen the role of the party. Clearly, differences between the high party leaders and territorial party functionaries, or among the high party leaders themselves, make it misleading to regard the party as a monolithic whole with homogeneous interests. Although party-state control was implicitly justified by the priority of "economics" over "politics," most economic administrators could only have regarded the innovation as an undesirable intrusion of party influence into technical production affairs. While party-state control was also intended to further policies that in time could lead to the liberalization of the Soviet system, "liberals," including many legal officials, were undoubtedly apprehensive about its immediate effect on the delicate fabric of "socialist legality." Most KGB officials probably favored party-state control, realizing that an expansion of "Soviet democracy" (i.e., "criticism from below") is not necessarily incompatible with an increase in secret police influence. The public at large, though not consulted on the matter, stood to gain from greater "democracy" but to lose from the general tightening of discipline.

Areas of Disagreement

1. Khrushchev as "first oligarch." If it is assumed, as it frequently has been, that Khrushchev was compelled after 1957 to struggle for the acceptance of his policies and to fight against repeated attempts to undermine his power, the following would be one possible interpretation of the instituting of party-state control.

Khrushchev's objectives, the argument might run, were to tighten bureaucratic discipline (as he said in his speeches) but also to strengthen his own position among the other oligarchs and to increase his ability to force the lower party apparatus to do his bidding—as he implied in his speeches and as the "historical" literature revealed. Party "unity" was a problem for him either because repeated policy failures made his own position increasingly insecure or because he wished to institute new and radical domestic or foreign policies that would inevitably provoke concerted attempts to unseat him. Repeated attacks on members of the Antiparty Group after their defeat in June, 1957, demonstrated Khrushchev's intention of gaining absolute power, just as the ineffectiveness of the attacks revealed that the opposition had successfully withheld from him the power to "liquidate" the losers in policy disputes and factional struggles. In order to circumvent this opposition, Khrushchev began to assemble the pieces of a purge machine, as Stalin had done in the 1920's, 1930's, and early 1950's. He promoted close followers into the key leadership positions in the secret police, Party Organs Department, Party Control Committee, and Goskontrol. He began expanding the functions of the PCC and Goskontrol, intending to merge the two into a single, party-police agency designed to spearhead the removal and punishment of inefficient, corrupt, or politically recalcitrant leaders in all branches of the party and state bureaucracy. Simultaneously, he campaigned to pack, or otherwise adulterate, the Central Committee as a first step in eliminating his opponents among the top leaders.

However, this theory would maintain that he achieved only partial success. The CPSC did not appear to emerge as a full-blown purging instrument. The concessions extracted from Khrushchev bore fruit by depriving local CPSC organs of power to act against influential economic managers and their party protectors—although CPSC influence might have been greater in unpublicized activities at higher levels. Published accounts have implied that petty officials and rank-and-file workers were taking the brunt of the attack. Perhaps, if a significant upturn in Khrushchev's political strength had occurred, he might have been able to "further develop Leninist principles" by merging the Party Commission with the CPSC and by tightening vertical subordination within the CPSC apparatus.

Certain tacit assumptions about how published Soviet sources should be analyzed underlie this understanding of party-state control. Great significance, it would be argued, should be attributed to differences in the "formulation" of ideas in the Soviet press. Such differences should be seen as surface manifestations of dissent and political combat. The fact that Kozlov never forcefully supported "party, state, and public control" ought to be seen as convincing evidence that he disagreed with the policy *and* opposed it. Ideology—in the present case, public references to party "history"— should be viewed as a medium of policy debate, a means of communicating disagreement and seeking support, and a weapon for attacking enemies while defending one's own claims. "Historical" references to the CCC-WPI should be read as an esoteric means of expressing and advancing disputed organizational and policy prescriptions that affected the distribution of political power among the oligarchs. Rabkrin was selected by Khrushchev because it was a convenient vehicle for advancing "rightist" policy objectives while claiming hard organizational power. Khrushchev's underlying objectives may be fathomed by analyzing his speeches and the course of events, for he consistently tried to achieve these objectives—beginning, perhaps, as early as the attacks on Goskontrol in 1954. The long delay in following "Lenin's instructions" once the issue of party-state control had

K. Eliseyev in *Krokodil*, April 20, 1965

ОТДЕЛ КАДРОВ

— Вообще-то я веду воспитательную работу среди цыплят...

The fox, being questioned by the Cadre Section: "Generally speaking, I am engaged in educational work among the chicks."

The two signs on the table say "Manager" and "Auditor." The caption reads: "So they agreed to call it a draw."

ДИРЕКТОР МАГАЗИНА

КОНТРОЛЕР

E. Shcheglov in *Krokodil*, May 10, 1963

E. Piho in *Krokodil*, February 28, 1962; reprinted from Estonian humor magazine, *Pikker*

— Укажите конкретно, чем мы ограничиваем вашу инициативу!

"Will you tell us concretely just how we inhibit your initiative?"

The volumes are all labeled "Complaint book." The caption reads: "The manager's private library."

Pravda, April 4, 1963

S. Kuzmin in *Krokodil*, January 30, 1965

Личная библиотека заведующего ателье.

Szpilki (Warsaw), April 15, 1956

This poster by artist Boris Leo for the party-state control "campaign" in the spring of 1963 shows a flashlight labeled "Control" pointed at a "Balance sheet," suggesting doctored accounts, graft, and false reporting.

"Comrades, the personality cult is a thing of the past. Now don't criticize me; criticize the collective!"

been raised indicated strongly that Khrushchev was blocked by opponents of this innovation. Departures from what Khrushchev wanted should be interpreted as concessions wrung from him by his opponents. The decisions of the November Plenum should therefore be regarded as riddled with compromises—on the question of the Party Commission; on the scope of CPSC functions; on organizational arrangements; and on the disciplinary powers assigned to the CPSC.

2. Khrushchev as "dictator." If, on the contrary, it is assumed that Khrushchev wielded dictatorial power after 1957, an entirely different meaning might be assigned to the history of party-state control.

Because he already had sufficient power (according to this theory) to effect whatever changes he desired in the composition of the Soviet political elite, Khrushchev did not need to institute purge machinery or tamper with the Central Committee. (In addition, would not influencing the choice of Central Committee members have provided an easier way to achieve the same objective?) Furthermore, the significance of the composition of the CPSC and its local organs is not entirely clear. Even if there was heavy KGB representation, in all likelihood this was simply a matter of degree and overtness, for Goskontrol probably continued to maintain some affiliation with the secret police even after 1953. If anything, Khrushchev's references to disciplining the party were numerically far fewer than his emphasis on overcoming inefficiency and corruption in the state administration. Party-state control was clearly designed simply to increase the weight of the party in the solution of economic difficulties—difficulties that were severe enough to justify the most drastic remedial measures.

It would be erroneous, then, so it might be argued, to assume that Khrushchev met with defeat in establishing party-state control. The measure of his power was the number of persons whose interests led them to oppose any change in control procedures. Important CPSC activities in the personnel field might well be concealed from public view. And equipping the party apparatus at each level with a special control organ permitted greater supervision of lower party bodies by higher party bodies.

This approach, too, involves certain assumptions about how the evidence should be interpreted. Differences in "formulation" may reveal divergent points of view, but they do not imply active opposition to Khrushchev. Excessive concern with imagined shades of meaning results in overinterpretation of the data. The fact that Kozlov never forcefully supported the establishment of "party, state, and public control" should not be taken as convincing proof that he could or did oppose it. Ideology, in the sense of public references to party "history," should be read more as propaganda directed at the general public than as a form of esoteric communication aimed at members of the elite. Rabkrin was used primarily to publicly justify a "re-Stalinizing" measure and to stimulate mass participation. It was selected as a propaganda vehicle because the "organization and management" problems with which Rabkrin dealt in the 1920's resemble those now plaguing the Soviet system. Can Khrushchev's genuine motives in fact be deduced from his public statements? Khrushchev never said precisely what he did want. Nor would it be correct to assume great consistency over time on his part. Khrushchev's various positions between 1956 and 1962 on party-state control, as on other issues, reflected disconnected and pragmatic adjustments to the exigencies of the moment. They were responses either to unique political situations or to "objective" social and economic developments. He was not tenaciously pursuing a predetermined course for seven years. As economic difficulties multiplied, he turned to more repressive measures, including party-state control. The delay in initiating party-state control was procrastination on his part, not the result of obstruction by alleged opponents. He had many more important problems on his mind than party-state control. It was characteristic of his style of rule that he did not ride roughshod over the opinions of others, as Stalin did, and that he encouraged experimentation before introducing policies on a nationwide scale. The argument that Khrushchev was forced to make concessions to opponents unwarrantedly assumes both consistency on his part and a knowledge of his unexpressed wishes. Did Khrushchev, for instance, really want the PCC merged into the CPSC? Apart from its fundamental underestimation of Khrushchev's power, a "concessions" interpretation ignores the situational factors that could have led him to support modifications of his own publicly proclaimed positions.

The same circularity attends both of these analyses of party-state control. Broad estimates of Khrushchev's power influence the interpretation of basic types of data: the expression of dissonant viewpoints in the press; "ideology"; Khrushchev's public statements; the consistency of these statements and of his underlying views; delays between words and deeds; and departures from expected courses of action. The pattern of interpreting these phenomena in turn largely determines the meaning assigned to the emergence of the CPSC. This interpretation then reinforces the original calculation of Khrushchev's power.

Each of these two approaches points to biases in the other, regardless of which is based upon the truer estimate of Khrushchev's strength during the years 1957–64. Both suffer, in varying degrees, from a fixation upon the problem of the leader's power.

The leading spokesman for the Soviet Union—whether "absolute" dictator or senior oligarch—must respond to numerous economic and social pressures if he is to act effectively in an increasingly complex environment. Hence, in some instances, the personal power issue can remain dormant; it may simply not be central to the actual solution of many concrete issues. In such cases, it is the practical issues that largely determine solutions, not power considerations. The declining rate of economic growth and increased costliness of technological backwardness may well be factors that falsify any purely power-centered analysis of party-state control.

Moreover, an analytic framework that focuses attention exclusively on Khrushchev may conceal the roles of other members of the cast. On occasion, Stalin allowed his lieutenants leeway to maneuver on their own, and Khrushchev followed suit, voluntarily or not. It may be assumed with some confidence that a perspective that slights autonomous action by Shelepin or Kozlov, for example, must produce a distorted picture of the emergence of party-state control.

The case of Khrushchev and party-state control illustrates the formidable nature of the problem of understanding Soviet domestic politics. The evidence culled from the press suggests, to be sure, the implausibility of single-factor explanations of Soviet political events. A combination of elements usually seems to be present: "neutral" efficiency considerations; horizontal and vertical conflicts of interest, uniting and dividing various officials in the party and other hierarchies; differing ideological perspectives; and the personal power stakes of top Soviet leaders. But how should these elements be *weighted*—even assuming (unrealistically) that all the critical factors are known? And how should the weights be adjusted to reflect changes that occur as time passes? To these questions there are no simple answers.

Postscript

At the December, 1965, Plenum of the Central Committee, First Secretary Leonid Brezhnev publicly criticized the CPSC and announced that the Party Presidium had decided to convert it into a system of "people's control," ostensibly in accord with "V. I. Lenin's instructions." "As is known," Brezhnev declared, "the Program of the CPSU . . . calls for the creation of a system of *people's control* in which *state control would be combined with public inspection* at the local level." He went on to insist that the "people's control" organs would be subordinate to the "party and government" and would not control the work of party agencies.

In December, 1965, at the Supreme Soviet session immediately following this Plenum, Pavel Kovanov, a former Second Secretary of the Georgian Communist Party, was appointed chairman of the new U.S.S.R. People's Control Committee. At the same time, Shelepin was relieved of his post as Deputy Chairman of the Council of Ministers. While observers debated whether the elimination of the CPSC was linked to a possible decline in Shelepin's political fortunes or merely reflected the judgment that a free-wheeling control agency was incompatible with the reestablishment of centralized ministerial direction of the economy already announced in September, 1965, it was clear in any event that the tamer conception of control propounded before 1962 was at last having its day.

Study Questions

1. What are the main strengths and weaknesses of attempts to attain a deeper understanding of Soviet politics through a careful sifting of the Soviet press?

2. Which of the two interpretations presented in the concluding part of the study seems more plausible? Are other interpretations possible?

3. Can the role ascribed to "ideology" in the present case be squared with the assumption that Soviet leaders are "dedicated Communists"? Why bother to pay attention to Soviet "ideological" discussions?

4. What interpretation of "Soviet democracy" is suggested at various points in the case? Does this interpretation help explain other manifestations of the post-Stalin policy of encouraging greater participation by the people in the conduct of public affairs?

5. How does the play of political interests in the Soviet Union (as sketched in this case) differ from that which occurs in the United States?

Selected Bibliography

The main sources for this case study are the published stenographic reports of Party Congresses and Central Committee Plenums; the two leading Soviet newspapers, *Pravda* and *Izvestia;* the two main party journals, *Kommunist* and *Partiinaia zhizn'* (Party Life); the major Russian-language newspapers for the constituent union-republics; and the following journals: *Voprosy istorii* (Problems of History); *Voprosy istorii KPSS* (Problems of the History of the CPSU); and *Sovetskoe gosudarstvo i pravo* (Soviet State and Law). Lenin's views on party and state control are scattered throughout his post-1917 writings. "How We Should Reorganize Rabkrin" and "Better Less, but Better" appear in V. I. Lenin, *Sochineniia* (Works), 4th ed., Vol. XXXIII (Moscow: Gospolitizdat, 1950). The draft versions of "How We Should Reorganize Rabkrin" were first published in *Leninskii sbornik* (The Lenin Collection), Vol. XXXVI (Moscow: Gospolitizdat, 1959).

The best non-Soviet source on the history of the CCC-WPI is Aleksandrov (pseud. for A. S. Michelson), *Kto upravliaet Rossiei?* (Who Rules Russia?), Berlin: Parabola, 1933. Also see Robert V. Daniels, *The Conscience of the Revolution* (Cambridge, Mass.: Harvard University Press, 1960). A recent Soviet work is G. A. Dorokhova, *Raboche-krest'ianskaia inspektsiia, 1920–*

1923), (The Worker-Peasant Inspection, 1920–1923), Moscow: Gosiurizdat, 1959. The proceedings of the November, 1962, Plenum, without Khrushchev's concluding speech, are contained in *Plenum tsentral'nogo komiteta kommunisticheskogo partii Sovetskogo Soyuza, 19–23 noiabria 1962* (Plenum of the Central Committee of the Communist Party of the Soviet Union, November 19–23, 1962), Moscow: Gospolitizdat, 1963. For a general description of the November Plenum see Herbert Ritvo, "Party Controls Reorganized," *Survey*, No. 49 (October, 1963).

Biographical data can be found in *Biographical Directory of the U.S.S.R.* (New York: Scarecrow Press, 1958); *Who's Who in the U.S.S.R.* (New York: Scarecrow Press, 1962); and in the various numbers of *Directory of Soviet Officials* (Washington, D.C.: Bureau of Intelligence and Research, Department of State). A stimulating discussion of the extent of Khrushchev's power is found in Carl Linden, "Khrushchev and the Party Battle" and a rejoinder by T. H. Rigby, "The Extent and Limits of Authority," in *Problems of Communism*, Vol. XII, No. 5 (September–October, 1963). This discussion is continued by Linden, Robert C. Tucker, Wolfgang Leonhard, and Michel Gordey in *Problems of Communism*, Vol. XII, No. 6 (November–December, 1963). A more extended treatment is Robert Conquest, *Power and Policy in the U.S.S.R.* (New York: St. Martin's Press, 1961).

5

Freedom and Control in Literature, 1962-63

Patricia Blake

During a visit to Moscow in August, 1962, I was witness to a spontaneous anti-Stalinist demonstration. It took place at one of the poetry readings that had become so popular with students and liberal-minded intellectuals of all ages. Here is how I described the incident at the time:

> This poetry reading was one of a series of six I attended in the public auditorium of Moscow's Polytechnical Museum which was filled to capacity—about 700 people, largely students. . . .
> Evgeny Evtushenko's appearance brought forth cries of "Hi, Zhenya!" and "Give us 'Babi Yar'!" and a barrage of paper pellets on which his admirers had written requests for their favorite poems. It was clear at once that this young man's popularity is extraliterary; although Evtushenko is gifted as a poet, it is the occasional boldness of his subjects that has made his national and international reputation—especially his protest against anti-Semitism. Moreover, he is marvelously handsome and engaging. Dressed in a wildly-patterned American sports shirt under a gray silk suit, he brushed back his blond forelock and waved familiarly at the audience. . . .
> Evtushenko read his now famous "The Heirs of Stalin" which appeared in *Pravda* two months later (October 21, 1962). For a year no editor had dared touch it, for the poem has a compelling message. It ends as follows:
>
>> We bore him out of the mausoleum.
>> But how, out of Stalin, shall we bear
>> > Stalin's heirs!
>> Some of his heirs trim roses in retirement

secretly thinking
                    their discharge is temporary.
Others,
            from rostrums, even heap abuse on Stalin
but,
        at night,
                    hanker after the good old days.
No wonder Stalin's heirs seem stricken
with heart attacks these days.
                                    They, once the stalwarts,
detest this time
                of empty prison camps
and halls packed with people listening
                                    to poets.
The party forbids me
                    to be smug.
"Why bother?"
                    some urge me—but I can't be quiet.
While the heirs of Stalin walk this earth,
Stalin,
        I fancy, still lurks in the mausoleum.

Evtushenko's reading of "The Heirs of Stalin" created an extraordinary disturbance that evening. During the *disput,* or public discussion, that took place after the recitations, a young man came to the microphone and said in a quavering voice: "Now I like Zhenya's poetry very much. It is very deep, very thought-provoking. But that poem about Stalin—well—I know Stalin did some very bad things, but he also did some very good things. . . ." A fearful deafening roar broke out in the hall. I thought the boy was about to be lynched. Somebody's protecting hands snatched him away.[1]

This incident is symptomatic of the mood of confidence in the future and indignation about the past that prevailed among many of Russia's liberal-minded young people and intellectuals during the "thaw" of 1962, on the eve of the Communist Party's vast public campaign, in the winter and spring of 1962–63, to reestablish fully effective control over literature and the arts.

Clearly, the removal of Stalin's body from the Lenin mausoleum on Red Square (following further revelations of his crimes at the Twenty-second Party Congress in October, 1961) was the most electrifying symbolic act of the Khrushchev era. No wonder, then, that the spectacular new thrust

---

[1] From *Half-way to the Moon,* edited by Patricia Blake and Max Hayward. Copyright © 1963 by Encounter Ltd. This and later excerpts from that book are abridged and reprinted by permission of Holt, Rinehart and Winston, Inc., and George Weidenfeld & Nicolson Ltd. The lines from "The Heirs of Stalin" were translated by George Reavey and are reprinted with the permission of Encounter Ltd.

toward "de-Stalinization" at the Twenty-second Party Congress was interpreted as a signal that Stalinist practices in the arts could at last be repudiated, together with the Stalinists.

Indeed, 1962 looked to be a year of unprecedented triumphs for the
liberal writers who had been striving for greater freedom of expression for
nearly a decade. Scarcely a week went by that a young writer or poet did
not publish a work of the imagination, each bolder in form and substance
than the last, each freer of the cant, the dreary didacticism, and the onward-
and-upward themes of "socialist realism."

The liberals had also captured many influential positions in the cultural
apparatus.[2] In April, 1962, for example, a group of liberal writers had

---

[2] Supreme control over cultural affairs—as over other areas of Soviet life—is
exercised by the *party* apparatus, manned by full-time, paid party professionals.
Three departments of the Central Committee's Secretariat share responsibility
for control over Soviet arts and letters:

1. the Department of Agitation and Propaganda (*agitprop*) for the R.S.F.S.R;
2. the Department of Agitation and Propaganda for the remaining fourteen
union republics;
3. the Department of Culture and Science.

The three departments are under the supervision of one of the Secretaries of the
Central Committee, who is responsible directly to the Party Presidium. In 1962–
63 this position was filled by Leonid Ilyichev. In November, 1962, he was made
head of the newly created Ideological Commission of the Central Committee,
established to coordinate party activities in the fields of political propaganda,
press, television, radio, cinema, the visual arts, and book publishing. This commission was abolished after Khrushchev's dismissal.

The staff of the three departments (each of which has subordinate sections
responsible for specific areas of culture, e.g., the Section of Literature and Art,
under the Department of Culture and Science) is relatively small but is recruited
from politically experienced and trusted party bureaucrats.

Five major institutions in the Soviet *government* deal with cultural affairs:
the Ministry of Culture (which, despite vast supervisory authority, appears to
have lost most of its power in the late 1950's and early 1960's); the State Committee for Cinematography; the State Committee for Cultural Relations with
Foreign Countries; the State Committee for Radio Broadcasting and Television;
and the State Committee for the Press.

One of the most powerful among the state organizations in literary affairs
is Glavlit (officially, the Main Administration for Literary Affairs and Publishing), which is in charge of censorship. Because of the secrecy surrounding its
work, even its place in the administrative structure is unclear. Its function, by
contrast, is clear: every Soviet publication must be approved by Glavlit before
going to the printers.

A third category of bodies supervising cultural affairs is the so-called self-
governing institutions, such as the various unions of writers, artists, composers,
cinematographers, and actors. The U.S.S.R. Writers' Union, with its headquarters
in Moscow, has as a member every published Soviet novelist, poet, literary
critic, and playwright. In addition (depending on his residence) a Soviet writer
may belong to a republic writers' union or its local branch. In recent years, the
writers' unions have taken over many of the functions formally assigned to
the Ministry of Culture. The leadership of the unions frequently decides what
is published and in how many copies.

played such skillful politics in the Moscow branch of the Writers' Union that they managed to elect eight of their own people to the board of the Union. Several well-known Stalinists were not even put up for reelection. One newspaper, *Literaturnaya gazeta,* and several journals, notably *Novyi mir,* were clearly in the "liberal camp." Such inroads into Stalinist strongholds are essential to liberalization of the arts, for the cultural apparatus, like all other Soviet administrative bureaucracies, is still replete with holdovers from the Stalin era—bureaucrats whom the novelist Konstantin Paustovsky, in a closed meeting of the Moscow Writers' Union in 1956, had accused of "betrayal, calumny, moral assassination, and just plain assassination."

The euphoria of the liberal writers was greatly heightened in October and November of 1962 when "The Heirs of Stalin" and Alexander Solzhenitsyn's powerful anti-Stalinist novel, *One Day in the Life of Ivan Denisovich,* were published on Khrushchev's personal authorization. The appearance of these works seemed to promise that some of the most wicked of Stalin's heirs might at last be dislodged from the cultural apparatus. This was, as it turned out, a vain hope. The significance of these events seems to be that Khrushchev was bidding for the liberal intelligentsia's support of his leadership and his policies, which, as we shall see, were then under attack in the Kremlin. "The Heirs of Stalin" includes an apparent reference to Frol Kozlov ("No wonder Stalin's heirs seem stricken / with heart attacks these days. . . ."), who was known to have suffered at least one heart attack; thus it appeared that Khrushchev was not above letting a 29-year-old poet take a pot shot at the Secretary of the Central Committee of the Communist Party. This was widely interpreted, in Russia and abroad, as one of several signs that Kozlov, Khrushchev's erstwhile choice to succeed him after his death, had become his opponent. The liberal intellectuals were encouraged by such speculations, for Kozlov was reputed to hold ultraorthodox views on the arts.

But as one American observer, Priscilla Johnson, has noted, this was one of those deceptive periods in Soviet history in which "a trend that appears to be on the rise is, like a wave, actually at its crest, about to flow into swift and perilous descent."

In December, 1962, Khrushchev launched a campaign against the liberal writers, artists, and intellectuals, which was to rage for seven months in the press and in public meetings throughout the country. Russia's most promising writers and poets were denounced. Control of the cultural apparatus was restored to the Stalinists and conservatives. And on March 8, 1963, less than a year after he had ordered the publication of *One Day in the Life of Ivan Denisovich,* a harrowing account of a Stalinist concentration camp, Khrushchev was to describe the Stalin era as "bright, happy years, years of struggle and victories, of the triumph of Communist ideas."

Resistance and, often, defiance were so widespread among the writers that Khrushchev indicated force might be used to bring the recalcitrant ones into line. But, again, another wave was at its crest and on the verge of descent. By the end of June, it was clear that the party had decided to settle for an undeclared truce with the liberals. The denunciations virtually ceased and the writers who had been under fire were gradually permitted to publish again, although by no means on such a scale as before.

The seven-month campaign (from December, 1962, until July, 1963) was, as we shall see, scarcely an unqualified success for Khrushchev and the party. In purely practical terms, the party did succeed in arresting the trend toward greater cultural and ideological freedoms—at least in its public manifestations. But the liberals won a moral victory that served to diminish further the authority of the party. And there were signs, after the cultural crackdown had come to a halt, that many liberal intellectuals and creative artists had lost all illusions about Khrushchev—and perhaps, indeed, about the system that had engendered him.

In sum, the situation on the literary scene which Khrushchev's successors inherited on October 15, 1964, was, as in so many other spheres of Soviet society, chaotic and highly inflammable.

This case will examine the dynamics of "thaw" and "freeze"—a climatic phenomenon which has been characteristic of the literary scene in the post-Stalin era. There have been three distinct periods during the post-Stalin decade (1953–54, 1956–57, 1962–63) in which the expectations of the writers and liberal intellectuals have risen to confront the party in inevitable and irremediable conflict. The period under consideration here is the most rewarding to students of Soviet affairs because the conflict was far more vocal—not only in the sense that it was more extensively reported in the Soviet press but, more importantly, because liberal intellectual opinion, which had been in the process of development since Stalin's death, was capable by 1962 of eloquent expression that met with broad public response. The literary field is, in fact, the area of Soviet life in which a spectrum of opinion may best be discerned by Western observers.[3]

The case of the cultural campaign of 1962–63 is also a dramatic illustration of Khrushchev's method and style of rule: his failure to deal with basic

---

[3] Such a spectrum of opinion does exist but is far less discernible in other forms of artistic expression, such as painting and music, in which the attitudes and opinions of the artist cannot be made explicit. Because of their special power to communicate ideas and move men to action, the writers were the principal target of the party's 1962–63 campaign (and hence are the principal subject of this study). Painters, composers, and cinematographers who had demanded greater freedom also came under fire during this period; and the rebellion against censorship, against the dogma of "socialist realism," and against other forms of party dictation or control was fundamentally the same in all the creative fields. The methods used to put down the rebellion and the results were also similar.

problems; his inability to cope with the forces he had let loose in the
nation when he de-Stalinized; his indecisiveness, his erraticism, and his
penchant for improvisation in the face of crisis.

This case presents a number of imponderables for the student of Soviet
politics. One is the cause-and-effect relation between power struggles behind the scenes in the Kremlin and events in the cultural sphere. There is
indirect evidence that such a relation did in effect exist in 1962–63. But
we know too little of Soviet power politics to do more than speculate about
the exact nature of the relation. Also, the student should not expect to find
a reasonable explanation of every event that took place in the cultural
sphere (as in other spheres), given the erratic and often so capricious style
of Khrushchev's rule. The imponderable element is particularly striking
in literature; the life of literature, although clearly part of a larger political
process in the Soviet Union, has its own momentum.

The Background: Stalin

The changes that have taken place in Soviet society in the post-Stalin
decade must be examined against the background of the Stalin era. On the
literary scene, the most important change since Stalin's death is that the
poets, the prose writers, and the playwrights—together with their public—
have gradually ceased to suffer from the old, fearful feeling of isolation.
This new sense of community and common cause—so striking in the face
of the onslaughts of 1963—seems very nearly miraculous when one considers how effectively Stalin's attempt to atomize Soviet society interrupted
intellectual and human discourse. The splendid upheaval of creative activity
in literature, as in all the arts, in the 1920's, had ended in massacre in the
1930's. The purges had decimated the intelligentsia of Russia and reduced
the survivors to silence or to humanly and artistically damaging compromise.

Poetry, as Pasternak remarked, ceased to exist. So indeed did literature,
with a few notable exceptions. While the canons of "socialist realism" required that literature be a pulpit for exhortation and instruction, it was
clear that the main function of the writer was to provide secular liturgies
for the worship of Stalin.

The damage done to literature *qua* literature in the Stalin era was accompanied by equally grave psychological and moral injury. The reflex of distrust, the habit of hypocrisy (even among members of the same family)
were symptoms of a fearful sickness: man's alienation from his own truth.
"They only ask you," said Pasternak of the Soviet authorities, "to praise
what you hate most and grovel before what makes you most unhappy."

Time to Tell the Truth?

The hopes of post-Stalin liberal intellectuals were perhaps best expressed by the poet Alexander Tvardovsky: "In art and literature, as in love, one can lie only for a while; sooner or later comes the time to tell the truth." By 1962, it seemed that that time might have come at last. Since Stalin's death in 1953, a genuine literary intelligentsia had come into being, composed not only of young writers whose experience with Stalinism had been slight but of some older authors, like Konstantin Paustovsky, who had endured the entire Stalin era. This intelligentsia dedicated itself to two related tasks: repairing Russia's deeply mutilated culture, and stripping away the cant and mendacity with which Stalinism had encrusted the nation.

Literature had come to offer what no totalitarian system can long tolerate, a forum for individual expression. As such the new writing had a resonance that is inconceivable in the West. Editions of 100,000 copies of Evtushenko's poetry, and books and magazines containing stories by young writers like Yuri Kazakov and Vasily Aksyonov sold out at once in the bookstores and on the newsstands. Poetry readings attracted mass audiences. For example, in November, 1962, 14,000 people gathered in a Moscow sports stadium to hear the poets Andrei Voznesensky, Bella Akhmadulina, and Boris Slutsky. What had happened was that the work of the young writers and poets found an echo among a vast number of people who discovered that they were no longer alone: that there existed others who could articulate and share their yearnings, their preoccupations, their tastes —and their hatred for the moral squalor of Stalinism.

It was this group of writers, and their public, that Khrushchev tried to court for his own political purposes in the fall of 1962. But their aspirations and his aims were so profoundly dissimilar that the attempt was bound to boomerang.

The immediate demand of those writers who in our study are called the liberals has been the freedom to write on a subject of their own choice and to handle it in accordance with the writer's own vision of reality, in a form that is congenial to his vision. Of course, such a demand collides with the party view that literature, like any other socially significant activity, must be integrated into the larger plan of building Communism. From the party's point of view, literature is merely a somewhat higher type of agitprop whose function is to elucidate, justify, and reinforce party policies for the reading public.

Among the liberal literary intelligentsia—the writers and readers who desire greater artistic and intellectual freedom—there exists a broad spectrum of opinion. It ranges from, at one extreme, dissatisfaction with censorship and other forms of artistic control to, at the other extreme, a general

disaffection with the basic values of the Soviet system coupled with a desire
for fundamental social and political change. Whatever their particular position on this spectrum, the liberals appear to share a powerful sense of revulsion against the Stalinist past and a desire to have the bloody history of the
Stalin era fully and publicly ventilated. Such attitudes are also held by
liberal artists, scientists, and other intellectuals—indeed, by men of conscience in many areas of Soviet life. The liberal writers have publicly and
privately asserted a sense of special mission in this respect. Some of them
hope to create a literature that could effect a kind of national catharsis that
would help cleanse Russia of the spirit and substance of Stalinism.

Such liberal demands are of course bound to come into conflict with
those of the "conservatives." Here too, there is a broad spectrum of opinion. On one side are those writers who have accepted the reality of the
changes that have taken place since Stalin's death (such as the liquidation
of mass terror, the greater rationality of the system, the wider margin for
free expression) but are opposed to any further moves in this direction. On
the other side are those writers (the "Stalinists") who yearn for a return to
the "good old days" when literature was in bondage, and they themselves
were its keepers.

On the Eve of the Crackdown

The publication of *One Day in the Life of Ivan Denisovich,* the first Soviet
literary work to describe Stalin's concentration camps, brought the liberal
intellectuals' euphoria to a climax and raised expectations that Khrushchev
had not anticipated and which he evidently had no intention of meeting.
Countless people believed that the full story of Stalin's crimes could now
be told. As Khrushchev later disclosed, manuscripts dealing with the horrors of Stalin's whole slave labor system were now being taken out of their
hiding places by their authors and were "flooding" magazine offices and
publishing houses.

Rumors raged in Moscow that some of the most powerful and malevo-
lent of Stalin's old cultural commissars, like Dmitri Polikarpov, now one of
the party's top ideological watchdogs, were about to be fired. It was even
widely believed that Polikarpov's agency, the Central Committee Section
of Literature and Art, would be abolished altogether. Liberals in all the
creative arts thought they now had license to stage revolts against the
Stalinist leadership of various cultural organizations, such as the Painters'
Union, the Academy of Fine Arts, the Union of Cinema Workers, and the
Dramatists' and Actors' Union. A Western observer, Peter Benno, who was
in Moscow at the time, described one of these revolts and interpreted the
whole phenomenon as follows:

In the Academy of Fine Arts, Polikarpov himself appeared to present the official party list for the forthcoming elections. Since it was known by this time that his position was greatly shaken, the public made so bold as to drive him from the stage with hoots and boos and remarks about his past. This incident amounted to a near riot. In view of the outpouring of "subversive" literature [about prison camps], this outburst could not but have created the deepest sort of panic among the ranks of [the Stalinists] Lesyuchevsky, Ermilov, etc. in literature, Serov, Gerasimov, etc. in painting, and their like in other domains of cultural activity; it also created the deepest alarm in the midst of various people at the very top, such as Kozlov.[4]

Khrushchev's decision to crack down on the rebellious writers and artists in December, 1962, can be better understood in the context of his insecure position at the time. During the preceding year, a series of foreign and domestic policy failures, and Khrushchev's announcements of intensely unpopular administrative reforms, had strengthened the hand of his competitors for power. Under Khrushchev's leadership, the Sino-Soviet conflict had burst into the open at the Twenty-second Party Congress and was constantly intensifying. A reorganization in agriculture in March, 1962, disrupted the administrative apparatus—and indicated how gravely Khrushchev's previous reforms in this area had failed. There were severe food shortages throughout the spring. In June came a substantial (25–30 percent) price increase on basic foodstuffs—the first such increase since Stalin's death; it can scarcely have enhanced Khrushchev's popularity with the urban consumer. Workers went out on illegal strikes in various large industrial complexes during the summer and fall. In October came the failure of Khrushchev's Cuban missile gamble, bringing the military leaders into the fray. Finally, in November, Khrushchev announced a basic reorganization of the Communist Party that split the bureaucracy into two parallel sectors, agricultural and industrial. Henceforth, the party would be closely involved with economic matters. This in turn greatly diminished the influence of the professional ideologues and of the party leaders in the provinces and threw the entire bureaucracy from top to bottom into a state of upheaval. Party opposition to the reorganization was widespread; one of the first acts of the post-Khrushchev regime was to reverse it.

Meanwhile, it seemed to the authorities that the liberal artists, writers, and intellectuals were running wild, demanding a purge of Stalinists, an end to censorship, to "socialist realism"—and heaven knows what other lunacies and heresies! Anarchy was at hand—so said the Stalinist cultural bureaucrats and their opposite numbers in the party apparatus. And Khrushchev's opponents in the Kremlin were almost certainly making capital

---

[4] Peter Benno, "The Political Aspect," in Max Hayward and Edward L. Crowley, eds., *Soviet Literature in the Sixties*.

out of the commotion—yet another example of Khrushchev's mismanagement, they must have been saying.

It did not take long for Khrushchev to see that things had got badly out of hand. His decision to crack down on the liberal intelligentsia may also have been a concession—not very costly for Khrushchev—to his critics in the party whom he was presently challenging on other fronts.

The Declaration of War

On December 1, 1962, Khrushchev, with a retinue of four Presidium members, and several members of the party Secretariat, visited the Moscow Manezh gallery where a number of nonrepresentational pictures were hanging among the standard "socialist realist" paintings of interminably smiling milkmaids milking unrelentingly contented cows.

On seeing the abstract pictures, Khrushchev, the Prime Minister of the Soviet State, the First Secretary of the Communist Party of the Soviet Union, and the Commander-in-Chief of the Soviet Armed Forces, turned to the painters who were standing nearby and addressed them in these terms:

> Your pictures just give a person constipation, if you'll excuse the expression. They don't arouse any other feelings at all. . . . Judging by these experiments, I am entitled to think that you are pederasts, and for that you can get ten years. You've gone out of your minds, and now you want to deflect us from the proper course. No, you won't get away with it. Gentlemen, we are declaring war on you.[5]

Khrushchev's outburst at the Manezh set the tone of the denunciations, the threats, and the abuse heaped on the artists and writers during the cultural campaign that followed.

Said Khrushchev of the paintings and the painters:

> What is this, anyway? You think we old fellows don't understand you. And we think we are just wasting money on you. Are you pederasts or normal people? I'll be perfectly straightforward with you; we won't spend a kopeck on your art. Just give me a list of those of you who want to go abroad, to the so-called free world. We'll give you passports tomorrow, and you can get out. Your prospects here are nil. What is hung here is simply anti-Soviet. It's amoral. Art should ennoble the individual and arouse him to action. And what have you set out here? Who painted this

---

[5] Although the full text of Khrushchev's remarks was never published in the Soviet Union, copies of the transcript circulated widely. The excerpts given here are taken from an English translation that appeared in *Encounter* (London), April, 1963. Reprinted with permission.

picture? I want to talk to him. What's the good of a picture like this? To cover urinals with?

Here Khrushchev established his own personal genre of art, music, and dance criticism. About "a picture of what was supposed to be a lemon":

> It consisted of some messy yellow lines that looked, if you will excuse me, as though some child had done his business on the canvas when his mother was away and then spread it around with his hands.

About jazz:

> I don't like jazz. When I hear jazz, it's as if I had gas on the stomach. I used to think it was static when I heard it on the radio.

About the dance:

> Or take these new dances which are so fashionable now. Some of them are completely improper. You wiggle a certain section of the anatomy, if you'll pardon the expression. It's indecent.

Khrushchev's Manezh remarks were obviously spontaneous and deeply felt. They offer a rare, unedited glimpse of Khrushchev's manner toward his colleagues, his subordinates, and others who incurred his displeasure. (He once publicly compared Mao Tse-tung to an old galosh mouldering in a corner.) Here too is revealed the ex-miner from Kalinovka, the product of a *Rabfak* (Workers' Faculty) education, whose views on the function of the arts developed, like his career, under Stalin's tutelage. Khrushchev was not only Russia's classic obscurantist whose attitude is still nicely summed up by the official in Saltykov-Shchedrin's nineteenth-century satire: "What I do not understand is dangerous for the state." He was also the archetypal Philistine whose detestation of modern art differs little from that of his counterparts in democratic societies—except in that Khrushchev had the will and the power to impose his tastes upon the nation.

Above all, Khrushchev's Manezh remarks revealed how wide was the gulf between Khrushchev and the liberal writers and artists, how unreasonable his hope that he might count on their support, and how foolish the notion—once shared by many of the liberals—that they might somehow accommodate themselves and their art to his regime.

The "Provocation Theory"

Some Western scholars and journalists have speculated that the Manezh affair was a "provocation" staged by Stalinist bureaucrats who wanted to undo the damage that had been done when Polikarpov had been booed off the stage at the Academy of Fine Arts. According to this theory, the provocators, knowing Khrushchev's hatred for modern art, had engineered his visit to the Manezh gallery, counting on an outburst from Khrushchev that they could then seize as a pretext for putting down the liberal revolt in all the arts. The conspirators are said to have included not only the cultural bureaucrats, like Polikarpov, who were directly concerned; some analysts have speculated that the plot may have been masterminded by Kozlov.

There is some evidence that disgruntled bureaucrats in the fine arts apparatus did engineer the Manezh visit.[6] (Kozlov's role remains unclear.) The pictures that Khrushchev was bound to detest had been brought, just before his visit, to the Manezh where a perfectly orthodox exhibition had been going on for a month. And two old-guard art bureaucrats, Vladimir Serov and Sergei Gerasimov, accompanied Khrushchev during his tour and egged him on with such comments as: "Some connoisseurs claim that these pictures are programmatic. We dispute that." Or: "People say, by the way, that pictures like these are supported in the press." Their immediate goal was abundantly realized. A few days later Serov was "elected" director of the Academy of Fine Arts, in place of the more moderate Boris Yoganson, and soon after, Gerasimov was made head of the Painters' Union.

Insofar as the "provocation theory" robs Khrushchev of a decisive role in the cultural crackdown, it is misleading. Whether Khrushchev was, in fact, deliberately provoked at the Manezh is not known; but in either event it is beside the point: the student of the cultural crackdown of 1962–63 has no need of the "provocation theory" in order to understand Khrushchev's motives. The events that led to the crackdown and Khrushchev's conduct throughout the campaign indicate that it was initiated by Khrushchev—not in response to a provocation, but for discernible political reasons.

This does not mean, of course, that Khrushchev was not under pressure from more conservative members of the party leadership to put down the liberals' revolt in all the arts. It is indeed likely that such pressure contributed to his decision. And certainly, the sight of the Manezh pictures must have reinforced his determination to launch an antimodernist campaign.

First Reactions

Just after Khrushchev's visit to the Manezh gallery, relevant but not obscene excerpts from the transcript of his remarks were quoted in the

---

[6] This view was so widely held in Moscow that Leonid Ilyichev, the party's chief cultural watchdog, mentioned it in his March 7, 1963, speech (see p. 186) in order to refute the story.

press. The immediate reaction was predictable. Newspapers began to publish editorials attacking modern art and jazz. Moderates and liberals began to be replaced by conservatives and Stalinists in top positions in the fine arts apparatus. And persons with reflexes well conditioned during Andrei Zhdanov's purge of the arts during 1946–48 took prophylactic measures. The first to do so was the composer Vano Muradeli, who wrote in *Pravda* (December 17, 1962) that Khrushchev's Manezh visit was "a new manifestation of the party's concern for the development of literature and art. Nikita Sergeyevich's [Khrushchev's] wise words stirred our thoughts and feelings." He added that "the friendly words addressed to certain persons in Soviet culture have once more demonstrated the Communist Party's paternal concern for the fate of the Soviet artistic intelligentsia."

Shades of 1948! At that time Muradeli's opera, *The Great Friendship,* which had displeased Stalin, had been the principal object of the Central Committee's famous resolution of February 10, 1948, which condemned experimentation in music. On that occasion, Muradeli had confessed his sins, thanking the Central Committee for its attack on him, which, he said, was "one more clear demonstration of the concern of our party for the fate of Soviet socialist culture."

But now such grovelings were scarce. In fact, well-known creative artists in every field promptly banded together and wrote letters of protest to Khrushchev. In a speech on December 17, Leonid Ilyichev, then head of the Ideological Commission of the Central Committee and the top party bureaucrat in charge of cultural affairs, was to disclose (for purposes of refutation) the text of one such letter, which read in part:

> If we all appeal to you through this letter, it is only because we wish to say in all sincerity that without the possibility of existence of various art trends, art is doomed.
>
> We are now seeing how artists of the very trend that alone flourished under Stalin, giving others no possibility of working or even living, are beginning to interpret the words you uttered at the art exhibition.
>
> We deeply believe that you did not desire this and that you are against it. We appeal to you to stop the swing in representational arts to past methods that are repugnant to the whole spirit of our times.[7]

The signers of the first letter numbered seventeen and included two Nobel prize winners, the scientists Igor Tamm and Nikolai Semyonov. Among the other signers were the writers Konstantin Simonov and Ilya Ehrenburg, the film director Mikhail Romm, and the composer Dmitri

---

[7] *Pravda,* December 22, 1962. Except as noted, translations of quoted material in this chapter are reprinted, with minor changes, from *The Current Digest of the Soviet Press,* published weekly at Columbia University; copyright 1963. By permission.

Shostakovich—men who seemed up to now to have little in common but their compromises under Stalin.

One of the signers of a second, similar letter (which was retracted) was later revealed to be none other than that Stalinist hack writer, Alexei Surkov, the former secretary of the Writers' Union. It would seem that, at this juncture, Surkov and at least some of the letter-writers had acted out of the conviction that the Manezh affair was merely a provocation and that Khrushchev had no intention of undertaking a full-scale campaign. The winds, they thought, were still favorable to the liberals.

The Call to Order

On December 17, 1962, some 400 creative artists in all fields were summoned to the Kremlin to meet with Khrushchev, Ilyichev, and other party leaders. (It was the first of several such meetings held in December but the only one in which Khrushchev participated.) Ilyichev's speech called for ideological purity and catalogued "formalist" (experimental) tendencies in all the arts. In music, there exists an "infatuation with the outlandish yowlings of various foreign jazz bands." In the cinema, films are being produced which are "ideologically immature" and suffer from "studied cleverness and complexity of form." In literature, the "vital content" is often emasculated and "the Russian language is mutilated and cluttered up." Moreover, "some writers are simply possessed with a passion for grubbing in backyards and will not see what is happening on the main highways of our development."

Ilyichev's speech (printed in *Pravda* on December 22) not only represented an unmistakable call to order in the arts. It also indicated the extent of the party's anxiety about the attitudes and demands of the liberal intelligentsia: some people were calling for an end to all censorship.

> Sometimes it is said: "Let us create as we ourselves wish, do not force any prescriptions upon us, do not restrict us." Hence the demand for exhibitions without juries, books without editors, the right of the artist to display, without an intermediary, anything he wishes. We have before us essentially nothing but an attempt to obtain an utterly unrestrained opportunity to force upon the people a swollen, subjectivist willfulness. This means placing one's own interests above the interests of the people, the interests of society as a whole.

In an extraordinarily revealing passage, Ilyichev indicated how deeply discredited were official party positions among some Soviet intellectuals:

> In the discussion of creative questions at one or another meeting a situation reportedly arises in which it is considered inconvenient and unfashion-

able to defend correct party positions; one might gain the reputation of being, so to say, retrograde and conservative; one might be accused of dogmatism, sectarianism, narrowness, backwardness, Stalinism, etc.

In a speech made later that month (December 26, 1962), Ilyichev added: "It is one thing to combat the consequences of the cult of personality in order to assert the Leninist standards of life . . . and another to deal blows, under the guise of the struggle against these consequences, to our life, our ideology—in a word, to socialism and Communism." (*Sovetskaya kultura,* January 10, 1963.)

Finally, Ilyichev himself defined what he believed to be at issue: *"We have complete freedom to struggle for Communism. We do not have and cannot have freedom to struggle against Communism."* (*Pravda,* December 22, 1962.)

Some Sharp Exchanges

These grave imputations of anti-Communism and disloyalty, which Khrushchev would soon make more explicit, were disputed during one of several sharp exchanges between Evtushenko and Khrushchev at the December 17 Kremlin meeting. Such exchanges had been inconceivable in Russia for thirty years. Clearly any antimodernist campaign in 1963 could no longer be regarded as a persecution of helpless writers and artists; it was a struggle—however unequal—between the authorities, and individuals and groups fighting for the right to defend their beliefs.

Evtushenko protested against the charge made at the meeting that Russia's foremost modern sculptor, Ernst Neizvestny, was guilty of producing unpatriotic, "formalist" art. Evtushenko is reported to have said: "Neizvestny came back from the war his body criss-crossed with wounds. I hope he will live many more years and produce many more fine works of art." Khrushchev retorted: "As people say, only the grave corrects a hunchback." Evtushenko answered: "I hope we have outlived the time when the grave is used as a means of correction." In one of the liberals' many displays of solidarity, the audience burst into applause at Evtushenko's rejoinder.

Neizvestny himself was bold enough to tell Khrushchev: "You may not like my work but it has the warm support of such eminent Soviet scientists as Kapitsa and Landau." Snapped Khrushchev: "That's not why we admire Kapitsa and Landau."

All this grim banter was, of course, not reported in the Soviet press, but it was immediately made known in Moscow by the hundreds of people who had been present. Several unofficial transcripts made their way abroad. Among them is the text of Evtushenko's courageous remarks to Khrushchev on anti-Semitism—a subject that had become, in recent years, an important moral issue for the liberal intelligentsia. Evtushenko began by reciting the last lines of "Babi Yar," a poem about the Nazi massacre of Jews that is, in effect, a protest against all anti-Semitism, including the Soviet variety:

> Let the Internationale ring out
> When the last anti-Semite on earth is buried!
> There is no Jewish blood in mine,
> But I am hated by every anti-Semite as a Jew,
> And for this reason
> I am a true Russian.[8]

After these lines were read, the following exchange (reported in *Commentary,* December, 1963) took place:

KHRUSHCHEV: Comrade Evtushenko, that poem has no place here.

EVTUSHENKO: Respected Nikita Sergeyevich, I especially selected this poem and with the following purpose in mind. We all know that no one has done more than you in the liquidation of the negative consequences of the Stalin cult of personality and we are all very grateful to you for this. However, one problem yet remains which is also a negative consequence of those times, but which today has not yet been resolved. This is the problem of anti-Semitism.

KHRUSHCHEV: That is not a problem.

EVTUSHENKO: It is a problem, Nikita Sergeyevich. It cannot be denied and it cannot be suppressed. It is necessary to come to grips with it time and again. It has a place. I myself was a witness to such things. Moreover, it came from people who occupy official posts, and thus it assumed an official character. We cannot go forward to Communism with such a heavy load as Judophobia. And here there can be neither silence nor denial.

This provoked Khrushchev into an outburst which was apparently not recorded. Witnesses, however, said that he retorted that anti-Semitism was "nonexistent" in the Soviet Union. But he was reported to have added that it is better for Jews not to hold important government jobs because this only stirs up resentment.

The Dangerous Theme

Anti-Semitism was by no means the only ticklish question raised and left unresolved during the cultural campaign. At issue was nothing less than the

---

[8] From Blake and Hayward, eds. *Half-way to the Moon,* p. 25.

responsibility of the Stalinist generation of officials and bureaucrats for the crimes of Stalin. Expressed in direct and indirect ways, this was the leit-motif of the entire campaign.

This round of troubles had begun with the publication of *A Day in the Life of Ivan Denisovich:* the response of intellectuals and of the general public to this concentration-camp novel had dismayed Khrushchev. In his March 8, 1963, speech Khrushchev revealed: ". . . periodicals and publishing houses are being flooded with manuscripts about the life of people in deportation, prisons, and camps. *This is a very dangerous theme.*" (Italics added.)

Clearly, the "danger" is that each time the crimes of Stalin are publicly ventilated a question is raised: who was responsible? Any consequential answer brings into the open the responsibility of Khrushchev as a high party official during and after the purges of the 1930's, and that of countless others among Stalin's associates and accomplices who still occupy positions on every level of the ruling bureaucracies. The question of responsibility is posed even more insistently by a work of art like *One Day in the Life of Ivan Denisovich* than by speeches at Party Congresses. Khrushchev was late in learning the lesson of Russian history that literature has the power to arouse the conscience of a people and disclose the essence of tyranny.

Khrushchev's personal authority depended as much on his profession of ignorance of Stalin's crimes at the time as on his "unmasking" of those crimes. Indeed, the very legitimacy of his regime rested on his claim to having "reestablished Leninist principles." In other words, if Stalin's regime was illegitimate, as Khrushchev declared, how then could people who had participated in that regime later claim legitimacy? This is why Khrushchev engaged, as we shall see, in such contortions in order to allege that even people in high places could not have known that Stalin's victims were innocent.

This also goes far to explain one particularly sinister aspect of the crackdown: the campaign against Ilya Ehrenburg. The 72-year-old Jewish writer and propagandist, whose own career was scarcely uncompromised by Stalinism in the past, was to serve as a scapegoat who might distract attention from the genuine accomplices in Stalin's crimes.

The first denunciation of Ehrenburg was made at the Kremlin meeting by the writer Galina Serebryakova. (Although herself a victim of Stalinism, she had been well known as an archconservative since her return from two decades spent in prison camps.) Many writers and artists present at the meeting, who, she said, were clamoring for more freedom, were taking a high moral tone about the past. But what had some of these moralists themselves been up to under Stalin? Take Ehrenburg, she went on. Not only was he one of Stalin's chief propagandists, but he had acted as an informer during Stalin's purges. And who had told her of this? None other, she said, than Alexander Poskrebyshev, Stalin's personal secretary whom Russians had long thought dead but who, in fact, was alive and writing his memoirs.

This speech created a dreadful sensation at the meeting. Serebryakova had made a criminal accusation against Ehrenburg—a man who, whatever his compromises with Stalinism, had been one of the liberals' most eloquent and effective champions in the post-Stalin era. Moreover, she had invoked the name of Poskrebyshev, whose "memoirs," if put to use, would damn many thousands of surviving Stalinist bureaucrats and nearly every member of the Party Presidium—including Khrushchev.

Serebryakova's denunciation was evidently a double-edged sword. Rumors were rife among Moscow intellectuals that her mention of Poskrebyshev was a veiled threat of Kozlov's against Khrushchev. Yet it might just as reasonably be interpreted the other way round. Several analysts pointed out that it was unlikely that Serebryakova could have resurrected Poskrebyshev on her own initiative. Since Poskrebyshev has not been heard from again, we remain in the dark as to who was doing what to whom.

The only evident target was Ilya Ehrenburg. Many Soviet intellectuals feared that Ehrenburg might even be put on trial in a further attempt to confuse the issue.

The Denunciators at Work

A number of persons immediately joined the pack against Ehrenburg. The fearful word, "cosmopolitanism,"[9] was again being pronounced in public. Nikolai Gribachev, a hack notorious for his zealous participation in "anticosmopolitan" campaigns of the late 1940's did not hesitate to use the word at the Kremlin meeting in connection with Ehrenburg's patronage of modern art. Laktyonov, a painter of patriotic scenes whose technique is indistinguishable from color photography, exulted in *Pravda* (January 4, 1963) over Ehrenburg's disgrace in highly chauvinistic terms: "If, let us say, we had listened to the voice of I. Ehrenburg, then we would long since have had to . . . deny our love for our Russian realist art and to espouse various 'isms,' mainly of French origin."

But these were mere pinpricks compared to the menace contained in two denunciations of Ehrenburg by the critic Vladimir Ermilov, which appeared in *Izvestia* (January 30 and February 6). Ermilov attacked Ehrenburg for unethical behavior during Stalin's purges. He objected to a statement Ehrenburg had made in his memoirs that he (Ehrenburg) and others

---

[9] During the last five years of the Stalin era, "cosmopolitanism" had often been used to connote treasonable associations with (or sympathies for) foreign countries and cultures, especially on the part of Jews.

had known that Stalin's victims were innocent but had had to keep silent, "teeth clenched." Here, again, the "dangerous theme" had been raised (perhaps inadvertently) by Ehrenburg. If Ehrenburg and others had known of Stalin's crimes at the time, then people in infinitely higher positions, like Khrushchev, must have known as well.

Ermilov wrote:

> Evidently, I. Ehrenburg had a great advantage over the overwhelming majority of ordinary Soviet people, who in those years had no doubts about the propriety of the actions of the "people in command." Ordinary Soviet people at that time felt bitter and shocked that there should prove to be so many enemies of the people. However, there were many who, doubting the propriety of some particular action, championed justice for a particular individual who they were certain was not an enemy; they fought, and fought not with silence. There were quite a few statements, too, at meetings and in the press, which, even though they were concerned with protest against a particular case, a particular occurrence, in reality related to the essence of the Stalin cult.

Ermilov was, of course, insinuating that because Ehrenburg enjoyed Stalin's favor (his "great advantage" over "ordinary people") he had dirtied (or bloodied) his hands with more than propaganda work. Ermilov also insinuated that anyone who remained silent while knowing of some injustice was somehow a party to the crime. Many people, he insisted, had spoken out when they happened to come across a particular injustice.

The effrontery of those who chose Ermilov for this particular hatchet job staggers the imagination. Ermilov, the man picked to defend the good name of Russia's leaders, is reputed to be one of the most notorious informers in the country. He began his career with a famous denunciation in 1930 of the poet Vladimir Mayakovsky, whom he called, in *Pravda* (March 9, 1930), a tool of the Trotskyist opposition. (Such a charge would ultimately have led to Mayakovsky's arrest, had the poet not committed suicide.) Ermilov's later victims included fellow-members of RAPP (the proletarian writers' organization) who were liquidated in the 1930's.

Ehrenburg responded, in a letter to *Izvestia* (February 6, 1963), by saying that Ermilov had insulted him "as a man and as a Soviet citizen." He also stated that he had never seen any sign of protest against Stalin's injustices:

> In my book I tell of how our military people fighting in Spain and our writers and journalists in Moscow learned with anguish of the arrest of one or another individual who they were sure was innocent. Often we would talk about it among ourselves, but it was not possible for us to protest publicly. I was not present at a single meeting at which people took the floor to protest the arbitrary persecution of comrades whose innocence they

never doubted; not once did I read an article protesting against a "case" or "occurrence."

Ermilov's rejoinder (which appeared the same day) was even more scurrilous than his earlier attack—and this time it was accompanied by a note by the editors of *Izvestia,* (the government newspaper, then edited by Khrushchev's son-in-law, Alexei Adzhubei) supporting Ermilov. This, of course, underscored the official nature of the denunciation. The matter at issue was put very plainly by Ermilov:

> How are the Soviet people who lived, worked, and fought in the time Ehrenburg is telling us about now made to look in the eyes of youth? After all, according to both his memoirs and his letter, it turns out that everybody, or at least the majority of people at that time [of the purges], already knew that evil was being done in the name of Stalin, that the mass repressions were unjustified—knew and were silent. *This represents an insult to a whole generation of Soviet people* in an effort to give oneself a clean bill of health. [Italics added.]

Lull and Confusion

At this point, there occurred something like a lull in the storm. Although the campaign against Ehrenburg was considered fearfully ominous by the liberals, there were no further denunciations of this gravity until early March.

On the other hand, the process of ousting liberals from positions of influence throughout the cultural apparatus was intensifying. The party naturally supposed that these firings and its warnings would be sufficient to cow the writers, as such measures always had in the past. Instead, the liberals counterattacked with acts of defiance which were not merely symbolic but substantive. For example, on December 29 *Literaturnaya gazeta* reported that the Moscow branch of the Writers' Union had elected a slate of well-known liberals to their board. In an even more striking act of defiance, the Moscow Union voted to reopen a case which, among many others, had been closed on orders from above. This case concerned the proposed expulsion of Nikolai Lesyuchevsky, a veteran Stalinist in a class with Ermilov and editor of one of the largest literary publishing houses, from the union.

The situation was evidently far more confused than when Andrei Zhdanov bore down upon the arts during 1946–48. Ilyichev, in his December speeches, had given the intellectuals "warning," but he had also assured them that there would be no more witch hunts. In the midst of this confusion, Evtushenko left for a tour of West Germany and France apparently still hopeful of the ultimate victory of the liberals over the Stalinists (or, as they are often called in Russia, the "dogmatists"). In the French left-wing (but non-Communist) weekly *L'Express,* he published a work he had written while abroad, *A Precocious Autobiography,* in which he made some compelling observations regarding the cynicism, the mendacity, the self-interest, and the anti-Semitism of the dogmatists who, he wrote, have betrayed not only the Revolution but Russia herself. At a huge poetry reading in Paris, he recited a poem, "The Dead Hand," which has never been published in Russia. Here are some excerpts from the poem:

> Someone is still living as of old,
> attempting to knife whatever's new.
> Someone still glares in the Stalin manner,
> looking at young men askance . . .
> Someone pines in impotent anger.
> That may be, but I for certain know
> it's harder to unclench a fist
> if the fist belongs to a dead hand.[10]

In his *Precocious Autobiography,* Evtushenko had made this remarkable statement: "In Russia all tyrants have believed poets to be their worst enemies."

On March 4, Evtushenko was summarily called home to Moscow to face the waiting dogmatists—and Nikita Khrushchev himself.

The Campaign Resumes

The lull was most definitely over. On March 7 and 8, some 600 writers, artists, and other intellectuals were summoned to the Kremlin to hear Ilyichev and Khrushchev address them in terms that were far less confused or confusing than in December.[11]

It was clear at once that the resistance of the liberals and their apparent nonchalance in the face of party criticism had greatly disconcerted the party leadership. Said Ilyichev:

> Unfortunately . . . the sharp and just criticisms of incorrect tendencies in artistic creative work have been incorrectly understood by some figures in Soviet art and literature. And they have not simply misunderstood but continue stubbornly to defend their erroneous views. Some people are

---

10 From *The Poetry of Yevgeni Yevtushenko, 1963–65,* translated with an introduction by George Reavey (New York: October House, 1965). Reprinted with permission.

11 Ilyichev's speech was printed in *Pravda* on March 9, 1963; translations of the excerpts printed below are from *The Current Digest of the Soviet Press,* copyright 1963. Khrushchev's speech was printed in *Pravda* on March 10, 1963; translations of the excerpts given below are from *Encounter,* Pamphlet No. 9, "Khrushchev on Culture." Reprinted with permission.

even attempting to win others to their point of view, to surround with a
wall of estrangement those artists who heed the wholesome voice of criticism. . . .

The incorrect views are expressed in different ways. Some still wish to
create the impression that nothing essentially has happened, simply that
someone incorrectly informed the party Central Committee, someone
secretly plotted to bring off the visit to the exhibition, someone "palmed
off" his point of view, etc.

People had found more than one way of resisting the party directives,
Ilyichev observed:

In serious conversation about serious matters the voices of some artists and
writers are not heard. But whom, strictly speaking, do they hope to embarrass by their "stance of silence"? The party, the people? Among creative
workers are there not a definite number who show no inclination to write,
to compose, to create for a time?

. . . .

After all, silence also means something, also expresses some point of
view.

This matter of "silence" then brought Ilyichev to the "dangerous theme"
that now seemed to obsess the party leadership. Ilyichev explicitly endorsed
Ermilov's denunciation of Ehrenburg and vehemently joined him in his
denial that people knew of Stalin's crimes at the time. He recalled that
Ehrenburg had slavishly praised Stalin, writing when he died that Stalin
"knew the thoughts and feelings of hundreds of millions of people, expressed their hopes, their will to happiness, their thirst for peace."

Ilyichev added:

If I quote your words, it is not in order to single you out from among the
many and blame you for the words quoted. We all spoke and wrote that
way at the time, without hypocrisy. We believed and we wrote. And you,
it turns out, did not believe but wrote! These are different positions.

However strenuous Ilyichev's contortions on March 7, Khrushchev out-
did him the following day.

Khrushchev and Stalin

On March 8, Khrushchev delivered a 15,000-word speech in which, among
other things, he confided to the nation his personal tastes in all the arts.[12]

---

[12] In music, Khrushchev was enraptured by the "Internationale" and the songs of
Budyonny's cavalry; in sculpture, by a monument to Karl Marx; in poetry, by
an agitprop jingle of Civil War days entitled "How my Mother saw me off to the
War." In sum, the arts are an "ideological weapon" whose function is to "crush
our enemies" and "summon people to military accomplishments and work."

Compelling as these preferences may be, Khrushchev's political concerns loomed far larger in his speech. First of all, he took up "the dangerous theme." Khrushchev's elaborate refutation of the offending passage in Ehrenburg's memoirs led him to a partial rehabilitation of Stalin.

Ehrenburg, he said, was not persecuted under Stalin, yet "he paints everything in gloomy colors." In fact, Ehrenburg has always been an "onlooker"—not a participant in Soviet life. How then can his judgments be taken seriously?

Then Khrushchev got down to the business at hand:

> A question often asked now is why the violations of the law and abuses of power were not exposed and cut short when Stalin was alive and whether it was possible then. Our point of view on this has been more than once stated, fully and with the utmost clarity, in party documents. Unfortunately, some people, including certain persons in cultural life, still try to present events in a false light. This is why we have to dwell on the question of the Stalin personality cult again today.
>
> The question arises whether the leading cadres of the party knew about, let us say, the arrests of people in that period. Yes, they did. But did they know that absolutely innocent people were arrested? No, they did not. They believed in Stalin and could not even imagine that repressive measures could be used against honest people devoted to our cause.

Khrushchev's imagination had, of course, failed him too. He said: "At Stalin's funeral, many, including myself, were in tears. These were sincere tears. Although we knew about some of Stalin's personal shortcomings, we believed in him."

Khrushchev took pains to recount two instances when, having become aware of Stalin's "personal shortcomings," Khrushchev had allegedly opposed him or mitigated his policy. (In June, Khrushchev was to return to this sort of defense of his past, in even greater detail.) He claimed to have helped prevent Stalin from purging the Moscow party organization in the early 1950's and to have mitigated a purge of Ukrainian intellectuals and suspected nationalists which Stalin was preparing in 1947.

Finally, Khrushchev chided Soviet writers for not regarding the Stalin era, as he then claimed to do, as a time of glorious progress: "I can say from my own experience, as a participant in the events of those years, which are sometimes painted in gloomy colors and dull shades, that those were bright, happy years, years of struggle and victories, of the triumph of Communist ideas."

Other Concerns

In addition to his central concern about the "dangerous theme," as raised —explicitly or implicitly—by the writers, Khrushchev expressed alarm about the erosion of ideological commitment and of party controls in the arts and letters. Thus, he assailed the defenders of "formalism" and abstractionism in Soviet art—among whom the chief culprit was the hapless Ehrenburg. In a direct reference to Ehrenburg, whom he had already accused in his speech of "jokingly" advocating "ideological coexistence," Khrushchev said:

> There can be no joking in matters of political policy. Anyone who advocates the idea of political coexistence in the sphere of ideology is, objectively speaking, sliding down to positions of anti-Communism. The enemies of Communism would like to see us ideologically disarmed. And they are trying to achieve this perfidious aim of theirs by propaganda for the peaceful coexistence of ideologies, with the help of this "Trojan horse," which they would gladly smuggle in among us.

Another of Khrushchev's worries was the alienation of young people from their elders whom they often consider contaminated, if not utterly compromised, by Stalinism. The authority of the party is threatened when Soviet youth is seen to respond with more enthusiasm to the young poetry than to agitprop. Khrushchev's repeated denials of any estrangement between "fathers and sons" was a measure of his alarm. Such an estrangement suggests, of course, that the fathers have something to be ashamed of— again, the "dangerous theme."

In this connection, Khrushchev criticized a young poet for allegedly having said that "the sentiments of our youth are expressed solely by a group of young authors and that these authors are the tutors of our youth." "That is certainly not so," said Khrushchev. "Our youth has been brought up by the party and sees in it its teacher and leader."

Evtushenko's *Precocious Autobiography,* which was to be denounced throughout the following month, had evidently not yet been shown to Khrushchev, as it had only just appeared in France. Khrushchev gave Evtushenko credit for behaving in a "worthy manner" in Europe, but he accused several other poets and writers, including Andrei Voznesensky and Viktor Nekrasov, of having been "imprudent" and "talking rubbish" when abroad. These criticisms, by far the mildest in Khrushchev's speech, were now seized upon and blown up to enormous proportions by the Stalinist die-hards in literature in order to strengthen their position.

The Stalinists Unleashed

The Stalinist hacks that Khrushchev had unleashed proceeded to vent their anger and jealousy on nearly every young author who had written works of any genuine quality and received public acclaim in the last years.

At this juncture, the cultural campaign took a somewhat different turn. Until now, Khrushchev and the party bureaucrats in charge of cultural and ideological matters had been conducting the campaign in accordance with their concerns. And, although the Stalinists in literature and the arts had been reaping jobs and other benefits, they had scarcely been in control of the campaign. Now, after Khrushchev's public tirade against the liberals on March 8, the Stalinist writers believed they had license to take over the campaign and put it at the service of their own personal and professional grievances.

In the press, and in writers' meetings held all over the country in March and April, the Stalinists called for an end to the editions of 100,000 copies, the favorable reviews, and the trips abroad for writers who play the game of bourgeois ideologists ("with one foot on Broadway and the other on Gorky Street") in their "rotten, overpraised, unrealistic, smelly writings."

The vindictive tone that prevailed at this stage of the campaign can readily be understood when one considers that most of the old-guard writers had attained their status, their jobs, their *dachas* (villas), and all their other prerogatives and perquisites through years of fearful infighting, and often enough, denunciation of others. Then, terror stalked even the most loyal commissars, and the most slavish writers; denunciators might even be arrested—and often were—together with their victims. It can truly be said that the Stalinist writers had come up the hard way. Since 1956, however, the "new wave" of young liberal writers threatened to wash away all their hard-won gains. These young writers were getting all the attention, making triumphal tours abroad, and attracting enormous audiences in the Soviet Union.

The Stalinist writers, on the other hand, were now profoundly discredited with the public. When they appeared to give lectures or read their poetry, they were often booed or interrupted from the floor by indignant questions about their past. Their books, although still printed in hundreds of thousands of copies, mouldered away, unsold, in the bookstores. And, as we have seen, the liberals, until recently, had threatened to dislodge them from the cultural apparatus.

The Invective

It is against this background that the Stalinist poet Alexander Prokofiev, the head of the archconservative Leningrad branch of the Writers' Union, said at a meeting of the U.S.S.R. Writers' Union at the end of March:

> Something should be done about book-trade policy. Books by the "innovators" are issued in enormous editions of 50,000 to 100,000 copies. Why?

> Who will answer these questions? Why did Sosnora's [a young modernist
> poet] first book receive fourteen reviews—it was grabbed right away!—
> while books by those who take a Soviet position receive almost no atten-
> tion?
>
> . . . Mountains of paper are devoted to the works of Evtushenko, Voz-
> nesensky—this group of four or five persons. There has not been a single
> magazine, a single newspaper, a single printed publication that did not
> speak in laudatory tones of anything concerning Evtushenko [and the
> young modernist poets] Voznesensky, Akhmadulina, Rozhdestvensky. [Lit-
> eraturnaya gazeta, March 28, 1963.]

Anatoli Sofronov, a playwright and editor of the magazine *Ogonyok,*
expressed the Stalinists' fury toward the rebels in the Moscow branch of
the Writers' Union. Sofronov said that "a great sin lies upon the Moscow
writers' organization." Its leaders, he added, and particularly its chairman,
Stepan Shchipachev, had encouraged the young writers in their mistakes.
He complained that writers with "a complete lack of foundation" go abroad
and, like Evtushenko and Voznesensky, give "vile interviews, insulting to
our society, which are simply revolting to read."

Even before Sofronov spoke, Shchipachev had been fired as chairman of
the Moscow Union and replaced by a Stalinist, Georgi Markov. Crowed
Sofronov over this important victory of the old guard:

> The Moscow organization of writers is not Evtushenko, is not Akhmadu-
> lina, is not Voznesensky. It is hundreds of really gifted, talented writers
> who have been with the Soviet power and the party for all the decades of
> Soviet rule. They have been, are, and will be with the Soviet power and
> will never depart from party positions. [*Literaturnaya gazeta*, March 28,
> 1963.]

Various Stalinist writers denounced Evtushenko at the writers' meetings.
Said Mikhail Sokolov: "Comrade Evtushenko dirtied his hands abroad."
Said Leonid Novichenko: "He has by his personal example introduced
into the poetry of the young a type of poet completely alien to our literature—the troublemaker, the politico, the self-advertiser. Evtushenko is a
very uneducated man, in general terms and in terms of Marxism."

Sergei Pavlov, the head of the Komsomol (Young Communist League),
also had his say about the young writers. It should be noted that Pavlov,
who was born in 1929, has shown himself to be one of the most promising
of Stalin's spiritual heirs. He spoke of literary matters not as a writer (his
entire higher education consists of an uncompleted course at the Moscow
Institute of Physical Culture) but as the man in charge of party guidance
of Soviet youth, and as head of a vast auxiliary police force composed of

Komsomol members. Pavlov's remarks carried particular weight because his Komsomol job had been, in the immediate past, a stepping stone to the job of chief of the secret police.

In an article in *Komsomolskaya pravda* (March 22, 1963), Pavlov gave a vivid picture of how the Stalinists—in the various administrative bureaucracies, we may take it—generally view the post-Stalin generation of writers and their enormous following. (The article is also noteworthy for Pavlov's direct attack on the magazine *Novyi mir,* whose editor, Alexander Tvardovsky, an older poet, was the only one among the liberal writers known to have had some influence on Khrushchev and the only liberal writer to be a member of the party's Central Committee.) Wrote Pavlov:

> The boundless love of Soviet young men and women for their socialist motherland, patriotism—this is what marks the true image of the young generation of our country. At the same time, we do not conceal the fact that there are still fools who are prepared to crawl on their bellies before the foreigner, begging him for foreign rags or chewing gum. There are insignificantly few of these. And everywhere the Komsomol gives resolute battle to them, since they trample human dignity in the mud.
>
> There is another kind of ignoramus who bites on the shiny bait of bourgeois propaganda. This kind wants the transoceanic "twist," abstract art, and cacophonous music.
>
> Both kinds are loathsome. But even greater indignation is aroused in our young people by those who, pretending to the role of "enlighteners," "talents," or even "spokesmen" of the generation, are prepared to forget about what is most sacred—about the people, who gave them literally everything; about the great achievements of Communism; about their motherland, on which all mankind gazes with pride—all, essentially, for the same cheap foreign goods: for a portrait in *Life,* an interview in *Der Stern,* or the publication of a book "over there." [These are direct references to Evtushenko.]

The Stalinists' rampage apparently obtained two unanticipated results. First of all, it alarmed Khrushchev; the campaign was threatening to get out of control, and the Stalinists (like the liberals in late 1962) now had expectations that Khrushchev had no intention of fulfilling. Khrushchev did not wish them to attain absolute dominance over Soviet cultural life. This would have been out of step with his entire program for modernization and rationalization of Soviet society. Khrushchev's basic policy vis-à-vis literature and the arts was to contain extremism on both the right and the left. This was almost certainly one of the reasons that the Stalinists began to be restrained by mid-April and that the campaign lost its momentum soon thereafter.

The second result obtained by the Stalinists was the stiffening of the liberal writers' resistance.

The Writers' Resistance

At the height of the campaign, in March and early April, party officials in charge of cultural affairs, together with the Stalinist writers, were putting formidable pressure on the liberal writers to recant in the classic purge style. Such recantations would have served both to dishonor the writers in the eyes of their reading public and to reestablish at least some degree of party authority. But if the bureaucrats expected that the new generation of writers would, like the old generation in 1948, fall on its collective knees and thank the party for its fatherly concern, benevolence, etc., they were wildly off the mark.

Many of the writers remained defiantly silent. Others defended themselves, or counterattacked, at the various writers' meetings held in March and April. The liberals were scarcely given a forum in the Soviet press, but their defiance was made known by their tormentors who publicly expressed their indignation at the writers' recalcitrance, and by foreign Communist and other observers from abroad who were on the scene at the time.

A few of the writers made recantations that were miracles of ambiguity. But only the novelist Vasily Aksyonov and Evtushenko yielded real recantations. Evtushenko's speech, at a meeting of the Writers' Union, was not, however, published in full. Reports indicate that the larger portion of his speech expressed more defiance than contrition. In the part of his speech considered fit to print in *Pravda* (March 29, 1963), Evtushenko was quoted as saying that he had "committed an irreparable mistake" and that he would try to correct his errors in the future. How powerful were the pressures applied to obtain this recantation may be gauged by the following report of the meeting in *Literaturnaya gazeta:* "Evtushenko attempted to dispute the sharp criticism directed at him . . . but under the influence of the exacting, principled atmosphere of the plenary session [of the U.S.S.R. Writers' Union] Evtushenko was nevertheless forced to talk of his mistakes."

The principal figure in the writers' resistance was, however, no foolhardy youngster untouched by memories of Stalinism, but the 51-year-old Viktor Nekrasov—war hero, Stalin Prize novelist, and party member. Khrushchev had attacked him on March 8 for his "absolutely impermissible writings." Now he was under very heavy fire for his friendly and objective essays on Italy and America, "On Both Sides of the Ocean."

Nekrasov's highly respected position in Soviet letters made it imperative, from the standpoint of reestablishing party authority, to bring him to heel. His reaction to efforts to make him recant were described by Nikolai Podgorny, then First Secretary of the Ukrainian party organization. At a writers' meeting in Kiev on April 9, Podgorny complained that Nekrasov had denied any wrongdoing and had said that he would write only "the truth, the great truth, the genuine truth." Nekrasov, Podgorny added, has learned nothing and indeed has no desire to do so. As all of you heard, he considers an admission of guilt to be demeaning to him as a Communist. For what truth do you stand, Comrade Nekrasov? Your speech and the ideas you continue to maintain have a strong flavor of petty-bourgeois anarchy. The party, the people cannot and will not tolerate this.[13]

The effect of the writers' resistance was reinforced by the protests expressed by leaders and representatives of eastern and western European Communist parties—notably the Italian Party. Foreign Communist newspapermen in Moscow were sending critical dispatches to their papers. Representations by various foreign party leaders were being made privately. Then at the end of April, Palmiro Togliatti, the head of the Italian Party, publicly disavowed the crackdown, saying that no one should "tell an artist how to write a poem, how to create music, or how to paint."

An Ambiguous Situation

The situation on the literary front from roughly mid-April until mid-June, 1963, was highly ambiguous. On the one hand, it seemed clear that the cultural campaign was flagging. No new antiliberal measures were being initiated. With the writers' meetings over, the Stalinists were no longer being offered public forums (and vast press coverage) for denunciations of the liberal writers. Alexander Tvardovsky, who had been criticized for publishing in *Novyi mir* many of the writers under fire during the crackdown, gave an interview (published in *Pravda* on May 12) in which he defended, albeit cautiously, most of the contributors to *Novyi mir*. The very publication of the Tvardovsky interview in *Pravda* appeared to be a sign that the party was ready to take a softer line vis-à-vis the liberal writers.

On the other hand, it was announced that two of the most important and most talented among the young writers were to be sent into temporary exile: Voznesensky was to go to the city of Vladimir and Aksyonov was on his way to a construction site in Siberia. And a statement issued by the party's Central Committee indicated that a major reform of the cultural apparatus was being planned, which would establish organizational safeguards to prevent the liberals from ever again making inroads into the cultural apparatus.

At a Soviet artists' congress in April, Ilyichev, speaking for the Central Committee, proposed that the individual unions of writers, artists, composers, and cinematographers be abolished altogether, in favor of a single organization of all creative artists. Such an organization would, of course, be easier to control. Details of this reform and other proposed changes

---

[13] *Pravda Ukrainy*, April 10, 1963; translation reprinted from *Half-way to the Moon*.

(such as the assimilation by *Pravda* and *Izvestia* of such literary newspapers as *Literaturnaya gazeta* and the establishment of a single organization to control all publishing activities), designed to tighten party controls of cultural life, were expected to be announced at a Central Committee Plenum on ideology scheduled for June 18.

The speeches made during the first days of the Plenum seemed to confirm that the amalgamation of the artistic unions was at hand. Ilyichev repeated his call for it, as did the heads of the Composers' Union and the Leningrad Party Committee. It was therefore most surprising that Khrushchev, in his major speech at the plenary session of June 21, showed no enthusiasm for the amalgamation proposal. All his remarks touching upon organizational reform were vague. He condemned "the scattering of leadership among various agencies" which, he said, harmed "ideological work." He added that "skilled people," instead of literary critics and art experts, should be recruited into the party apparatus to evaluate works of art and literature from the point of view of the party. This was as far as Khrushchev would go in committing himself to a reorganization of the cultural apparatus: "We must arrange this [ideological] work otherwise and organize it better." The result was that no organizational reforms were adopted at the Plenum.

Following the Plenum, several reforms were instituted, but, with one exception, they took place within the framework of the existing cultural apparatus. The Moscow Writers' Union, for example, was reorganized to tighten controls over its wayward liberal members. The exception was the establishment, in August, of a State Committee for the Press, headed by the former chief of Glavlit, the censorship agency. This committee, which was put in charge of book publishing throughout the country, was designed to centralize authority and responsibility for all editorial decisions, thus rendering impossible such extremely common occurrences as the acceptance of a work by one publishing house after it had been turned down by another. The committee, which was merely fastened onto the vast literary bureaucracy, does not seem to have been outstandingly successful in this function. Judging from books published, publishing houses, like literary journals, had by 1964 again begun to reflect a spectrum of editorial policy, ranging from archconservative to near-liberal.

The paltriness of these reforms, in the face of problems that had engaged the party's attention for seven months, is striking—the more so when one considers Khrushchev's mania for administrative reorganizations. It would be expected that Khrushchev's usual panacea for economic and political problems would have been applied to the troublesome cultural sphere, i.e., a sweeping bureaucratic shakeup that would create new impressive-sounding agencies, with new men in charge who would attempt to establish better controls and carry out party policy more effectively. And, indeed, as we have seen, Ilyichev had indicated that a drastic reorganization *was* being planned.

Why did the reorganization plan miscarry? We may attempt to formulate and weigh some hypotheses:

1. The indications that a large-scale reorganization was imminent were misleading. They, in fact, represented an overzealous approach by individual party officials and cultural bureaucrats that had not been coordinated in inner party circles.

2. There existed a difference of opinion in the top leadership (Ilyichev being the spokesman of the pro-reorganization elements), which was resolved in favor of the status quo.

3. Kozlov's crippling heart attack in mid-April, 1963, removed literature from the arena of internal party struggles. (This hypothesis is based on the purely speculative assumption that Kozlov was the instigator or at least a major sponsor of the cultural crackdown.) Therefore, Kozlov's eclipse removed one of the effective pressures in favor of a "hard line" in cultural affairs.

4. The change of policy stood in close relation to the changed Soviet relationship with Communist China, which seemed to reach a climax on the eve of the June Plenum.

5. Literary policies shifted from left to right as a function or by-product of a broader and more general shift back to a more moderate orientation—perhaps in hostile response to the exacerbation of the Sino-Soviet relationship cited above; perhaps for other, internal reasons.

6. At a time when several critical political issues—from bloc unity to nuclear weapons agreements—demanded the sustained attention of the Soviet leadership, it was natural and necessary to put first things first and to suspend what, in the last analysis, was not an equally vital contest with the liberal intelligentsia.

These hypotheses are not mutually exclusive, and, indeed, some of them are complementary. And there may have been others as well.

Khrushchev on the Defensive

Whatever the reasons behind the decision not to reorganize the cultural apparatus, it is clear that in June Khrushchev was prepared to deal less harshly with the arts than he had been in March. In his June 21 speech, he did not return to the earlier blanket condemnation of the liberal intelligentsia.

While he made no further attempts to rehabilitate Stalin, he showed him-

Marc Riboud, Magnum

On the left, Evgeny Evtu-shenko, one of the heroes of the "liberal" youth. Below, poet Alexander Tvardovsky, editor of *Novyi mir,* with Ni-kita Khrushchev.

Sovfoto

ПОРТРЕТ ЖЕНЫ

— Гениально! Только, мне кажется, я выгляжу здесь чуточку старше!..

The artist's wife: "Wonderful! Only I think it makes me look a little too old!"

V. Zhitnikov in *Molodoi Kommunist*, January, 1962

This drawing accompanied a bitter attack on "trash" and "pygmies," "parasites playing the esthete," and "homegrown demigods" with "half-baked little thoughts"—the participants in the improvised poetry readings on Mayakovsky Square in Moscow.

— Ну и темные люди!

N. Lisogorsky in *Krokodil*, February 28, 1962

The coming generation expresses the official view toward devotees of both religion and modern art: "What benighted people!"

self as defensive as ever about the "dangerous theme." Still thrashing about in search of means of disassociating himself from Stalin's crimes, he took credit for the decision to de-Stalinize in 1956 and indicated that he had faced great opposition among his colleagues, some of whom "felt much guilt for the crimes they had committed together with Stalin." They had therefore resisted having those crimes revealed, "fearing that they themselves would be unmasked."

Khrushchev and his son-in-law, Alexei Adzhubei, sought to cite various examples from the Stalin era to show how Khrushchev had allegedly tried to condemn or contain the "personality cult." Only once in his June 21 speech did Khrushchev take the offensive: he ferociously denounced Nekrasov for not recanting: "He has wallowed so deeply in his ideological errors, has so degenerated, that he does not acknowledge what the party requires." He expressed his characteristic indignation about all those people who "hold their own mistaken opinions higher than the decisions of the party." He called for Nekrasov's expulsion from the party and, to illustrate how far he might go in dealing with recalcitrants, he drew an example from Gogol: "Taras Bulba killed his own son, Andrei, for going over to the side of the enemy. Such is the logic of the struggle."

This was an empty threat. Nekrasov was *not* expelled from the party. By this time it was amply clear that nothing short of violence could have put down the liberals' resistance. But the price of using overt Stalinist methods was too high for Khrushchev; such a decision would have compromised the entire domestic program he had advanced since 1956 on the ideological basis of de-Stalinization.

Khrushchev obviously had had enough by now of all the tumult and the intrigues on the cultural scene. Far more pressing problems demanded his attention, such as the greatly aggravated Sino-Soviet dispute that, as it turned out, was the main concern of the Plenum on ideology—and not the arts, as anticipated. On the domestic scene, Khrushchev's policies were increasingly vulnerable to criticism by top party leaders. For example, the anticipation of the Soviet Union's worst harvest in ten years was then forcing Khrushchev to make the decision to buy millions of tons of wheat from abroad, thus admitting the failure of his agricultural policy.

Insofar as the arts were concerned, Khrushchev had come to the June Plenum with the intention of cutting his losses. As force was not contemplated against the writers and artists, threats and abuse had shown themselves to be unavailing. Moreover, Khrushchev, as we have seen, was unwilling or unable to establish truly substantive organizational controls over the liberals. Khrushchev had to settle for an undeclared truce with the liberals who, it was hoped, could now at least be expected to understand the limits of their actions in the present and of their expectations in the future. Thus did the cultural campaign lose its momentum.

Some Western analysts have pointed to a connection between the amelioration of the campaign beginning in mid-April and Kozlov's heart attack on or about April 11. There are, however, sufficient reasons to explain the end of the campaign without relying on this purely speculative supposition.

Although the resistance of the writers and other creative artists appears to have been the crucial factor in the cessation of hostilities, there were certainly other factors at work. The increasingly fierce Sino-Soviet quarrel not only distracted the leadership from the cultural scene, but also required an appearance of national unity and solidarity among Communist parties against the common enemy. (The first reappearances in print of the condemned writers included veiled attacks on the Chinese by Ehrenburg, Evtushenko, and Voznesensky.) This was scarcely the moment to alienate Moscow's Communist allies abroad, who had expressed their strong distaste for the cultural crackdown. Moreover, the Sino-Soviet polemics made the cultural campaign appear ideologically incongruous; when the Soviet Communist Party is attacked by the Chinese for revisionism and retaliates with accusations of dogmatism, it is patently absurd to be carrying on a public campaign against revisionist heresies among the Soviet Union's own writers!

The Aftermath

It seems clear that the cultural offensive resulted in an overwhelming moral victory for most of the liberal writers. They emerged from their seven-month ordeal unbroken, unrepentant, and uncompromised in the eyes of their public by servile concessions to the Establishment.

In practical terms, however, the liberals' losses had been grave. They had been removed from most positions of influence in the cultural apparatus. (One notable exception was Alexander Tvardovsky, who remained in the important post of editor of the literary journal *Novyi mir*.) And although all of the condemned writers appeared in print before the Khrushchev era came to an end, these publications represented only a small part of their production. Indeed, little writing of any significant literary quality passed the censor in the year following the crackdown, in contrast to the wide choice of excellent poetry and prose published in the three years preceding the cultural campaign. Public poetry readings, which were banned during 1963, resumed in 1964 on a much reduced scale. The authorities evidently wished to prevent these gatherings from becoming pretexts for extraliterary demonstrations.

Although works by some of the best-known modern poets and writers circulate continually in typescript and mimeograph form, systematic attempts have been made to stop this flow of unauthorized literature, which increased with the cutback in publications of genuine interest to the reading public. Such attempts have included the arrest of a number of second-hand book dealers charged with selling the material. And in 1964 Iosif Brodsky, a talented young poet whose unpublished verse circulates widely, was charged with "parasitism" (i.e., not doing socially useful work) and, after a sensational trial, sentenced to five years in a labor camp.

The writers' works indicate that they have made no concessions to their critics in style or substance. Voznesensky, for example, who was consistently attacked for being obscure, ambiguous, and "formalistic" (i.e., too experimental), published a brilliant long poem, "Oza," full of the amazing and arcane associations, allusions, and images for which the young poet is famous. The case of "Oza" is a dramatic example of how difficult it has proved to maintain control over the liberals in the post-crackdown period. "Oza," a strikingly *avant-garde* work, appeared in the November, 1964, issue of *Molodaya gvardiya,* a magazine published by the Komsomol organization headed by Voznesensky's erstwhile enemy, Sergei Pavlov. The fact that "Oza" was later criticized in *Literaturnaya gazeta* and *Pravda* suggests that coordination of editorial policies had scarcely become more effective.

The liberal writers continued to express in their work—often in necessarily allegorical and Aesopian language—both their determination to pursue the struggle and their contempt for their adversaries.

In "The Long Suffering of Russia," a poem that circulated widely in the Soviet Union, until it was published in a censored version, Evtushenko writes of Russia's agony through the ages. Russia has been "kneaded, like clay, in blood," and has suffered from "famine, forced labor, and the knout." "But I cannot understand," says the poet, "how she has suffered her own long suffering." The poem ends:

> Russia's patience is the bravery of a prophet
> who is wisely forebearing.
> Russia suffers all. But only for a certain time,
> like a mine. And then
> > there is
> > an explosion![14]

In a satiric prose passage included in the poem "Oza," Voznesensky thus lampoons the cultural bureaucrats:

> The chairmen of the Committee of the Quasi-Arts Section were able to preserve order only at public meetings. Its members shone like eggs in one

---

[14] A variant of this poem later appeared in print (*Yunost,* No. 6, 1965) as a part of a long epic, *The Bratsk Hydroelectric Station.* In the published version, the last line has been changed to "And then/there was/an explosion."

of those X-ray gadgets used for determining the sex of chicks. They were all round and hence identical, whichever way you looked at them. Except that one of them had his leg sticking up above the table where his torso should have been—like a periscope.

But nobody noticed this.

The speaker stuck his chest out. But his head, like a celluloid doll's, was back to front. "Forward to the Art of the Future!" Everybody agreed with him. But which way was forward?

An arrow, pointing perhaps to the toilet or else to the Art of the Future, was sloping upwards like the minute hand at ten to three.

The mood and attitude of Evtushenko in the post-crackdown period is most strikingly expressed in a poem, "Letter to Esenin," which is unpublished but widely known in the Soviet Union and which ultimately appeared in print abroad (in *Russkaya mysl* [Paris], November 13, 1965).

The poem is addressed to Sergei Esenin, one of Russia's greatest twentieth-century poets, who, in deep disillusionment with the Revolution, committed suicide in 1925. Here Evtushenko suggests that things are no better (and perhaps even worse) for Russia since the Revolution, and, in this connection, evokes the enormity of the "war upon the nation," i.e., the imprisonment and death of millions in concentration camps under Stalin.

> Russia has changed, Esenin my friend,
> but, to my mind, shedding tears is purposeless:
> I hesitate to say that things are on the mend—
> and to say they're worse is dangerous.
> There's no end of new buildings and sputniks to spare,
> but the going was rough and on the way
> we lost twenty millions in the war—
> and millions more in war upon the nation.
>
> To forget this we'd have to cut out our memories,
> but where's the axe to hack off recollection?
> No one helps others as much as we Russians—
> and no one's so given to self-destruction.

Evtushenko also defies the Sergei Pavlovs of this world in his poem.

> When pink-cheeked Komsomol bigwigs
> bang their fists and shout at us poets,
> hoping to mould our souls like bees-wax
> in order to recreate us in their likeness,
> their words don't frighten us, Esenin. . . .

The poem ends on a note of pride in the accomplishment of Russia's new poets.

And the poetry of Russia goes
ahead, under suspicion and attack,
yet, with a Esenin hold, it throws
the West, as Poddubny[15] does, flat upon its back.[16]

Conclusions

The events on the literary scene permit us to formulate some assumptions about

1. The efficacy of controls of a totalitarian regime which is in the process of evolution from police terror to a more rational system of rule;

2. The special character of the "literary sector," compared to other sectors of Soviet society;

3. The mechanism of attempted reforms from above which modify not administrative structures but ideological beliefs.

Efficacy of Controls

The Stalinist model of rule has been drastically modified in the post-Stalin decade. Reforms in the economic and political structure of the country have taken place and the outstanding characteristic of the Stalin era, mass terror directed against both the bureaucracy and the people, has been abolished. Thus has the "stability" of the Stalin era given way to a period of dynamic change.

The failure of the cultural campaign suggests that Western analysts have underestimated the significance of mass terror as an everyday method of rule and overestimated the efficacy of nonterroristic means of control by a totalitarian regime. The lesson of the campaign appears to be that, when terror is absent, all other instruments of control are less effective, and, often, altogether useless.

It would also seem that the efficacy of nonterroristic controls decreases in proportion to the ability of individuals and groups to cast off the habit of servitude, master the reflex of terror, and brave the ever-present possibility of a return to mass police terror. Moreover, a totalitarian regime that is unwilling to restore terror is repeatedly obliged to undertake more threatening measures in order to reestablish controls, which are then effective until the disintegration of authority recommences. The efficacy of these measures is also seen to be reduced each successive time they are applied. In sum, party "offensives" may, thus far, be interpreted as defensive measures against the erosion of effective authority. But, it should be emphasized

---

[15] Soviet wrestling champion.
[16] Translated by Max Hayward. Reprinted with permission.

that, no matter how compelling the disintegration of party controls may appear to the student of the post-Stalin decade, the renewal of such offensives should never be regarded as a mere rear-guard action; they may as well portend a return to terror.

Special Character of the "Literary Sector"

The autonomy of literary life in the Soviet Union was destroyed in the early 1930's. From that time until Stalin's death, literature, like all other socially significant activities in Soviet society, was integrated into the mainstream of Soviet policy. In the post-Stalin decade, literature has acquired a measure of autonomy that appears to be appreciably greater than that achieved by any other activity. Moreover, in periods of "thaw," literature serves as a unique forum for individual expression.

The cultural campaign of 1962–63 represented a forceful attempt to reintegrate literature into the body politic. Its failure suggests that, short of terror, further attempts along these lines will also fail.

The special character of the "literary sector" is all the more striking for the fact that its autonomy is largely drawn from moral sources. In their demands for greater freedoms, the writers are concerned with far more than the narrow, professional issues at stake when a manager, say, struggles to obtain some economic reform. The writers have repeatedly and eloquently shown themselves to be concerned with fundamental issues of conscience and fundamental freedoms of personal and intellectual life. The moral autonomy of the writers has now been greatly enhanced by their resistance to the onslaughts of 1963—a fact which can only serve to diminish still further the authority of the party, which continues to proclaim itself the "standard bearer" of all humanist ideals and the enemy of every injustice known to man.

Ideological Reforms

The evolution of Soviet society in the post-Stalin decade had been largely the result of reforms from above, wherein the initiative for change, and the degree and the rate of change, were all defined by the men in charge of the political establishment.

Whenever these reforms have been applied to the economic and political structure, the leadership has been able to prescribe the dosage of change desired. Despite the fact that these reforms have often failed and that important interest groups have pressed for more radical solutions, there is no evidence that the top Soviet decision-makers have been unable, by and large, to keep a tight rein on the numerous Soviet bureaucracies involved in these reforms.

The leadership has scarcely been as successful in containing the effect of ideological reforms put forward to serve limited political objectives. The mistake of Khrushchev and his colleagues was to treat ideological revisions as if they were, say, administrative or agricultural reforms. They evidently believed that small, controlled doses of de-Stalinization could be administered, as with a medicine dropper, whenever political expediency demanded. A measure of the morally and intellectually stupefying effect of the Stalinist past on the post-Stalin leadership is seen in the persistence of the assumption that people's beliefs can be turned on and off by decree.

Of course, Khrushchev's revelations of Stalin's crimes in 1956 and 1961 (however fragmentary in terms of the total reality) set off a reaction that was incalculably far-reaching and absolutely irreversible. The myth of Stalin, inculcated for three decades and fortified by the full weight of a modern, terroristic totalitarian state, was shattered. The scope of public reaction may be appreciated when one considers that the whole ideological schema of Communism and the entire Soviet political and economic system had been for thirty years inextricably linked with the person of Stalin. The destruction of the Stalin myth put into question the legitimacy of the post-Stalin leadership and, indeed, the *raison d'être* of the Soviet system.

The fact that the cultural campaign was, in a significant part, an exercise in obfuscation and justification of the leadership's Stalinist past indicates that Soviet leaders have recently felt endangered by the reach of the ideas and questions raised by de-Stalinization. Indeed, each of their successive attempts to contain the "dangerous theme" by a show of force may merely have deepened the skepticism of the public.

The tensions and conflicts described in this case study will influence the evolution of Soviet society for a long time to come. For Khrushchev's successors they pose problems that are no less difficult of solution and no less decisive for the stability of the regime than the other crises that the new Soviet leadership inherited from Khrushchev.

Study Questions

1. In what fundamental ways does the relation between politics and literature in the Soviet Union differ from the relation between politics and literature in the United States?

2. Describe the methods used by the Communist Party in its attempt to reestablish full control over the liberal writers in 1962–63.

3. Evaluate the effectiveness of these methods.

4. In what ways did the demands and the actions of the liberal writers in 1962–63 undermine the totalitarian character of the Soviet system?

5. Why, under Soviet conditions, would freedom of literary expression threaten the stability of the Soviet political system, while democratic societies can reconcile the existence of such freedom with a stable political system?

Selected Bibliography

The most important speeches, articles, and documents of the cultural campaign are available in English in *Khrushchev and the Arts: The Politics of Soviet Culture, 1962–1964*, edited by Priscilla Johnson and Leopold Labedz (Cambridge, Mass.: M.I.T. Press, 1965). Miss Johnson's detailed introduction to this volume provides a brilliant interpretive account of the cultural campaign.

For an extremely valuable on-the-scene view of the crackdown, with political and Kremlinological interpretations not entirely shared by this writer, see the chapter, "The Political Aspect," by Peter Benno, in *Soviet Literature in the Sixties,* edited by Max Hayward and Edward L. Crowley (New York: Praeger, 1964). This volume also contains several chapters on the Soviet literary scene, which provide useful background for the events of 1962–63.

The anthology, *Half-way to the Moon: New Writings from Russia,* edited by Patricia Blake and Max Hayward (New York: Holt, 1964), includes writings, by Evtushenko, Voznesensky, Nekrasov, and others, that are directly relevant to the cultural offensive. The introduction to this volume provides a journalistic account of the literary scene on the eve of the crackdown.

The central literary work of the period examined in this case is *One Day in the Life of Ivan Denisovich* by Alexander Solzhenitsyn (New York: Praeger, 1963). *A Precocious Autobiography* by Evgeny Evtushenko (New York: Dutton, 1963) offers considerable insight into the psychology and the attitudes of this famous young poet.

Harold Swayze's excellent study, *Political Controls of Literature in the U.S.S.R., 1946–1959* (Cambridge, Mass.: Harvard University Press, 1962), provides the historical and institutional background on Soviet literary policies.

6

Social Control Through Law

John N. Hazard

On March 4, 1963, in a small town of the Russian Republic, two women—mother and daughter—walk to work along the highway under the cheerless rays of the morning sun. Suddenly a young man approaches and begins an animated conversation with the younger woman. Their voices rise; the man's gesticulating becomes wilder; the young woman points an accusing finger. Then the man, in a fit of rage, draws a knife from his coat and in a sudden motion plunges it into her breast. As she sinks to the ground, he strikes her once more in the back. The mother stands stunned, frozen with horror.

The scene, which takes but a few moments, is the tragic climax of an unhappy, turbulent marriage entered into seven years earlier. For the wife, it was a succession of merciless beatings by her unstable husband, violent arguments, and ultimately threats of death. His behavior became a public scandal, and as a result of it he was fined three times and sentenced to two terms in a labor camp. Finally, after four years of marriage, the wife returned to her parents and obtained a divorce.

But this was not the end. Abusive letters threatening death followed the unhappy woman. Soon after her former husband's release from camp, he accosted her on the street and cursed and threatened her. One night he arrived at her home in a drunken rage and pounded on the door, shouting curses and threats of murder at her and her parents. In panic, the woman ran to the local police office and to the chairman of her "street committee." But the next morning her tormentor returned, saying that if she did not withdraw her complaint, he would kill her. It was two days later that he met her in the street. When she refused to return to him, he struck the fatal blow.

The trial court sentenced him to death. On appeal, the Chamber for Criminal Cases of the Supreme Court of the Russian Republic[1] concluded that the sentence was too severe and had been issued without full consideration of the man's personality, his creditable record at his place of work, and the fact that the motive for the crime was entirely personal and not broadly antisocial. But the Supreme Court, sitting as a full bench, thought its Chamber for Criminal Cases in error, and concluded that the personal motive did not exclude the elements of heightened social danger in the crime that had been committed. On retrial, the trial court was ordered to consider the recurring crimes of the defendant and the ineffectiveness of the various "measures of social restraint" applied to him.

In another case, which came before the Supreme Court of the U.S.S.R. at the same time—in 1963—a band of thieves had terrorized the Central Asian countryside. They were accused of armed robberies of several homes. In one instance, they had threatened the home owner with death while seizing his food, clothing, cattle, and valuables. On another occasion, they had entered a collective-farm tractor park and stolen two tractor covers. Twice they had tried to steal sheep from a collective-farm flock but were thwarted by the cries of the shepherd. Over four years, they had obtained the equivalent of $25,000 in loot from individuals and organizations.

The trial court here also sentenced the ringleader to death. On review, the Supreme Court of the U.S.S.R. found the death sentence inappropriate: the defendant was a first offender, and no especially dangerous consequences had followed from his acts. Referring to the formula in the Criminal Code that the death penalty is exceptional and not mandatory, the

---

[1] Soviet courts are organized in two systems, one being that of the fifteen union republics and the other a federal system. Criminal prosecutions, except for espionage and offenses committed by members of the armed services, are tried by republic courts. These have three levels: the lowest one trying charges for which penalties less than capital punishment may be levied, and the intermediate one trying the cases considered especially serious. Appeals by the convict may be taken to one higher level than the court of trial, but there may be a still higher review of the sentence on appeal if the Procurator General of the Republic or the Procurator General of the U.S.S.R. requests it by a "protest," or when a President of a Supreme Court of a republic or of the U.S.S.R. desires it. When a Supreme Court reviews a sentence on appeal, its judges sit as a bench of three in what is called a Chamber for Criminal Cases. If this Chamber's opinion is questioned, the reviewing body becomes the entire membership of the Supreme Court, sitting together. The case cited was tried in an intermediate court since the death penalty was authorized by the code. Then it was heard on appeal by the Chamber for Criminal Cases, and subsequently reviewed by all of the judges of the Supreme Court of the republic, sitting together. The Supreme Court of the U.S.S.R. may also review a case involving high principle if requested by its President or by the Procurator General of the U.S.S.R. Such reviews of murder convictions occur rarely, but one is considered below.

Supreme Court reduced the sentence to fifteen years in a labor camp of the strictest regime and ordered the confiscation of the convict's personal property.

In both cases, the Criminal Code authorized the death sentence: in one case, for murder under aggravating circumstances, and in the other, for threats when made by a group of bandits. What then accounted for the different results—one court reaffirming the "hard" line, the other upholding the principle that the death sentence was an exceptional penalty that must not be applied in any but the most extreme cases?

The answer is not easy to give, for it springs from nearly fifty years of dispute among Communists on the ways and means of keeping law and order. The answer is the more difficult because in Soviet legal thought, offenses against individuals, such as "crimes of passion," have traditionally been considered less serious than those that—like economic crimes or crimes against the state—are assumed to be "socially dangerous." The position taken in the current cases appears to reverse this traditional position.

While the lines of argument have shifted, there were, during the Revolution and later, those who had come to the Bolshevik movement with humanitarian ideals and impulses—as well as those who were prepared to strike terror among their foes. There were those who would re-educate the convicts, whom they saw as unfortunate victims of circumstances, and those who would make deterrent examples of the criminals they proposed to punish. There were those who would let the punishment fit the crime without regard to the personality of the criminal, and those who argued for subjective "individualization" of sentences with consequent leniency when the situation suggested its efficacy in rehabilitation. In its many forms and mutations, what was at stake was the balance between politics and law, between duress and persuasion, between "class justice" (or "revolutionary justice") on the one hand and the advocacy of definite, uniform, and predictable penal norms, on the other.

Leaning on the Marxist view of the state apparatus as a device to perpetuate the dominance of the ruling class, Lenin had once declared that "law is politics." Surely, in the Soviet state, the cause of the Revolution —and the authority of the party—must be the supreme law. But even while this principle continued to be recognized, conflicts developed in practice. A member of the Supreme Court and of the Central Control Commission told the Party Congress in 1927, "throughout the [Soviet] Union we have a struggle on our hands between the courts and the executive." This was but one of the many dimensions over which Soviet officials and lawyers, professors and practitioners, differed in the field of law.

In its many ramifications the problem has not yet been solved in the minds of Soviet jurists. In reaching their decisions they must be aware of

the long and tortuous history of these debates, for on these debates the
ultimate solution rests.

Soviet Penal Law: From Lenin Through Stalin

Crime, Marxists argued, was a product of the environment; once a good
society was built, crime would disappear. To the penologist of the first
decade after the Bolshevik Revolution, therefore, law was a transient phenomenon, and the only "incorrigible" criminal was one who sought to
bring down the Communist Party and the Soviet regime. To be sure, the
basic approach and the key issue of "intent" were sometimes muddied
when the courts dealt with acts committed by members of "hostile" classes
—former landowners or petty businessmen taking advantage of the period
of limited private enterprise sanctioned in the 1920's under the so-called
New Economic Policy. But, however severe the treatment of "class
enemies," Soviet law professed to follow the belief that peasants and workers needed no death penalties to keep them on the straight and narrow
road to Communism. When members of the working class erred, education
(or re-education) was expected to restore proper respect for social order.
The period of "deprivation of liberty" prescribed in the sentence was
primarily designed—it was said—to provide an opportunity to work such
a metamorphosis.

In those years, the policy of rehabilitation was reflected dramatically in
the youth colonies established to provide a "road to life" for wayward
orphans—children deprived of their parents during the violent upheavals of
the Civil War and the ensuing famine. It was also reflected in the erasure of
such words as "imprisonment" from the vocabulary of the Criminal Code:
the traditional term connoted a hateful, injust, or, at the very least, point-
less and unproductive sitting in jail, and conjured up no image of rehabilitation through the teaching of trades and the giving of lectures on socialist
morality.

The decade of enlightened penology attracted the attention of experts
from many parts of the Western world; but for many observers this ceased
to be the image of Soviet law soon after Stalin changed his policies to end
the period of the NEP. There was, to be sure, something in the Leninist
heritage that had paved the way for this shift. Society required protection,
some leading Bolsheviks had argued, and humanism was to motivate the
courts only when they dealt with people who *could* be redeemed. But until
society was remade, terror alone would protect man—and the Revolution
—from the seasoned foe. Lenin instructed his Commissar of Justice in
1922 that the future criminal code must furnish "a basis for the essence and
justification of terror, its necessity, its limits. The court must not do away

with terror—to promise that would be self-deception, or deception—but must ground it and legalize it in a principled way, clearly, without humbug and without coloring over."

But Lenin had probably anticipated nothing like what Stalin instituted when he launched the forcible collectivization of agriculture in 1929. One of its facets was the "liquidation of the kulaks as a class." The kulaks were in no sense "landlords" like the estate owners of tsarist times, who had long since been driven from their confiscated lands. At most, they used a few hired hands to glean a modest livelihood from their small, or occasionally middle-sized, farms.

Stalin's "liquidation of the kulaks as a class" became the rock on which the policy of re-educating the wayward foundered. The liquidation marked the first formal departure from the earlier rule restricting the punishment of individual members of the "toiling" classes to cases involving intention to damage or unseat the regime, and allowing for sentencing only after judicial determination of that intention. The new policy also marked the first departure from the concept which had restricted severity of punishment to presumably hostile classes.

Having broken the barrier against the ruthless and wholesale exercise of power without regard to individual guilt, Stalin moved with speed to put into effect his policy of terror. The institution of capital punishment for property crimes was one aspect of it. A decree of August 7, 1932, introduced for the first time the death penalty for theft of property from collective farms. After this wedge was driven, the death penalty for property crimes was extended by degrees through application of the concept of punishment by "analogy." The analogy clause of the 1922 and 1926 Criminal Codes—which was to be used to sanction punishment of a wide variety of activities—permitted the punishment of acts not expressly listed in the Code: when a court found an act not heretofore defined as a crime to be dangerous (or when the prescribed penalty was thought to be too low), it could act, at its discretion, by "analogizing" the event to some crime that *was* punishable. In consequence of this practice, a theft—not only of collective-farm property but also of any property owned by the state—became punishable by death on many occasions.

The assassination of Sergei Kirov[2] in December, 1934, was followed by the increased activity of the Special Boards of the NKVD created five months earlier. They had authority by summary and secret trial—without any right of appeal and without publicity—to sentence anyone hauled before them to exile or terms in forced labor camps. The roster of Stalin's victims quickly extended well beyond the defendants in the much-publicized political show trials. By 1936, hundreds, if not thousands, of industrial

---

[2] On Kirov's assassination and Stalin's probable role in it, see Chapter 2, "De-Stalinization and the Heritage of Terror."

managers, engineers, and foremen had been accused of "wrecking" the Soviet economy. As the terror rose in an incredible and seemingly senseless crescendo, ever wider groups of citizens were enveloped by it. Even law professors who, in earlier years, had counselled moderation in punitive policy now reaped execution. By early 1937, those who had been arrested and executed after secret proceedings included both the Commissar of Justice of the U.S.S.R., Nikolai V. Krylenko, and the imaginative Director of the Institute of State and Law, Evgeny B. Pashukanis.

Even when, at last, on the eve of the war, the terror abated, those of its innumerable victims who remained alive continued to be kept in forced labor camps. No move was made to free those unfortunates or to restore the reputation of the executed innocents until after Stalin died.

Voices in the Wilderness

Stalin's tyranny never completely cowed his penologists, even when they could not—or dared not—speak out. Utilizing the mandate given them by the 1936 Constitution, they began to discuss the principles to be reflected in the new Soviet codes of law (which were to replace the ones adopted in the 1920's by the individual union republics). Pashukanis was made the scapegoat. Ostensibly under the spell of another posthumous whipping boy, the eminent economic historian Mikhail N. Pokrovsky, Pashukanis was now said to have forgotten Lenin's admonition that, though man is the product of social conditions, he nevertheless can reason and has a conscience and must therefore be held responsible for his actions. It was argued that, while class interests define the main course of human activity, it is people who make their history and, in consequence, men must be held accountable for what they do. Even during Stalin's purges some penologists had argued that, in all but a few exceptional cases, Soviet courts should punish only criminal negligence and intent, and must refuse to punish because of objective factors alone.

Pashukanis' desire to trim the Criminal Code to some simple definitions of forms of "social danger," without prescribing specific punishment for given acts, was criticized in the late 1930's as neglecting the subjective factors in each individual's behavior. Application of the principle of analogy was decried by many law professors, the most noted being Professor A. A. Gertsenzon, who specialized in criminology. The Supreme Court of the U.S.S.R. expressed itself in favor of narrowing the use of analogy (although murder could still be punished by death by analogizing sadistic murder to the crime of banditry, for which the Code prescribed death).

To some extent all this was facilitated by the shift in political and legal theorizing which accompanied Stalin's argument that in the new phase of "socialism"—which he claimed the U.S.S.R. had entered by 1936—conflicts would become more severe; more, not less, terror would be required; and, rather than withering away, the state apparatus was bound to become stronger than ever before. As Soviet jurists were told in 1938, "under socialism . . . law is raised to the highest level of development." No longer considered a temporary necessity, law—to quote a recent observer—"was converted by Stalin into an instrument of party dictatorship."

Re-education of offenders remained the formal aim of Soviet penal legislation even during the Stalin era, but legal authors remained understandably silent about Stalin's widespread application of capital punishment for political crime—or for no crime at all. Nor did anyone attack the system of Special Boards. By silence the penologists sought to protect themselves, but even during Stalin's most oppressive period some of them gave the impression that they were—not only literally—able to keep their heads. They continued to foster policies inherited from the optimistic days of 1917, when it had been assumed that toilers could be redirected to useful lives, largely by "corrective labor." From this relatively courageous nucleus of scholars was to come, after World War II, another effort to draft all-union codes that could reflect ideas on the control of crime, associated in the West with individualization of penalties to facilitate rehabilitation.

While it prompted more drastic and summary punishment for certain offenses, the war also provided an opportunity to reaffirm hope for less severe policies after its end. In arguing for application of severe penalties "by analogy" to theft, illegal manufacture of intoxicating liquors, and the resale of articles purchased for consumption, the Procurator General declared that there was no need to amend the Code so as to increase penalties in wartime. Presumably, it would be easier to return to milder penalties after the war by terminating or limiting application of analogy than by initiating the protracted procedures necessary to obtain an amendment to the Code. There was widespread hope that such opinions were a portent of things to come.

During the final phase of the war, the judiciary was already moving in the direction of fitting penalties to the individual offender. In one case, which the Supreme Court of the U.S.S.R. considered in 1944, the Procurator had secured a reversal of a worker's acquittal in a lower court. The Supreme Court struck a note of moderation, though not of absolution: it returned the case for new trial with instructions that the accused man's personal history *was* pertinent in determining the sentence. It did not order him released, however, for it maintained that he must not be relieved of all responsibility for his acts.

Indeed, the advocates of judicial moderation scored their signal success with the decree of May 26, 1947, abolishing capital punishment in peacetime and substituting, as maximum punishment for crimes previously punishable by death, 25-year sentences in corrective-labor camps. Not since 1920, when capital punishment was abandoned for a two-year period in anticipation of peace following the defeat of anti-Bolshevik forces in the Civil War, had the moderates been able fully to carry the day. The end of World War II offered them a somewhat similar opportunity to speak out successfully, perhaps because of a similar revulsion against killing. Millions had been killed at the front and had died of exposure, disease, and famine in the rear. To the Soviet government's announced figure of seven million deaths, population experts abroad have added many more, and even Soviet experts put the figure at twenty million when conversing with foreigners. The end of the war thus marked a time of exhaustion but also of hope for the Soviet people—hope that the terror (which some Communist intellectuals had deplored but accepted as necessary while fighting enemies at home and abroad) could at last be abandoned.

Early in 1947, Soviet law journals had carried letters from readers proposing a revision of the Criminal Code and of the Code of Criminal Procedure. They seemed to reflect a smouldering hostility to some of the institutional aspects of terror, such as the analogy clause and the lack of precision in the code's provisions relating to political crimes. Being unable to mount a frontal attack on the analogy article, which was evidently favored by Stalin, the letter writers argued that application of analogy resulted in lack of uniformity in the administration of justice, and that Lenin had once, when writing his Commissar of Justice, made a much-publicized statement in favor of uniform standards of sentences.

The criticism, as voiced, was directed not only against analogy but also against indefiniteness. One school of thought argued that the Code should be lengthened so as to include a larger number of specifically defined crimes rather than kept short in continuation of the policy of applying a few broadly stated provisions to a wide variety of acts. One such proposed revision called for differentiation of degrees of murder, so that, e.g., a separate article might treat mothers who murdered newborn children. Another proposal urged separate treatment of threats designed to influence the decision of a court. To meet the need for more precision in application of penalties, it was proposed to define new crimes rather than apply inappropriate articles by analogy. Thus, it was proposed that penalties be added for larceny of personal property, for fraudulently entering upon marriage before terminating a prior marriage, for concealing impediments to marriage from a spouse, for lying before a court, and for failure to answer a summons to appear as a witness.

In addition to these criticisms, the Code of Criminal Procedure was subjected to sharp criticism by the senior specialist in the field, Professor Mikhail S. Strogovich. He wanted, for instance, to narrow the work of administrative agencies, namely the police, that conduct the first study of a case, before it goes to the court investigator for so-called pretrial examination and preparation of the indictment.[3] This was essentially a jurist's vote of no-confidence in the procedures of the police and of the security services.

Similarly, the role of the defense attorney came in for some public reconsideration. One prosecutor, after recounting his many years of experience, urged that a defense attorney be permitted to participate in the entire pretrial examination. His view was disputed by others who claimed that such participation would nullify the value of secrecy during the pretrial stage, and without secrecy co-conspirators might be able to conceal evidence. Others took a compromise position, urging that the defense attorney be excluded during the assembly of evidence by the investigator but that he be admitted when the indictment was concluded so that he might have time to prepare his defense for the trial.

Similarly, the presumption of innocence—which, some Soviet jurists had maintained, was accepted by Soviet law because of the 1936 guarantee of counsel at the trial but which in fact was not respected in letter or in spirit —became an issue during the early postwar years. One jurist urged that the principle needed new emphasis in future codes because some judges were not adhering to the existing requirement that the trial review all the evidence in the record of the pretrial examination.

All these proposals and criticisms seemed to bear in the same direction.

---

[3] Soviet court procedure provides two pretrial stages: a police inquest and a preliminary investigation. The police inquest has the function of discovery and preservation of material evidence, such as weapons, blood-stained clothing, and fingerprints, as well as identification of potential witnesses. The preliminary investigation is required by law to be much more than an assembly of the state's case in extension of the police inquest. The code obliges the official charged with the investigation to act as if he were judge—that is, to be impartial in developing both the case for the state and the case for the suspect. Witnesses for both sides are heard, material evidence is examined as collected by the police, and the suspect himself is interrogated if he will speak. The investigator is required to inform the suspect of his procedural rights, but no lawyer is allowed to provide counsel. During the preliminary investigation, a documentary record is assembled, and an indictment is prepared if one seems justified. It is the indictment and the record that are examined again at the trial in open court with the recall of essential witnesses and the hearings of the accused, of his attorney, and of the prosecutor. Pressure has been constant throughout Soviet legal history to telescope the two stages of inquest and investigation, not only for inconsequential crimes seemingly requiring no exhaustive preparation but for crimes against state security for which security-conscious officials lacked confidence in the ability of preliminary investigators of the usual sort. During Stalin's time the security-conscious school triumphed, but on his death some law professors successfully separated the two stages in the procedural reforms of 1958. Their victory was short-lived, for by decree of July 21, 1961, the security police regained the function of preliminary investigator as well as of inquest for a wide variety of offenses thought to endanger state security. They presented again to the professors the seemingly improbable combination in one individual of the vigilant security official and the preliminary investigator charged with the duty of being impartial.

Invariably, during periods of relative relaxation of political tension, greater diversity of views—and greater advocacy of moderation—became evident. But in addition, during the years immediately following the war, the jurists drafting the new Soviet codes of law seemed to be giving less credence to the perils previously claimed to be lurking in every act and to have concluded that there was no longer cause for such alarm. There was an emerging desire among Soviet law professors to proceed methodically and with care in handling cases so as to avoid catching the innocent in dragnet procedures. In short, some Communist legal specialists considered the system sufficiently strong to survive the careful determination of guilt. They recalled that re-education rather than conformity through fear had been the original aim of Soviet penology.

The moderates were never in complete control; they had many influential enemies within Stalin's bureaucracy, judging by the slowness of reform. Yet for a while their influence seemed to be increasing. This interlude came to a sudden end with the decree of January 12, 1950, reestablishing capital punishment. The very brief preamble to the decree stated that labor unions, peasant organizations, and people working in the arts had demanded a change in the 1947 decree abolishing the death sentence. Capital punishment was reinstituted, effective immediately, for "traitors, spies, and those seeking to undermine the state."

One easy explanation for the 1950 decree, suggested by Khrushchev's later revelations, was that Stalin had gone mad. Even Stalin's senior collaborators, Khrushchev told his colleagues, had feared for their lives. A form of paranoia had seized the aging party chief with increasing intensity, until in the autumn of 1952 he had ordered the trial of his medical doctors and prepared the way for what his colleagues subsequently identified as the beginning of a new great purge.

That the sole explanation for the reversal of policy in 1950 was Stalin's "illness" is doubtful. The new "hard line" coincided with the stiffening all along the front—from the series of purges against men like Voznesensky in the U.S.S.R. and the real and imaginary Titoists in eastern Europe, to the new crisis mood engendered by the Korean War. The cold war was approaching its peak. At any rate, observers noted that proposals for law reform disappeared from the Soviet press, the last one being carried in the April, 1949, issue of the principal Soviet journal on legal theory. Once again, it seems, as terror mounted across the Soviet land, the pall of fear had fallen on the legal fraternity, and no one felt sufficiently attuned to Stalin's ideas to risk drafting a new Criminal Code.

Not until 1954, a year after Stalin's death, were proposals again advanced in public. As in other fields, they picked up the arguments of 1947–48, as if to indicate that the advocates of reform and moderation had continued to do their own thinking throughout Stalin's final years and now could resume the debates.

The first themes to appear in legal criticism after Stalin's death were familiar. An early target was the principle of analogy. One month prior to Stalin's death, Andrei Vyshinsky—spokesman of Stalinist legal thought— had submitted to the editors of the Academy of Sciences' law review his critique of a new textbook on criminal law. He had castigated the book because its authors had not supported with sufficiently detailed argument the retention of the analogy principle. In short, their defense was too luke- warm to please him, and Vyshinsky's criticism provides us with another clue to what was happening in the Academy's Institute of Law. It appears that the authors of the textbook in question opposed the analogy principle but, not daring to say so openly, hoped to damn it with faint praise. Vyshinsky's book review, although written before Stalin's death, appeared after it. It stands as the final monument in legal literature to Stalin's policy of terror.

The Revival of Argument

Stalin's death was the crucial precondition for the public expression of individual and independent views. Yet it took time for Soviet citizens to explore, and adjust to, the limits of the new tolerance. There was a lapse of years before people spoke out in public on sensitive issues and before authors began to write—and publishing houses to issue their writings— about their experiences under Stalinism, especially those that dealt with jails and labor camps. But gradually the barriers were lowered, and the gates were opened guardedly to the flow of literature and other influences from abroad. No doubt one of the most widespread, intensive, and per- sistent impulses to introduce reform was inspired by the revulsion against terror and arbitrariness—the hallmarks of the Stalin era.

In an environment in which the more daring were beginning to attack the "excesses" of the "personality cult," with the Stalinists waging what seemed to be a losing rear-guard action, Soviet legal specialists also called up their courage to assail anew the abuses in the field of penology. One by one, the issues raised after the war again came to the fore.

In the legal profession, the first to break into print with a courageous but well-modulated call for reform was Viktor Chkhikvadze, a young Georgian lawyer then in his early forties. A decade later he was to be named Director of the Institute of Law of the U.S.S.R. Academy of Sciences, a post once held by Andrei Vyshinsky. In April, 1954, Chkhikvadze published a criti- cism openly urging the complete elimination of the doctrine of analogy from the Criminal Code. He buttressed his appeal with an argument that may be presumed to have appealed to some of his official readers. He de- clared that the "imperialist states" were moving in the direction of ill- defined, broad, general provisions under which the courts could punish whom they wished; and, he cleverly argued, the U.S.S.R. should by contrast demonstrate the superiority of *its* system of government by establishing more definite norms in criminal law.

To this argument, Chkhikvadze appended something that smacked of self-protection in the event that a new Stalin should emerge: Soviet judges must apply the law not with dogmatic formality or addiction to legalism but with all the flexibility necessary for the individualization of punishment.

Considering the freeze that had obtained in Soviet legal theory and writing, this was a significant article. But there was much more that Chkhikvadze failed to say. He remained silent even on the issue of adding definiteness to the article on political crime. This, it is likely, was still deemed a matter too sensitive for public discussion.

On April 30, 1954, a decree was adopted establishing the death sentence for murder when there are attendant circumstances showing complete disrespect for human dignity and social order. With the benefit of hindsight, it is now apparent that this decree was related to the emerging pressures for greater definiteness in the Code and for the abandonment of analogy. Previously the courts had used the analogy clause to order the execution of individuals, for instance, who had committed "sadistic" murder in analogy to banditry, for which the Code provided capital punishment. What the new decree did was to make superfluous the use of analogy and instead to provide warning to prospective "sadistic murderers" that henceforth they could expect death rather than imprisonment. Studies then published suggested an increasing concern with the incidence of brutal crime; and Soviet newspapers chose to publicize cases to show that the new decree was being applied.

In one instance, reported in *Pravda,* a young man had invited a girl to walk home with him from a club, had attempted to rape her during the walk, and on her resistance had slashed her face and strangled her. His record showed that he had been released from prison only a short time before, probably under the March 27, 1953, amnesty promulgated after Stalin's death. A second case, also reported by *Pravda,* involved the prosecution for murder of a young man who had been ejected from a dormitory party in an intoxicated condition. He returned with a knife to inflict fifty knife wounds upon the Komsomol member who had ejected him. In both cases, capital punishment would probably have been imposed even prior to the new decree through application of the doctrine of analogy. With the April 30 decree, the death sentence became a virtual certainty, and a modest victory had been scored by the advocates of greater definiteness of penal norms.

Stalin's heirs seemed eager to dispense with the terror and harshness of punishment that had become endemic. The 1953 amnesty provided, among other things, for the optional use, in place of the more severe punishment stipulated in the Criminal Code, of administrative and disciplinary measures such as expulsions, suspensions, and fines for crimes committed by officials in their official capacity, and for economic, social, and relatively less dangerous other crimes.

There was still, in the first post-Stalin years, a rigid screen of political taboos. The first legal commentaries on the proposed new Code, in 1954, still denied the need to reduce the penalties for political crimes. Even Chkhikvadze reminded his readers of the continued threat posed by the "capitalist environment": the implication was that the propriety of the 1950 decree continued, since presumably the danger of foreign spies and saboteurs still existed.

A second commentator, V. S. Tadevosian, fifteen years Chkhikvadze's senior, urged a more cautious course, opposing the elimination of analogy. He recalled Stalin's dictum that the security services were needed to meet with due vigilance the efforts of enemies from abroad. He argued, therefore, that the changes to be put into effect should be limited to crimes unrelated to politics or to the stability of the regime. It was in these non-political areas that government agencies were to devote their attention to re-educating offenders, whose labor was to be used for purposes of economic development.

Re-education suggested short sentences. Under Stalin, the position of severity had been symbolized by a decree of January 4, 1949, which had increased the penalty for rape from the previous maximum of eight to a new maximum of fifteen years, with penalties from fifteen to twenty years if committed by several persons or on a minor, or when it prompted suicide. The decree coincided with reports in the press of a crime wave and suggested that policy-makers had lost their patience with hardened criminals, believing that severe penalties could deter men from crime. Thus, in 1949 the Soviet Union had contradicted the evidence reported by many other nations and reflected in studies sponsored by the United Nations, that severe penalties and, notably, capital punishment do not diminish or prevent crime. The severity of punishment understandably became through this evolution another issue in the reviving debate among advocates of "hard" and "soft" penal policies.

Tadevosian argued in 1954 that a 25-year term was unrealistic for "corrective" purposes. Ten years was deemed a maximum for "social" crimes; mild crimes, he proposed, should be made the basis of a prison sentence only if they were serious enough to require seclusion for at least three months. Interestingly enough, in the course of disputing the contention of those who favored sweeping uniformity of sentences, he explicitly referred to the existence of a group who believed (as Stalin had) that severe penalties would ultimately reduce the incidence of crime. These people, he explained, wanted to eliminate all forms of mild penalties, leaving only

imprisonment. They would, moreover, eliminate the possibility of individualization of punishment under Code articles providing maxima and minima,
favoring instead a single penalty to be applied to all committing a given
offense.

In his view, such a rigid approach overlooked the change of circumstances, such as the recent amassing of economic wealth and the growth
of public education in the U.S.S.R. He seemed to be saying that, since the
public could now be expected to be well informed of the social consequences of individual acts and could no longer plead economic want as a
mitigating circumstance, the criminal no longer needed to be pitied as the
unconscious tool of forces which he could neither understand nor influence.
He must be regarded as a conscious being, to be dissuaded from crime by
penalties fitted to his special situation.

Under this view, those who had stolen public property in 1932 had
been properly punished for it by death. Likewise, the penalty imposed in
1954 for those murdering under aggravating circumstances could be justified. But for lesser crimes, this jurist argued, it was time to decrease penalties so as to foster rehabilitation through corrective labor and education.
Above all he hoped for a return to the suspended sentence, long since abandoned by Soviet judges.

History was to repeat itself, but with a twist. After two years of experimentation with its abolition, capital punishment had been restored in 1922,
with the justification that it was necessary as a protection of the proletarian
dictatorship at a time when the "retreat on the economic front" had made
necessary some concessions to the capitalists. The expansion of the death
penalty in 1954 was also a victory for the "hard" line, but under vastly
different circumstances. In 1922, it was taken for granted that the capitalist
"class enemies" were fundamentally incorrigible insofar as the goals and
values of Soviet society were concerned. By 1954, the capitalists had long
since been driven from the social order, but a new threat seemed to stem
from the working people themselves—namely, from those who in the eyes
of their leaders had become despicable offenders in that they refused to
accept the opportunities for self-improvement offered by an expanding full-
employment economy. Once they had demonstrated themselves to be incorrigible, society would have to rid itself of their presence—not as an act of
rehabilitation, of course, but as a safety measure against the repetition of
their offense. Their execution would stand as a warning to others that the
socialist state was not becoming soft even while it espoused a policy of
lessened penalties for the vast majority of offenders. Such at least was the
tenor of official arguments.

The balance between the advocates of a milder policy and those opposing it remained precarious and uncertain. But, especially after the Twentieth
Party Congress, law benefited from the general spirit of de-Stalinization

from above and from below. The years 1956 and 1957 witnessed relatively greater frankness in public criticism with regard to legal problems, much as in other areas of Soviet life.

Legislating the New Moderation

A decision to return with determination to the drafting of a new Code gave the advocates of reform their chance to recommence their campaign for lessening of penalties, abolition of analogy, introduction of precision into the definition of crime, and the creation of rights (under the Code of Criminal Procedure) which would facilitate proof of innocence. Characteristically for the Khrushchev round of limited decentralization in Soviet administration and economy in 1956–58, the decision took the form of an amendment to the Soviet Constitution. Effective February 11, 1957, it retransferred to the fifteen constituent republics of the U.S.S.R. the right they had lost in 1936 to draft their own codes. Under this amendment, the central Soviet government would adopt "Fundamentals" in each branch of law, and the union republics would enact codes introducing detail consistent with these Fundamentals. No constitutional provisions drew a distinction between what the federal government might include in the Fundamentals and what the republics might include in their codes. Some items moved back and forth during the months of discussion that were to follow (the most noted being the age of responsibility for juveniles, which was first left to the republics for determination but was in the end made the concern of the federal Fundamentals).

Seizing upon the policy change regarding the role of the republics in the legislative process, the legal specialists began rediscussion of the principles to be incorporated in the Fundamentals. When the draft appeared for public examination in June, 1958, it became apparent that by and large the advocates of reform had scored a victory.

Analogy was the principal loser. While the new Fundamentals were not entirely explicit on the ending of analogy, they forbade criminal responsibility and punishment except for acts constituting a crime as provided by law. Along with other Soviet commentators, the chief editor of the U.S.S.R. Supreme Court bulletin interpreted this to mean the end of the concept of analogy.

A second major change was the abolition of penalties inflicted by any agency other than a court. This was taken to mean the formal end of the Special Boards of the NKVD (later the MVD), which Stalin's heirs had abolished—without publicity—in September, 1953. There were to be no more of these hated tribunals, which had functioned since 1934 to condemn citizens to labor camps on a charge of "social danger" without the necessity of adhering to the Code of Criminal Procedure or the definitions of the Criminal Code.

The third significant change in principle related to the retroactivity of criminal legislation—that is, to the question of whether penalties specified by new legislation should be imposed on those who had committed crimes before the legislation was passed. So long as the analogy concept had existed, retroactivity of legislation had no meaning, as any act could be punished, whether defined by the Code or not. With the abolition of analogy, retroactivity became an issue. The moderates won here as well, although only in establishing an attitude which could be negated or ignored under extreme provocation, as the record later was to prove.

A further change was to restate the duty of the court to find "fault" as the basis of punishment. There had previously been nothing but scorn for efforts of Soviet jurists to establish the necessity of finding fault; the dread chief of Stalin's personal secretariat, A. N. Poskrebyshev, had ridiculed these endeavors. Now there was no more doubt that punishment could not be decreed merely on the basis of an individual's belonging to a hostile class or associating with hostile elements. An individual had to be shown to intend to violate the Code or to evidence such dangerous negligence in his conduct that the Code could punish it as criminal.

The moderates likewise seemed to have carried the day on the problem of capital punishment. The fact that it was declared an "exceptional penalty" was no cause for rejoicing, since it had been described in just the same phrase in all previous codes. The new element was the narrowed field of its application. Death was now permitted only for treason, espionage, terrorism, acts of "diversion," "especially serious military crimes in wartime," and intentional killing under aggravating circumstances.

At the same time, imprisonment was limited to a new maximum of ten years for ordinary crimes and fifteen for especially serious crimes. This meant that the maximum term of twenty-five years, which had been designated in 1947 as the limit for crimes previously punishable by death, had been reduced by ten years.

A Chance To Prove Innocence

Criminal procedure was similarly revised to increase the opportunities for the defendant to prove his innocence. The burden of proof was placed upon the prosecutor, and the accused was given the right to defense counsel from the moment he received the indictment. Both of these provisions had been anticipated in the discussions of earlier years. Indeed, some of the same jurists now argued the same causes they had advocated in 1947–48.

The formulation in the Fundamentals represented something of a compromise. To the disappointment of some of the reform-minded law professors, counsel was still not to be permitted throughout the preliminary investigation, and there was to be no explicit statement that the accused was presumed innocent until proven guilty.

While on the preceding issues the West knows little of the exact dynamics and mechanics of conflicting opinions and pressures—though it is clear that diverse opinions existed and were voiced, that some issues were warmly debated even in public and certainly even more so behind closed doors, and that, at this juncture, the moderate views tended to prevail—the record is a little more ample concerning the presumption of innocence, which has turned out to be the subject of continuing debate.

The veteran spokesman for the moderates, Professor Strogovich, appeared before the Legislative Commission of the Supreme Soviet of the U.S.S.R. to urge that the presumption of innocence be stated in specific terms. He was opposed, in the Commission's hearings, by a battery of others, who included Dimitry S. Karev, Dean of the Moscow Law Faculty, I. E. Zagurskaia, Minister of Justice of the Ukrainian Republic, and Dr. M. A. Cheltsov. In a summary of the proceedings published in 1959 as an explanation to lawyers of the meaning to be given the legislative reforms, Cheltsov is reported to have said that general declarations had no place in the Code, but there should be very specific statements of rights which might be differentiated for each stage of judicial proceedings. The presumption of innocence was a general declaration, while the Code's purpose—namely, the determination of crime—would be served better if the right of the accused to counsel were defined for each stage of the proceedings.

The Commission was reported to have come to the conclusion that "legislative formulation of the presumption of innocence would provide nothing except formal [and] purely declaratory propositions that could only serve to disorient the personnel of the investigation and of the court." In short, a statement of the presumption of innocence could confuse the courts, which might not understand why the criminal was brought to trial if the investigator had not concluded that there was guilt.

The desire to vary the circumstances under which the accused might have counsel also prevailed over Strogovich's plea that counsel be permitted at *all* times, even during the entire preliminary investigation, that is, from the moment of the presentation of the charge. The Commission rejected this proposal on the ground that this would lead to a lengthening of the investigation period, because the lawyer for the defense could be expected to interpose objections and make requests for the gathering of additional evidence, and "would put fetters on the efficiency of the investigator in gathering the evidence."

The accounts show clearly that in 1958 there were among the politicians who make up the Legislative Commission of the Supreme Soviet—and even among the legally trained experts who advise them—elements who firmly opposed the views of the moderates. The final formulation in the Fundamentals reflected the compromise that was struck: "The court, procurator, investigator, and person conducting the inquiry do not have the right to shift the burden of proof onto the accused." (Article 14.) The ambiguity of this formula was illustrated by the conflicting views expressed during the (otherwise perfunctory) discussion prior to the adoption of the Fundamentals by the Supreme Soviet in December, 1958. While one deputy, A. F. Gorkin, who was also President of the Supreme Court of the U.S.S.R., praised the draft for providing that "the accused is not obliged to prove his innocence," another deputy, B. S. Sharkov, bitterly assailed "certain scholars" who, "from their ivory towers," were trying to introduce "outworn dogmas of bourgeois law such as the presumption of innocence." Proclaiming that it was patently absurd to consider an accused innocent even when the evidence against him was overwhelming, he said, "The only thing that defies understanding is, why is this not clear to these theoreticians?"

The issue was not settled, for the presumption of innocence remained in dispute until December, 1964, when an unexpected court case resolved it. That case bears examination as an example of the trend that made itself felt soon after Nikita Khrushchev's ouster in October, 1964. It will be discussed in its chronological place below.

The Balance: 1958

Virtually all the changes contained in the 1958 Fundamentals could have been—in fact, were—predicted by close observers of the Soviet scene: so much had been published prior to final enactment that the discussion on most points had prepared the observer for what occurred.

Not all the decisions had gone against radical change in official attitudes. In the Legislative Commission, one deputy had expressed the view not only that judges should assess evidence impartially but that the Fundamentals should place such a duty on police officers, investigators, and prosecutors. In short, he had hoped to overcome prosecution bias in those who dealt with a case prior to trial, and this was indeed reflected in the formulation of the Fundamentals at his request. There had always been such an obligation of prosecutors and investigators, but the concise restatement in the Fundamentals may have been evidence of increased pressure to observe the rule.

The Commission also rejected a proposal of two legal experts to exclude from the Fundamentals the long-existing requirement that the police obtain a warrant from the prosecutor before search of premises. The Commission thought that its exclusion would weaken the guarantee of the inviolability of homes contained in the Constitution. One of the experts proposed that the testimony of the accused and of the victim be excluded from the sources of evidence and, therefore, be placed outside the protection provided to witnesses by the Code. The Commission declined, declaring that it would not leave the accused without rights.

At the same time, a significant number of liberal proposals also failed to carry. As was shown above, the death sentence was not entirely abolished. If anything, the criteria for parole were tightened. In practice, the strictures against the retroactive application of laws were officially circumvented by a few specially enacted exceptions adopted by the Supreme Soviet to permit severe punishment of individuals who aroused the anger of Nikita Khrushchev.

The rights of defense counsel fell far short of what some of the moderate lawyers had hoped for. Neither a jury system nor even a significantly enlarged number of lay assessors, as some jurists had advocated, was adopted. Contrary to some reform proposals, the prosecuting agency, known as the Office of Procuracy, remained highly centralized so that no local official could influence its activities. Pretrial investigations remained under the supervision of the procurator rather than being transferred to the control of the courts themselves. The concept of "social danger" remained vague and open to potential abuse, as did the novel extragovernment machinery such as the comrades' courts and the social assemblies authorized to act against so-called parasites and hooligans.

The compromises struck were exemplified in a variety of areas, such as the problem of presumed innocence. They were similarly illustrated in the stated purposes of punishment incorporated into the Fundamentals of Criminal Law: rather than choose among conflicting theories, it listed three. Punishment according to it is, first, "a penalty for the crime committed"; second, it "aims at the correction and rehabilitation of those convicted"; and, third, "at the deterrence of those convicted as well as of others from new crimes."

The hearings on the Fundamentals and the subsequent discussion, in the latter part of 1958, showed clearly that there were different points of view struggling for recognition—basically, that of the moderates and that of those who continued to advocate severe treatment of suspects, the accused and those who were convicted. This was not a split between Communists and non-Communists: as had been true in earlier years, it was a split among party members. The moderate wing, by no means itself unanimous on all issues, found it possible to express its views loudly and with many voices, as it could not under Stalin.

One gains the impression that the moderates' views were in many cases accepted by the Legislative Commission in 1958, not because they seemed

necessary as concessions to a growing and unmanageable segment of party
—or public—opinion, but because Stalin's terror and the revelations about
it after his death had convinced a majority of opinion leaders within the
party that something needed to be done to protect themselves from the
reemergence of another dictator of a similar brand. At the same time, there
was still evident among them a fear that in some unforeseen manner crime
might get out of hand if "complete liberalization" were made the order of
the day.

The Soviet Lawyer

After forty years, the Soviet bar was still not fully trusted to participate in
the investigation; nor were judges expected by those who made the laws
either to understand what lawyers meant when they favored the presumption of innocence, or to make the sophisticated distinction between a rebut-
table presumption of innocence and an incontrovertible fact.

In no society does the lay public have full confidence in its professional
lawyers. The Russian Revolution only intensified this universal distrust.
After 1917, lawyers were at first banned from the courts, and they were
permitted to return only after experience had proved that they could help
a busy judge determine the facts in a case. But many of these men had been
lawyers before the Revolution; during the NEP they inevitably defended
the accused—including "class enemies"—against charges raised by the
state. There was a dilemma here that has baffled Soviet jurists to this day:
if the lawyer helped the defendants accused by the state, he—by definition
—acted "objectively" as an enemy of the Revolution. If he put foremost the
interests of "revolutionary expediency," he failed to fulfill the true purpose
of counsel for the defense. Communists of Stalin's persuasion were therefore
inclined to look down on lawyers as men who stood in the way of quick
realization of policies of terror, which could be effective only if merciless.
Law professors fared no better, for they tended to favor theoretical positions which seemed to the Communist leadership unrelated to the needs
of the real world of forced development.

With Stalin's death and the subsequent revelation of his atrocities, the
public temper changed, but slowly. Lenin's short career as a lawyer in
St. Petersburg at the turn of the century was retold to prove the value of
lawyers in defending the innocent worker. Medals were awarded to elderly
professors for outstanding service to the state. The living conditions of jurists
were improved, and increasing respect for legal scholarship was in the air.

In spite of the measures taken to upgrade the legal profession and to enhance the status of defense attorneys, respect for the views and services of
these experts was not yet firmly rooted in the consciousness of some top

leaders; while his position has not been fully disclosed, it is likely that Khrushchev himself was one of these. There was lacking, moreover, any tradition that would recognize the lawyer as a middleman between state and society, or between society and the individual. Indeed, even in his report to the Supreme Soviet, the chairman of the Legislative Commission argued against unnamed advocates of broader—and, it seems, fundamentally different—functions of the defense counsel:

> Soviet defense counsel must serve the great humane cause of the defense of socialist society, law, truth, and justice. . . . That is where the task of defense counsel lies, and not in the defense of illegal chicanery by the accused, which would inevitably grow into defense of a criminal and thus of crime.

The victory of the moderates rested on shaky ground, and the lawyers knew it.

The Reaction Against the Moderates

The discussions of 1958 set the stage for the reversal of policy that was to begin in 1961. The first steps in this reversal related to speculation in foreign currencies. By a federal decree of February 24, 1961, the punishment for this offense was increased by adding to the existing maximum of eight years imprisonment an additional penalty—confiscation of the offender's property. Within a month, the penalty for the same crime was increased to lengthen the maximum term from eight to fifteen years. These changes coincided with widely publicized charges of alleged foreign-currency deals by Olga Ivinskaya, who had been a close friend of Boris Pasternak, and who was rumored to have assisted in obtaining royalties for foreign publication of *Doctor Zhivago*.

These increases in penalties did not cause an international stir until a third decree, on May 5, 1961, reestablished capital punishment as a possible maximum for a list of crimes from which this penalty had been removed in 1958. These were: theft of property of the state or of public organizations in especially large amounts, counterfeiting of currency and bonds when conducted as a business, and crimes not otherwise so punishable if committed by especially dangerous repeaters. It also sought to strengthen discipline in the prison camps by introducing the death penalty for persons convicted of terrorizing convicts "on the road to reform" in the prison camps, or of committing or organizing attacks on prison guards.

This decree marked a reversion to the 1932 policy of capital punishment for economic crimes. The resistance of the moderates had been overcome. The gate was down, and the Stalinist-oriented policy-makers rushed through. Within little more than a month, they were able to obtain enactment of a decree further increasing the maximum penalty for speculation in currency or bonds as a business or in large amounts, as well as for violation of the foreign-currency regulations by second offenders: the maximum penalty for such offenses became death.

More importantly, this decree was applied retroactively to some offenders, in spite of the 1958 prohibition of retroactive application of legislation. Soviet leaders were notably cautious about the retroactive application of the decree, and they took the matter to the legislature, that is, to the Supreme Soviet, rather than leaving it to the Supreme Court. In each case of retroactive application they have since obtained a special decree of the Presidium of the Supreme Soviet authorizing its application. By virtue of the fact that special legislation is now necessary for retroactive application of law, the leadership indicated that 1958 is still to be a dividing line between Stalin's policies and those of the current day, for there must be a high policy decision in every case rather than a decision by a lowly judge. Still, the potential criminal is put on notice that his acts may be punished more severely than he had thought possible at the time of commission. An element of "limited terror," if that term can be used appropriately to describe uncertainty in the application of penalties, has been reintroduced.

Other articles of the codes were amended in fact by federal statutes to increase the severity of penalties. Thus, in subsequent months the death penalty was established as a maximum for the receiving of bribes under exceptionally aggravating circumstances; for attacks with intent to kill members of the police and of the voluntary militia; and for rape when committed by a group or by a particularly dangerous repeater, or of a minor, or when especially severe consequences followed.

Each of these increases in penalty was enacted by the federal parliament, and the republics were directed by the decrees to incorporate the new penalty in their Criminal Codes. It was in fulfillment of this obligation that the Supreme Soviet of the Russian Republic on July 25, 1962, voted to amend its own Criminal Code so as to incorporate provisions already put into effect as a result of federal legislation. The purely formal nature of the process accounts for the lack of discussion or even of explanation by the legislative committee of the R.S.F.S.R. Supreme Soviet. The record cites the words of the president:

> Is there some deputy who wishes to take the floor to speak on the report of the Legislative Commission? There are none. Let us proceed to the vote. The drafts have been circulated. Need they be read? (*Voices:* No.) . . . I present for the vote the draft law "on changes and additions to the Criminal Code of the R.S.F.S.R." Shall we vote on it as a whole? We shall vote

on it as a whole. Will those who vote for it please raise their hands? Put them down. Who is against? No one. Who abstains? No one. The law introducing changes and additions into the Criminal Code of the R.S.F.S.R. has been adopted unanimously.

Application of the death penalty for economic crimes has been frequent since the amendments. Tabulation of reports in Soviet newspapers shows that between July, 1961, and February, 1963, for instance, there were 131 death sentences reported for economic crimes, and the number has continued to rise since that time.

Reconsidering the Issues

Soviet penologists have sought to find answers to the seeming conflict between the severity of penalties introduced in 1961 and the general framework of relative leniency suggested by the 1958 reforms (and, according to some of them, confirmed by the new Communist Party Program, which declared for the first time that the Soviet state was no longer a dictatorship of the proletariat but a "state of the whole people"). They have simultaneously had to cope with the theoretical underpinning of the "voluntary" extragovernmental institutions, such as the comrades' courts, which amounted to a novel form of "social control." It was opportune for the authorities to describe these moves as steps on the road to "full Communism," which presupposed the ultimate withering of the state and institutions of compulsion—including courts, police, and other forms of duress.

The dilemma that some of the jurists faced amounted to the fact that the more utopian views—attractive though they may have been in their idealism—also opened the door to abuse: the shift from the court system and regularized "socialist legality" to "subjectivity" and informal moot courts without rules of evidence or procedure, without professional judges or attorneys, manifestly caused concern even to those jurists who could not afford to take issue publicly with what seemed to be a pet project of the Khrushchev regime.

Thus Professor Sergei Golunsky, a widely respected specialist on criminal law and procedure who had served as a public prosecutor in the U.S.S.R. and as Soviet representative among the prosecutors of war criminals in Tokyo after World War II, very carefully avoided endorsing the new policy. "The task of our legal scholarship," he declared in an article published in November, 1962, in the Law Institute's journal, "is to find criteria that would enable us to determine rightly in each particular instance whether it is expedient in that case to establish norms of law presupposing the possibility of coercion or to apply a complex of other measures of an organizational and educational character. So far, our legal science has not gone beyond general statements about the union of persuasion and coercion in Soviet law."

Golunsky summed up his position in terms of the alternatives before the Soviet public. As he put it, "It would be incorrect to interpret the proposition that during the period of developing Communism the instruments of state compulsion should be reduced in number, to mean that the apparatus of the state should be weakened, in the sense that the compulsory nature of the norms of socialist law should be weakened." The public was officially expected to assume some of the duties of maintaining order, but the state would remain strong, being reduced only in size of its civil service, that is, in this instance, in the number of paid judges, prosecutors, and police.

Others continued the discussion of sanctions, their purpose, and their efficacy. Professor O. E. Leist approved the increases in penalties for hardened criminals, justifying the death sentence by saying, "Socialist humanism cannot permit any weakening with regard to repeaters, dangerous criminals, and persons who gravely violate public order." He believed increases in severity to be "in full accord with the moral and legal conscience of the Soviet people," and cited the Communist Party Program of 1961 to the effect that "in a society that is building communism there must be no place for violation of law and for crime."

Another noted criminologist, Dr. Boris S. Nikiforov, took issue with the direction and quality of Soviet research on the causes of crime. He tried to relate the increased penalties to psychological factors of the individual criminal. This position required some reorientation of Marxist positions, and he attempted this by saying, "It would be a grave vulgarization to claim that antisocial acts, just as is true of other human conduct, are to be explained solely by social factors." He argued that individuals have relative freedom of choice in their course of conduct, and that this choice depends upon traits of character, temperament, and ease of adjustment to changing conditions. On this basis, it is possible to argue that since individuals have choice and are not prisoners of their environment, penalties can be used to influence that choice in the direction of acceptable rather than unacceptable activity.

This authority is critical of the completely hard line, for he says it would be a mistake to think, as some Soviet courts seem to be thinking, that the threat of severe punishment is the only means of controlling crime. He opposes long prison sentences because these cannot re-educate prisoners and instead tend to develop in them a bitter approach to life. He says nothing of the death penalty, but his argument suggests that he wants only sanctions that facilitate re-education. Death would be only for the incorrigibles from whose depredations society must protect itself.

Old arguments of penologists in the 1920's and the early 1930's were restored by Dr. B. S. Utevsky, another penologist, who is willing even to consider biological factors of crime. For Vyshinsky, such theories had been anathema, for everything was related by him to "social environment." Utevsky asks for study of the extent to which the serious threat of punishment has value in preventing crime. He quotes Lenin to the effect that Communists must know how to frighten, but that they must limit themselves in application of this measure when working with elements not engaged in counterrevolution. Fear can strengthen respect for law, this author says, but if it is used without education, it leads not to development of social consciousness but to nothing more than fear with no beneficial consequences.

The hard line has been more popular with the President of the Criminal College of the U.S.S.R. Supreme Court, G. Z. Anashkin. He has redefined socialist humanism as "great love for the toilers but hatred for oppressors and enslavers and for all who fill man's life with trouble and suffering." Such persons are the criminal repeaters in Soviet society. To Judge Anashkin the increase in number of the types of crime subject to capital punishment is justified by the complete intolerability of such crimes at the present moment. He takes the position rejected by the United Nations' experts when he says that the new laws "in considerable measure pursue a general preventive purpose; they have a great importance in rooting out crime that is especially dangerous to society."

Judge Anashkin's position provides contrast with the questions being asked by the professors. The judge thinks he knows the answers, while the professors want to research and rethink the matter. The split of opinion can cause no surprise to those who know the situation in other lands. It was the Lord Chief Justice of England who supported the death penalty in the early 1950's as necessary to discourage crime and who applied it in a much publicized case to two young offenders who had shot a policeman. It was the professors of the University of Cambridge who thought it necessary at that time to create a research institute to determine the deterrent effects of capital punishment, and many of their findings have been substantiated by parallel research throughout the world.

Soviet policy-makers have been dividing along similar lines for many years on the major questions of our time in the field of criminal law. During Stalin's years of tyranny, the debate was muted but not silenced completely. Some brave souls dared raise the issue of the efficacy of capital punishment in social control, but they were few. Now that Stalin is dead, the moderates speak out with louder voices. They are overruled at times by those of the judiciary and even by some from among their own number who are convinced that softness breeds contempt for state authority; but they continue to press for acceptance of their views. Curiously, their position may have been strengthened by developments in an unexpected quarter —China.

Since the summer of 1963, the Chinese Communists have castigated publicly the Soviet Communists for a wide variety of policies, including that relating to crime. The Chinese argue that by adopting the concept of the "state of the whole people" (in abandonment of the "dictatorship of the proletariat"), Soviet policy-makers have made it impossible to consider criminals as enemies of the people and have put them all into the category of wayward workers. To the Chinese, this creates a weakness that is not counterbalanced by recent Soviet decrees increasing penalties for crime. The Soviet policy-makers, in the Chinese view, have fallen into the pattern of bourgeois states in fostering the concept of presumption of innocence and definiteness in describing crime, in permitting the right of counsel after presentation of the indictment, and in prohibiting the use of the concept of analogy.

What the Chinese seem to be saying is that terror, in the sense of lack of predictability in the application of penalties, is necessary to the complete success of a true social revolution. In renouncing terror, the Soviet policy-makers have betrayed the revolution, in Chinese eyes, and initiated a trend that will lead inevitably to the degeneration of Soviet society, to its acquiescence in the continuation of black markets, speculation in stolen state property, and even a return to the private enterprise system. The acquisitive habits of centuries cannot be overcome by ordinary means, the Chinese believe, and social control is impossible through law—if that word is taken to mean what Soviet penologists now wish to read into it. In a Chinese court complete flexibility must be preserved so that the judges may terrorize those elements who seek to unseat or subvert the regime. And Peking proclaims that what is good for its society is good for all Marxist-oriented societies. In this Khrushchev and his successors refuse to acquiesce.

If the quarrel with the Chinese accelerates the modernizing of Soviet attitudes toward crime and punishment—polarizing viewpoints in this, as in other, fields—the Sino-Soviet dispute may have an unexpected but significant impact upon the lives of many millions. Already Communist leaders in eastern Europe have dared to reassert traditions inherited in their respective countries from liberal thinkers who, in earlier days, played a prominent part in determining the substance of Criminal Codes and Codes of Criminal Procedure. Hungarians, Poles, Yugoslavs, and Rumanians have been benefitting from the Sino-Soviet quarrel in various ways, not the least of which is the opportunity to restore definiteness to their codes and a chance to prove innocence in court. As in the Soviet Union, this approach is not without challenge from groups within each ruling elite who still look upon Stalin's approach as necessary to the achievement of the radical change in social and economic structure to which they are committed; some of them may indeed have favored the Chinese position but have found it politic to keep silent in view of the official condemnation of the Peking line. As a result, the liberals have had somewhat more opportunity to make themselves heard.

Post-Khrushchev Developments

During Khrushchev's tenure as First Communist Party Secretary so much was done to de-Stalinize the Soviet legal system that it was often assumed abroad that he was the principal support for the law reformers who spoke out in favor of such features as definiteness in description of crime, recognition of a presumption of innocence, and a system of punishments that would reemphasize rehabilitation of the criminal rather than his extermination. Still, events proved that not all of these reforms were adopted. Khrushchev himself favored the expansion of the comrades'-courts system and the social assemblies, both of which operated on a base that did not include a clear definition of a "social offense." Khrushchev expressed doubt as to the desirability of procedural protection for persons whom he thought clearly guilty under the circumstances of their detection. The legislature, which he presumably influenced greatly, refused to accept the statement of presumption of innocence prepared for it by the law professors; it increased penalties sharply in 1961 and soon made some of them retroactive, while enlarging at the same time the powers of the security police. The record suggests that Khrushchev believed in some moderation of Stalin's repressive measures, but that he would not accept fully the reforms urged upon him by the law professors.

Further evidence that it was Khrushchev who had influenced some of the legislative restraints on the professors and some of the judges came to light in December, 1964, and in the spring of 1965. Both events concerned the courts, which began to introduce a new measure of moderation in penology. The catalyst in the December events was again Professor Strogovich, who had played such a prominent and only partially successful part in establishing the reforms of December, 1958. In May, 1964, he published again (in *Literaturnaya gazeta*) his arguments for the presumption of innocence.[4] He supported his arguments with attacks on current Soviet practice, saying: "Frequently, the source of error of investigatory and judicial organs is the identification of the accused person with a guilty one; of a person on trial with one convicted." From this he argued that "the court may not declare the accused to be guilty if his guilt is not established beyond a doubt, however plausible it may seem," and he inveighed against the Vyshinsky doctrine of the Stalin era which permitted conviction in the event of establishment of a "high probability" of guilt. Strogovich reminded his readers, "Everyone knows the damage this 'theory' did to our society."

Having established his case in the faulty practice of the time, Strogovich proceeded to interpret the 1958 Fundamentals as incorporating the presumption of innocence, in spite of specific rejection of this phrase by the

---

[4] The translations of quoted material to the end of this chapter are reprinted, with minor changes, from *The Current Digest of the Soviet Press,* published weekly at Columbia University; copyright 1964 and 1965. By permission.

A 1959 divorce case being tried before a judge and two lay assessors in a Leningrad People's Court.

M. Cheremnykh in *Krokodil*

Лекарство горькое, но для здоровья необходимое.

A spoonful from the bottle labeled "Criticism" is identified in the caption as "Bitter medicine, but essential for good health." The label reads, "For gullibility, prattling, complacency, conceit, sycophancy, bureaucratism, and other dangerous maladies."

E. Shcheglov in *Krokodil*, November 10, 1964

— Обещаю жить в мире с моей соседкой. Слова больше не скажу об этой дряни!

The reformed defendant in court: "I promise to live in peace with my neighbor. I won't say another word about that bitch!"

Boris Leo in *Krokodil*, May 30, 1961

Не трогать! Смертельно!

The drawing labeled "Don't touch! Lethal!" shows an electrified strongbox displaying the Decree on Strengthening the Struggle Against Especially Dangerous Crimes, from which it cites the provision restoring the death sentence.

legislators, and he said that this presumption was implied by the right to counsel guaranteed in the Constitution. He noted that "there are also pseudo jurists who believe that the defense counsel merely draws out the investigation and the court proceedings unnecessarily and hinders the exposure of criminals." He noted in refutation of this position that defendants had in numerous instances confessed crimes they never committed because they had no counsel. He concluded that he had touched on only a few of the many problems of judicial error, which can and must be avoided under "socialist legality."

Strogovich's renewed pressure for open recognition of the presumption of innocence might have attracted little attention had it not been followed in August, 1964, by a reply written for the same journal by an assistant prosecutor from Siberia. He attacked Strogovich and argued that the preliminary investigation was the stage at which criminal guilt is established, and the courts only subsequently verify the findings. He took a position much like that of many non-Soviet authors who have commented on the Soviet approach to the preliminary investigation under Stalin, for he said,

> The law gives the investigatory agencies the right to bring charges against someone, to interrogate him as the accused, and hence to recognize him as guilty. The prosecutor brings the person to trial, and in criminal proceedings accuses an individual who is already guilty in the eyes of the investigatory agencies, i.e., of the authorities. The court merely verifies to what extent the individual brought to trial and accused by the prosecutor is guilty and whether or not this offender deserves criminal punishment.

The prosecutor's attack on Strogovich was published in the same issue with a reply from the professor, restating his position of many years' standing, reasserting the essential supremacy of the court, and warning against the prejudicial consequences of the prosecutor's views. Strogovich was supported by a columnist for the government newspaper *Izvestia*, O. Chaikovskaia, who on September 9, 1964, attacked the Siberian prosecutor's views as a product of the Stalin era and added, "The ignorance with which we are dealing here is malignant. In the years of the personality cult they would have come for a man in the night and by the morning he would already be called an enemy of the people."

The support for Strogovich expanded with an article from the President of the Supreme Court of the U.S.S.R., A. F. Gorkin, published in *Izvestia* on December 2, 1964. He had always fought for the principle and had been willing to say at the time of adoption of the 1958 Fundamentals that they incorporated it, even though they had excluded it in so many words. Now he declared, "In present-day conditions . . . the strengthening of the citizen's rights and of the inviolability of the person, freedom, honor, and dignity of man constitute one of the most important demands of the party."

Referring to the exchange between Strogovich and the Siberian prosecutor he stated, "Some investigatory and court officials obviously underestimate the role of Soviet defense counsel. Correct jurisprudence and the most complete and all-round quest for truth by the courts demand a qualified accusation and a corresponding defense of the accused." He denounced his lower courts by adding, "Time and again, the norms of criminal procedure are being violated; not all the evidence in a given case is verified or it is only superficially or one-sidedly examined. . . . Yes, there are even cases of unfounded conviction. In court sessions, sometimes tendencies become apparent revealing a priori support of accusations."

Gorkin's intervention in the dispute was the first from a very high official after Khrushchev's ouster, and it suggests that a man who had expressed the position as early as 1958 was either authorized to speak out by the new party leaders or felt the time was ripe to use his weight in favor of measures to oppose remnants of Stalinist thinking among some elements of the apparatus in charge of social order.

Strogovich returned to the journal in which he had previously written to hail the support he was getting, and noted that he was receiving letters from readers. One from the Volga town of Kazan said, "Guilt is above all an objective category. The guilt of the criminal begins the moment he commits the crime. The criminal is guilty, not because he has been convicted or brought before a court but because he has committed a crime." Strogovich thought this shocking and chose the occasion also to attack Dr. Cheltsov, who had testified contrary to his view before the Legislative Commission of the Supreme Soviet in 1958 when it was holding hearings on the presumption of innocence. He quoted Cheltsov as having said that a judge naturally tends to see a criminal in every accused before him.

In refutation of this view Strogovich added, "There is one further, extremely important quality of the court that has outstanding importance: the independence of the judiciary and the subordination of judges exclusively to the law. Neither officials nor public organizations may interfere with judicial decisions." Public organizations in Soviet terminology include not only trade unions, cooperative associations and the Communist Youth League, but also the Communist Party. This was not as bold a statement as it might seem, for the party had itself told its local secretaries never to interfere in court work, and this order had been issued in 1954 to the Tula party organization. It stated that the party's function was to provide political guidance and control over courts but not to dictate court sentences. It may be that Strogovich knew that the order was being ignored in some places, and it required restating at what seemed to be an opportune moment when the pendulum was swinging his way.

The Strogovich article was followed by an informative account by the paper's editors that to their surprise the dispute had moved from the pages of the press to the courts. The Siberian prosecutor had sued the newspaper *Izvestia* and its columnist for libel under a provision introduced into the civil law in December, 1961, and never previously used, at least to the knowledge of foreigners. The people's court of Moscow had decided on December 14 that there was no basis for recovery of damages as the prosecutor's position was in conflict with the principles of "socialist legality," and that the columnist's characterization of the prosecutor's views as the manifestation of ignorance was correct. Therefore, he deserved the opprobrium he had received.

The matter was not closed, for Strogovich wrote again and restated his position in response to further articles by individuals from the prosecutor's side who feared being handicapped in their work by the emerging trend. His hand was strengthened, however, by an article published in the March, 1965, issue of the law journal of the Academy of Sciences' Institute of Law revealing as never before the full extent of Vyshinsky's condoning, if not supporting, the work of the security police during Stalin's epoch. This article, written by the Deputy Procurator General of the U.S.S.R., N. V. Zhogin, revealed that when Vyshinsky's subordinates in the Office of the Procurator General of the U.S.S.R. had complained about the violations of the procedural code by the security police, he had not defended them, and had even conducted what was described as a "mass purge" in which "many prominent workers in the Office of the Procuracy who had tried in one way or another to mitigate repressive measures and stop the lawlessness and arbitrariness were arrested and subsequently perished."

Stalin's laws of 1934 and 1937 relieving courts of the necessity of observing various procedural protections in the event of counterrevolutionary crimes were justified by Vyshinsky, so the 1965 article stated, on the ground that security required such departures. The work of the Special Boards of the Ministry of Internal Affairs were said to have functioned with his direct participation and to have received from him cases for which the evidence was insufficient for a conviction in court. He is said to have required that counterrevolutionary intent be imputed to all cases of arson and those having to do with destruction of the harvest, and to have scorned procedural guarantees by approving illegal measures taken to force suspects to confess their guilt.

Zhogin ended with an appeal for complete exposure of the harmful theories and concepts of Vyshinsky as a contribution to the strengthening of socialist legality and of the defense of the rights and the lawful interests of citizens.

The Supreme Court of the R.S.F.S.R. at the same time published in its March, 1965, bulletin a November, 1964, case on the death sentence indicating that it was to be used with discrimination in cases of economic crime. One Petrov had been convicted of swindling state property as dispatcher of a railway warehouse. He accomplished this by organizing a conspiracy, together with the managers of warehouses and directors of retail stores, in which the money received for goods distributed by them was paid over to the members of the conspiracy. Petrov had been found guilty of forty-seven cases of misappropriation and had received personally rubles equivalent to nearly $11,000.

The guilt of the accused had been proved satisfactorily at the trial in the opinion of the Supreme Court, but the sentence of death seemed to the Supreme Court to have been without foundation. It was noted that Petrov had admitted his guilt and had turned state's witness against the others. In addition, he was a first offender. Under the circumstances the death sentence was not necessary. The death sentence was reduced to fifteen years imprisonment.

Decision-Making and the Law

The evidence suggests that Khrushchev's successors are prepared to press further than Khrushchev in establishing procedures that give the accused a chance to state his case and in moderating the severe penalties associated with his relatively primitive ideas of how to discourage crime. This does not mean that the legal scholars can make their voice effective on every issue or that it can be expected that the severe sanctions introduced by the Khrushchev-inspired legislation of 1961 will be repealed, but courts may well have started on a new direction in the 1965 case of Petrov that will cause them to choose penalties less than death when the circumstances of crime or its revelation merit moderation.

Soviet courts can be expected to continue to differ, as they were shown to have differed in the cases presented at the outset of this chapter, on the desirable "line" for Soviet penal policy. Their members, Communists specializing in social controls, will make the decisions. They may establish their policy changes either by court order, or they may ask for new legislation under their constitutional right of legislative initiative, if they think dramatic change in policies desirable. The law professors may also make their demands for procedural reforms more vocal through their specialized press and even in the national newspapers. Change is in the air in the U.S.S.R., and these scholars may think the occasion ripe to press for adoption of points they have not yet been able to incorporate in the codes.

The decision-making process will be affected by considerations other than philosophical views on "socialist humanism" or sociological studies on the efficacy of fear as a deterrent. Not all crime is caused by need or greed, as every penologist knows, but the economic offenses currently punished by the most severe penalties in the Soviet Union bear more than casual relationship to the economic situation there. Shortages, caused by poor harvests, inadequate organization of production, and allocation of resources to military supplies, moon shots, and foreign aid provide the perfect circumstances for black market operations in stolen state stocks. A sharp increase in consumer goods could reduce incentives to crime and the justification for severe penalties to strike fear into the hearts of those who contemplate illegal acts.

True, there are aspects of Soviet life to which other authors have already pointed that cannot but influence the prospects for change: the lack of long tradition of a judiciary steeped in the protection of the rights of accused; the dangers of abuse and prejudice inherent in the preliminary investigation, to which Soviet authors have given much attention; the long tradition of reliance on security police to perform investigative functions reserved elsewhere for state officials of the standing of magistrates; the relatively low prestige of the professional lawyer and his nearly fifty years of experience in a system that has suggested that he be cautious in the defense; and finally what might be called a "vested interest," on the part of some and perhaps many bureaucrats within the state and party apparatus, in arbitrary action without regard to the legal provisions designed to restrain their activity.

Yet there is room for expectation that a change is in the offing. The law professors are not alone. Strogovich has been joined not only by many of his colleagues, but by the press representing the generalists of the party. There is even a willingness today to go beyond the simplistic thinking of Stalinist Marxists who laid all crime to capitalism, first as it existed during the period of the New Economic Policy of the 1920's and thereafter as "capitalism in the minds of men." Judge Anashkin, whose earlier article has already been cited as evidence of judicial attitudes toward punishment of hardened criminals, published a paper (in *Izvestia,* March 3, 1965) opposing harsh treatment for rowdies, noting that their antisocial attitudes had been caused mainly by poor upbringing, which he thought beyond the reach of strict law or harsh justice. He noted what has so frequently been noted in recent years, that 80 percent of crimes of rowdiness are committed in a state of intoxication, and he made no mention of the previously popular formula of crime as a survival of capitalist mentality. In this article, he showed that the judiciary was catching up with the thinking of the law professors as it had been expressed some years earlier.

"Socialist legality" has gained considerably in stature since Stalin's time. It is still developing under pressures both from within the U.S.S.R. and from abroad, especially from the sister states that have accepted Marxian socialism as a way of life while holding persistently to the legal traditions of humanism inherited from their forebears who shared in the thinking underlying the French Declaration of the Rights of Man as it was formulated in 1789. These men have rejected the property concepts of the French bourgeoisie, but not the humanism of their philosophy, and Soviet policy-makers are now sharing in a debate inspired by such pressures. It is to this debate that many Soviet intellectuals look for their complete liberation from the thinking of Stalin's time. The Soviet youth think that return to the past is out of the question in view of the current state of Soviet public opinion. Their elders who remember Stalin are not so sure, for they know that those who shared his views have not yet passed completely from political life, but they hope that, barring some catastrophe requiring the mobilization of resources to meet a security threat of obviously large proportions, the current trend will continue and become so firmly imbedded that a reversal will become as impossible as the young generation now thinks.

Study Questions

1. Have the leaders of the Soviet system of government made use of law as the West understands it in attempting to control and discourage crimes of violence against the person?

2. Do professional lawyers play any part in the determination of policy relating to the control of criminals, or is the decision solely that of Communist party chiefs?

3. Can you see any reason why Soviet policy-makers take murderers to court rather than shooting them on the spot or after a police investigation to make sure that they committed the act without the assistance of others who ought also to be punished?

4. What alternatives can you imagine to a policy of frightening potential criminals away from the commission of a crime by a severe Criminal Code providing the death penalty for a wide variety of crimes endangering society?

5. Has the socialist type of society that Soviet leaders profess to be directing had any impact on the types of problems faced by penologists in any society wishing to limit the commission of crimes?

Selected Bibliography

Materials for this analysis of Soviet law have been drawn largely from the Russian-language sources, as they alone keep up to date. Many of these are, however, published with delays. Periodical literature from Soviet journals is published weekly in English in the *Current Digest of the Soviet Press*. This can be supplemented by translations from the quarterly *Soviet Law and Government* and *The Soviet Review,* the latter two published in New York by the International Arts and Sciences Press. Translations of codes also appear in the latter's series entitled *Soviet Statutes and Decisions,* the first two numbers of which contain translations of both the Criminal Code and the Code of Criminal Procedure of the R.S.F.S.R. currently in force.

Relatively popular descriptions of the Soviet legal system appear in standard political science texts, such as Merle Fainsod, *How Russia Is Ruled,* 2nd ed. (Cambridge, Mass.: Harvard University Press, 1963) and John N. Hazard, *The Soviet System of Government,* 3rd ed. (Chicago: University of Chicago Press, 1964). Analysis of the historical and political influences upon which the Soviet legal system is based is provided by Harold J. Berman, *Justice in the U.S.S.R.,* rev. ed. (Cambridge, Mass.: Harvard University Press, 1963), while the practice as evidenced by 150 judicial decisions is set forth in John N. Hazard, *Law and Social Change in the U.S.S.R.* (London: Stevens, 1953). Translations of these decisions appear in John N. Hazard and Isaac Shapiro, *The Soviet Legal System* (Dobbs Ferry, N.Y.: Oceana, 1962).

Popular Soviet books in English on the Soviet legal system are *Fundamentals of Soviet Law,* edited and published in Moscow in 1960 by Peter S. Romashkin, and *Soviet State Law* by Andrei I. Denisov and M. Kirichenko, published in Moscow in 1960 and in New York in 1962 by International Publications Service. A highly readable account of some fifty Soviet trials observed by a young American political scientist who was at the time a foreign exchange student in Moscow is George Feifer, *Justice in Moscow* (New York: Simon and Schuster, 1964).

For more technical accounts of the system, the reader may turn to Kazimierz Grzybowski, *Soviet Legal Institutions: Doctrines and Social Functions* (Ann Arbor, Mich.: University of Michigan Press, 1962) or John N. Hazard, *Settling Disputes in Soviet Society* (New York: Columbia University Press, 1960). The role of the Office of the Procurator General is set forth in Glenn G. Morgan, *Soviet Administrative Legality: The Role of the Attorney General's Office* (Stanford, Calif.: Stanford University Press, 1962). Current trends are analyzed by legal experts from the United States and abroad in two special issues of periodicals, *The Illinois Law Forum* for Spring, 1964, and *Problems of Communism* for March–April, 1965.

7

Khrushchev and the Military

Raymond L. Garthoff

Cheered by the successful conclusion of the nuclear test-ban treaty and other agreements that seemed to herald a *détente* in Soviet-American relations, Chairman Khrushchev told the Supreme Soviet in mid-December, 1963, that his government was again considering a "reduction in the numerical strength of our armed forces." He coupled this statement with the announcement that the Soviet military budget (or at least its public part) would be reduced from 13.9 to 13.3 billion rubles for 1964.

While, under Soviet conditions, no one could take public exception to his pronouncement, leading spokesmen for the Soviet military establishment soon made it clear that they were distinctly unhappy about the projected decrease in the size of the armed forces. The nonmilitary press repeatedly referred—with approval—to the Khrushchev statement, but the military papers, such as *Red Star* (in Russian, *Krasnaya zvezda*), the daily newspaper of the Soviet armed forces, carefully avoided mentioning it and the public statements of virtually all senior military commanders studiously ignored the question of possible force reductions.

Less than ten days after the Khrushchev speech, the commander of the Soviet ground forces, Marshal Vasily I. Chuikov, published an article that at first glance might have seemed unrelated to the issues raised by Khrushchev. However, a closer look showed that Chuikov was actually challenging the Premier's views. Citing a rarely noted message in which Stalin, in 1920, had accused the party leadership of throwing away hard-won military victories, Chuikov in effect argued that Western countries, even while building up their nuclear arsenals (much as the Soviet Union was doing), were "not only not liquidating ground forces but on the contrary were

steadily developing them." Chuikov implied that experience had taught the
NATO countries—and presumably must teach the Soviet Union—that
nuclear weapons and missiles alone cannot win (or prevent) a future war.
Although Chuikov acknowledged the importance of strategic missile forces
in a world conflict, he concluded that "in modern conditions the ground
forces continue to be not only a necessary but also a highly important
integral part of the armed forces." Any experienced reader of the Soviet
press was sure to interpret this as a dissent from Khrushchev's plan to
reduce the size of the Soviet armed forces.

This was, of course, by no means the first time that disagreement with
Khrushchev's policies had been expressed (or implied) by some of the
military commanders. Indeed, the whole Khrushchev decade (1954–64)
had witnessed considerable flux—cooperation, conflict, and compromise—
between the civil and military leaderships, as well as sharp ups and downs
in the role of the military in policy-making.

A study of the relationships between Khrushchev and the Soviet marshals
offers considerable insight into the interconnection of Soviet military
policies and Soviet political and economic policies. Though Khrushchev
was ultimately deposed, the fundamental problems of Soviet civil-military
relations have remained, and the history of these problems during the
Khrushchev era provides a window for looking into the Soviet political
process as a whole.

"Politics" in the Soviet Union includes both conflicts among institutions
contending for economic resources and competition for personal power.
Although internal political conflicts erupt into the open only from time to
time, they are constantly active beneath the deceptively calm surface of
Soviet affairs; the military as an interested institution and its leaders as its
representatives and as individuals play a part in the political process. Ordinarily, the military are concerned chiefly with meeting their requirements in
the process of resource allocation. But when political differences among
civilian party and government leaders become sharp, the military or its
leaders may become involved, and the course of events may reflect an
awareness that the military (and sometimes the police) have unique potential power through their monopoly of weapons.

One of the most important Soviet issues concerns the essence of relations
between the political and the military: how much power shall each be allowed in the affairs of the others? Khrushchev's arms-reduction plan is a case
in point: was it—or should it have been—primarily a political or a military
problem?

The supremacy of the Communist Party in the Soviet Union has been
axiomatic since 1917. Within as well as outside the armed forces, the party
has maintained tight control. The assignment of political commissars to
each low-level military unit has been abolished, but there has remained in

the military establishment an autonomous political administration responsible only to the party's Central Committee. There is also a counter-intelligence network operated by the secret police. Both these organs, paralleling the regular command hierarchy, were developed to instill and ensure the loyalty of the military to the system.

The drive of the professional military men—as of other groups of experts in Soviet society—for greater autonomy, that is, for greater freedom from political interference, has been a perennial feature of Soviet civil-military relations. It was bound to be resumed after Stalin's death.

The "thaw" that allowed some expression of divergent views after Stalin's death was also bound to extend to the areas of military doctrine and policies. Here the problems included a definition of the very nature of war: how adequate was the traditional view of war as a continuation of policy by other means? What was the significance of the destructive power of nuclear weapons? What were the ideological and political implications of the new awareness that in a nuclear war there could be no "winners" in the usual sense?

If, on the one hand, this complex included the pervasive problem—familiar in other countries as well—of the roles of nuclear and conventional weapons, on the other it acquired a special coloration from Russia's traditional position as a continental power. The land army has remained the dominant military service in Russia despite changes in technology and political relations. Although considerable attention was paid to the development of nuclear weapons, missiles, and long-range aircraft after World War II, the ground forces remained dominant in the Soviet high command, and they continued to claim a large share of Soviet military resources. Because of the buildup during the Korean War (1950–53) the Soviet armed forces at the time of Stalin's death numbered nearly six million men—most of them in the ground forces, which comprised some 175 divisions.

This supremacy was inevitably challenged on both military and political grounds. Thus, the debate of the Khrushchev era involved many problems: the sufficiency of the current Soviet defense posture; the possible role of surprise in future wars and the likelihood of short or protracted wars; the relative importance of the deterrent or the war-performance value of weapons; the formulation of a "winning" strategy against the major potential enemy of the U.S.S.R., the United States. Closely related to these problems were the size of Soviet armed forces; the size of the Soviet military budget; and the relative priority commanded by the military within the whole military-industrial complex. This last problem, often referred to as the struggle over resource allocation, of course involved many people and institutions outside the military; it was also, for a number of years, one of the most visible and most persistent areas of conflict among the Soviet elite.

It is not surprising that the political views of Soviet military leaders reflected, at least in part, their institutional commitments and functional orientations. Where these views clashed with those of political leaders—as they did, for instance, regarding American intentions, disarmament proposals, and military expenditures—they revealed potential weaknesses in the political fabric. But the marshals were nonetheless increasingly inclined to assume that the military had to be heard before important policy decisions were made. The problem arises whether, given the broad spectrum of opinions both among the political leaders and among the marshals, there was or could be a congruence—or an alliance—between those civil and military leaders whose views or interests seemed to invite similar policies.

While many of the key issues debated during the Khrushchev era might have been predicted, the extent to which they were articulated or publicly aired, the sophistication of the argument, and the alignments of individuals, issues, and institutions could not have been foretold—and neither, of course, could the results.

The Legacy of Stalin

Soviet military doctrine before 1953 was little more than a canonization of military thought as it had developed during the war. The only accepted foundation had been laid down by Stalin in an order of February, 1946, which declared that "the whole preparation of the army" and "the development of military science" in the future "must be conducted on the basis of a skillful mastering of the experience of the recent war." For nearly a decade, Soviet experience in the war did become the basis of doctrine, and —most significantly—it was virtually forbidden to develop military thought on any other basis.

A misguided and intensive censorship prevented discussion in the military press of atomic weapons, missiles, and other new weapons. Stalin did, of course, move ahead with the development of new weaponry. But the oppressive atmosphere of postwar Russia was hardly conducive to novel interpretations of the doctrinal implications of developments in military technology. Stalin's injunction to rely on Soviet experience in the war served also to sanctify his own alleged military genius in wartime strategic planning, command, and doctrinal formulation. Consequently, there was room for no creative thinking that would appear to conflict with "Stalinist military science." A year *before* Khrushchev's famous "secret speech" in February, 1956, denouncing the cult of Stalin's personality, an authoritative General Staff journal had admitted: "It is necessary to say frankly that in connection with the cult of the individual no science sinned so much as did military science." (*Military Thought,* March, 1955.) In short, the years from 1945 to 1953 were a period of stagnation in Soviet military doctrine.

The Malenkov Period, 1953–55

Politics

Within a week after Stalin's death the former Ministries of War and the Navy were merged into a new Ministry of Defense. The "political" Marshal Nikolai Bulganin was placed in charge, but his three First Deputies (Soviet political arithmetic is flexible) were all top professional officers: Marshals of the Soviet Union Georgi Zhukov and Alexander Vasilevsky, and Admiral Nikolai Kuznetsov.

In the next few years, the military acquired increased importance simply because of the change in the relationships of other Soviet institutions. A drastic decline in the importance of the secret police followed the purge of Lavrenty Beria in June, 1953. It has been rumored that Marshals Zhukov and Konev personally played a role in Beria's arrest; whether the rumor is true or not is less important, however, than the fact that the military *did* acquire new status after the decline of the police. The same Plenum of the Central Committee that sanctioned the arrest of Beria named Zhukov to Beria's seat on the Committee. During the next three months, at least ten senior generals and admirals were promoted, in the first series of high-level promotions since the end of World War II, and military men in disgrace were rehabilitated (Chief Marshal of Aviation Novikov, for example, was released from a forced-labor camp). Finally, the power of the political officers in the armed forces was gradually curbed.

All this did not necessarily presage a change in real political power. In fact, although such a change *did* occur between 1953 and 1955, it resulted from a struggle for power between two *political* factions rather than from a divergence over strictly military problems.

One of the first indications of opposition to the "Malenkov line" was the publication in *Military Thought* (September and October, 1953) of articles emphasizing heavy-industry requirements for defense and referring only in passing to the new consumer-goods orientation of the Soviet economy. By late 1954, Khrushchev and his associates had launched a campaign against the Malenkov policy and endorsed a return to higher investment in heavy industry; the military press supported this drive and stressed, in addition, that continued priority for heavy industry was required in order to raise the level of armaments.

In 1953 and 1954, Malenkov reduced the announced annual military budget, and actual military spending (as estimated abroad) fell still further. Late in 1954, when deliberations on the 1955 budget began, the conflict was intensified. Military men began to emphasize in public speeches the need for constant attention to military preparedness, while Malenkov and several of his associates, in March and again in November, 1954, pointedly and unprecedentedly failed to give it that attention.

The February, 1955, Plenum of the Central Committee removed Malenkov from the premiership and replaced him with Bulganin. It also adopted a budget for 1955 that raised total military appropriations by 12 percent and increased the proportion allotted to heavy industry. Malenkov's practice of dipping into the state reserves (stockpiles of food and materials) to accelerate the consumer-goods program was also stopped after his fall. "Reserves comprise our might and strengthen the defense capability of the country," Bulganin reassured the military in his first address as Prime Minister. "To increase the state reserves is . . . our most important task."

With the triumph of Khrushchev and Bulganin over Malenkov at the February Plenum, Marshal Zhukov became Minister of Defense. A month later, twelve generals and marshals were promoted, six of them to the highest rank, Marshal of the Soviet Union. Soon six more were advanced to General of the Army. Among those promoted in 1955 were a conspicuously large number (from a group that we will later call the "Southern clique") likely to have been included at the behest of Khrushchev.

Thus, at the close in early 1955 of the initial Beria-Malenkov phase of the succession struggle after Stalin's death, the military leadership seemed to have won its place in the new post-Stalin order.

The Renaissance in Military Theory

The most important element in the revitalization of Soviet military thinking after Stalin was the belated recognition of the significance of the revolution in military technology. In 1954, the Soviet military leaders began systematically to inform themselves (and lower-ranking Soviet officers as well) of the nature and effects of new weapons and technical developments, and of their implications for military doctrine.

A debate on "the laws of military science," conducted from late 1953 to early 1955 in the pages of a confidential General Staff journal, *Military Thought,* disclosed the lively interest of military personnel in questions of military theory, but it also revealed their difficulties in breaking with the Stalinist concepts that had long been impressed upon them. For example, one major issue was whether "the laws of military science" apply equally to the armies of socialist and capitalist countries. The conclusion reached was that the same laws do apply, but superiority in understanding and in utilizing the laws was still attributed to the socialist system and Marxist-Leninist leadership of the Soviet Union.

The main issue in the debate, however, was whether military science should limit its focus to the study of the "laws of war as armed conflict" or should also embrace a whole complex of politico-military questions. The conclusion was that military science should concern itself primarily with the narrower range of technical problems, while of course retaining as its base general Marxist-Leninist views on war as a political process.

The Soviet Union has never expressed military doctrine in a list of "principles of war," as Western armies usually do. It has, however, enumerated the elements that, Soviet military men have argued, in the last analysis are decisive in war. From 1942 until 1956, these factors were officially imbedded in a formulation by Stalin, who had labeled them "the permanently operating factors" that "decide the course and outcome of wars." Stalin had first referred to these "factors" early in the war to boost Soviet morale, since they were contrasted with transitory factors such as surprise or advance mobilization. During the postwar Stalin years, discussions of military science and strategy inevitably invoked this formulation, and they rarely went beyond it. During the doctrinal debates of the mid-1950's, the basic concept was reiterated, but after 1956 the stereotyped formulation of "permanently operating factors" was generally discarded. Considerable attention continued to be given, however, to the "decisive" factors themselves.

The discussion of the key factors in war was accompanied by consideration of a factor formerly considered "transitory," surprise. After early 1955, it was recognized that in a nuclear war surprise *could* be decisive. However, it was also concluded that surprise alone was no foundation for a *blitzkrieg* ("lightning") victory, even in the thermonuclear era. Surprise could be decisive against an enemy neither vigilant nor ready for combat. But against a prepared major power, surprise could not succeed if one did not also possess superiority in the decisive (i.e., underlying political, military, and economic) factors. *Blitzkrieg* was, therefore, specifically rejected as a feasible strategy for either side.

At this same time, the even more important concept of "preemptive" action in the case of an enemy attack was developed. This concept was not discussed in the open military press, but the classified discussions in *Military Thought* make clear that preemptive action was specifically distinguished from deliberate preparation for and initiation of a preventive war. A preemptive strike was defined as the last-minute seizure of the initiative in order to prevent a surprise attack planned by the enemy. It meant forestalling a surprise attack at a time of the *enemy's* choosing.

In this early post-Stalin period, the doctrinal adjustments to the nuclear age did not question the belief that a major war would be long, that it would require the combined operations of all military components, or that it would be waged in large-scale campaigns. Soviet military doctrine continued to stress the need for such campaigns, in which victory would finally be won by destroying the enemy's armed might and then by having conventional forces seize and occupy his territory. Despite the new emphasis on nuclear weapons, they were not regarded as "ultimate weapons." Soviet military thought continued to be conservative.

The Zhukov-Khrushchev Alliance, 1955–57

The alliance between Khrushchev and Zhukov began with the downfall of Malenkov in February, 1955, and lasted until October, 1957, when Khrushchev concluded that Zhukov was usurping, or might usurp, too much power. (The question of equal power, of course, never arose: Khrushchev was always the more powerful of the two.) It was an alliance of mutual convenience, born of common opposition to the policies of Malenkov, in which each enjoyed the other's support in consolidating his hold on matters of his own direct concern. Khrushchev was building his personal power within the party and the power of the party within the state; Zhukov, as the new Minister of Defense, was developing Soviet military thought and building a modern military establishment. All was well while they had a common enemy against whom each felt he needed the other, and for a time they were able to follow a policy of "live and let live" toward their separate bases of power. But once their common enemy had been disposed of, they clashed over the practical problem of the dividing line between the authority of the party in military affairs and the autonomy of the military in its own domain.

Various maneuvers by military and political figures were undertaken during the period of Khrushchev's rise in the mid-1950's. Although Khrushchev's role as a wartime leader was not heavily stressed until after the defeat of the Antiparty Group that included Malenkov and Molotov, and Zhukov's fall from power, in 1957, efforts to rewrite history to Khrushchev's advantage began as early as 1955. References began to appear, particularly in political articles, to Khrushchev's role at Stalingrad, while references to Malenkov's presence there, frequent in studies written in 1953 and 1954, had become rare by 1955. During the first half of 1955, in particular, political figures sent by the party to the front during the war were singled out for praise—a device intended, among other things, to divert attention from the wartime State Defense Committee in Moscow, of which Malenkov and Beria had been key members. Most often, praise of living persons was restricted to Khrushchev and Bulganin. On one highly important occasion, however, Marshals Zhukov, Vasilevsky, Sokolovsky, Biryuzov, and Admiral Kuznetsov studiously avoided reference to any living political figures.

Through the late 1940's and 1950's remarkably few differences between members of the Soviet military establishment and between the military and the political leadership over strategy were articulated. Even when new doctrinal approaches were undertaken after Stalin's death, there was apparently no serious conflict of opinion in the armed forces. In 1955, however, a dispute did develop over the value of a modern, conventional ocean-navy. Both Zhukov (and his army associates) and Khrushchev decided that investment in a conventional navy should be cut sharply, and Admiral of the Fleet Nikolai Kuznetsov, who objected, was replaced by Admiral Sergei Gorshkov. Construction of new cruisers was halted, and the uncompleted vessels (as well as obsolete battleships and cruisers) were later scrapped.

Changes in organization and personnel suggest that there may also have been disputes over the operational control of long-range ballistic rockets and over future manned-bomber programs. In 1956, Chief Marshal of Aviation Pavel Zhigarev was relieved and named Chief of the Civil Air Fleet to manage the development of modern jet transports built instead of bombers. Long-range missile development was organized under Chief Marshal of Artillery Mitrofan Nedelin. Later, in 1960, a separate Strategic Rocket Forces command was organized, headed by Marshal Nedelin (until his death in an unexplained accident, which was in fact due to a missile failure). A parallel unified strategic Air Defense Command, amalgamating the detection and warning service, fighter interceptors, and antiaircraft artillery and missiles, had been created as early as 1955, apparently without provoking disagreement.

The Twentieth Party Congress in February, 1956, marked both the endorsement of past leaders and policies—in the military establishment as well as in the party—and the initiation of new ones. Marshal Zhukov became the first professional officer to be made a candidate member of the Presidium of the party. Zhukov, Konev, Sokolovsky, and Vasilevsky were retained as members of the Central Committee; Malinovsky and Moskalenko were added. Twelve other military leaders were made candidate members, a considerable decrease from the military's former representation. One revealing fact was that no senior officers of the party's Main Political Administration in the armed forces were made members or candidate members. This was unprecedented and shows their decline in importance under Zhukov's administration of the Ministry of Defense.

It was of political significance that the Congress selected for political office a number of military men acceptable to Khrushchev. In the course of World War II there had been extensive contact among various political and military leaders, and strong ties (and antipathies) sometimes resulted. For example, the important "Southern clique" of marshals and generals originated during the famous Stalingrad campaign in late 1942 and lasted through and beyond the war. This group developed a resentment against the wartime Moscow Headquarters (*Stavka*) headed by Zhukov, Vasilevsky, and Kuznetsov. It happened that the senior political adviser with the Stalingrad front was Lieutenant General Nikita Khrushchev—while the chief advisers around Stalin included Malenkov, Beria, and Bulganin. The Twentieth Congress, in addition to raising Malinovsky and Moskalenko to the Central Committee (the latter had not even been a candidate previously), gave candidate status to Bagramyan, Chuikov, and Yerëmenko—all from the "Southern clique."

Nonetheless, although Khrushchev showed some favor to personal friends and political supporters, the Khrushchev-Zhukov alliance remained in force during the Congress. In his "secret speech" denouncing the cult of Stalin, Khrushchev praised the wartime commanders in general and Marshal Zhukov in particular, presenting himself as Zhukov's loyal defender against Stalin's hints that he was not a good soldier. The military were gratified by the opportunity afforded them by the deflated Stalin image to further the revision of military history and doctrine, and by the quiet rehabilitation of military men whom Stalin had purged.

During the year preceding and the year following the Twentieth Party Congress, the military managed to score—quite undramatically—a major success. The authority of the professional commanders and of professional military theory was largely freed from political interference. In late 1955, the position of political officer at the company level was abolished, and senior officers were permitted to meet their compulsory political education by what was euphemistically termed individual study. But the relationship between the party organizations and the professional commanders needed clarification. Accordingly, in April, 1957, by decree of the Central Committee, "Instructions to the CPSU Organizations in the Soviet Army and Navy" were issued, replacing those issued ten years before. This decree, and an accompanying order from the Minister of Defense, marked a compromise between military and party views on the division of authority. The compromise did not, however, settle the issue; various commentaries still emphasized the restrictions either on the political organs or on the officers, depending on the point of view of the author.

At all times, of course, the four lines of command—the professional military, the political administration, the party organization in the armed forces, and the secret-police counterintelligence—extended from the Ministry of Defense itself into every battalion of the armed forces. By 1957, the last three had all declined in influence, both absolutely and in relation to the professional command cadres.

The Fall of the Antiparty Group—and Zhukov

In June, 1957, the various opponents of Khrushchev in the party leadership joined in an effort to depose him. When Malenkov, Molotov, and Kaganovich obtained a majority in the Presidium, Khrushchev was in critical danger. Although he had the support of many key party officials, it was without question of great, and conceivably crucial, importance that he also had the full support of Marshal Zhukov. Zhukov is reliably reported to have told the Central Committee Plenum itself that the Soviet armed forces would not "permit" anyone to "bid for power." Zhukov, now elected to full membership in the Presidium, was soon to speak "on behalf of the armed forces" in pledging continued support to the party leadership under Khrushchev.

This was the apogee of the Khrushchev-Zhukov alliance. Indeed, these two now appeared, to many observers, to be the most powerful men in the Soviet Union. But could the newly successful party chief permit Zhukov such a position? In particular, although Zhukov had on this occasion extralegally pledged the army to Khrushchev's support, might he not on some future occasion attempt to range this power against him? Could Party Presidium member Zhukov be permitted to make charged political statements "on behalf of the armed forces"?

This was one aspect of the new situation from June to October, 1957—Khrushchev's wariness of the Marshal's rising power and popularity. But there were two other factors that also deeply affected the civil-military relationship.

Under Zhukov, the military had acquired a substantial degree of autonomy. The whole trend of his administration of the military establishment was, while not antiparty, nonparty. "Military science" itself was defined in terms stressing purely professional military competence. This development clashed with party policy—not because the military sought to usurp political prerogatives, but because it threatened to become a self-contained professional body within the state. Khrushchev and the party refused to accept this, since their whole aim was to revitalize the party as the driving force in all activities of the state. The growing tendency toward an autonomous, professional governmental and economic bureaucracy, a would-be independent intelligentsia, and a professionally autonomous military establishment—this is precisely what the party has considered a threat to its own control of the state.

Just as Zhukov pressed for recognition of the principle that the professional competence of career officers could not be criticized in party meetings or by political officers, he evidently began to assume that as the leading military strategist he was unchallengeable on strategic judgments in the Presidium of the party. Although the evidence is not conclusive, there are reasons to believe that from June to October, 1957, Zhukov spoke with authority not only on military strategy in the specific sense of doctrine and plans (over which there had been no dispute), but also on the strategic implications of other policies.

Marshal Zhukov was sent on a visit to Yugoslavia in October, 1957;

while he was in Belgrade, a weeklong extension of his trip to Albania was announced. Thus Zhukov was kept out of Moscow for a three-week period, during which Khrushchev lined up Malinovsky and others in the military and political leadership in support of Zhukov's removal. On October 26, Zhukov returned to Moscow and was met at the airport by a delegation of military and political leaders who informed him of his dismissal from the post of Defense Minister, a move immediately made public. During the next several days an extended discussion of the whole matter of military-political relations took place in the Central Committee. On November 2, 1957, it was announced that Zhukov had also been removed from the Presidium and the Central Committee; he was castigated for fostering a "personality cult" and for attempting to "abolish the leadership and control of the party" over the armed forces. When Zhukov fought the issue, Khrushchev insisted on his capitulation, disgrace, and complete retirement.

It seemed likely to many that Marshal Konev would succeed Zhukov. He was the senior First Deputy, a rival of Zhukov's, and, moreover, a man who had shown his readiness to support Khrushchev in the latter's rewriting of his wartime service. But Khrushchev selected instead Marshal Malinovsky, the third-ranking military man and the senior marshal of the "Southern clique"—who, of course, thus also profited directly from Zhukov's removal. As a consequence of Malinovsky's appointment and other shifts in the high command, the "Southern clique" came to hold most of the key military positions. At the same time, Zhukov's Chief of Staff, Sokolovsky, who had been Chief of the General Staff of the armed forces since the late days of Stalin, and all the other deputy ministers were retained in office. This allayed any suspicion the military leaders may have had about the possibility of a wholesale purge of the high command: Khrushchev was, in a sense, showing that he recognized the political importance of the military institution and that he did not intend to assault it. However, Malinovsky was not given Presidium membership, and Khrushchev thus retained the final voice on matters of national security to which Marshal Zhukov had evidently been aspiring before his fall.

The Advent of the ICBM

By late 1957, Khrushchev seemed to be in full control. Within the Soviet Union and the CPSU he had successfully coped with the powerful coalition of his political enemies and disposed of what he viewed as the source of potential military challenge, Marshal Zhukov. In the Communist bloc he had rallied from the humiliations and crises of 1956 and succeeded in establishing a new equilibrium in relations with the east European states. Representatives of sixty-four Communist Parties, including Mao Tse-tung, came to Moscow for the fortieth anniversary of the 1917 Revolution.

Among the dramatic tokens of the new Soviet power (which Khrushchev exploited fully) were breakthroughs in science and technology: in the second half of 1957 the Soviet Union launched the world's first space satellite—the sputnik—and the first inter-continental ballistic missile—the ICBM.

Though the first Soviet nuclear device had been tested in 1949, the Soviet armed forces did not have more than a very small operational inventory of nuclear weapons, or even begin to consider seriously the strategic and tactical significance of nuclear weapons, until after Stalin's death. Yet research and development proceeded rapidly. The first Soviet thermonuclear test was in August, 1953, only nine months after the first American test of a thermonuclear device (and before American testing of an air-delivered H-bomb).

Thus the initial period of review and modification of military doctrine coincided with the introduction of nuclear weapons and jet-aircraft delivery systems into the Soviet armed forces. The doctrinal adjustment was, however, both belated and abrupt because of the previous restriction and constriction of Soviet military thought.

Particularly from 1955 to 1957, these and other new weapons were integrated into the Soviet armed forces and, to a considerable extent, into military doctrine. The process of integrating new weapons with doctrine was primarily carried out through an adaptation of the new weapons to traditional doctrinal concepts rather than the reverse, despite some modifications in operational doctrine. Military theory was developed and perfected with an eye to the use of new tools, but there was little real doctrinal ferment until the end of the decade. Thus, while the ICBM and sputnik had a tremendous impact on popular attitudes, on Soviet foreign relations, and even on Sino-Soviet differences, their development was not to affect military doctrine markedly for some time to come.

"More Rubble for the Ruble"

A new phase—in military doctrine and in civil-military relations—was opened with the development of a new policy by Khrushchev, one which was first mentioned and secretly debated in the Central Committee in December, 1959, and which formed the basis for Khrushchev's public statement to the Supreme Soviet on January 14, 1960. This public statement represented a major party and government decision on military policy. It marked a compromise between, on the one hand, the doctrinal views and force structure desired by the military leadership, and on the other, the desire of Khrushchev and others to retrench on expenditures by reducing the size of standing forces and to rely more heavily on nuclear-missile deterrence and counterdeterrence.

Khrushchev was evidently able to insist that the ground forces, tactical and naval air forces, and surface fleet could be pared—in some cases sharply—without adversely shifting the Soviet Union's general strategic balance vis-à-vis comparable Western forces. One of the chief motivations for this move was to reduce the cost of maintaining a mammoth standing army while adding expensive new offensive and defensive systems. The program he outlined provided for a one-third reduction in military manpower, and also for alterations in the structure of the Soviet armed forces.

Khrushchev stressed that "under present conditions wars would not be carried out as before, and there would be little to resemble previous wars. . . . War would begin in the hearts of warring countries; there would not be a single capital, not a single major industrial or administrative center, not a single strategic area that would not be subjected to attack." He justified the force cuts on this basis: "As before, we shall have all the essential means for the defense of the country, and the enemy knows this well; if he does not know it, we warn him and openly state that in reducing the numbers of the armed forces we are not diminishing their firepower. On the contrary, it increases by several times." While falsely claiming superiority, Khrushchev did feel compelled to admit that the West might catch up. At the same time, he posed—and answered—the question whether, under such parity, the enemy might not gain victory by using surprise in a nuclear-missile attack: "No, modern means of waging war do not give *any* country such advantages." Any major, prepared power, he contended, "will *always* be able to give a powerful rebuff to the aggressor," even after being subjected to a successful surprise attack. (*Pravda,* January 15, 1960.)

The new military policy provoked a "parting of the ways" between Khrushchev and the bulk of the military leadership. In order to understand why this was so, it is useful first to consider what led Khrushchev to advance his new military program. The primary cause was the scarcity of resources and tautness of the economy; military demands collided with or forestalled economic and political programs that Khrushchev regarded as highly desirable if not essential. If Khrushchev was to succeed in substantially improving the lot of the Soviet consumer, if he was to gain the desperately needed new capital investment for agriculture, if he was to meet his own promises on improved housing, it was necessary to cut back on military outlays. But these domestic desiderata were not all. If Khrushchev was to continue his blossoming program of large-scale economic aid to underdeveloped countries, and, above all, if the U.S.S.R. was going to make good its ideological claim to demonstrate the superiority of socialism over capitalism in peaceful competition on the world stage, resources must be released from essentially nonproductive military expenditures.

These were the chief incentives for some reorientation of economic disbursements. Were the international situation and the strategic confrontation such that these considerations could be allowed to outweigh military claims? By 1959, Khrushchev and his chief associates were convinced that the United States had no aggressive designs on the U.S.S.R. or the socialist camp; "men of reason," who understood the impermissibility of nuclear war, were recognized to rule in the West. Khrushchev's own visit to the United States in September, 1959, confirmed these impressions, and his faith in them was so strong that he insisted on the validity of his opinion despite the fact that this contributed greatly to the growing rift between the Soviet Union and Communist China. Even some progress on disarmament agreements—the subject of a major new Soviet campaign launched in September, 1959—seemed not beyond the realm of possibility (again despite vigorous Chinese dissent). Finally, recognizing the need to maintain Soviet military security and to have politically exploitable military power, Khrushchev saw no reason not to rely on nuclear-missile deterrence and counterdeterrence—and to cut back on expensive, traditional forms of Soviet military strength. The military leaders were less persuaded than Khrushchev of American peaceful intentions, less eager to try for disarmament, less ready to trade tried military forces for the new weapons, and less prepared to skimp on military requirements in order to allow domestic economic growth or foreign economic investment for political purposes. But Khrushchev rammed his program through.

Thus Khrushchev embraced the doctrines of reliance on massive strikes by strategic nuclear armed missiles, reduction of conventional forces, and mutual deterrence. But Soviet military *theory,* written by military men, bore little relation to these governmental statements of Soviet military *policy.*

Following Khrushchev's announcement of a "new look," extended debate among senior Soviet military officers in the early 1960's resulted in a more penetrating reconsideration of the nature of modern war than had the revisions of the 1950's. Although willingness of the political leadership to take the initiative encouraged those military men who believed that more drastic changes in doctrine, strategy, and force structure were called for in the missile age, most military men were strongly conservative.

The result of this intensive review was a compromise between the radical, "modern" school that has stressed the role of nuclear weapons, and the conservative, "traditional" one that continues to see an important role for other arms as well. The "Khrushchev doctrine," with its stress on *deterrence* and the political uses of military power, began even in 1960 to be modified to meet requirements seen by the military for *waging* a nuclear war, should one occur. These requirements both for ready forces to be used in case of a relatively short and largely inter-continental war *and* for forces to wage a protracted general nuclear war with extensive land campaigns compound the problem of drawing on strained resources.

Military reservations concerning the Khrushchev program were evident. On the day after Khrushchev's speech, Marshal Malinovsky, while supporting the new line, also pointedly reiterated the importance of maintaining a balance of *all* arms in the military establishment.

In April, 1960, in the wake of dissatisfactions among many military men with Khrushchev's plan for substantial reduction in the armed forces and for alterations in force structure, the two leading military men who had failed to speak publicly in support of his program—the senior First Deputy Ministers, Marshals Sokolovsky and Konev—were retired. Thus, the two remaining holdovers from the Zhukov administration were removed. They were replaced by Khrushchev's protégé, Marshal Grechko, and Malinovsky's wartime Chief of Staff, Marshal Zakharov. From that time on, despite some reshuffling of assignments, *all* the key places in the Soviet military high command have been filled by members of the "Southern clique."

After 1960, the military leadership was a more cohesive group than in any other recent period, though there were probably personal and service differences on some issues. All the military chiefs owed their status in part to Khrushchev's favor—but then, so did many of Khrushchev's political successors. Although the fortunes of individuals are politically relevant because of Khrushchev's association with the "Southern clique," the main question at all times remains the institutional one. Malinovsky and his colleagues, after all, are marshals absorbed with military interests and charged with defining, advocating, and fulfilling military requirements. The institutional autonomy of the military establishment had not been basically altered by Zhukov's fall.

With the passage of time, the significance of cliques arising in World War II has faded. Differences over policy issues both among the military leaders and between them and the political leadership have become more important. For example, in March, 1963, Marshal Matvei Zakharov was replaced as Chief of the General Staff of the Armed Forces by Marshal Sergei Biryuzov. Zakharov may have been in ill health, but it is likely that his continuing opposition to Khrushchev's renewed pressures for force reductions contributed to the decision to replace him. In any case, his successor—while also a member of the "Southern clique"—was evidently more sympathetic to Khrushchev's stress on strategic deterrence. (Marshal Biryuzov had the advantage of having served as commander-in-chief of the air defense forces, and then as commander-in-chief of the strategic rocket forces, before becoming Chief of the General Staff.) The diminution of relevance of the clique alignments was particularly evident when, in February, 1963, Marshal Malinovsky went so far as to recall favorably Marshal Zhukov's role in the Stalingrad campaign and indirectly to slight Khrushchev's own role.

There have been differences over the question of military force requirements between the *political* leadership most concerned with the *political* use of military power short of major war, and the *military* leadership most concerned with the *military* requirements for waging war if it should come. The compromise between these views and interests was in turn affected by developments in the domestic and international political arenas, by changes in the leadership, and by fluctuations in international tension. Moreover, considerations of the international relation of forces—including the military "balance"—are intertwined with internal policy issues such as the priority of heavy and defense industry, issues on which the Soviet leaders are not always of one mind and on which military considerations may carry considerable weight.

During 1959 and 1960—and, indeed, until Khrushchev's ouster in October, 1964—the Soviet leadership seemed to many to be firmly in his hands. There were, however, discernible differences among political leaders, although these were difficult to analyze because they appeared not to reflect clear and consistently feuding factions but, rather, shifting alignments on various issues. Nonetheless, on the key complex of issues related directly to resource allocation, there was always a group that was relatively conservative, and thus closer in thought to the military than was Khrushchev. Frol Kozlov, who rose to the "number two" spot in the leadership in early 1960, favored such a conservative approach until his sudden illness and abandonment of an active role in the spring of 1963.

Alignments of coinciding (if not common) interests arose between the politico-economic and military conservatives, although it would be inaccurate to lump them together as one group. Nor can one neatly place the military "modernists" or radicals next to Khrushchev; both they and Khrushchev were ready to reduce conventional arms, but the military radicals sought military superiority in the new weapons, while Khrushchev accepted slower and smaller strategic force goals as sufficient for deterrence and (erroneously, as it turned out) for political pressure. Rapid large-scale acquisition of the new weapons would have cut across development of some of the other nonmilitary economic programs. Nonetheless, it can be said that the main body of military leaders, led by Malinovsky, took a more conservative view of international politics, domestic economic priorities, *and* military requirements for deterrence and for waging war than did Khrushchev or even the political leadership as a whole.

As the Sino-Soviet rift widened from 1958 on, and publicly after 1960, the Russians were castigated by the Chinese for their unwillingness to take risks on behalf of the world revolution. But on this issue there have been no signs of division within the political leadership since the fall of Molotov, nor any indications of diverging views by the military leaders, who appreciate the facts of war in the nuclear age.

Crosscurrents and Compromises on Force Levels

Khrushchev's address on military policy in January, 1960, called for a manpower cut of one-third (some 1.2 million men). Since he had justified this reduction in part on the basis of the improved international situation (as well as on increased nuclear-missile firepower), later trouble on the international scene—such as the downing of a United States U-2 reconnaissance plane over the U.S.S.R. on May 1, 1960—offered opportunities for the military leaders to seek reconsideration. Khrushchev, however, was evidently successful in insisting that the reductions in force continue as planned, and by the end of 1960 perhaps one-half of the total announced cut had been made.

During the first half of 1961, the program of reductions was greatly slowed down. The new Kennedy Administration was committed to the acquisition of a more balanced military posture, redressing an earlier neglect of conventional forces. But the Soviet reversal was evidently also the result of internal problems, such as those presented by the rapid release of many thousands of professional military men into the civilian labor force. Then, during the summer and fall of 1961, the serious politico-military confrontation over Berlin led the United States and the U.S.S.R. to make a series of military "demonstration" moves and countermoves. One such move occurred in July, 1961, when the Soviet Union publicly announced suspension of further implementation of the 1960 program of reductions. Two months later, the Soviet Union broke the three-year informal moratorium on nuclear testing and resumed a series of tests climaxed by 30- and 60-megaton super H-bomb detonations. These moves were clearly favored by the military leaders, but they were decided upon by the political leaders both as politico-military demonstrations and as measures to meet the military requirements of Soviet deterrence policy.

The Missile Gap and the Cuban Missile Gambit

In view of the high importance attributed by Khrushchev to the Soviet achievement as the first nation to test an ICBM and to the continuing alleged Soviet superiority in strategic missiles, and in view of the evident political as well as military advantages of superior missiles, it is understandable that most Western observers assumed that the Soviet Union would press for and attain at least a transient advantage in this field. Even military and intelligence analysts (more aware than outsiders of the complexities involved in translating an early advance in long-range rocketry into an operational capability) were concerned about the possibility that the Soviet Union could, with maximum effort, produce larger numbers of such weapons for a time than could the United States. Thus was born the idea that a missile gap between American and Soviet strength could occur in the early 1960's.

From 1958 to 1961, during the period of widespread American concern over an impending (in popular eyes, even an existing) missile gap, Khrushchev may have been counting his missiles before they were hatched. Trading in rocket futures, he attempted the overambitious task of dislodging the Western powers from West Berlin. By the time of Khrushchev's ouster, six years had passed since his initial demand for a new status for West Berlin "within six months." By the fall of 1961, the swollen image of the missile gap had been punctured by official and unofficial disclosures from Washington, and during 1962 it became evident to all that in fact the only missile gap of the mid-1960's would be one favoring the United States. The Soviet military leaders—who must have had doubts about the comparatively slow rate of Soviet ICBM buildup and who had probably also had doubts about brandishing missiles not yet in operation—could not have been pleased at having their weakness revealed.

Khrushchev was obviously disappointed and concerned over his repeated failure to make any concrete political gains from the Soviet Union's impressive—and universally acknowledged—leadership in space exploration and in the development of inter-continental-range rockets. But beyond this he was also beset by the effect this political failure had on his prestige within the party leadership at home and within the world Communist movement. Moreover, Soviet military planners were concerned over the growing American strength in strategic missiles.

Sometime in the spring of 1962, Khrushchev apparently decided to offset the American missile gap by a daring "end-run" emplacement of intermediate-range missiles in Cuba. From the standpoint of the Soviet military leadership, the move—if it succeeded—would transform cheap and readily available medium- and intermediate-range missiles into *ersatz* ICBM's, of which the Russians still had very few, and would considerably complicate the defense of the North American continent. Although the military leaders knew full well that they were in no position to do anything if the United States intervened, Khrushchev was strongly drawn to the prospect of a sudden dramatic improvement in the Soviet strategic military posture vis-à-vis the United States. Moreover, by reducing Western confidence and cohesiveness with this move, Khrushchev expected that the U.S.S.R. would gain increased political leverage, in particular for a new confrontation on Berlin.

As it happened, of course, Washington proved determined to effect the removal of the missiles from Cuba by whatever means were necessary. Khrushchev's only real choice quickly boiled down to this: to pull the missiles out under the humiliating circumstances of an effective United

States naval quarantine and escort, or to have them destroyed by the United States. While Khrushchev cut his diplomatic losses fairly effectively, he had certainly attained neither the political nor the military aims of the missile gambit. American strategic superiority was doubly confirmed: Khrushchev's ploy showed his need for such substitute ICBM's, and its failure not only prevented the substitution but impressively demonstrated the American strength that compelled him to capitulate. Moreover, the prestige of the military had been damaged, and the "missile gap" within the Soviet Union had been revealed by the political adventurism of Khrushchev.

Deterrence has become the key strategic concept in the United States, and under Khrushchev's auspices it became so in the Soviet Union as well. However, in accordance with the differing foreign policies of the two countries, the concept in turn is somewhat differently defined. Khrushchev and his successors are interested in maintaining enough defensive strength to deter any opponent from launching an attack or otherwise offensively compelling a retreat—as is the United States. At the same time, the Russians are eager to use their military power as a political weapon to deter their opponents from defensively resorting to military means to check the Communist use of nonmilitary economic, political, and subversive instruments. This may be termed "counterdeterrence," that is, countering and neutralizing the opponent's use of his own deterrent to meet indirect challenges. Put in other terms, deterrence in the Soviet conception is a double-edged sword, to be used for offense as well as for defense.

The way military power is used as a political instrument is often more important than its war-making capacity. Thus Khrushchev, as a bluff, engaged in "ballistic blackmail" as early as the Suez crisis of November, 1956. The limits of bluff, of course, are well known, and the Cuban missile crisis showed the insufficiency of a bare minimum deterrent for a confrontation provoked by an adventurous gamble.

"Military Strategy"

The early fall of 1962 also saw the publication of *Military Strategy,* an authoritative treatise written by fifteen leading Soviet military theoreticians headed by Marshal Vasily Sokolovsky, the retired former Chief of the General Staff. This volume set out in some detail, and publicly, the compromise military doctrine—"enlightened conservatism"—that had emerged from the debate prompted by Khrushchev's "new look" in January, 1960. Strategic nuclear missile strikes in the initial period of a war were now recognized as "decisive," in the sense that one could not lose in this initial nuclear exchange and win the war. On the other hand, it was not assumed that either side could "win" in such a phase if both were alert and prepared, and success to the extent of merely *not losing* in the initial period would mean that the final outcome would still be decided in a war of undetermined duration. A war *might* be won or lost quickly, but it also might involve extended campaigns waged by huge armies. Hence *Military Strategy* stressed nuclear missiles but cautioned that large armies would be needed too, as would military economic production in the course of the war. There is only one reflection of Khrushchev's theme of "more rubble for the ruble," and it is not consistent even with the rest of the chapter on peacetime preparations for war in which it appears: "The availability of megaton nuclear-rocket weapons reduces expenditures for military preparations in peacetime, since it permits a significant cutback in production of other types of armament without lowering the firepower of the armed forces."[1]

The authors of *Military Strategy* could not, of course, have directly challenged the Soviet political leadership even had they wanted to do so. But there were in 1962–64 indirect indications of a new sensitivity concerning the familiar problem of defining the proper line dividing the responsibilities of the political leaders from those of the military professionals. This problem became more evident when, in the fall of 1963, a revised edition of the volume was published.

In the fifteen months between editions, the Cuban crisis had occurred, and in its wake Khrushchev had decided upon a new *détente*. During the summer of 1963 a direct "hot line" teletype between Washington and Moscow was agreed on; the ban on nuclear testing in the atmosphere, oceans, and outer space was signed; and in the early fall, agreement was reached on joint American and Soviet support of a United Nations resolution banning the placement of nuclear and other weapons of mass destruction in outer space. These limitations served to circumscribe the arms race. Partly because of the military's dissatisfaction with these developments and partly because of Khrushchev's dissatisfaction with the low political payoff of the very high investment in the military, the problems of 1960–61 were posed again.

The second edition of *Military Strategy* showed very little change and no significant new departures in military doctrine. There was, however, a new emphasis on the dominant role of politics and the political leadership in ultimate decisions on strategy. For example, there appeared in the first edition a sentence clearly aimed at limiting the value of Khrushchev's 1960 contribution to military theory: "Military doctrine is not thought out or compiled by a single person or group of persons." Not only was this sentence deleted in the second edition, but in its place it was explicitly stated

---

[1] Marshal V. D. Sokolovsky *et al.*, eds., *Voyennaya strategiya* (*Military Strategy*), Moscow, 1962, p. 363.

that "the basic theses of military doctrine are determined by the political leadership of a state." And, in the final analysis, this is indeed true.

Continued Controversy and the Fall of Khrushchev

Khrushchev's position had indeed been weakened by the outcome of the Cuban missile affair. In late 1962 and early 1963 he was compelled to accept a new annual budget and an allocation of economic priorities more in line with the views of the conservatives. However, by April—with the sudden illness of Kozlov—Khrushchev recovered his balance. At this time he again began to rein in the military leaders, and he replaced Marshal Zakharov as Chief of the General Staff.

Perhaps Khrushchev's most striking successes were in the field of disarmament, seeming to justify his belief that agreements could be reached with the "imperialists" in spite of both military (and perhaps conservative political) doubts in the U.S.S.R. and the increasingly vocal Chinese Communists. The "hot line" between Moscow and Washington, the test ban, and the ban on bombs in orbit have already been mentioned; the last of these, though less formal and less dramatic than the ban on atmospheric nuclear testing, was significant in another way. From the spring of 1962 until the fall of 1963, a number of articles in the military press had argued that the United States was planning to station nuclear rockets in space and had implied that the Soviet Union should therefore do likewise. The military leaders were probably not united in favor of such a measure, but a group of them was apparently able to form an effective "lobby." One can imagine that, after Cuba, a new image of strategic military power would have been welcome. But Khrushchev must have considered that if the United States would not tolerate Soviet nuclear warheads ninety miles to the south, it would not be likely to tolerate them ninety miles overhead. Accordingly, he agreed to the UN Resolution against placing nuclear warheads in space, avoiding a probably risky and certainly expensive new dimension of the arms race while adding to the achievements of *détente*.

In December, 1963, Khrushchev had again announced imprecisely that the Soviet Union was planning or considering further reductions of military force levels, and at that time the U.S.S.R. and the United States each announced reductions in their military budgets of about 5 percent. After Khrushchev's statement, Soviet military leaders such as Marshals Malinovsky and Chuikov were notably silent on any possibility of reducing forces, although they did acknowledge the budget reduction.

However, the very fact of Khrushchev's success in *détente* and disarmament, the sharp polemic with the Chinese Communists, the proposed crash program for the chemical industry, and the ever more vocal appeals for "goulash Communism"—all these concerned his more conservative colleagues, and even his "centrist" associates. In addition to this concern, especially over *détente* and disarmament, the military were unhappy at the new pressures for force reductions and the armaments cutback implied in the renewed shift toward consumer-goods industry.

Military doctrinal discussion reflected these shifting currents. As we have seen, the publication of the comprehensive *Military Strategy* in 1962, and of a revised version in 1963, had evidenced a working compromise between the more conservative and more radically "modernist" military thinkers, and also between the enlightened conservatism of the military leadership as a whole and the "ultraradicalism" of Khrushchev. The debate continued during 1963 and 1964, and in the summer of 1964, two especially interesting works showed at least a tactical division among the military leaders and possibly reflected the development of a real new divergence.

In July, 1964, *The Nuclear Age and War,* edited by the First Deputy Minister of Defense, Marshal Grechko, was published. Even though Grechko had earlier been particularly close to Khrushchev, he has shared the dominant, enlightened conservative view of the leading military men. The book, a collection of articles by a number of the senior marshals and leading military thinkers, had a decidedly conservative thrust. A key article by Marshal Chuikov, Deputy Minister of Defense and Commander-in-Chief of the Ground Forces at the time it was written, had in fact been revised after its first appearance six months earlier to defend even more staunchly large multimillion-man armies ready to wage extensive campaigns in nuclear war. (Chuikov, incidentally, was soon thereafter relieved as Commander-in-Chief of the Ground Forces.)

A month later the armed forces' newspaper, *Red Star,* carried two articles written by Marshal Sokolovsky and one of his collaborators on *Military Strategy,* Major General Cherednichenko. It was noted that "not all" would agree with the views expressed, and that they were not official. One of the articles, in the issue of August 28, 1964, contained a major concession to the radical viewpoint—and to Khrushchev. The article stated that "it is an indisputable conclusion, in our opinion, that a thermonuclear war cannot last long. Hence it is necessary, in our opinion, above all to make preparations for a short war." Sokolovsky, at least, appeared to be converted to the radical viewpoint—but not to Khrushchev's corollary view on reducing the size of the standing army. But other military writers continued to stress that a general nuclear war could be short or long, and that it was necessary to prepare for both contingencies.

While Sokolovsky conceded that a general nuclear war would be short and, by implication, that large armies (or at least wartime mobilization) would not be needed to wage such a war, he proceeded in the very next sentence to take back any inference that large armies *in general* were un-

IRBM's on parade in Moscow's Red Square. On the reviewing stand above the Lenin Mausoleum (within a fortnight after the 1962 Cuban missile crisis), the Soviet leaders: Khrushchev, flanked on his right by Malinovsky, Voroshilov, and other marshals; on his left, by Party Presidium members (l. to r.) Brezhnev, Kozlov, Kosygin, Polyansky, Voronov, Kuusinen, Kirilenko, Grishin, Ilyichev, and Ponomarev.

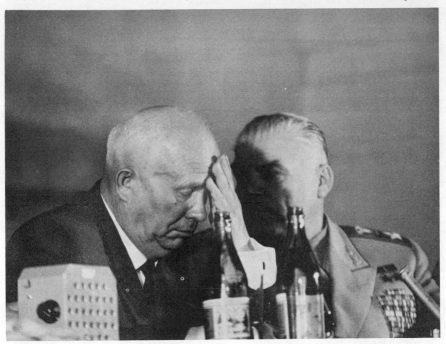

The First Secretary and the Minister of Defense (Paris, May, 1960).

On his seventieth birthday (April 17, 1964), Khrushchev receives the congratulations of the Soviet marshals: (l. to r.) Malinovsky, Moskalenko, Biryuzov, Yeremenko, Voroshilov, Timoshenko, and Sokolovsky.

necessary. A new possibility, not discussed in known Soviet military discourse since the mid-1950's, was now noted—a major, long *non*-nuclear war. He continued: "At the same time, it is not possible to exclude the possibility of the outbreak of a relatively protracted war. This may apply to a war in which nuclear weapons are not used—for example, a local war which may escalate into a world war; therefore preparations for a relatively protracted war must not be neglected." Was Sokolovsky really so converted to the "radical" view that he came full circle (as some Western strategic thinkers have done) to seeing nuclear weapons not used at all in a future major war? Or did he believe that, if Khrushchev was able to wear down resistance to force cuts by arguing the power of the strategic nuclear arsenals, it was better tactics to defend the need for large armies on different doctrinal grounds? In either case, there followed neither rebuttal nor support for this position from other military writers.

In late September, 1964, a meeting of several score leading Soviet government and party officials had discussed a new major economic development plan. Khrushchev delivered a speech that, as can be seen even from the truncated version published in *Pravda* on October 2, called for a drastic shift away from heavy—and defense—industry. It is clear that on this occasion not only conservative party leaders and the military chiefs, but even some of those who usually proved to be supporters of more consumer-goods industry, were unconvinced by Khrushchev's proposals. The issue posed by his intention to urge this radical shift at the coming November Central Committee Plenum very likely contributed to the decision to remove Khrushchev in mid-October. On this, as on many earlier occasions, the military were an interested party, but only as a part of a coalition of individual leaders and interest groups.

The sudden removal of Khrushchev from power in October, 1964, was evidently not opposed or regretted by the military leaders whom he had been pressing hard on disputed military policy issues. There is, however, no indication that the military played any *active* role in the conspiracy to remove Khrushchev. Indeed, on the very eve of his removal, a number of the leading marshals included, in articles commemorating the twentieth anniversary of the liberation of the Ukraine, standard statements praising Khrushchev's wartime role. Had they known of his imminent displacement, they would probably have omitted these references. Marshal Malinovsky may well have been informed by the party leaders shortly before they acted, but we do not know. In any case, in the reshuffling of posts after Khrushchev's dismissal no professional military men were promoted (in contrast to the rise to full membership in the Presidium of former secret police chief Alexander Shelepin, and the rise to full membership in the Central Committee of both KGB chief Vladimir Semichastny and chief political commissar in the armed forces, General Alexander Yepishev).

Nonetheless, beginning with their very first pronouncements, both the new party chief, Leonid Brezhnev, and the new Prime Minister, Alexei Kosygin, affirmed that "the CPSU Central Committee and the government have taken *and will take* measures to *strengthen* the defense capacity of our great motherland." This formulation offered more promise to the military than Khrushchev's usual statements on "maintaining" defense capacity. No doubt the new leaders did not want to add to their other immediate problems by confronting the already discontented military leaders. On the other hand, the problem of holding down rising military expenditures is bound to lead to new frictions.

We do not know if Khrushchev had planned to replace Malinovsky; there were rumors to that effect not long before Khrushchev's fall. Purely by coincidence, only a few days after Khrushchev was dropped, the Chief of the General Staff, Marshal Biryuzov, was killed in an aircraft accident. Biryuzov was apparently the most prominent military leader to have supported Khrushchev's reliance on strategic missile deterrence and counter-deterrence (though he himself may have favored a larger strategic missile force). The new leadership, after a month's delay, named Marshal Matvei Zakharov as his successor—undoubtedly Malinovsky's selection. Marshal Zakharov had been Malinovsky's chief of staff at Stalingrad, later during World War II, and then in the Far East. He had, moreover, served as Chief of the General Staff from the time of Sokolovsky's compulsory retirement in April, 1960, until he in turn was replaced (probably at least in part because of his opposition to Khrushchev's pressures for more force cuts) by Biryuzov in March, 1963. On doctrinal matters Zakharov, like Malinovsky, has been an "enlightened conservative."

The Khrushchev era marked a significant transformation in military thought, and in the military establishment. Politico-military relations moved through several stages; at the end of the Khrushchev period, the military leadership was still excluded from the top councils, but it had a significant voice at least in the key decisions on resource allocation that underlie so much of Soviet political decision-making.

Conclusions

The Khrushchev decade saw dramatic developments of Soviet military doctrine, policy, and forces. The armed forces were reduced from six to three million men, and they have substantially shifted from a non-nuclear to a nuclear basis, and from a continental to an inter-continental force. But even more significant were the changes in Soviet views on the role of military power.

Six major contributing elements helped to shape this decade of change:

1. De-Stalinization.   The liberation of Soviet military thought from the

constraints both consciously and unconsciously imposed by Stalin's dictatorship was surely basic to the changes that occurred. It was, however,
more in the nature of a precondition for the task of dealing with the problems of the nuclear age than it was a solution.

2. The revolution in military technology. The main raw material for
the refashioning of Soviet military doctrine has been provided by the exceptional development of new weapons and military technology. After its initial
attempt to "catch up" in the early post-Stalin period, the Soviet Union
developed the nuclear strategic air-delivery systems that formed the basis
for doctrinal revision in the mid-1950's. The next major jump forward was
the development of long-range rockets in the late 1950's. During the 1960's,
instead of being held back by the political leadership, the military were the
more conservative force. They were strongly pressed by Khrushchev, who
was impatient for the realization of military potentialities and tried pre-
maturely to derive political benefits abroad from technical military
advances. The military-technological revolution has also had global geo-
strategic consequences. In particular, the technical foundation for mutual
deterrence was provided by the rise of inter-continental ballistic missiles
with multi-megaton thermonuclear warheads, which spelled the end of
American continental invulnerability even though it did not, of course, re-
ice Soviet vulnerability.

3. Western military thought. Western military thought has come to
play a more and more important role in Soviet doctrine. In the initial phase
of revision, the question even arose as to whether there were common laws
of military science between the capitalist and socialist countries. Once that
question had been answered in the affirmative, a large number of Western
military and politico-military writings were translated and published in the
Soviet Union. Despite frequent sharp Soviet refutations and distortions,
Western thought has clearly had a substantial impact on Soviet doctrine.
Indeed, it is probably not an overstatement to say that the Khrushchev era
saw the beginnings of a "dialogue" between East and West on questions of
military strategy.

4. Soviet political developments. Soviet politics have affected not only
the dramatis personae but also the plot of the military-doctrinal drama. As
we have seen, one of the first consequences of the death of Stalin was the
rise—unsought—of the military institution in the post-Stalin political leadership. Personal relationships among military men, and between military
and political leaders, became important in policy issues where the political
and economic views of some leaders were related to the military interests
of others. Thus, developments in the Soviet political leadership and in
Soviet society were affected by and in turn affected politico-military relationships. In the interval between two highly significant events, the abrupt
dismissal of Marshal Zhukov and the sudden removal of Khrushchev, the
military leadership fought a not wholly ineffective rear-guard action against

Khrushchev's efforts to substitute the more limited requirements of deterrence for the traditional military goal of a war-winning strategy and capability. This rear-guard resistance did not assume the form of direct challenge, but it is notable that it was possible at all. It did prove possible only because of the differing views of political leaders and the somewhat volatile course of Soviet politics.

5. World political developments.   World politics have played a considerable role in influencing Soviet military policy. The swings from *détente* to confrontation to *détente* in Soviet relations with the United States have been important, as have the shifts, real and anticipated, in the military strategic balance. Moreover, Soviet political strategy in other parts of the world gave birth to military aid programs totalling well over three billion dollars in the Khrushchev decade. Changes in Soviet relations with Communist China and with the Communist regimes of eastern Europe have partly arisen from differences over policy, risks, and military cooperation, and these changes have, in turn, greatly affected military cooperation, aid, and even alliance commitments. Finally, there have been the beginnings of arms-control agreements.

6. The political role of the marshals.   In the post-Stalin period, all institutions in Soviet society have assumed new, though in many cases fluctuating, significance. The military leaders have not sought or been accorded political power, although under the pressure of Khrushchev's rise to power against the various elements that finally coalesced to form the Antiparty Group in 1957, Marshal Zhukov was given—briefly—membership in the ruling Party Presidium. However, soon after reaching this political pinnacle, Zhukov was removed by Khrushchev and disgraced, and his successor, Marshal Malinovsky, has never been granted even candidate membership in that body.

The importance of the military in Soviet politics comes not from their political ambitions or activities, but from policy issues and the general constellation of political power at the time the issues arise. When political leaders disagree—and especially when they form shifting coalitions rather than firm factions by taking different stands on various issues, as they did during the Khrushchev period—there is more scope for influence by the representatives of a major "outside" institution such as the military. The military leaders have sometimes differed among themselves, but on the main political issues—above all, on the share of industrial and other resources to be devoted to defense needs—they have tended to take a common line, and one that remains consistent. The military do not oppose, for example, increased production of consumer goods per se, but they do oppose any measures that require sharp restrictions or cutbacks in their forces or in the availability of weapons. The ups and downs in the fortunes of the military on these issues have depended on shifting political alignments rather than on differing (or changing) military preferences. And when the political leadership does decide upon a given policy, even one the military opposes, the latter of course accepts it.

The military leadership itself has not, of course, been monolithic. There have been personal differences and clashes of ambitions and personalities, and there have been cliques and competitions for influence among them, though these latter differences tended to fade in the Khrushchev period. Although inter-service rivalries have probably been more widespread within the Soviet military establishment than we in the West would suppose, there are several reasons that such rivalries are fewer and less intense than those in major Western countries. One is the historical tradition of the land-oriented, continental horizon of the Russian military and the dominance of the ground soldiers. A second is the constraints on the development of any point of view which has not already been sanctioned by the party leadership. Moreover, the nature of the Soviet political system does not encourage (though neither does it entirely prevent) lobbying for views that are at variance with established doctrines. A third reason is the sociological and psychological difficulty of developing new ideas when one cannot refine them though expression and debate; a corollary of this difficulty is the reluctance of some military personnel to adopt unofficial ideas. Finally, the ideological-political foundation of Soviet military thought is the military's conviction of the need for a balanced and varied military capability, a conviction that has discouraged interest in theories proclaiming the superiority or sufficiency of any particular service.

From 1960 to 1964, the military leadership, in spite of the fact that it had been installed by Khrushchev, fought his persistent efforts to retrench on military expenditures. And they had some success. Certainly the motivations of the military were not basically "political," but rather derived from their views of the Western threat, the world military balance, the military technological prospect, the nature of future war, and, finally, the requirements of the military establishment that they believed were justified on the basis of these considerations. From the standpoint of most political leaders, military requirements were more limited than the military believed; moreover, not all the political leaders saw the same requirements. But in the political arena, controversy centered on economic policy and resource allocation, and to a lesser extent on tactics of foreign policy. When diverging political voices were heard, the military could support (and be courted by) those political leaders whose views on economic policy or foreign policy most closely coincided with their own.

Policy questions over Soviet relations with Communist China and the other Communist states (and with the underdeveloped states) were often relevant to military concerns, but there are no indications that the military leaders were given any role in deciding these matters. Disarmament rarely became more than propaganda or a political weapon, but some specific disarmament issues did affect military interests directly. The discussions in 1962 and 1963 of a ban on nuclear weapons tests probably caused divergence within the political leadership and thus permitted the military a voice, though not a strong enough voice to prevent Soviet acceptance of the limited test ban.

Thus the political role of the marshals has depended on the nature of policy issues, and on the degree of consensus among political leaders. Civil-military relations in more general terms has not been an issue; the party is supreme. The military leadership has never challenged political primacy, and it has been much more discreet than the military in most Western countries in public "lobbying" for its preferences. However, the political role of the marshals has become increasingly significant as collective leadership, and often an unstable balance within that leadership, has come to characterize Soviet politics.

Soviet military doctrine serves the policy of the U.S.S.R. and thus reflects those ideological and institutional features which are peculiar to that state and its elite. Nonetheless, it deals with the basic military and political facts of international life. The tendency now to think in terms of deterrence and counterdeterrence—that is, of political rather than military *objectives* for military power—is transforming the whole meaning of military policy. Taking into account past and prospective developments (internal and external) in Soviet politics and also present and future technical developments and the state of the world military balance, we can see that the past decade may have marked a transition whose importance goes beyond even the manifest modernization of military capability and the projection of Soviet military presence onto a global scope. No doubt Soviet military doctrine will continue to develop and to change, but it crossed a watershed in the Khrushchev decade.

Study Questions

1. In what significant ways do civil-military relationships differ in the Soviet Union and the United States?

2. What are the chief issues that have arisen between political and military leaders in the Soviet Union? What differences and continuities have characterized these issues under successive postwar Soviet leaders?

3. To what extent was Khrushchev personally responsible for framing Soviet military doctrine and policy? For stirring up political-military differences?

4. How are institutional and personal differences over policy questions among military leaders, and between military and political leaders, posed? How are they resolved?

5. To what extent is Soviet military doctrine determined by "national" (e.g., geographic, economic) factors, to what extent by ideological (i.e., specifically Communist) factors, or by technological factors such as the state of the art of weapon development?

Selected Bibliography

For the background development of Soviet military doctrine and policy before 1953, see: John Erickson, *The Soviet High Command: A Military-Political History, 1918–1941* (New York: St. Martin's Press, 1962), an excellent institutional and politico-military study; Daniel D. Fedotoff-White, *The Growth of the Red Army* (Princeton, N.J.: Princeton University Press, 1940), a good account of policy and actual force developments; Raymond L. Garthoff, *Soviet Military Doctrine* (New York: Free Press, 1953), a comprehensive treatise; Garthoff, *Soviet Military Policy: A Historical Analysis* (New York: Praeger, 1966), a wide-ranging study of the role of military institutions, instruments, and influence in Soviet foreign and internal policy, with particular attention to changing ideological views on the roles of war, revolution, and peace.

On the period since 1953, see: Herbert S. Dinerstein, *War and the Soviet Union* (New York: Praeger, 1962), a study of politico-military relations between 1953 and 1955; Dinerstein, Leon Gouré, and Thomas W. Wolfe, eds., *Soviet Military Strategy,* translated from the Soviet *Military Strategy,* edited by Marshal of the Soviet Union V. D. Sokolovsky *et al.* (New York: Dutton, 1963), the main Soviet work of this period, with an extensive commentary by the American editors. Raymond L. Garthoff, *Soviet Strategy in the Nuclear Age,* rev. ed. (New York: Praeger, 1962), a general analysis covering the period from 1953 through 1961; Roman Kolkowicz, *Conflicts in Soviet Party-Military Relations: 1962–1963* (Santa Monica, Calif.: The RAND Corporation, RM-3760-PR, August, 1963), an interesting account of politico-military relations in the period following the Cuban missile crisis; Thomas W. Wolfe, *Soviet Strategy at the Crossroads* (Cambridge, Mass.: Harvard University Press, 1964), an intensive and excellent review of changes in Soviet military thought from 1962 into early 1964.

INDEX

Italic page numbers refer to illustrations

B 7
C 8
D 9
E 0
F 1
G 2
H 3
I 4
J 5